T0091815

Computer Aided Verification:
Techniques and Applications

Computer Aided Verification: Techniques and Applications

Edited by Jordan Dean

CLANRYE INTERNATIONAL
www.clanryeinternational.com

Clanrye International,
750 Third Avenue, 9ᵗʰ Floor,
New York, NY 10017, USA

ISBN: 978-1-64726-586-1

Cataloging-in-publication Data

Computer aided verification : techniques and applications / edited by Jordan Dean.
    p. cm.
Includes bibliographical references and index.
ISBN 978-1-64726-586-1
1. Computer software--Verification. 2. Computer programs--Verification.
3. Electronic digital computers--Evaluation. 4. Computer-aided design.
I. Dean, Jordan.
QA76.76.V47 C663 2023
005.14--dc23

For information on all Clanrye International publications
visit our website at www.clanryeinternational.com

Contents

Preface

This book was inspired by the evolution of our times; to answer the curiosity of inquisitive minds. Many developments have occurred across the globe in the recent past which has transformed the progress in the field.

Computer aided verification is a branch of computer science that focuses on creating tools and techniques to help programmers in verifying whether the software designed by them works correctly or not. These tools have been developed sufficiently to the point where they are being incorporated in the system design of firms. Computer aided verification strives to improve the quality of digital systems through the analysis of software designs using logical reasoning and software tools. The goal is to create a mathematical model of a system and then attempt to prove formal properties that either certifies the system's correctness or, at the very least aid in the detection of bugs. This book discusses the techniques and applications of computer aided verification. For all readers who are interested in computer aided verification, the studies included herein will serve as an excellent guide to develop a comprehensive understanding.

This book was developed from a mere concept to drafts to chapters and finally compiled together as a complete text to benefit the readers across all nations. To ensure the quality of the content we instilled two significant steps in our procedure. The first was to appoint an editorial team that would verify the data and statistics provided in the book and also select the most appropriate and valuable contributions from the plentiful contributions we received from authors worldwide. The next step was to appoint an expert of the topic as the Editor-in-Chief, who would head the project and finally make the necessary amendments and modifications to make the text reader-friendly. I was then commissioned to examine all the material to present the topics in the most comprehensible and productive format.

I would like to take this opportunity to thank all the contributing authors who were supportive enough to contribute their time and knowledge to this project. I also wish to convey my regards to my family who have been extremely supportive during the entire project.

Editor

Formal Reasoning About the Security of Amazon Web Services

Byron Cook[1,2(✉)]

[1] Amazon Web Services, Seattle, USA
byron@amazon.com
[2] University College London, London, UK

Abstract. We report on the development and use of formal verification tools within Amazon Web Services (AWS) to increase the security assurance of its cloud infrastructure and to help customers secure themselves. We also discuss some remaining challenges that could inspire future research in the community.

1 Introduction

Amazon Web Services (AWS) is a provider of *cloud services*, meaning on-demand access to IT resources via the Internet. AWS adoption is widespread, with over a million active customers in 190 countries, and $5.1 billion in revenue during the last quarter of 2017. Adoption is also rapidly growing, with revenue regularly increasing between 40–45% year-over-year.

The challenge for AWS in the coming years will be to accelerate the development of its functionality while simultaneously increasing the level of security offered to customers. In 2011, AWS released over 80 significant services and features. In 2012, the number was nearly 160; in 2013, 280; in 2014, 516; in 2015, 722; in 2016, 1,017. Last year the number was 1,430. At the same time, AWS is increasingly being used for a broad range of security-critical computational workloads.

Formal automated reasoning is one of the investments that AWS is making in order to facilitate continued simultaneous growth in both functionality and security. The goal of this paper is to convey information to the formal verification research community about this industrial application of the community's results. Toward that goal we describe work within AWS that uses formal verification to raise the level of security assurance of its products. We also discuss the use of formal reasoning tools by externally-facing products that help customers secure themselves. We close with a discussion about areas where we see that future research could contribute further impact.

Related Work. In this work we discuss efforts to make formal verification applicable to use-cases related to cloud security at AWS. For information on previous work within AWS to show functional correctness of some key distributed algorithms, see [43]. Other providers of cloud services also use formal verification to establish security properties, *e.g.* [23,34].

Our overall strategy on the application of formal verification has been heavily influenced by the success of previous applied formal verification teams in industrial settings that worked as closely with domain experts as possible, *e.g.* work at Intel [33,50], NASA [31,42], Rockwell Collins [25], the Static Driver Verifier project [20], Facebook [45], and the success of Prover AB in the domain of railway switching [11].

External tools that we use include Boogie [1], Coq [4], CBMC [2], CVC4 [5], Dafny [6], HOL-light [8], Infer [9], OpenJML [10], SAW [13], SMACK [14], Souffle [37], TLA+ [15], VCC [16], and Z3 [17]. We have also collaborated with many organizations and individuals, *e.g.* Galois, Trail of Bits, the University of Sydney, and the University of Waterloo. Finally, many PhD student interns have applied their prototype tools to our problems during their internships.

2　Security of the Cloud

Amazon and AWS aim to innovate quickly while simultaneously improving on security. An original tenet from the founding of the AWS security team is to never be the organization that says *"no"*, but instead to be the organization that answers difficult security challenges with *"here's how"*. Toward this goal, the AWS security team works closely with product service teams to quickly identify and mitigate potential security concerns as early as possible while simultaneously not slowing the development teams down with bureaucracy. The security team also works with service teams early to facilitate the certification of compliance with industry standards.

The AWS security team performs formal security reviews of all features/services, *e.g.* 1,430 services/features in 2017, a 41% year-over-year increase from 2016. Mitigations to security risks that are developed during these security reviews are documented as a part of the security review process. Another important activity within AWS is ensuring that the cloud infrastructure *stays* secure after launch, especially as the system is modified incrementally by developers.

Where Formal Reasoning Fits In. The application security review process used within AWS increasingly involves the use of deductive theorem proving and/or symbolic model checking to establish important temporal properties of the software. For example, in 2017 alone the security team used deductive theorem provers or model checking tools to reason about cryptographic protocols/systems (*e.g.* [24]), hypervisors, boot-loaders/BIOS/firmware (*e.g.* [27]), garbage collectors, and network designs. Overall, formal verification engagements within the AWS security team increased 76% year-over-year in 2017, and found 45% more pre-launch security findings year-over-year in 2017.

To support our needs we have modified a number of open-source projects and contributed those changes back. For example, changes to CBMC [2] facilitate its application to C-based systems at the bottom of the compute stack used in AWS data centers [27]. Changes to SAW [13] add support for the Java programming language. Contributions to SMACK [14] implement automata-theoretic constructions that facilitate automatic proofs that s2n [12] correctly implements the *code balancing* mitigation for side-channel timing attacks. Source-code contributions to OpenJML [10] add support for Java 8 features needed to prove the correctness of code implementing a secure streaming protocol used throughout AWS.

In many cases we use formal verification tools *continuously* to ensure that security is implemented as designed, *e.g.* [24]. In this scenario, whenever changes and updates to the service/feature are developed, the verification tool is re-executed automatically prior to the deployment of the new version.

The security operations team also uses automated formal reasoning tools in its effort to identify security vulnerabilities found in internal systems and determine their potential impact on demand. For example, an SMT-based semantic-level policy reasoning tool is used to find misconfigured resource policies.

In general we have found that the internal use of formal reasoning tools provides good value for the investment made. Formal reasoning provides higher levels of assurance than testing for the properties established, as it provides clear information about what has and has not been secured. Furthermore, formal verification of systems can begin long before code is written, as we can prove the correctness of the high-level algorithms and protocols, and use under-constrained symbolic models for unwritten code or hardware that has not been fabricated yet.

3 Securing Customers *in* the Cloud

AWS offers a set of cloud-based services designed to help customers be secure *in* the cloud. Some examples include AWS Config, which provides customers with information about the configurations of their AWS resources; Amazon Inspector, which provides automated security assessments of customer-authored AWS-based applications; Amazon GuardDuty, which monitors AWS accounts looking for unusual account usage on behalf of customers; Amazon Macie, which helps customers discover and classify sensitive data at risk of being leaked; and AWS Trusted Advisor, which automatically makes optimization and security recommendations to customers.

In addition to automatic cloud-based security services, AWS provides people to help customers: *Solutions Architects* from different disciplines work with customers to ensure that they are making the best use of available AWS services; *Technical Account Managers* are assigned to customers and work with them when security or operational events arise; the *Professional Services* team can be hired by customers to work on bespoke cloud-based solutions.

Where Formal Reasoning Fits In. Automated formal reasoning tools today provide functionality to customers through the AWS services Config, Inspector, GuardDuty, Macie, Trusted Advisor, and the storage service S3. As an example, customers using the S3 web-based console receiving alerts—via SMT-based reasoning—when their S3 bucket policies are possibly misconfigured. AWS Macie uses the same engine to find possible data exfiltration routes. Another application is the use of high-performance datalog constraint solvers (*e.g.* [37]) to reason about questions of reachability in complex virtual networks built using AWS EC2 networking primitives. The theorem proving service behind this functionality regularly receives 10s of millions of calls daily.

In addition to the automated services that use formal techniques, some members of the AWS Solutions Architects, Technical Account Managers and Professional Services teams are applying and/or deploying formal verification directly with customers. In particular, in certain security-sensitive sectors (*e.g.* financial services), the Professional Services organization are working directly with customers to deploy formal reasoning into their AWS environments.

The customer reaction to features based on formal reasoning tools has been overwhelmingly positive, both anecdotally as well as quantitatively. Calls by AWS services to the automated reasoning tools increased by four orders of magnitude in 2017. With the formal verification tools providing the semantic foundation, customers can make stronger universal statements about their policies and networks and be confident that their assumptions are not violated.

4   Challenges

At AWS we have successfully applied existing or bespoke formal verification tools to both raise the level of security assurance *of* the cloud as well as help customers protect themselves *in* the cloud. We now know that formal verification provides value to applications in cloud security. There are, however, many problems yet to be solved and many applications of formal verification techniques yet to be discovered and/or applied. In the future we are hoping to solve the problems we face in partnership with the formal verification research community. In this section we outline some of those challenges. Note that in many cases existing teams in the research community will already be working on topics related to these problems, too many to cite comprehensively. Our comments are intended to encourage and inspire more work in this space.

Reasoning About Risk and Feasibility. A security engineer spends the majority of their time informally reasoning about risk. The same is true for any corporate Chief Information Security Officer (CISO). We (the formal verification community) potentially have a lot to contribute in this space by developing systems that help reason more formally about the consequences of combinations of events and their relationships to bugs found in systems. Furthermore, our community has a lot to offer by bridging between our concept of a counterexample and the security community's notion of a *proof of concept* (PoC), which is a constructive realization of a security finding in order to demonstrate its feasibility. Often security engineers will develop partial PoCs, meaning that they combine reasoning about risk and the finding of constructive witnesses in order to increase their confidence in the importance of a finding. There are valuable results yet to be discovered by our community at the intersection of reasoning about and synthesis of threat models, environment models, risk/probabilities, counterexamples, and PoCs. A few examples of current work on this topic include [18, 28, 30, 44, 48].

Fixes Not Findings. Industrial users of formal verification technology need to make systems more secure, not merely find security vulnerabilities. This is true both for securing the cloud, as well as helping customers be secure in the cloud. If there are security findings, the primary objective is to find them *and* fix them quickly. In practice a lot of work is ahead for an organization once a security finding has been identified. As a community, anything we can do to reduce the friction for users trying to triage and fix vulnerabilities, the better. Tools that report false findings are quickly ignored by developers, thus as a community we should focus on improving the fidelity of our tools. Counterexamples can be downplayed by optimistic developers: any assistance in helping users understand the bugs found and/or their consequences is helpful. Security vulnerabilities that require fixes that are hard to build or hard to deploy are an especially important challenge: our community has a lot to offer here via the development of more powerful synthesis/repair methods (*e.g.* [22,32,39]) that take into account threat models, environment models, probabilities, counterexamples.

Auditable Proof Artifacts for Compliance. Proof is actually two activities: *searching* for a candidate proof, and *checking* the candidate proof's validity. The searching is the art form, often involving a combination of heuristics that attempt to work around the undecidable. The checking of a proof is (in principle) the boring yet rigorous part, usually decidable, often linear in the size of the proof. Proof artifacts that can be re-checked have value, especially in applications related to compliance certification, *e.g.* DO-333 [26], CENENLEC EN 50128 SIL 4 [11], EAL7 MILS [51]. Non-trivial parts of the various compliance and conformance standards can be checked via mechanical proof, *e.g.* parts of PCI and FIPS 140. Found proofs of compliance controls that can be shared and checked/re-checked have the possibility to reduce the cost of compliance certification, as well as reduce the time-to-market for organizations who require certification before using systems.

Tracking Casual or Unrealistic Assumptions. Practical formal verification efforts often make unrealistic assumptions that are later forgotten. As an example, most tools assume that the systems we are analyzing are immune to *single-event upsets*, *e.g.* ionizing particles striking the microprocessor or semiconductor memory. We sometimes assume compilers and runtime garbage collectors are correct. In some cases (*e.g.* [20]) the environment models used by formal verification tools do not capture all possible real-world scenarios. As formal verification tools become more powerful and useful we will increasingly need to reason about what has been proved and what has not been proved, in order to avoid misunderstandings that could lead to security vulnerabilities. In applications of security this reasoning about assumptions made will need to interact with the treatment of risk and how risk is modified by various mitigations, *e.g.* some mitigations for single-event upsets make the events so unlikely they they are not a viable security risk, but still not impossible. This topic has been the focus of some attention over the years, *e.g.* CLINC stack [41], CompCert [3], and DeepSpec [7]. We believe that this will become an increasingly important problem in the future.

Distributed Formal Verification in the Cloud. Formal verification tools do not take enough advantage of modern data centers via distributing coordinated processes. Some examples of work in the right direction include [21,35,36,38,40, 47]. Especially in the area of program verification and analysis, our community still focuses on procedures that work on single computers, or perhaps *portfolio* solvers that try different problem encodings or solvers in parallel. Today large formal verification problems are often decomposed manually, and then solved in parallel. There has not been much research in methods for automatically introducing and managing the reasoning about the decompositions automatically in cloud-based distributed systems. This is in part perhaps due to the rules at various annual competitions such as SV-COMP, SMT-COMP, and CASC. We encourage the participants and organizers of competitions to move to cloud-based competitions where solvers have the freedom to use cloud-scale distributed computing to solve formal verification problems. Tool developers could build AMIs or CloudFormation templates that allow cloud distribution. Perhaps future contestants might even make Internet endpoints available with APIs supporting SMTLIB or TPTP such that the competition is simply a series of remote API calls to each competitor's implementation. In this case competitors that embrace the full power of the cloud will have an advantage, and we will see dramatic improvements in the computational power of our formal verification tools.

Continuous Formal Verification. As discussed previously, we have found that it is important to focus on *continuous verification*: it is not enough to simply prove the correctness of a protocol or system once, what we need is to *continuously* prove the desired property during the lifetime of the system [24]. This matches reports from elsewhere in industry where formal verification is being applied, *e.g.* [45]. An interesting consequence of our focus on continuous formal verification is that the time and effort spent finding an initial proof before a system is deployed is not as expensive as the time spent maintaining the proof later, as the up-front human cost of the pre-launch proof is amortized over the lifetime of the system. It would be especially interesting to see approaches developed that synthesize new proofs of modified code based on existing proofs of unmodified code.

The Known Problems are Still Problems. Many of the problems that we face in AWS are well known to the formal verification community. For example, we need better tools for formal reasoning about languages such as Ruby, Python, and Javascript, *e.g.* [29,49]. Proofs about security-oriented properties of many large open source systems remain an open problem, *e.g.* Angular, Linux, OpenJDK, React, NGINX, Xen. Many formal verification tools are hard to use. Many tools are brittle prototypes only developed for the purposes of publication. Better understanding of ISAs and memory models (*e.g.* [19,46]) are also key to prove the correctness of code operating on low-level devices. Practical and scalable methods for proving the correctness of distributed and/or concurrent systems remains an open problem. Improvements to the performance and scalability of formal verification tools are needed to prove the correctness of larger modules without manual decomposition. Abstraction refinement continues to be a problem, as false bugs are expensive to triage in an industrial setting. Buggy (and thus unsound) proof-based tools lose trust in formal verification with the users who are trying to deploy them.

5 Conclusion

In this paper we have discussed how formal verification contributes to the ability of AWS to quickly develop and deploy new features while simultaneously increasing the security of the AWS cloud infrastructure. We also discussed how formal verification techniques contribute to customer-facing AWS services. In this paper we have outlined some challenges we face. We actively seek solutions to these problems and are happy to collaborate with partners in this pursuit. We look forward to more partnerships, more tools, more collaboration, and more sharing of information as we try to bring affordable, efficient and secure computation to all.

References

1. Boogie program prover. https://github.com/boogie-org/boogie
2. CBMC model checker. https://github.com/diffblue/cbmc
3. CompCert project. http://compcert.inria.fr
4. Coq theorem prover. https://github.com/coq/coq
5. CVC4 decision procedure. http://cvc4.cs.stanford.edu
6. Dafny theorem prover. https://github.com/Microsoft/dafny
7. DeepSpec project. https://deepspec.org
8. HOL-light theorem prover. https://github.com/jrh13/hol-light
9. Infer program analysis. https://github.com/facebook/infer
10. OpenJML program prover. https://github.com/OpenJML
11. Prover Certifier. https://www.prover.com/software-solutions-rail-control/prover-certifier
12. s2n TLS/SSL implementation. https://github.com/awslabs/s2n
13. SAW program prover. https://github.com/GaloisInc/saw-script
14. SMACK software verifier. http://smackers.github.io/
15. TLA+ theorem prover. https://github.com/tlaplus
16. VCC program prover. https://vcc.codeplex.com
17. Z3 decision procedure. https://github.com/Z3Prover/z3
18. Aldini, A., Seigneur, J.M., Ballester Lafuente, C., Titi, X., Guislain, J.: Design and validation of a trust-based opportunity-enabled risk management system. Inf. Comput. Secur. **25**(2), 2–25 (2017)
19. Alglave, J., Cousot, P.: Ogre and Pythia: an invariance proof method for weak consistency models. In: POPL (2017)
20. Ball, T., Bounimova, E., Cook, B., Levin, V., Lichtenberg, J., McGarvey, C., Ondrusek, B., Rajamani, S.K., Ustuner, A.: Thorough static analysis of device drivers. In: EuroSys, pp. 73–85 (2006)
21. Beyer, D., Dangl, M., Dietsch, D., Heizmann, M.: Correctness witnesses: exchanging verification results between verifiers (2016)

22. Griesmayer, A., Bloem, R., Cook, B.: Repair of Boolean programs with an application to C. In: Ball, T., Jones, R.B. (eds.) CAV 2006. LNCS, vol. 4144, pp. 358–371. Springer, Heidelberg (2006). https://doi.org/10.1007/11817963_33

23. Bouchenak, S., Chockler, G., Chockler, H., Gheorghe, G., Santos, N., Shraer, A.: Verifying cloud services: present and future. ACM SIGOPS Oper. Syst. Rev. **47**(2), 6–19 (2013)

24. Chudnov, A., Collins, N., Cook, B., Dodds, J., Huffman, B., Magill, S., MacCarthaigh, C., Mertens, E., Mullen, E., Tasiran, S., Tomb, A., Westbrook, E.: Continuous formal verification of Amazon S2N. In: CAV (2018)

25. Cofer, D., Gacek, A., Miller, S., Whalen, M.W., LaValley, B., Sha, L.: Compositional verification of architectural models. In: Goodloe, A.E., Person, S. (eds.) NFM 2012. LNCS, vol. 7226, pp. 126–140. Springer, Heidelberg (2012). https://doi.org/10.1007/978-3-642-28891-3_13

26. Cofer, D., Miller, S.: DO-333 certification case studies. In: Badger, J.M., Rozier, K.Y. (eds.) NFM 2014. LNCS, vol. 8430, pp. 1–15. Springer, Cham (2014). https://doi.org/10.1007/978-3-319-06200-6_1

27. Cook, B., Khazem, K., Kroening, D., Tasiran, S., Tautschnig, M., Tuttle, M.R.: Model checking boot code from AWS data centers. In: CAV (2018)

28. Dullien, T.F.: Weird machines, exploitability, and provable unexploitability. IEEE Trans. Emerg. Top. Comput. **PP**(99) (2017)

29. Eilers, M., Müller, P.: Nagini: a static verifier for Python. In: CAV (2018)

30. Ganesh, V., Banescu, S. and Ochoa, M.: The meaning of attack-resistant programs. In: International Workshop on Progamming Languages and Security (2015)

31. Goodloe, A.E., Muñoz, C., Kirchner, F., Correnson, L.: Verification of numerical programs: from real numbers to floating point numbers. In: Brat, G., Rungta, N., Venet, A. (eds.) NFM 2013. LNCS, vol. 7871, pp. 441–446. Springer, Heidelberg (2013). https://doi.org/10.1007/978-3-642-38088-4_31

32. Gulwani, S., Polozov, O., Singh, R.: Program synthesis. In: Foundations and Trends in Programming Languages, vol. 4 (2017)

33. Harrison, J.: Formal verification of IA-64 division algorithms. In: TPHOLs (2000)

34. Hawblitzel, C., Howell, J., Kapritsos, M., Lorch, J.R., Parno, B., Roberts, M.L., Setty, S., Zill, B.: IronFleet: proving practical distributed systems correct. In: SOSP (2015)

35. Heule, M.J.H., Kullmann, O., Marek, V.W.: Solving and verifying the Boolean Pythagorean triples problem via cube-and-conquer. In: Creignou, N., Le Berre, D. (eds.) SAT 2016. LNCS, vol. 9710, pp. 228–245. Springer, Cham (2016). https://doi.org/10.1007/978-3-319-40970-2_15

36. Holzmann, G.J., Joshi, R., Groce, A.: Tackling large verification problems with the swarm tool. In: Havelund, K., Majumdar, R., Palsberg, J. (eds.) SPIN 2008. LNCS, vol. 5156, pp. 134–143. Springer, Heidelberg (2008). https://doi.org/10.1007/978-3-540-85114-1_11

37. Jordan, H., Scholz, B., Subotic, P.: Towards proof synthesis by neural machine translation. In: CAV (2016)

38. Kumar, R., Ball, T., Lichtenberg, J., Deisinger, N., Upreti, A., Bansal, C.: CloudSDV enabling static driver verifier using Microsoft azure. In: Ábrahám, E., Huisman, M. (eds.) IFM 2016. LNCS, vol. 9681, pp. 523–536. Springer, Cham (2016). https://doi.org/10.1007/978-3-319-33693-0_33

39. Le Goues, C., Forrest, S., Weimer, W.: Current challenges in automatic software repair. Softw. Qual. J. **21**, 421–443 (2013)

40. Lopes, N.P., Rybalchenko, A.: Distributed and predictable software model checking. In: Jhala, R., Schmidt, D. (eds.) VMCAI 2011. LNCS, vol. 6538, pp. 340–355. Springer, Heidelberg (2011). https://doi.org/10.1007/978-3-642-18275-4_24

41. Moore, J.S.: Machines reasoning about machines: 2015. In: Finkbeiner, B., Pu, G., Zhang, L. (eds.) ATVA 2015. LNCS, vol. 9364, pp. 4–13. Springer, Cham (2015). https://doi.org/10.1007/978-3-319-24953-7_2

42. Narkawicz, A., Muñoz, C.A.: Formal verification of conflict detection algorithms for arbitrary trajectories. Reliab. Comput. **17**, 209–237 (2012)

43. Newcombe, C., Rath, T., Zhang, F., Munteanu, B., Brooker, M., Deardeuff, M.: How Amazon web services uses formal methods. Commun. ACM **58**(4), 66–73 (2004)

44. Ochoa, M., Banescu, S., Disenfeld, C., Barthe, G., Ganesh, V.: Reasoning about probabilistic defense mechanisms against remote attacks. In: IEEE European Symposium on Security and Privacy (2017)

45. O'Hearn, P.: Continuous reasoning: scaling the impact of formal methods. In: LICS (2018)

46. Reid, A., Chen, R., Deligiannis, A., Gilday, D., Hoyes, D., Keen, W., Pathirane, A., Shepherd, O., Vrabel, P., Zaidi, A.: End-to-end verification of processors with ISA-formal. In: Chaudhuri, S., Farzan, A. (eds.) CAV 2016. LNCS, vol. 9780, pp. 42–58. Springer, Cham (2016). https://doi.org/10.1007/978-3-319-41540-6_3

47. Rozier, K.Y., Vardi, M.Y.: A Multi-encoding approach for LTL symbolic satisfiability checking. In: Butler, M., Schulte, W. (eds.) FM 2011. LNCS, vol. 6664, pp. 417–431. Springer, Heidelberg (2011). https://doi.org/10.1007/978-3-642-21437-0_31

48. Rushby, J.: Software verification and system assurance. In: IEEE International Conference on Software Engineering and Formal Methods, pp. 3–10 (2009)

49. Santos, J.F., Maksimović, P., Naudžiūnienė, D., Wood, T., Gardner, P.: JaVerT: JavaScript verification toolchain. In: POPL (2017)

50. Seger, C.-J.H., Jones, R.B., O'Leary, J.W., Melham, T., Aagaard, M.D., Barrett, C., Syme, D.: An industrially effective environment for formal hardware verification. IEEE Trans. Comput. Aided Des. Integr. Circuits Syst. **24**(9), 1381–1405 (2005)

51. Wilding, M.M., Greve, D.A., Richards, R.J., Hardin, D.S.: Formal verification of partition management for the AAMP7G microprocessor. In: Hardin, D. (ed.) Design and Verification of Microprocessor Systems for High-Assurance Applications. Springer, Boston (2010). https://doi.org/10.1007/978-1-4419-1539-9_6

Propositional Dynamic Logic for Higher-Order Functional Programs

Yuki Satake[(✉)] and Hiroshi Unno

University of Tsukuba, Tsukuba, Japan
{satake,uhiro}@logic.cs.tsukuba.ac.jp

Abstract. We present an extension of propositional dynamic logic called HOT-PDL for specifying temporal properties of higher-order functional programs. The semantics of HOT-PDL is defined over Higher-Order Traces (HOTs) that model execution traces of higher-order programs. A HOT is a sequence of events such as function calls and returns, equipped with two kinds of pointers inspired by the notion of justification pointers from game semantics: one for capturing the correspondence between call and return events, and the other for capturing higher-order control flow involving a function that is passed to or returned by a higher-order function. To allow traversal of the new kinds of pointers, HOT-PDL extends PDL with new path expressions. The extension enables HOT-PDL to specify interesting properties of higher-order programs, including stack-based access control properties and those definable using dependent refinement types. We show that HOT-PDL model checking of higher-order functional programs over bounded integers is decidable via a reduction to modal μ-calculus model checking of higher-order recursion schemes.

1 Introduction

Temporal verification of higher-order programs has been an emerging research topic [12,14,18,22–24,26,27,31,34]. The specification languages used there are (ω-)regular word languages (that subsume LTL) [12,18,26] and modal μ-calculus (that subsumes CTL) [14,24,31], which are interpreted over sequences or trees consisting of events. (Extended) dependent refinement types are also used to specify temporal [23,27] and branching properties [34]. These specification languages, however, cannot sufficiently express specifications of control flow involving (higher-order) functions. For example, let us consider the following simple higher-order program $D_{\mathtt{tw}}$ (in OCaml syntax):

```
let tw f x = f (f x) in let inc x = x + 1 in let r = * in tw inc r
```

Here, $*$ denotes a non-deterministic integer, and the higher-order function $\mathtt{tw}$: $(\mathtt{int} \to \mathtt{int}) \to \mathtt{int} \to \mathtt{int}$ applies its function argument $\mathtt{f}$: $\mathtt{int} \to \mathtt{int}$ to the integer argument $\mathtt{x}$ twice. For example, for $\mathtt{r} = 0$, the program $D_{\mathtt{tw}}$ exhibits the following call-by-value reduction sequence (with the redexes underlined).

$$\underline{\mathtt{tw\ inc}\ 0} \longrightarrow \underline{(\lambda x.\mathtt{inc\ (inc}\ x))\ 0} \longrightarrow \mathtt{inc\ (\underline{inc\ 0})} \longrightarrow^* \underline{\mathtt{inc\ 1}} \longrightarrow^* 2$$

Example properties of the program $D_{\tt tw}$ that cannot be expressed by the previous specification languages are:

Prop.1. If the function returned by a partial application of $\tt tw$ to some function (e.g., $\lambda x.{\tt inc}\ ({\tt inc}\ x)$ in the above sequence) is called with some integer n, the function argument passed to $\tt tw$ (i.e., $\tt inc$) is eventually called with n.

Prop.2. If the function returned by a partial application of $\tt tw$ to some function is never called, then the function argument passed to $\tt tw$ is never called.

To remedy the limitation, we introduce a notion of Higher-Order Trace (HOT) that captures the control flow of higher-order programs and propose a dynamic logic over HOTs called Higher-Order Trace Propositional Dynamic Logic (HOT-PDL) for specifying temporal properties of higher-order programs.

Intuitively, a HOT models a program execution trace which is a possibly infinite sequence of events such as function calls and returns with information about actual arguments and return values. Furthermore, HOTs are equipped with two kinds of pointers to enable precise specification of control flow: one for capturing the correspondence between call and return events, and the other for capturing higher-order control flow involving a function that is passed to or returned by a higher-order function. The two kinds of pointers are inspired by the notion of justification pointers from the game semantics of PCF [1,2,19,20].

For the higher-order program $D_{\tt tw}$, for ${\tt r} = 0$, we get the following HOT $G_{\tt tw}$:[1]

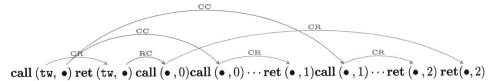

Here, $\bullet$ represents some function value, $\mathbf{call}(f, v)$ represents a call event of the function f with the argument v, and $\mathbf{ret}(f, v)$ represents a return event of the function f with the return value v. This trace corresponds to the previous reduction sequence: the call events $\mathbf{call}({\tt tw}, \bullet)$, $\mathbf{call}(\bullet, 0)$, $\mathbf{call}(\bullet, 0)$, and $\mathbf{call}(\bullet, 1)$ that occur in the trace in this order correspond respectively to the redexes $\tt tw\ inc$, $(\lambda x.{\tt inc}\ ({\tt inc}\ x))\ 0$, ${\tt inc}\ 0$, and ${\tt inc}\ 1$. The three important points here are that (1) the call events have pointers labeled with $\mathbf{CR}$ to the corresponding return events $\mathbf{ret}({\tt tw}, \bullet)$, $\mathbf{ret}(\bullet, 2)$, $\mathbf{ret}(\bullet, 1)$, and $\mathbf{ret}(\bullet, 2)$, (2) the call event $\mathbf{call}({\tt tw}, \bullet)$ has two pointers labeled with $\mathbf{CC}$, where $\bullet$ represents the function argument $\tt f$ of $\tt tw$ and the pointed call events $\mathbf{call}(\bullet, 0)$ and $\mathbf{call}(\bullet, 1)$ represent the two calls to $\tt f$ in $\tt tw$, and (3) the return event $\mathbf{ret}({\tt tw}, \bullet)$ has a pointer labeled with $\mathbf{RC}$, where $\bullet$ represents the partially-applied function $\lambda x.{\tt inc}\ ({\tt inc}\ x)$ and the pointed call event $\mathbf{call}(\bullet, 0)$ represents the call to the function.

To allow traversal of the pointers, HOT-PDL extends propositional dynamic logic with new path expressions (see Sect. 3 for details). The extension enables

---

[1] The symbol $\cdots$ indicates the omission of a subsequence. The two omitted subsequences are $\overset{\mathbf{CR}}{\overbrace{\mathbf{call}({\tt inc}, 0)\ \mathbf{ret}({\tt inc}, 1)}}$ and $\overset{\mathbf{CR}}{\overbrace{\mathbf{call}({\tt inc}, 1)\ \mathbf{ret}({\tt inc}, 2)}}$ in this order.

HOT-PDL to specify interesting properties of higher-order programs, including stack-based access control properties and those definable using dependent refinement types. Here, stack-based access control is a security mechanism implemented in runtimes like JVM for ensuring secure execution of programs that have components with different levels of trust: the mechanism ensures that a *security-critical* function (e.g., file access) is invoked only if all the (immediate and indirect) callers in the current call stack are *trusted*, or one of the callers is a *privileged* function and its callees are all *trusted*. We introduce a new variant of stack-based access control properties for higher-order programs, formalized in HOT-PDL from the point of view of interactions among callers and callees.

Compared to the previous specification languages with respect to the expressiveness, HOT-PDL subsumes (ω-)regular languages because PDL interpreted over words is already as expressive as them [15]. Temporal logics over nested words [6] such as CaRet [5] and NWTL [4] can capture the correspondence between call and return events (i.e., pointers labeled with **CR**) but cannot capture higher-order control flow (i.e., pointers labeled with **CC** and **RC**). Branching properties (expressible in, e.g., CTL), however, are out of the scope of the present paper, and such an extension of HOT-PDL remains an interesting future direction. Dependent refinement types are often used to specify properties of higher-order programs for partial- and total-correctness verification [29, 33, 39, 40]. For example, the following properties of the program D_{tw} are expressible:

Prop.3. The function yielded by applying tw to a strictly increasing function is strictly increasing.

Prop.4. The function yielded by applying tw to a terminating function is terminating.

This paper shows that HOT-PDL can encode such dependent refinement types.

We also study HOT-PDL model checking: given a higher-order program D over bounded integers and a HOT-PDL formula ϕ, the problem is to decide whether ϕ is satisfied by all the execution traces of D modeled as HOTs. We show the decidability of HOT-PDL model checking via a reduction to modal μ-calculus model checking of higher-order recursion schemes [21, 28].

The rest of the paper is organized as follows. Section 2 formalizes HOTs and explains how to use them to model execution traces of higher-order functional programs. Section 3 defines the syntax and the semantics of HOT-PDL and Sect. 4 shows how to encode stack-based access control properties and dependent refinement types in HOT-PDL. Section 5 discusses HOT-PDL model checking. We compare HOT-PDL with related work in Sect. 6 and conclude the paper with remarks on future work in Sect. 7. Omitted proofs are given in the extended version of this paper [30].

2   Higher-Order Traces

This section defines the notion of Higher-Order Trace (HOT), which is used to model execution traces of higher-order programs. To this end, we first define (Σ, Γ)-*labeled directed graphs* and *DAGs*.

Definition 1 ((Σ, Γ)-labeled directed graphs). *Let Σ be a finite set of node labels and Γ be a finite set of edge labels. A (Σ, Γ)-labeled directed graph is defined as a triple (V, λ, ν), where V is a countable set of nodes, $\lambda : V \to \Sigma$ is a node labeling function, and $\nu : V \times V \to 2^{\Gamma}$ is an edge labeling function. We call a (Σ, Γ)-labeled directed graph that has no directed cycle (Σ, Γ)-labeled DAG.*

Note that an edge may have multiple labels. For nodes $u, u' \in V$, $\nu(u, u') = \emptyset$ means that there is no edge from u to u'. We use σ and γ as meta-variables ranging respectively over Σ and Γ. We write V_{σ} for the set $\{u \in V \mid \sigma = \lambda(u)\}$ of all the nodes labeled with σ. We also write V_{Σ} for the set $\bigcup_{\sigma \in \Sigma} V_{\sigma}$. For $u, u' \in V$, we write $u \prec_{\gamma} u'$ if $\gamma \in \nu(u, u')$. A binary relation $\prec_{\gamma}^{+}$ (resp. $\prec_{\gamma}^{*}$) denotes the transitive (resp. reflexive and transitive) closure of $\prec_{\gamma}$.

Definition 2 (HOTs). *A HOT is a (Σ, Γ)-DAG, $G = (V, \lambda, \nu)$ that satisfies:*

1. *$V \neq \emptyset$, $\Gamma = \{\mathbf{N}, \mathbf{CR}, \mathbf{CC}, \mathbf{RC}\}$, $\Sigma = \Sigma_{\mathbf{call}} \uplus \Sigma_{\mathbf{ret}}$, and $\Sigma_{\mathbf{call}} = \Sigma_{\mathbf{call}}^{T} \uplus \Sigma_{\mathbf{call}}^{A}$.*
2. *$\prec_{\mathbf{CR}} \subseteq (V_{\Sigma_{\mathbf{call}}} \times V_{\Sigma_{\mathbf{ret}}})$, $\prec_{\mathbf{CC}} \subseteq (V_{\Sigma_{\mathbf{call}}} \times V_{\Sigma_{\mathbf{call}}^{A}})$, and $\prec_{\mathbf{RC}} \subseteq (V_{\Sigma_{\mathbf{ret}}} \times V_{\Sigma_{\mathbf{call}}^{A}})$.*
3. *The elements of V are linearly ordered by $\prec_{\mathbf{N}}$.*
4. *If $u \prec_{\mathbf{CR}} u'$ and $u \prec_{\mathbf{CR}} u''$, then $u' = u''$.*
5. *For all $u' \in V_{\Sigma_{\mathbf{ret}}}$, there uniquely exists $u \in V_{\Sigma_{\mathbf{call}}}$ such that $u \prec_{\mathbf{CR}} u'$ holds.*
6. *For all $u' \in V_{\Sigma_{\mathbf{call}}^{A}}$, there uniquely exists $u \in V$ such that $u \prec_{\mathbf{CC}} u'$ or $u \prec_{\mathbf{RC}} u'$ holds.*

Intuitively, $\Sigma_{\mathbf{call}}$ (resp. $\Sigma_{\mathbf{ret}}$) represents a set of call (resp. return) events. $\Sigma_{\mathbf{call}}^{T}$ (resp. $\Sigma_{\mathbf{call}}^{A}$) represents a set of call events of top-level functions (resp. functions that are returned by or passed to (higher-order) functions). $u \prec_{\mathbf{N}} u'$ means that u' is the next event of u in the trace. $u \prec_{\mathbf{CR}} u'$ indicates that u' is the return event corresponding to the call event u. $u \prec_{\mathbf{CC}} u'$ represents that u' is a call event of the function argument passed at the call event u. $u \prec_{\mathbf{RC}} u'$ means that u' is a call event of the partially-applied function returned at the return event u. We call the minimum node of a HOT G with respect to $\prec_{\mathbf{N}}$ the *root node*, denoted by 0_G. For HOTs G_1 and G_2, we say G_1 is a *prefix* of G_2 and write $G_1 \preceq G_2$, if G_1 is a sub-graph of G_2 such that $0_{G_1} = 0_{G_2}$. Note that the HOT $G_{\mathtt{tw}}$ in Sect. 1, where $\mathbf{N}$-labeled edges are omitted, satisfies the above conditions, with $\{\mathbf{call}(\mathtt{tw}, \bullet), \mathbf{call}(\mathtt{inc}, 0), \mathbf{call}(\mathtt{inc}, 1)\} \subseteq \Sigma_{\mathbf{call}}^{T}$, $\{\mathbf{call}(\bullet, 0), \mathbf{call}(\bullet, 1)\} \subseteq \Sigma_{\mathbf{call}}^{A}$, and $\{\mathbf{ret}(\mathtt{tw}, \bullet), \mathbf{ret}(\mathtt{inc}, 1), \mathbf{ret}(\mathtt{inc}, 2), \mathbf{ret}(\bullet, 1), \mathbf{ret}(\bullet, 2)\} \subseteq \Sigma_{\mathbf{ret}}$.

2.1 Trace Semantics for Higher-Order Functional Programs

We now formalize our target language $\mathcal{L}$, which is an ML-like typed call-by-value higher-order functional language. The syntax is defined by

$$
\begin{aligned}
\text{(programs)} \quad & D ::= \{f_1 \mapsto \lambda x.e_1, \ldots, f_m \mapsto \lambda x.e_m\} \\
\text{(expressions)} \quad & e ::= x \mid f \mid \lambda x.e \mid e_1\, e_2 \mid n \mid \mathsf{op}(e_1, e_2) \mid \mathtt{ifz}\ e_1\ e_2\ e_3 \\
\text{(values)} \quad & v ::= f \mid \lambda x.e \mid n \\
\text{(types)} \quad & \tau ::= \mathtt{int} \mid \tau_1 \to \tau_2
\end{aligned}
$$

Here, x and f are meta-variables ranging respectively over term variables and names of top-level functions. The meta-variable n ranges over the set of bounded integers $\mathbb{Z}_b = \{n_{\min}, \cdots, n_{\max}\} \subset \mathbb{Z}$. For simplicity of presentation, $\mathcal{L}$ has the type int of bounded integers as the only base type. op represents binary operators such as $+, -, \times, =$, and $>$. The binary relations $=$ and $>$ return an integer that encodes a boolean value (e.g., 1 for true and 0 for false). A program D maps each top-level function name f_i to its definition $\lambda x.e_i$. We write dom(D) for $\{f_1, \ldots, f_m\}$. We assume that D has the main function main of the type int $\to$ int. The functions in D can be mutually recursive. Expressions e comprise variables x, function names f, lambda abstractions $\lambda x.e$, function applications $e_1\, e_2$, bounded integers n, binary operations $\mathbf{op}(v_1, v_2)$, and conditional branches ifz $e_1\, e_2\, e_3$. We assume that expressions are simply-typed. As usual, the simple type system guarantees that an evaluation of a typed expression never causes a runtime type mismatch like $1 + \lambda x.x$. An expression ifz $e_1\, e_2\, e_3$ evaluates to e_2 (resp. e_3) if e_1 evaluates to 0 (resp. a non-zero integer). For example, the program $D_{\mathtt{tw}}$ in Sect. 1 is defined in $\mathcal{L}$ as follows:

$$D_{\mathtt{tw}} \triangleq \{\mathtt{tw} \mapsto \lambda f.\lambda x.f\ (f\ x), \mathtt{inc} \mapsto \lambda x.x + 1, \mathtt{main} \mapsto \lambda r.\mathtt{tw}\ \mathtt{inc}\ r\}$$

Domains

(configurations) $C ::= (I, E[e])$
(eval. contexts) $E ::= [\ ] \mid E\, e \mid v\, E \mid \mathbf{op}(E, e) \mid \mathbf{op}(v, E) \mid \mathtt{ifz}\, E\, e_1\, e_2 \mid \mathbf{ret}(h, i, E)$
(interfaces) $I ::= \left\{ h_1 \overset{i_1}{\mapsto} v_1, \ldots, h_m \overset{i_m}{\mapsto} v_m \right\}$
(handles) $h ::= n \mid f \mid \lfloor h \rfloor_i \mid \lceil h \rceil_i$
(events) $\alpha ::= \mathbf{call}(h_1, i, h_2) \mid \mathbf{ret}(h_1, i, h_2)$

Derivation Rules

$(I, E[(\lambda x.e)\, v]) \overset{\epsilon}{\to} (I, E[[v/x]e])$ (APP)

$$\frac{n = [\![\mathbf{op}]\!](n_1, n_2)}{(I, E[\mathbf{op}(n_1, n_2)]) \overset{\epsilon}{\to} (I, E[n])} \quad (\mathrm{OP})$$

$$\frac{(h \overset{i}{\mapsto} v) \in I \qquad \alpha = \mathbf{call}(h, i, n) \qquad I' = I\left\{ h \overset{i+1}{\mapsto} v \right\}}{(I, E[h\, n]) \overset{\alpha}{\to} (I', E[\mathbf{ret}(h, i, v\, n)])} \quad (\mathrm{CINT})$$

$(I, E[\mathtt{ifz}\, 0\, e_1\, e_2]) \overset{\epsilon}{\to} (I, E[e_1])$ (IFZ)

$$\frac{n \neq 0}{(I, E[\mathtt{ifz}\, n\, e_1\, e_2]) \overset{\epsilon}{\to} (I, E[e_2])} \quad (\mathrm{IFN})$$

$$\frac{v \text{ is a function} \qquad (h \overset{i}{\mapsto} v') \in I \qquad \alpha = \mathbf{call}(h, i, \lfloor h \rfloor_i) \qquad I' = I\left\{ h \overset{i+1}{\mapsto} v', \lfloor h \rfloor_i \overset{0}{\mapsto} v \right\}}{(I, E[h\, v]) \overset{\alpha}{\to} (I', E[\mathbf{ret}(h, i, v'\, \lfloor h \rfloor_i)])} \quad (\mathrm{CFUN})$$

$C \overset{\epsilon}{\Rightarrow} C$ (REFL)

$$\frac{\alpha = \mathbf{ret}(h, i, n)}{(I, E[\mathbf{ret}(h, i, n)]) \overset{\alpha}{\to} (I, E[n])} \quad (\mathrm{RINT})$$

$$\frac{C \overset{\varpi_1}{\Longrightarrow} C'' \qquad C'' \overset{\varpi_2}{\Longrightarrow} C'}{C \overset{\varpi_1 \cdot \varpi_2}{\Longrightarrow} C'} \quad (\mathrm{TRAN})$$

$$\frac{v \text{ is a function} \qquad \alpha = \mathbf{ret}(h, i, \lceil h \rceil_i) \qquad I' = I\left\{ \lceil h \rceil_i \overset{0}{\mapsto} v \right\}}{(I, E[\mathbf{ret}(h, i, v)]) \overset{\alpha}{\to} (I', E[\lceil h \rceil_i])} \quad (\mathrm{RFUN})$$

$$\frac{C \overset{\varpi}{\Rightarrow} C' \qquad C' \overset{\pi}{\Rightarrow} \bot}{C \overset{\varpi \cdot \pi}{\Longrightarrow} \bot} \quad (\mathrm{TRAN}\omega)$$

Fig. 1. Labeled transition relations ($\overset{\varpi}{\Rightarrow}$) and ($\overset{\pi}{\Rightarrow}$) for $\mathcal{L}$

$$(I_1, \text{main } 0) \qquad\qquad I_1 \triangleq \left\{ \begin{array}{l} \text{tw} \xmapsto{0} e_{\text{tw}}, \\ \text{inc} \xmapsto{0} \lambda x.x+1, \\ \text{main} \xmapsto{0} \lambda r.\text{tw inc } r \end{array} \right\}$$

$$\xrightarrow{\text{call}(\text{main},0,0)} (I_2, E_{\text{main}}[(\lambda r.\text{tw inc } r)\ 0]) \qquad I_2 \triangleq I_1\left\{\text{main} \xmapsto{1} \lambda r.\text{tw inc } r\right\}$$

$$\longrightarrow (I_2, E_{\text{main}}[\text{tw inc } 0])$$

$$\xrightarrow{\text{call}(\text{tw},0,\lfloor\text{tw}\rfloor_0)} (I_3, E_{\text{tw}}[(\lambda f.\lambda x.f\ (f\ x))\ \lfloor\text{tw}\rfloor_0]) \quad I_3 \triangleq I_2\left\{\text{tw} \xmapsto{1} e_{\text{tw}}, \lfloor\text{tw}\rfloor_0 \xmapsto{0} \text{inc}\right\}$$

$$\longrightarrow (I_3, E_{\text{tw}}[\lambda x.\lfloor\text{tw}\rfloor_0\ (\lfloor\text{tw}\rfloor_0\ x)])$$

$$\xrightarrow{\text{ret}(\text{tw},0,\lceil\text{tw}\rceil_0)} (I_4, E_{\text{main}}[\lceil\text{tw}\rceil_0\ 0]) \qquad I_4 \triangleq I_3\left\{\lceil\text{tw}\rceil_0 \xmapsto{0} e'_{\text{tw}}\right\}$$

$$\xrightarrow{\text{call}(\lceil\text{tw}\rceil_0,0,0)} (I_5, E_{\lceil\text{tw}\rceil_0}[(\lambda x.\lfloor\text{tw}\rfloor_0\ (\lfloor\text{tw}\rfloor_0\ x))\ 0]) \quad I_5 \triangleq I_4\left\{\lceil\text{tw}\rceil_0 \xmapsto{1} e'_{\text{tw}}\right\}$$

$$\longrightarrow (I_5, E_{\lceil\text{tw}\rceil_0}[\lfloor\text{tw}\rfloor_0\ (\lfloor\text{tw}\rfloor_0\ 0)])$$

$$\xrightarrow{\text{call}(\lfloor\text{tw}\rfloor_0,0,0)} (I_6, E_{\lfloor\text{tw}\rfloor_0}[\text{inc } 0]) \qquad I_6 \triangleq I_5\left\{\lfloor\text{tw}\rfloor_0 \xmapsto{1} \text{inc}\right\}$$

$$\xrightarrow{\text{call}(\text{inc},0,0)} (I_7, E_{\text{inc}}[(\lambda x.x+1)\ 0]) \qquad I_7 \triangleq I_6\left\{\text{inc} \xmapsto{1} \lambda x.x+1\right\}$$

$$\Longrightarrow (I_7, E_{\text{inc}}[1])$$

$$\xrightarrow{\text{ret}(\text{inc},0,1)\cdot\text{ret}(\lfloor\text{tw}\rfloor_0,0,1)} (I_7, E_{\lceil\text{tw}\rceil_0}[\lfloor\text{tw}\rfloor_0\ 1])$$

$$\xrightarrow{\text{call}(\lfloor\text{tw}\rfloor_0,1,1)} (I_8, E_{\lfloor\text{tw}\rfloor_0'}[\text{inc } 1]) \qquad I_8 \triangleq I_7\left\{\lfloor\text{tw}\rfloor_0 \xmapsto{2} \text{inc}\right\}$$

$$\xrightarrow{\text{call}(\text{inc},1,1)} (I_9, E_{\text{inc}'}[(\lambda x.x+1)\ 1]) \qquad I_9 \triangleq I_8\left\{\text{inc} \xmapsto{2} \lambda x.x+1\right\}$$

$$\Longrightarrow (I_9, E_{\text{inc}'}[2])$$

$$\xrightarrow{\text{ret}(\text{inc},1,2)\cdot\text{ret}(\lfloor\text{tw}\rfloor_0,1,2)\cdot\text{ret}(\lceil\text{tw}\rceil_0,0,2)\cdot\text{ret}(\text{main},0,2)} (I_9, 2)$$

$$e_{\text{tw}} \triangleq \lambda f.\lambda x.f\ (f\ x) \qquad\qquad e'_{\text{tw}} \triangleq \lambda x.\lfloor\text{tw}\rfloor_0\ (\lfloor\text{tw}\rfloor_0\ x)$$
$$E_{\text{main}} \triangleq \text{ret}(\text{main},0,[\,]) \qquad\qquad E_{\text{tw}} \triangleq E_{\text{main}}[\text{ret}(\text{tw},0,[\,])\ 0]$$
$$E_{\lceil\text{tw}\rceil_0} \triangleq E_{\text{main}}[\text{ret}(\lceil\text{tw}\rceil_0,0,[\,])] \qquad E_{\lfloor\text{tw}\rfloor_0} \triangleq E_{\lceil\text{tw}\rceil_0}[\lfloor\text{tw}\rfloor_0\ \text{ret}(\lfloor\text{tw}\rfloor_0,0,[\,])]$$
$$E_{\text{inc}} \triangleq E_{\lfloor\text{tw}\rfloor_0}[\text{ret}(\text{inc},0,[\,])] \qquad E_{\lfloor\text{tw}\rfloor_0'} \triangleq E_{\lceil\text{tw}\rceil_0}[\text{ret}(\lfloor\text{tw}\rfloor_0,1,[\,])]$$
$$E_{\text{inc}'} \triangleq E_{\lfloor\text{tw}\rfloor_0'}[\text{ret}(\text{inc},1,[\,])]$$

Fig. 2. Example trace of D_{tw}

We now introduce a trace semantics of the language $\mathcal{L}$, which will be used in Sect. 5 to define our model checking problems of higher-order programs. In the trace semantics, a program execution trace is represented by a sequence of function call and return events without an explicit representation of pointers but with enough information to construct them. We will explain how to model traces of $\mathcal{L}$ as HOTs by presenting a translation.

The trace semantics $[\![D]\!]$ of the language $\mathcal{L}$ is defined as $[\![D]\!]_{\text{fin}} \cup [\![D]\!]_{\text{inf}}$ where $[\![D]\!]_{\text{fin}} = \left\{ \varpi \mid (I, \text{main } n) \xRightarrow{\varpi} C \right\}$ and $[\![D]\!]_{\text{inf}} = \left\{ \pi \mid (I, \text{main } n) \xRightarrow{\pi} \bot \right\}$ are respectively the sets of *finite* and *infinite* execution traces obtained by evaluating $\text{main } n$ for some integer n using *trace-labeled* multi-step reduction relations $\xRightarrow{\varpi}$ and $\xRightarrow{\pi}$, which are presented in Fig. 1, under the program $I = \left\{ f \xmapsto{0} v \,\middle|\, (f \mapsto v) \in D \right\}$ annotated with the number of calls to each function occurred so far (i.e., initialized to 0). There, we use ϖ (resp. π) as a meta-variable ranging over finite sequences $\alpha_1 \cdots \alpha_m$ (resp. infinite sequences $\alpha_1 \cdot \alpha_2 \cdots$) of events α_i. We write ϵ for the empty sequence, $\varpi_1 \cdot \varpi_2$ for the concatenation of the sequences ϖ_1 and ϖ_2, and $|\varpi|$ for the length of ϖ. An *event* α is either of the form $\mathbf{call}(h_1, i, h_2)$ or $\mathbf{ret}(h_1, i, h_2)$, where a *handle* h represents a top-level function or a runtime value exchanged among functions. An event $\mathbf{call}(h_1, i, h_2)$ represents the $(i+1)^{\text{th}}$ call to the function h_1 with the argument h_2. On the other hand, an event $\mathbf{ret}(h_1, i, h_2)$ represents the return of the $(i+1)^{\text{th}}$ call to the function h_1 with the return value h_2. We thus equip call and return events of h_1 with the information about (1) the number i of the calls to h_1 occurred so far and (2) the runtime value h_2 passed to or returned by h_1, so that we can construct pointers (see Definition 3 for details). Note here that handles h are also equipped with meta-information necessary for constructing pointers. More specifically, h is any of the following: a bounded integer n, a top-level function name $f \in \text{dom}(D)$, the special identifier $\lfloor h \rfloor_i$ for the function argument of the $(i+1)^{\text{th}}$ call to the higher-order function h, or the special identifier $\lceil h \rceil_i$ for the partially-applied function returned by the $(i+1)^{\text{th}}$ call to h. We thus use handles to track for each function value where it is constructed and how many times it is called. We shall assume that the syntax of expressions e and values v is also extended with handles h. As we have seen, the finite traces $[\![D]\!]_{\mathtt{fin}}$ of a program D are collected using the *terminating* trace-labeled multi-step reduction relation $\overset{\varpi}{\Rightarrow}$ on configurations. A *configuration* $(I, E[e])$ is a pair of an interface I and an expression $E[e]$ consisting of an evaluation context E and a sub-expression e under evaluation. A special evaluation context $\mathbf{ret}(h, i, E)$ represents the calling context of the $(i+1)^{\text{th}}$ call to h that waits for the return value computed by E. An *interface* I is defined to be $\left\{ h_1 \overset{i_1}{\mapsto} v_1, \ldots, h_m \overset{i_m}{\mapsto} v_m \right\}$ that maps each function handle h_j to its definition v_j, where i_j records the number of calls to the function h_j occurred so far. In the derivation rules for $\overset{\varpi}{\longrightarrow}$, $[\![\mathsf{op}]\!]$ represents the integer function denoted by op, and $I\left\{ h \overset{i}{\mapsto} v \right\}$ represents the interface obtained from I by adding (or replacing existing assignment to h with) the assignment $h \overset{i}{\mapsto} v$. In the rule CINT (resp. RINT) for function calls (resp. returns) with an integer n, the reduction relation is labeled with $\mathbf{call}(h, i, n)$ (resp. $\mathbf{ret}(h, i, n)$). By contrast, in the rule CFUN (resp. RFUN) for function calls (resp. returns) with a function value v, the special identifier $\lfloor h \rfloor_i$ (resp. $\lceil h \rceil_i$) for v is used in the label $\mathbf{call}(h, i, \lfloor h \rfloor_i)$ (resp. $\mathbf{ret}(h, i, \lceil h \rceil_i)$) of the reduction relation, and v in the expression is replaced by the identifier. For example, as shown in Fig. 2, the following finite trace $\varpi_{\mathtt{tw}}$ is generated from the program $D_{\mathtt{tw}}$:

$\mathbf{call}(\mathtt{main}, 0, 0) \cdot \mathbf{call}(\mathtt{tw}, 0, \lfloor \mathtt{tw} \rfloor_0) \cdot \mathbf{ret}(\mathtt{tw}, 0, \lceil \mathtt{tw} \rceil_0) \cdot \mathbf{call}(\lceil \mathtt{tw} \rceil_0, 0, 0) \cdot$

$\mathbf{call}(\lfloor \mathtt{tw} \rfloor_0, 0, 0) \cdot \mathbf{call}(\mathtt{inc}, 0, 0) \cdot \mathbf{ret}(\mathtt{inc}, 0, 1) \cdot \mathbf{ret}(\lfloor \mathtt{tw} \rfloor_0, 0, 1) \cdot \mathbf{call}(\lfloor \mathtt{tw} \rfloor_0, 1, 1) \cdot$

$\mathbf{call}(\mathtt{inc}, 1, 1) \cdot \mathbf{ret}(\mathtt{inc}, 1, 2) \cdot \mathbf{ret}(\lfloor \mathtt{tw} \rfloor_0, 1, 2) \cdot \mathbf{ret}(\lceil \mathtt{tw} \rceil_0, 0, 2) \cdot \mathbf{ret}(\mathtt{main}, 0, 2)$

Similarly, the infinite traces $[\![D]\!]_{\mathtt{inf}}$ of a program D are collected using the *non-terminating* trace-labeled reduction relation $C \overset{\pi}{\Rightarrow} \bot$ on configurations. Intuitively, $C \overset{\pi}{\Rightarrow} \bot$ means that an execution from the configuration C diverges, producing an infinite event sequence π. In the rule TRANω, the double horizontal line represents that the rule is interpreted co-inductively.

We now define the translation from traces $[\![D]\!]_{\mathtt{fin}}$ to HOTs with $\Sigma^T_{\mathbf{call}} = \{\mathbf{call}(f, n), \mathbf{call}(f, \bullet) \mid f \in \mathrm{dom}(D), n \in \mathbb{Z}_b\}$, $\Sigma^A_{\mathbf{call}} = \{\mathbf{call}(\bullet, n), \mathbf{call}(\bullet, \bullet) \mid n \in \mathbb{Z}_b\}$, and $\Sigma_{\mathbf{ret}} = \{\mathbf{ret}(f, n), \mathbf{ret}(f, \bullet), \mathbf{ret}(\bullet, n), \mathbf{ret}(\bullet, \bullet) \mid f \in \mathrm{dom}(D), n \in \mathbb{Z}_b\}$. We shall write $\Sigma(D)$ for $\Sigma^T_{\mathbf{call}} \cup \Sigma^A_{\mathbf{call}} \cup \Sigma_{\mathbf{ret}}$. Note that $\Sigma(D)$ is finite because $\mathrm{dom}(D)$ and $\mathbb{Z}_b$ are finite. We write $|\alpha|$ for the element of $\Sigma(D)$ obtained from the event α by dropping the second argument and replacing $\lfloor h \rfloor_i$ and $\lceil h \rceil_i$ by $\bullet$. For example, we get $|\mathbf{call}(\mathtt{tw}, 0, \lfloor \mathtt{tw} \rfloor_0)| = \mathbf{call}(\mathtt{tw}, \bullet)$.

Definition 3 (Finite Traces to HOTs). *Given a finite trace $\varpi = \alpha_1 \cdots \alpha_m \in [\![D]\!]_{\mathtt{fin}}$ with $m > 0$, the corresponding HOT $G_\varpi = (V_\varpi, \lambda_\varpi, \nu_\varpi)$ is defined by:*

- *$V_\varpi = \{1, \ldots, m\}$,*
- *$\lambda_\varpi = \{j \mapsto |\alpha_j| \mid j \in V_\varpi\}$, and*
- *ν_ϖ is the smallest relation that satisfies: for any $j_1, j_2 \in V_\varpi$,*
  - *$j_1 \prec_{\mathbf{N}} j_2$ if $j_2 = j_1 + 1$,*
  - *$j_1 \prec_{\mathbf{CR}} j_2$ if $\exists h, h', h'', i.\ \alpha_{j_1} = \mathbf{call}(h, i, h') \wedge \alpha_{j_2} = \mathbf{ret}(h, i, h'')$,*
  - *$j_1 \prec_{\mathbf{CC}} j_2$ if $\exists h, h', h'', i, i'.\ \alpha_{j_1} = \mathbf{call}(h', i, h) \wedge \alpha_{j_2} = \mathbf{call}(h, i', h'')$,*
  - *$j_1 \prec_{\mathbf{RC}} j_2$ if $\exists h, h', h'', i, i'.\ \alpha_{j_1} = \mathbf{ret}(h', i, h) \wedge \alpha_{j_2} = \mathbf{call}(h, i', h'')$.*

For example, the HOT $G_{\mathtt{tw}}$ in Sect. 1 is translated from the finite trace $\varpi_{\mathtt{tw}}$ defined above (with the call and return events of $\mathtt{main}$ omitted).

For an infinite trace $\pi = \alpha_1 \cdot \alpha_2 \cdots \in [\![D]\!]_{\mathtt{inf}}$, the HOT $G_\pi = (V_\pi, \lambda_\pi, \nu_\pi)$ is defined similarly for $V_\pi = \{j \in \mathbb{N} \mid j \geq 1\}$ and $\lambda_\pi = \{j \mapsto |\alpha_j| \mid j \in V_\pi\}$.

3   Propositional Dynamic Logic over Higher-Order Traces

This section presents HOT-PDL, a propositional dynamic logic (PDL) defined over HOTs (see [16] for a general exposition of PDL). HOT-PDL extends path expressions of PDL with $\rightarrow_{\mathbf{ret}}$ and $\rightarrow_{\mathbf{call}}$ for traversing edges of HOTs labeled respectively with $\mathbf{CR}$ and $\mathbf{CC}/\mathbf{RC}$. The syntax is defined by:

$$
\begin{aligned}
\text{(formulas)}\quad & \phi ::= p \mid \phi_1 \wedge \phi_2 \mid \neg\phi \mid [\pi]\,\phi \\
\text{(path expressions)}\quad & \pi ::= \rightarrow \mid \rightarrow_{\mathbf{call}} \mid \rightarrow_{\mathbf{ret}} \mid \{\phi\}? \mid \pi_1 \cdot \pi_2 \mid \pi_1 + \pi_2 \mid \pi^*
\end{aligned}
$$

Here, p is a meta-variable ranging over atomic propositions $\mathcal{AP}$. Let $\top$ and $\bot$ denote tautology and contradiction, respectively. Path expressions π are defined using a syntax based on regular expressions: we have concatenation $\pi_1 \cdot \pi_2$, alternation $\pi_1 + \pi_2$, and Kleene star π^*. We write π^+ for $\pi \cdot \pi^*$. Path expressions $\rightarrow$, $\rightarrow_{\mathbf{ret}}$, and $\rightarrow_{\mathbf{call}}$ are for traversing edges labeled with $\mathbf{N}$, $\mathbf{CR}$, and $\mathbf{CC}$ or $\mathbf{RC}$, respectively. A path expression $\{\phi\}?$ is for testing if ϕ holds at the current node. A formula $[\pi]\,\phi$ means that ϕ always holds if one moves along any path represented by the path expression π. The dual formula $\langle \pi \rangle\,\phi$ is defined by $\neg\,[\pi]\,\neg\phi$ and means that there is a path represented by π such that ϕ holds if one moves along the path. $\langle \pi \rangle$ and $[\pi]$ have the same priority as $\neg$.

We now define the semantics of HOT-PDL. For a given HOT $G = (V, \lambda, \nu)$ with $\Sigma = \mathcal{AP}$, $\lambda(u)$ represents the atomic proposition satisfied at the node $u \in V$. We define the semantics $[\![\phi]\!]_G$ of a formula ϕ as the set of all nodes $u \in V$

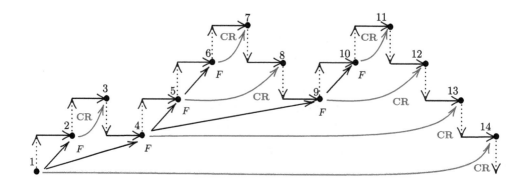

$1 : \mathbf{call}(\mathtt{main}, 0), 2 : \mathbf{call}(\mathtt{tw}, \bullet), 3 : \mathbf{ret}(\mathtt{tw}, \bullet), 4 : \mathbf{call}(\bullet, 0), 5 : \mathbf{call}(\bullet, 0),$
$6 : \mathbf{call}(\mathtt{inc}, 0), 7 : \mathbf{ret}(\mathtt{inc}, 1), 8 : \mathbf{ret}(\bullet, 1), 9 : \mathbf{call}(\bullet, 1), 10 : \mathbf{call}(\mathtt{inc}, 1),$
$11 : \mathbf{ret}(\mathtt{inc}, 2), 12 : \mathbf{ret}(\bullet, 2), 13 : \mathbf{ret}(\bullet, 2), 14 : \mathbf{ret}(\mathtt{main}, 2)$

Fig. 3. The pairs of nodes in $G_{\mathtt{tw}}$ related by $\mathbf{CR}$ or $\nearrow_F$

where ϕ is satisfied, and the semantics $[\![\pi]\!]_G$ of a path expression π as the set of all pairs $(u_1, u_2) \in V \times V$ such that one can move along π from u_1 to u_2.

$$[\![p]\!]_G = \{u \in V \mid p = \lambda(u)\} \quad [\![\phi_1 \wedge \phi_2]\!]_G = [\![\phi_1]\!]_G \cap [\![\phi_2]\!]_G \quad [\![\neg\phi]\!]_G = V \setminus [\![\phi]\!]_G$$
$$[\![[\pi]\,\phi]\!]_G = \{u \in V \mid \forall u'. ((u, u') \in [\![\pi]\!]_G \Rightarrow u' \in [\![\phi]\!]_G)\}$$
$$[\![\rightarrow]\!]_G = \prec_{\mathbf{N}} \qquad [\![\rightarrow_{\mathbf{ret}}]\!]_G = \prec_{\mathbf{CR}} \qquad [\![\rightarrow_{\mathbf{call}}]\!]_G = \prec_{\mathbf{CC}} \cup \prec_{\mathbf{RC}}$$
$$[\![\{\phi\}?]\!]_G = \{(u, u) \in V \times V \mid u \in [\![\phi]\!]_G\}$$
$$[\![\pi_1 \cdot \pi_2]\!]_G = \{(u_1, u_3) \in V \times V \mid \exists u_2 \in V. (u_1, u_2) \in [\![\pi_1]\!]_G \wedge (u_2, u_3) \in [\![\pi_2]\!]_G\}$$
$$[\![\pi_1 + \pi_2]\!]_G = [\![\pi_1]\!]_G \cup [\![\pi_2]\!]_G \qquad [\![\pi^*]\!]_G = \bigcup_{m \geq 0} [\![\pi]\!]_G^m$$

Here, for a binary relation R, R^m denotes the m-th power of R. Note that this semantics can interpret a given HOT-PDL formula over both finite and infinite HOTs. $[\![p]\!]_G$ consists of all nodes labeled by p. $[\![[\pi]\,\phi]\!]_G$ contains all nodes from which we always reach to a node in $[\![\phi]\!]_G$ if we take a path represented by π. $[\![\rightarrow]\!]_G$, $[\![\rightarrow_{\mathbf{ret}}]\!]_G$, and $[\![\rightarrow_{\mathbf{call}}]\!]_G$ contain the pairs of nodes linked by an edge labeled by $\mathbf{N}$, $\mathbf{CR}$, and $\mathbf{CC}$ or $\mathbf{RC}$, respectively. We write $G \models \phi$ if $0_G \in [\![\phi]\!]_G$. For example, let us consider the HOT $G_{\mathtt{tw}}$ and $\mathcal{AP} = \Sigma(D_{\mathtt{tw}})$. Then, $[\![\langle\rightarrow\rangle\,\mathbf{ret}(\mathtt{tw}, \bullet)]\!]_{G_{\mathtt{tw}}}$ consists of the node labeled by $\mathbf{call}(\mathtt{tw}, \bullet)$. $[\![\langle\rightarrow_{\mathbf{ret}}\rangle\,\mathbf{ret}(\bullet, 2)]\!]_{G_{\mathtt{tw}}}$ consists of a node labeled by $\mathbf{call}(\bullet, 0)$ and the node labeled by $\mathbf{call}(\bullet, 1)$. $[\![\langle\rightarrow_{\mathbf{call}}\rangle\,\mathbf{call}(\bullet, 0)]\!]_{G_{\mathtt{tw}}}$ consists of the two nodes respectively labeled by $\mathbf{call}(\mathtt{tw}, \bullet)$ and $\mathbf{ret}(\mathtt{tw}, \bullet)$. The example properties of $D_{\mathtt{tw}}$ discussed in Sect. 1 can be expressed as follows:

Prop. 1.: $[\rightarrow^*]\,\bigwedge_{x \in \mathbb{Z}_b} ((\mathbf{call}(\mathtt{tw}, \bullet) \wedge \langle\rightarrow_{\mathbf{ret}} \cdot \rightarrow_{\mathbf{call}}\rangle\,\mathbf{call}(\bullet, x)) \Rightarrow \langle\rightarrow_{\mathbf{call}}\rangle\,\mathbf{call}(\bullet, x))$
Prop. 2.: $[\rightarrow^*]\,((\mathbf{call}(\mathtt{tw}, \bullet) \wedge \neg\,\langle\rightarrow_{\mathbf{ret}} \cdot \rightarrow_{\mathbf{call}}\rangle\,\top) \Rightarrow \neg\,\langle\rightarrow_{\mathbf{call}}\rangle\,\top)$

Here, $\bigwedge_{x \in \mathbb{Z}_b} \phi$ abbreviates $[n_{\mathbf{min}}/x]\,\phi \wedge \cdots \wedge [n_{\mathbf{max}}/x]\,\phi$.

In Sect. 4, we show further examples that express interesting properties of higher-order programs, including stack based access control properties and those

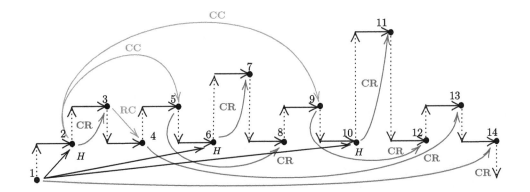

$1 : \mathbf{call}(\mathtt{main}, 0), 2 : \mathbf{call}(\mathtt{tw}, \bullet), 3 : \mathbf{ret}(\mathtt{tw}, \bullet), 4 : \mathbf{call}(\bullet, 0), 5 : \mathbf{call}(\bullet, 0),$

$6 : \mathbf{call}(\mathtt{inc}, 0), 7 : \mathbf{ret}(\mathtt{inc}, 1), 8 : \mathbf{ret}(\bullet, 1), 9 : \mathbf{call}(\bullet, 1), 10 : \mathbf{call}(\mathtt{inc}, 1),$

$11 : \mathbf{ret}(\mathtt{inc}, 2), 12 : \mathbf{ret}(\bullet, 2), 13 : \mathbf{ret}(\bullet, 2), 14 : \mathbf{ret}(\mathtt{main}, 2)$

Fig. 4. The pairs of nodes in $G_{\mathtt{tw}}$ related by **CR**, **CC**, **RC**, or $\nearrow_H$

definable using dependent refinement types. We here prepare notations used there. First, we overload the symbols $\Sigma_{\mathbf{call}}$, $\Sigma_{\mathbf{ret}}$, and $\Sigma_{\mathbf{call}}^T$ to denote the path expressions $\{\bigvee \Sigma_{\mathbf{call}}\}?$, $\{\bigvee \Sigma_{\mathbf{ret}}\}?$, and $\{\bigvee \Sigma_{\mathbf{call}}^T\}?$, respectively. We write $\rightarrow_F$ for the path expression $\rightarrow_{\mathbf{ret}} \cdot \rightarrow$, which is used to move from a call event to the next event of the caller (by skipping to the next event of the corresponding return event). We also write $\nearrow_F$ for the path expression $\Sigma_{\mathbf{call}} \cdot \rightarrow \cdot \rightarrow_F^* \cdot \Sigma_{\mathbf{call}}$, which is used to move from a call event to any call event invoked by the callee. Figure 3 illustrates the pairs of nodes in $G_{\mathtt{tw}}$ related by $\nearrow_F$. To capture control flow of higher-order programs, where function callers and callees may exchange functions as values, we need to use **CC**- and **RC**-labeled edges. For example, an event raised by the function argument f_{arg} of a higher-order function f could be regarded as an event of the caller g of f, because f_{arg} is constructed by g. Similarly, an event raised by the (partially-applied) function f_{ret} returned by a function f could be regarded as an event of f. To formalize the idea, we introduce variants $\rightarrow_H$ and $\nearrow_H$ of $\rightarrow_F$ and $\nearrow_F$ with higher-order control flow taken into consideration: $\rightarrow_H$ denotes $(\rightarrow_{\mathbf{ret}} \cdot \rightarrow) + (\rightarrow_{\mathbf{call}} \cdot \rightarrow)$ and $\nearrow_F$ denotes $\Sigma_{\mathbf{call}}^T \cdot \rightarrow \cdot \rightarrow_H^* \cdot \Sigma_{\mathbf{call}}^T$. Note that the source and the target of $\nearrow_H$ are restricted to call events of top-level functions. Figure 4 illustrates the pairs of nodes in $G_{\mathtt{tw}}$ related by $\nearrow_H$, where nodes labeled with events of the same function (in the sense discussed above) are arranged in the same horizontal line.

4 Applications of HOT-PDL

We show how to encode dependent refinement types and stack-based access control properties using HOT-PDL.

4.1 Dependent Refinement Types

HOT-PDL can specify pre- and post-conditions of higher-order functions, by encoding dependent refinement types τ for partial [29,33,40] and total [23,27,34, 36,39] correctness verification, defined as: $\tau ::= \{\nu \mid \psi\} \mid (x : \tau_1) \to \tau_2^Q$. Here, Q is either $\forall$ or $\exists$. An integer refinement type $\{\nu \mid \psi\}$ is the type of bounded integers ν that satisfy the refinement formula ψ over bounded integers. A dependent function type $(x : \tau_1) \to \tau_2^\forall$ is the type of functions that, for any argument x conforming to the type τ_1, *if terminating*, return a value conforming to the type τ_2. By contrast, $(x : \tau_1) \to \tau_2^\exists$ is the type of functions that, for any argument x conforming to τ_1, *always terminate* and return a value conforming to τ_2. For example, Prop.3 and Prop.4 of $D_{\mathtt{tw}}$ are expressed by the following types of $\mathtt{tw}$:

Prop.3.: $(f : (x : \mathtt{int}) \to \{\nu \mid \nu > x\}^\forall) \to \left((x : \mathtt{int}) \to \{\nu \mid \nu > x\}^\forall\right)^\forall$

Prop.4.: $(f : (x : \mathtt{int}) \to \mathtt{int}^\exists) \to \left((x : \mathtt{int}) \to \mathtt{int}^\exists\right)^\forall$

We here write $\mathtt{int}$ for $\{\nu \mid \top\}$. These types can be encoded in HOT-PDL as:

Prop.3.: $\mathbf{call}(\mathtt{tw}, \bullet) \Rightarrow ([\to_{\mathbf{call}}]\,\mathtt{incr}(\bullet)) \wedge [\to_{\mathbf{ret}}]\,(\mathbf{ret}(\mathtt{tw}, \bullet) \Rightarrow [\to_{\mathbf{call}}]\,\mathtt{incr}(\bullet))$

Prop.4.: $\mathbf{call}(\mathtt{tw}, \bullet) \Rightarrow ([\to_{\mathbf{call}}]\,\mathtt{term}(\bullet)) \wedge [\to_{\mathbf{ret}}]\,(\mathbf{ret}(\mathtt{tw}, \bullet) \Rightarrow [\to_{\mathbf{call}}]\,\mathtt{term}(\bullet))$

Here, $\mathtt{incr}(g) = \bigwedge_{x \in \mathbb{Z}_b} \mathbf{call}(g, x) \Rightarrow [\to_{\mathbf{ret}}] \bigwedge_{y \in \mathbb{Z}_b} (\mathbf{ret}(g, y) \Rightarrow y > x)$ and $\mathtt{term}(g) = \bigwedge_{x \in \mathbb{Z}_b} (\mathbf{call}(g, x) \Rightarrow \langle \to_{\mathbf{ret}} \rangle \top)$ for $g \in \{\bullet\} \cup \{f \mid f \in \mathrm{dom}(D)\}$. We now define a translation F from types to HOT-PDL formulas as follows:

$$F(g, (x : \tau_1) \to \tau_2^Q) = \bigwedge_{x \in |\tau_1|} \left(\mathbf{call}(g, x) \Rightarrow F_{arg}(x, \tau_1) \wedge F_{ret}(g, \tau_2^Q)\right)$$

$$|(x : \tau_1) \to \tau_2^Q| = \{\bullet\} \qquad\qquad |\{x \mid \psi\}| = \mathbb{Z}_b$$

$$F_{arg}(\bullet, \tau) = [\to_{\mathbf{call}}]\,F(\bullet, \tau) \qquad F_{arg}(n, \{x \mid \psi\}) = \begin{cases} \top & (\text{if } \models [n/x]\psi) \\ \bot & (\text{if } \not\models [n/x]\psi) \end{cases}$$

$$F_{ret}(g, \tau^\forall) = [\to_{\mathbf{ret}}] \bigwedge_{x \in |\tau|} (\mathbf{ret}(g, x) \Rightarrow F(x, \tau))$$

$$F_{ret}(g, \tau^\exists) = (\langle \to_{\mathbf{ret}} \rangle \top) \wedge F_{ret}(g, \tau^\forall)$$

4.2 Stack-Based Access Control Properties

As briefly summarized in Sect. 1, stack-based access control [13] ensures that a *security-critical* function (e.g., file access) is invoked only if all the (immediate and indirect) callers in the current call stack are *trusted*, or one of the callers is a *privileged* function and its callees are all *trusted*. We here use HOT-PDL to specify stack-based access control properties for higher-order programs. Let **Critical**, **Trusted**, and **Priv** be HOT-PDL formulas that tell whether the current node is labeled with a call event of security-critical, trusted, and privileged functions, respectively. We assume that **Critical**, **Priv**, and ¬**Trusted** do not overlap each other, and a function in **Priv** can be directly called only from a function in **Trusted**. Then, one may think we can express the specification as:

$$\neg \left\langle \nearrow_F^* \cdot \{\neg\mathbf{Trusted}\}? \cdot (\nearrow_F \cdot \{\neg\mathbf{Priv}\}?)^+ \right\rangle \mathbf{Critical}$$

Here, the path expression $\nearrow_F$ introduced in Sect. 3 is used to traverse the call stack bottom-up. The above formula says that an invalid call stack never occurs, where a call stack is called *invalid* if it contains a call to an untrusted function (represented by the part $\nearrow_F^* \{\neg\mathbf{Trusted}\}?$), followed by a call to a critical function (represented by **Critical**), with no intervening call to a privileged function (represented by $(\nearrow_F \cdot \{\neg\mathbf{Priv}\}?)^+$).

This definition, however, is not sufficient for our higher-order language. Let us consider the following program D_{pa}, which involves a partial application:

```
let untrusted () = λu.critical u
let main () = untrusted () ()
```

Here, untrusted $\notin$ **Trusted** and critical $\in$ **Critical**. Intuitively, D_{pa} should be regarded as *unsafe* because critical in the body of untrusted is called. However, D_{pa} satisfies the specification above (under the assumption that anonymous functions are in **Trusted**), because the partial application untrusted () never causes a call to critical but just returns the anonymous (and trusted) function $\lambda u.\mathtt{critical}\ u$. The following higher-order program D_{ho} is yet another unsafe example that satisfies the specification:

```
let privileged f = f ()
    let trusted f = if test () then privileged f else ()
 let untrusted () = trusted (λx.crash (); critical ())
        let main () = untrusted ()
```

Here, privileged $\in$ **Priv**, trusted $\in$ **Trusted**, untrusted $\notin$ **Trusted**, and critical $\in$ **Critical**. Note that critical in the body of untrusted is called as follows: the anonymous function $\lambda x.\mathtt{crash}\ ();\mathtt{critical}\ ()$ is first passed to trusted and then to privileged (if test () returns true), and is finally called by privileged, causing a call to critical.

To remedy the limitation, we introduce a new refined variant of stack-based access control properties for higher-order programs, formalized in HOT-PDL from the point of view of interactions among callers and callees as follows:

$$\neg \left\langle \nearrow_H^* \cdot \{\neg\mathbf{Trusted}\}? \cdot (\nearrow_H \cdot \{\neg\mathbf{Priv}\}?)^+ \right\rangle \mathbf{Critical}$$

Note that this is obtained from the previous version by just replacing $\nearrow_F$ with $\nearrow_H$, which takes into account which function constructed each function value exchanged among functions. The refined version rejects the unsafe D_{pa} and D_{ho} as intended: D_{pa} (resp. D_{ho}) is rejected because the call event of $\lambda u.\mathtt{critical}\ u$ (resp. $\lambda x.\mathtt{crash}\ ();\mathtt{critical}\ ()$) is regarded as an event of untrusted.

Fournet and Gordon [13] have studied variants of stack-based access control properties for a call-by-value higher-order language. We conclude this section by comparing ours with one of theirs called "stack inspection with frame capture".[2] The ideas behind the two are similar but what follows illustrates the difference:

```
let untrusted f = crash (); f ()
    let trusted x = untrusted (λx.if test () then critical () else ())
        let main () = trusted ()
```

This program satisfies ours but violates theirs. Note that ours allows a function originally constructed by a trusted function to invoke a critical function even if the function is passed around by an untrusted function. By contrast, in their definition, a trusted function value gets "contaminated" (i.e., disabled to invoke a critical function) once it is passed to or returned by an untrusted function. In some cases, their conservative policy is useful, but we believe ours would be more semantically robust (e.g., even works well with the CPS transformation).

5   HOT-PDL Model Checking

In this section, we define HOT-PDL model checking problems for higher-order functional programs over bounded integers and sketch a proof of the decidability.

Definition 4 (HOT-PDL model checking). *Given a program D and a HOT-PDL formula ϕ with $\mathcal{AP} = \Sigma(D)$, HOT-PDL model checking is the problem of deciding whether $G_\varpi \models \phi$ and $G_\pi \models \phi$ for all $\varpi \in [\![D]\!]_{\mathtt{fin}}$ and $\pi \in [\![D]\!]_{\mathtt{inf}}$.*

Theorem 1 (Decidability). *HOT-PDL model checking is decidable.*

We show this by a reduction to modal μ-calculus (μ-ML) model checking of higher-order recursion schemes (HORSs), which is known decidable [21,28]. A HORS is a grammar for generating a (possibly infinite) ranked tree, and HORSs are essentially simply-typed lambda calculus with general recursion, tree constructors, and finite data domains such as booleans and bounded integers.

In the reduction, we encode the set of HOTs that are generated from the given program D as a single tree (generated by a HORS). For example, Fig. 5 shows such a tree that encodes the HOTs of $D_{\mathtt{tw}}$.[3] There, a node labeled with **end** represents the termination of the program. Note that the branching at the root node is due to the input to the function **main**. The subtree with the root node labeled with **call**(main, 0) is obtained from the HOT $G_{\mathtt{tw}}$ by appending a special node labeled with **end**, adding, for each edge with the label $\gamma \in \{\mathbf{N}, \mathbf{CR}, \mathbf{CC}, \mathbf{RC}\}$, a new node labeled with γ, and expanding the resulting DAG into a tree. Thus, the edge labels of $G_{\mathtt{tw}}$ are turned into node labels of the tree.

---

[2] We do not compare with the other variants in [13] because they are too syntactic to be preserved by simple program transformations like inlining.

[3] There, for simplicity, we illustrate an *unranked* tree and omit the label of branching nodes. In the formalization, we express an unranked tree as a binary tree using a special node label **br** of the arity 2 representing a binary branching.

It is also worth mentioning here that we are allowed to expand DAGs into trees because the truth value of a HOT-PDL formula is not affected by node-sharing in the given HOT. This nice property is lost if we extend the path expressions of HOT-PDL, for example, with intersections. Thus, the decidability of model checking for extensions of HOT-PDL is an open problem.

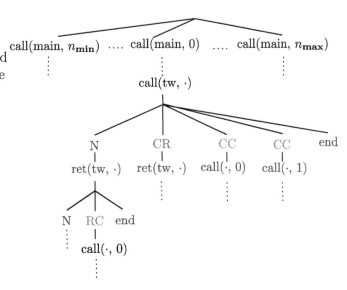

Fig. 5. A tree encoding the HOTs generated from D_{tw}

We next explain our translation from a HOT-PDL formula into a μ-ML formula interpreted over trees that encode HOTs. Our translation is based on an existing one for ordinary PDL [11]. The syntax of μ-ML is defined as follows:

$$\varphi ::= X \mid p \mid \neg\varphi \mid \varphi \wedge \varphi \mid \Box\varphi \mid \nu X.\varphi \mid \mu X.\varphi$$

Here, X represents a propositional variable and p represents an atomic proposition. A formula $\Box\varphi$ means that φ holds for any child of the current node. A formula $\mu X.\varphi$ (resp. $\nu X.\varphi$) represents the least (resp. greatest) fixpoint of the function $\lambda X.\varphi$. Here, we assume X occurs only positively in φ. For example, the HOT-PDL formulas $[\rightarrow] p$, $[\rightarrow_{\mathbf{ret}}] p$, and $[\rightarrow_{\mathbf{call}}] p$ are respectively translated to μ-ML formulas: $\Box(\nu X.(\mathbf{N} \Rightarrow \Box p) \wedge (\mathbf{br} \Rightarrow \Box X))$, $\Box(\nu X.(\mathbf{CR} \Rightarrow \Box p) \wedge (\mathbf{br} \Rightarrow \Box X))$, and $\Box(\nu X.((\mathbf{CC} \vee \mathbf{RC}) \Rightarrow \Box p) \wedge (\mathbf{br} \Rightarrow \Box X))$, where the greatest fixpoints are used to skip the branching nodes labeled with $\mathbf{br}$ (that may repeat infinitely).

Finally, we explain how to obtain a HORS for generating a tree that encodes the set of HOTs generated from the given program D. We here need to simulate pointer traversals of HOT-PDL by using purely functional features of HORSs because μ-ML does not support pointers. Intuitively, we obtain the desired HORS from D by embedding an event monitor and an event handler. Whenever the monitor detects a function call or return event during the execution of D, the handler creates a new node labeled with the event or ignores the event until a certain event is detected by the monitor, depending on the current mode of the handler. The handler has the following three modes:

$m_{\mathbf{N}}$: The handler always creates and links two new nodes $u_{\mathbf{N}}$ and u_α labeled respectively with $\mathbf{N}$ and the event α observed. The handler then continues as follows, depending on the form of the event α:

$\mathbf{call}(g, n)$: Spawns a new handler with the mode $m_{\mathbf{ret}}$. Then, the two handlers of the modes $m_{\mathbf{N}}$ and $m_{\mathbf{ret}}$ continue to create subtrees of u_α.

$\mathbf{call}(g, \bullet)$: Spawns two new handlers with the modes $m_{\mathbf{ret}}$ and $m_{\mathbf{call}}$. The three handlers of $m_{\mathbf{N}}$, $m_{\mathbf{ret}}$, and $m_{\mathbf{call}}$ continue to create subtrees of u_α.

$\mathbf{ret}(g, n)$: The handler of the mode $m_{\mathbf{N}}$ continues to create a subtree of u_α.

$\mathbf{ret}(g, \bullet)$: Spawns a new handler with the mode $m_{\mathbf{call}}$. Then, the two handlers of the modes $m_{\mathbf{N}}$ and $m_{\mathbf{call}}$ continue to create subtrees of u_α.

$m_{\mathbf{ret}}$: The handler ignores all events but the return event corresponding to the call event that caused the spawn of the handler. If not ignored, the handler creates and links new nodes $u_{\mathbf{CR}}$ and u_α labeled with $\mathbf{CR}$ and the event α. The handler changes its mode to $m_{\mathbf{N}}$ and continues creating a subtree of u_α.

$m_{\mathbf{call}}$: The handler ignores all events but the call event of the function passed to or returned by the call or return event that caused the spawn of the handler. If not ignored, the handler creates and links new nodes u and u_α labeled respectively with $\mathbf{CC}$ or $\mathbf{RC}$ and the event α, duplicates itself, and changes the mode of the original to $m_{\mathbf{N}}$. The handler of the mode $m_{\mathbf{N}}$ (resp. $m_{\mathbf{call}}$) continues to create a subtree of u_α (resp. the parent of u).

For simplicity of the construction, we assume that D is in the Continuation-Passing Style (CPS). This does not lose generality because we can enforce this form by the CPS transformation. Because CPS explicates the order of function call and return events, it simplifies event monitoring, handling, and tracking of the current mode of the monitors, which often changes as monitoring proceeds.

6   Related Work

HOT-PDL can specify temporal trace properties of higher-order programs. An extension for specifying branching properties, however, remains a future work.

There have been proposed logics and formal languages on richer structures than words. Regular languages of nested words, or equivalently, Visibly Pushdown Languages (VPLs) have been introduced by Alur and Madhusudan [7]. An (ω-)nested word is a (possibly infinite) word with additional well-nested pointers from call events to the corresponding return events. Compared to temporal logics CaRet [5] and NWTL [4] over (ω-)nested words, HOT-PDL is defined over HOTs that have richer structures. Recall that a HOT is equipped with two kinds of pointers: one kind with the label $\mathbf{CR}$, which is the same as the pointers of nested words, and the other kind with the label $\mathbf{CC}$ or $\mathbf{RC}$, which is newly introduced to capture higher-order control flow. Bollig et al. proposed nested traces as a generalization of nested words for modeling traces of concurrent (first-order) recursive programs, and presented temporal logics over nested traces [8]. Nested traces, however, cannot model traces of higher-order programs. We expect a combination of our work with theirs enables us to specify temporal trace properties of concurrent and higher-order recursive programs. Cyriac et al. have recently introduced an extension of PDL defined over traces of *order-2* collapsible pushdown systems (CPDS) [3]. Interestingly, their traces are also equipped with two kinds of pointers: one kind of pointers captures the correspondence between ordinary push and pop stack operations, and the other captures the correspondence between order-2 push and pop operations for second-order stacks. Our work deals with higher-order programs that correspond to order-n CPDS for arbitrary n.

Finally, we compare HOT-PDL with existing logics defined over words. It is well known that LTL is less expressive than ω-regular languages [38]. To remedy the limitation of LTL, Wolper introduced ETL [38] that allows users to define new temporal operators using right-linear grammars. Henriksen and Thiagarajan proposed DLTL [17] that generalizes the until operator of LTL using regular expressions. Leucker and Sánchez proposed RLTL [25] that combines LTL and regular expressions. Vardi and Giacomo have introduced Linear Dynamic Logic (LDL), a variant of PDL interpreted over infinite words [15,35]. LDL$_f$, a variant of PDL interpreted over finite words, has also been studied in [15]. ETL, DLTL, RLTL, and LDL are as expressive as ω-regular languages. Note that HOT-PDL subsumes (ω-)regular languages because LDL and LDL$_f$ can be naturally embedded in HOT-PDL. (ω-)VPLs strictly subsume (ω-)regular languages. Though CaRet [5] and NWTL [4] are defined over nested words, they do not capture the full class of VPLs [10]. To remedy the limitation, VLTL [10] combines LTL and VRE [9] in the style of RLTL, where VRE is a generalization of regular expressions for VPLs. VLDL [37] extends LDL by replacing the path expressions with VPLs over finite words. VLTL and VLDL exactly characterize ω-VPLs. Because VPLs and HOT-PDL are incomparable, it remains future work to extend HOT-PDL to subsume (ω-)VPLs.

7 Conclusion and Future Work

We have presented HOT-PDL, an extension of PDL defined over HOTs that model execution traces of call-by-value and higher-order programs. HOT-PDL enables a precise specification of temporal trace properties of higher-order programs and consequently provides a foundation for specification in various application domains including stack-based access control and dependent refinement types. We have also studied HOT-PDL model checking and presented a reduction method to modal μ-calculus model checking of higher-order recursion schemes.

To further widen the scope of our approach, it is worth investigating how to adapt HOTs and HOT-PDL to call-by-name and/or effectful languages. To this end, it is natural to incorporate more ideas from achievements of game semantics [1,20,32] and extend HOTs with new kinds of events and pointers for capturing call-by-name and/or effectful computations.

Acknowledgments. We would like to thank anonymous referees for their useful comments. This work was supported by JSPS KAKENHI Grant Numbers 15H05706, 16H05856, 17H01720, and 17H01723.

References

1. Abramsky, S., Jagadeesan, R., Malacaria, P.: Full abstraction for PCF. Inf. Comput. **163**, 409–470 (2000)
2. Abramsky, S., McCusker, G.: Call-by-value games. In: Nielsen, M., Thomas, W. (eds.) CSL 1997. LNCS, vol. 1414, pp. 1–17. Springer, Heidelberg (1998). https://doi.org/10.1007/BFb0028004
3. Aiswarya, C., Gastin, P., Saivasan, P.: Nested words for order-2 pushdown systems. arXiv:1609.06290 (2016)
4. Alur, R., Arenas, M., Barcelo, P., Etessami, K., Immerman, N., Libkin, L.: First-order and temporal logics for nested words. Log. Methods Comput. Sci. **4**(4), 1–44 (2008)
5. Alur, R., Etessami, K., Madhusudan, P.: A temporal logic of nested calls and returns. In: Jensen, K., Podelski, A. (eds.) TACAS 2004. LNCS, vol. 2988, pp. 467–481. Springer, Heidelberg (2004). https://doi.org/10.1007/978-3-540-24730-2_35
6. Alur, R., Madhusudan, P.: Visibly pushdown languages. In: STOC 2004, pp. 202–211. ACM (2004)
7. Alur, R., Madhusudan, P.: Adding nesting structure to words. J. ACM **56**(3), 16:1–16:43 (2009)
8. Bollig, B., Cyriac, A., Gastin, P., Zeitoun, M.: Temporal logics for concurrent recursive programs: satisfiability and model checking. J. Appl. Log. **12**(4), 395–416 (2014)
9. Bozzelli, L., Sánchez, C.: Visibly rational expressions. In: FSTTCS 2012. LIPIcs, vol. 18, pp. 211–223. Schloss Dagstuhl-Leibniz-Zentrum fuer Informatik (2012)
10. Bozzelli, L., Sánchez, C.: Visibly linear temporal logic. In: Demri, S., Kapur, D., Weidenbach, C. (eds.) IJCAR 2014. LNCS (LNAI), vol. 8562, pp. 418–433. Springer, Cham (2014). https://doi.org/10.1007/978-3-319-08587-6_33
11. Carreiro, F., Venema, Y.: PDL inside the μ-calculus: a syntactic and an automata-theoretic characterization. Adv. Modal Log. **10**, 74–93 (2014)
12. Disney, T., Flanagan, C., McCarthy, J.: Temporal higher-order contracts. In: ICFP 2011, pp. 176–188. ACM (2011)
13. Fournet, C., Gordon, A.D.: Stack inspection: theory and variants. In: POPL 2002, pp. 307–318. ACM (2002)
14. Fujima, K., Ito, S., Kobayashi, N.: Practical alternating parity tree automata model checking of higher-order recursion schemes. In: Shan, C. (ed.) APLAS 2013. LNCS, vol. 8301, pp. 17–32. Springer, Cham (2013). https://doi.org/10.1007/978-3-319-03542-0_2
15. Giacomo, G.D., Vardi, M.Y.: Linear temporal logic and linear dynamic logic on finite traces. In: IJCAI 2013, pp. 854–860. AAAI Press (2013)
16. Harel, D., Tiuryn, J., Kozen, D.: Dynamic Logic. MIT Press, Cambridge (2000)
17. Henriksen, J.G., Thiagarajan, P.: Dynamic linear time temporal logic. Ann. Pure Appl. Log. **96**(1), 187–207 (1999)
18. Hofmann, M., Chen, W.: Abstract interpretation from Büchi automata. In: CSL-LICS 2014, pp. 51:1–51:10. ACM (2014)
19. Honda, K., Yoshida, N.: Game theoretic analysis of call-by-value computation. In: Degano, P., Gorrieri, R., Marchetti-Spaccamela, A. (eds.) ICALP 1997. LNCS, vol. 1256, pp. 225–236. Springer, Heidelberg (1997). https://doi.org/10.1007/3-540-63165-8_180

20. Hyland, J.M.E., Ong, C.H.L.: On full abstraction for PCF: I, II, and III. Inf. Comput. **163**, 285–408 (2000)
21. Kobayashi, N., Ong, C.H.L.: A type system equivalent to the modal Mu-calculus model checking of higher-order recursion schemes. In: LICS 2009, pp. 179–188. IEEE (2009)
22. Kobayashi, N., Tsukada, T., Watanabe, K.: Higher-order program verification via HFL model checking. In: Ahmed, A. (ed.) ESOP 2018. LNCS, vol. 10801, pp. 711–738. Springer, Cham (2018). https://doi.org/10.1007/978-3-319-89884-1_25
23. Koskinen, E., Terauchi, T.: Local temporal reasoning. In: CSL-LICS 2014, pp. 59:1–59:10. ACM (2014)
24. Lester, M.M., Neatherway, R.P., Ong, C.H.L., Ramsay, S.J.: Model checking liveness properties of higher-order functional programs (2011). http://mjolnir.comlab.ox.ac.uk/papers/thors.pdf
25. Leucker, M., Sánchez, C.: Regular linear temporal logic. In: Jones, C.B., Liu, Z., Woodcock, J. (eds.) ICTAC 2007. LNCS, vol. 4711, pp. 291–305. Springer, Heidelberg (2007). https://doi.org/10.1007/978-3-540-75292-9_20
26. Murase, A., Terauchi, T., Kobayashi, N., Sato, R., Unno, H.: Temporal verification of higher-order functional programs. In: POPL 2016, pp. 57–68. ACM (2016)
27. Nanjo, Y., Unno, H., Koskinen, E., Terauchi, T.: A fixpoint logic and dependent effects for temporal property verification. In: LICS 2018. ACM (2018)
28. Ong, C.H.L.: On model-checking trees generated by higher-order recursion schemes. In: LICS 2006, pp. 81–90. IEEE (2006)
29. Rondon, P., Kawaguchi, M., Jhala, R.: Liquid types. In: PLDI 2008, pp. 159–169. ACM (2008)
30. Satake, Y., Unno, H.: Propositional dynamic logic for higher-order functional programs (2018). http://www.cs.tsukuba.ac.jp/~uhiro/
31. Suzuki, R., Fujima, K., Kobayashi, N., Tsukada, T.: Streett automata model checking of higher-order recursion schemes. In: FSCD 2017. LIPIcs, vol. 84, pp. 32:1–32:18. Schloss Dagstuhl-Leibniz-Zentrum fuer Informatik (2017)
32. Tzevelekos, N.: Nominal game semantics. Ph.D. thesis, University of Oxford (2008)
33. Unno, H., Kobayashi, N.: Dependent type inference with interpolants. In: PPDP 2009, pp. 277–288. ACM (2009)
34. Unno, H., Satake, Y., Terauchi, T.: Relatively complete refinement type system for verification of higher-order non-deterministic programs. Proc. ACM Program. Lang. **2**(POPL), 12:1–12:29 (2017)
35. Vardi, M.Y.: The rise and fall of LTL. GandALF (2011)
36. Vazou, N., Seidel, E.L., Jhala, R., Vytiniotis, D., Peyton Jones, S.L.: Refinement types for Haskell. In: ICFP 2014, pp. 269–282. ACM (2014)
37. Weinert, A., Zimmermann, M.: Visibly linear dynamic logic. In: FSTTCS 2016. LIPIcs, vol. 65, pp. 28:1–28:14. Schloss Dagstuhl-Leibniz-Zentrum fuer Informatik (2016)
38. Wolper, P.: Temporal logic can be more expressive. Inf. Control **56**(1), 72–99 (1983)
39. Xi, H.: Dependent types for program termination verification. In: LICS 2001, pp. 231–242. IEEE (2001)
40. Xi, H., Pfenning, F.: Dependent types in practical programming. In: POPL 1999, pp. 214–227. ACM (1999)

3

Exploiting Synchrony and Symmetry in Relational Verification

Lauren Pick[(✉)], Grigory Fedyukovich[iD],
and Aarti Gupta

Princeton University, Princeton, USA
{lpick,grigoryf,aartig}@cs.princeton.edu

Abstract. Relational safety specifications describe multiple runs of the same program or relate the behaviors of multiple programs. Approaches to automatic relational verification often compose the programs and analyze the result for safety, but a naively composed program can lead to difficult verification problems. We propose to exploit relational specifications for simplifying the generated verification subtasks. First, we maximize opportunities for synchronizing code fragments. Second, we compute symmetries in the specifications to reveal and avoid redundant subtasks. We have implemented these enhancements in a prototype for verifying k-safety properties on Java programs. Our evaluation confirms that our approach leads to a consistent performance speedup on a range of benchmarks.

1 Introduction

The verification of relational program specifications is of wide interest, having many applications. Relational specifications can describe multiple runs of the same program or relate the behaviors of multiple programs. An example of the former is the verification of security properties such as non-interference, where different executions of the same program are compared to check whether there is a leak of sensitive information. The latter is useful for checking equivalence or refinement relationships between programs after applying some transformations or during iterative development of different software versions.

There is a rich history of work on the relational verification of programs. Representative efforts include those that target general analysis using relational program logics and frameworks [4,5,8,27,31] or specific applications such as security verification [1,7,9], compiler validation [16,32], and differential program analysis [17,19,21–23]. These efforts are supported by tools that range from automatic verifiers to interactive theorem-provers. In particular, many automatic verifiers are based on constructing a *composition* over the programs under consideration, where the relational property over multiple runs (of the same or different programs) is translated into a functional property over a single run of a composed program. This has the benefit that standard techniques and tools for program verification can then be applied.

However, it is also well known that a naively composed program can lead to difficult verification problems for automatic verifiers. For example, a *sequential* composition of two loops would require effective techniques for generating loop invariants. In contrast, a *parallel* composition would provide potential for aligning the loop bodies, where relational invariants may be easier to establish than a functional loop invariant. Examples of techniques that exploit opportunities for such alignment include use of type-based analysis with self-composition [29], allowing flexibility in composition to be a mix of sequential and parallel [6], exploiting structurally equivalent programs for compiler validation [32], lockstep execution of loops in reasoning using Cartesian Hoare Logic [27], and merging Horn clause rules for relational verification [13,24].

In this paper, we present a compositional framework that leverages relational specifications to further simplify the generated verification tasks on the composed program. Our framework is motivated by two main strategies. The first strategy, similar to the efforts mentioned above, is to exploit opportunities for *synchrony*, i.e., aligning code fragments across which relational invariants are easy to derive, perhaps due to functional similarity or due to similar code structure, etc. Specifically, we choose to *synchronize* the programs at conditional blocks as well as at loops. Similar to closely related efforts [6,27], we would like to execute loops in lockstep so that relational invariants can be derived over corresponding iterations over the loop bodies. Specifically, we propose a novel technique that analyzes the relational specifications to infer, under reasonable assumptions, *maximal sets of loops* that can be executed in lockstep. Synchronizing at conditional blocks in addition to loops enables simplification due to relational specifications and conditional guards that might result in infeasible or redundant subtasks. Pruning of such infeasible subtasks has been performed and noted as important in existing work [27], and synchronizing at conditional blocks allows us to prune eagerly. More importantly, aligning different programs at conditional statements sets up our next strategy.

Our second strategy is the exploitation of symmetry in relational specifications. Due to control flow divergences or non-lockstep executions of loops, even different copies of the same program may proceed along different code fragments. However, some of the resulting verification subtasks may be indistinguishable from each other due to underlying symmetries among related fragments. We analyze the relational specifications, expressed as formulas in first-order theories (e.g., linear integer arithmetic) with multi-index variables, to discover symmetries and exploit them to prune away redundant subtasks. Prior works on use of symmetry in model checking [11,14,15,20] are typically based on symmetric states satisfying the same set of indexed atomic propositions, and do not consider symmetries among different indices in specifications. To the best of our knowledge, ours is the first work to *extract* such symmetries in relational specifications, and to *use* them for pruning redundant subtasks during relational verification. For extracting these symmetries, we have lifted core ideas from symmetry-discovery and symmetry-breaking in SAT formulas [12] to richer formulas in first-order theories.

The strategies we propose for exploiting synchrony and symmetry via relational specifications are fairly general in that they can be employed in vari-

```
if (y_j > 20) {
    while (i_j < 10) {
        x_j *= i_j;
        i_j++;
    }
} else {
    while (i_j < 10) {
        x_j++;
        i_j++;
    }
}
```

$y_1 > 20 \wedge y_2 > 20 \wedge y_3 > 20$

$y_1 > 20 \wedge y_2 > 20 \wedge y_3 \leq 20$

$y_1 > 20 \wedge y_2 \leq 20 \wedge y_3 > 20$

$y_1 > 20 \wedge y_2 \leq 20 \wedge y_3 \leq 20$

$y_1 \leq 20 \wedge y_2 > 20 \wedge y_3 > 20$

$y_1 \leq 20 \wedge y_2 > 20 \wedge y_3 \leq 20$

$y_1 \leq 20 \wedge y_2 \leq 20 \wedge y_3 > 20$

$y_1 \leq 20 \wedge y_2 \leq 20 \wedge y_3 \leq 20$

Fig. 1. Example program (left), and eight possible control-flow decisions (right).

ous verification methods. We provide a generic logic-based description of these strategies at a high level (Sect. 4), and also describe a specific instantiation in a verification algorithm based on forward analysis that computes strongest-postconditions (Sect. 5). We have implemented our approach in a prototype tool called SYNONYM built on top of the DESCARTES tool [27]. Our experimental evaluation (Sect. 6) shows the effectiveness of our approach in improving the performance of verification in many examples (and a marginal overhead in smaller examples). In particular, exploiting symmetry is crucial in enabling verification to complete for some properties, without which DESCARTES exceeds a timeout on all benchmark examples.

2   Motivating Example

Consider three C-like integer programs $\{P_j\}$ of the form shown in Fig. 1 (left). They are identical modulo renaming, and we use indices $j \in \{1, 2, 3\}$ as subscripts to denote variables in the different copies. We assume that each variable initially takes a nondeterministic value in each program.

A *relational verification problem* (RVP) is a tuple consisting of programs $\{P_j\}$, a relational precondition *pre*, and a relational postcondition *post*. In the example RVPs below, we consider the three conditionals, which in turn lead to eight possible control-flow decisions (Fig. 1, right) in a composed program. Each RVP reduces to subproblems for proving that *post* can be derived from *pre* for each of these control-flow decisions. In the rest of the section, we demonstrate the underlying ideas behind our approach to solve these subproblems efficiently.

Maximizing Lockstep Execution. Given an RVP (referred to as RVP_1) with precondition $x_1 < x_3 \wedge x_1 > 0 \wedge i_1 > 0 \wedge i_2 \geq i_1 \wedge i_1 = i_3$ (*pre*) and postcondition $(x_1 < x_3 \vee y_1 \neq y_3) \wedge i_1 > 0 \wedge i_2 \geq i_1 \wedge i_1 = i_3$ (*post*), consider a control-flow decision $y_1 > 20 \wedge y_2 > 20 \wedge y_3 > 20$. This leads to another RVP, consisting of three programs of the following form:

```
assume(y_j > 20); while (i_j < 10) {x_j *= i_j; i_j++;}
```

where $j \in \{1, 2, 3\}$, and the aforementioned *pre* and *post*. From *pre*, it follows that $i_1 = i_3$ and $i_2 \geq i_1$. We can thus infer that the first and third loops are always executed the same number of times, while the second loop may be executed for fewer iterations. This knowledge lets us infer a single relational invariant for the first and third loops and handle the second loop separately. Clearly, the relational invariant $x_1 < x_3 \wedge i_1 = i_3 \wedge i_1 \leq 10$ and the non-relational invariant $i_2 \leq 10$ are enough to derive *post*. If we were to handle the first and third loop separately, we would need complex nonlinear invariants such as $x_1 = \frac{x_{1,init} \times i_1!}{i_{1,init}!}$ and $x_3 = \frac{x_{3,init} \times i_3!}{i_{3,init}!}$, which involve auxiliary variables $x_{j,init}$ and $i_{j,init}$ denoting the initial values of x_j and i_j respectively.

Symmetry-Breaking. For the same program, and an RVP (referred to as RVP_2) with precondition $i_1 > 0 \wedge i_2 \geq i_1 \wedge i_1 = i_3$ and postcondition $i_1 > 0 \wedge i_2 \geq i_1 \wedge i_1 = i_3$, consider a control-flow decision $y_1 > 20 \wedge y_2 > 20 \wedge y_3 \leq 20$. We generate another RVP involving the following set of programs:

```
assume(y₁ > 20); while (i₁ < 10) {x₁ *= i₁; i₁++;}
assume(y₂ > 20); while (i₂ < 10) {x₂ *= i₂; i₂++;}
assume(y₃ ≤ 20); while (i₃ < 10) {x₃++; i₃++;}
```

Similarly, decision $y_1 \leq 20 \wedge y_2 > 20 \wedge y_3 > 20$ generates yet another RVP over the following:

```
assume(y₁ ≤ 20); while (i₁ < 10) {x₁++; i₁++;}
assume(y₂ > 20); while (i₂ < 10) {x₂ *= i₂; i₂++;}
assume(y₃ > 20); while (i₃ < 10) {x₃ *= i₃; i₃++;}
```

Both RVPs have the same precondition and postcondition as RVP_2. We can see that both RVPs differ only in their subscripts; by taking one and swapping the subscripts 1 and 3 due to symmetry, we arrive at the other. Thus, knowing the verification result for either RVP allows us to skip verifying the other one, by discovering and exploiting such symmetries.

3 Background and Notation

Given a loop-free program over input variables $\vec{x}$ and output variables $\vec{y}$ (such that $\vec{x}$ and $\vec{y}$ are disjoint), let $Tr(\vec{x}, \vec{y})$ denote its symbolic encoding.

Proposition 1. *Given two loop-free programs, $Tr_1(\vec{x}_1, \vec{y}_1)$ and $Tr_2(\vec{x}_2, \vec{y}_2)$, a precondition $pre(\vec{x}_1, \vec{x}_2)$, and a postcondition $post(\vec{y}_1, \vec{y}_2)$, the task of relational verification is reduced to checking validity of the following formula.*

$$pre(\vec{x}_1, \vec{x}_2) \wedge Tr_1(\vec{x}_1, \vec{y}_1) \wedge Tr_2(\vec{x}_2, \vec{y}_2) \implies post(\vec{y}_1, \vec{y}_2)$$

Given a program with one loop (i.e., a transition system) over input variables $\vec{x}$ and output variables $\vec{y}$, let $Init(\vec{x}, \vec{u})$ denote a symbolic encoding of the block of code before the loop, $Guard(\vec{u})$ denote the loop guard, and $Tr(\vec{u}, \vec{y})$ encode the loop body. Here, $\vec{u}$ is the vector of local variables that are live at the loop guard. For example, consider the program from our motivating example:

```
assume(y₁ > 20); while (i₁ < 10) {x₁ *= i₁; i₁++;}
```

In its encoding, $\vec{x} = \vec{u} = (i_1, x_1, y_1)$, $\vec{y} = (i'_1, x'_1)$, $Init(\vec{x}, \vec{u}) = y_1 > 20$, $Guard(\vec{u}) = i'_1 < 10$, and $Tr(\vec{u}, \vec{y}) = x'_1 = x_1 \times i_1 \wedge i'_1 = i_1 + 1$.

Proposition 2 (Naive parallel composition). *Given two loopy programs,* $\langle Init(\vec{x}_1, \vec{u}_1), Guard(\vec{u}_1), Tr(\vec{u}_1, \vec{y}_1) \rangle$ *and* $\langle Init(\vec{x}_2, \vec{u}_2), Guard(\vec{u}_2), Tr(\vec{u}_2, \vec{y}_2) \rangle$, *a precondition* $pre(\vec{x}_1, \vec{x}_2)$, *and a postcondition* $post(\vec{y}_1, \vec{y}_2)$, *the task of relational verification is reduced to the task of finding (individual) inductive invariants* $\boldsymbol{I_1}$ *and* $\boldsymbol{I_2}$:

$$pre(\vec{x}_1, \vec{x}_2) \wedge Init(\vec{x}_1, \vec{u}_1) \Longrightarrow \boldsymbol{I_1}(\vec{u}_1)$$
$$pre(\vec{x}_1, \vec{x}_2) \wedge Init(\vec{x}_2, \vec{u}_2) \Longrightarrow \boldsymbol{I_2}(\vec{u}_2)$$
$$\boldsymbol{I_1}(\vec{u}_1) \wedge Guard_1(\vec{u}_1) \wedge Tr_1(\vec{u}_1, \vec{y}_1) \Longrightarrow \boldsymbol{I_1}(\vec{y}_1)$$
$$\boldsymbol{I_2}(\vec{u}_1) \wedge Guard_2(\vec{u}_2) \wedge Tr_2(\vec{u}_2, \vec{y}_2) \Longrightarrow \boldsymbol{I_2}(\vec{y}_2)$$
$$\boldsymbol{I_1}(\vec{y}_1) \wedge \boldsymbol{I_2}(\vec{y}_2) \wedge \neg Guard_1(\vec{y}_1) \wedge \neg Guard_2(\vec{y}_2) \Longrightarrow post(\vec{y}_1, \vec{y}_2)$$

Note that the method of naive composition requires handling of multiple invariants, which is known to be difficult. Furthermore, it might lose some important relational information specified in $pre(\vec{x}_1, \vec{x}_2)$. One way to avoid this is to exploit the fact that loops could be executed in lockstep.

Proposition 3 (Lockstep composition). *Given two loopy programs,* $\langle Init(\vec{x}_1, \vec{u}_1), Guard(\vec{u}_1), Tr(\vec{u}_1, \vec{y}_1) \rangle$ *and* $\langle Init(\vec{x}_2, \vec{u}_2), Guard(\vec{u}_2), Tr(\vec{u}_2, \vec{y}_2) \rangle$, *a precondition* $pre(\vec{x}_1, \vec{x}_2)$, *and a postcondition* $post(\vec{y}_1, \vec{y}_2)$. *Let **both loops iterate exactly the same number of times**, then the task of relational verification is reduced to the task of finding one (relational) inductive invariant* $\boldsymbol{I}$:

$$pre(\vec{x}_1, \vec{x}_2) \wedge Init(\vec{x}_1, \vec{u}_1) \wedge Init(\vec{x}_2, \vec{u}_2) \Longrightarrow \boldsymbol{I}(\vec{u}_1, \vec{u}_2)$$
$$\boldsymbol{I}(\vec{u}_1, \vec{u}_2) \wedge Guard_1(\vec{u}_1) \wedge Tr_1(\vec{u}_1, \vec{y}_1) \wedge Guard_2(\vec{u}_2) \wedge Tr_2(\vec{u}_2, \vec{y}_2) \Longrightarrow \boldsymbol{I}(\vec{y}_1, \vec{y}_2)$$
$$\boldsymbol{I}(\vec{y}_1, \vec{y}_2) \wedge \neg Guard_1(\vec{y}_1) \wedge \neg Guard_2(\vec{y}_2) \Longrightarrow post(\vec{y}_1, \vec{y}_2)$$

In this paper, we do not focus on a specific method for deriving these invariants – a plethora of suitable methods have been proposed in the literature, and any of these could be used.

4   Leveraging Relational Specifications

In this section, we describe the main components of our compositional framework where we leverage relational specifications to simplify the verification subtasks. We first describe our novel algorithm for inferring maximal sets of loops that can be executed in lockstep (Sect. 4.1). Next, we describe our technique for handling conditionals (Sect. 4.2). While this is similar to other prior work, the main purpose here is to set the stage for our novel methods for exploiting symmetry (Sect. 4.3).

4.1 Synchronizing Loops

Given a set of loopy programs, we would like to determine which ones can be executed in lockstep. As mentioned earlier, relational invariants over lockstep loops are often easier to derive than loop invariants over a single copy.

Our algorithm CHECKLOCKSTEP takes as input a set of loopy programs $\{P_1, \ldots, P_k\}$ and outputs a set of *maximal* classes of programs that can be executed in lockstep. The algorithm partitions its input set of programs and recursively calls CHECKLOCKSTEP on the partitions.

First, CHECKLOCKSTEP infers a relational inductive invariant over the loop bodies, synthesizing $\boldsymbol{I}(\vec{u}_1, \ldots, \vec{u}_k)$ in the following:

$$pre(\vec{x}_1, \ldots, \vec{x}_k) \wedge \bigwedge_{i=1}^{k} Init(\vec{x}_i, \vec{u}_i) \implies \boldsymbol{I}(\vec{u}_1, \ldots, \vec{u}_k)$$

$$\boldsymbol{I}(\vec{u}_1, \ldots, \vec{u}_k) \wedge \bigwedge_{i=1}^{k} Guard_i(\vec{u}_i) \wedge Tr_i(\vec{u}_i, \vec{y}_i) \implies \boldsymbol{I}(\vec{y}_1, \ldots, \vec{y}_k)$$

CHECKLOCKSTEP then poses the following query:

$$\neg\left(\left(\boldsymbol{I}(\vec{u}_1, \ldots, \vec{u}_k) \wedge \bigvee_{i=1}^{k} \neg Guard(\vec{u}_i)\right) \implies \bigwedge_{i=1}^{k} \neg Guard(\vec{u}_i)\right) \tag{1}$$

The left-hand side of the implication holds whenever one of the loops has terminated (the relational invariant holds, and at least one of the loop conditions must be false), and the right-hand side holds only if all of the loops have terminated. If the formula is unsatisfiable, then the termination of one loop implies the termination of all loops, and all loops can be executed simultaneously [27]. In this case, the entire set of input programs is one maximal class, and the set containing the set of all input programs is returned.

Otherwise, CHECKLOCKSTEP gets a satisfying assignment and partitions the input programs into a set *Terminated* and a set *Unfinished*. The *Terminated* set contains all programs P_i whose guards $Guard(\vec{u}_i)$ are false in the model for the formula, and the *Unfinished* set contains the remaining programs. The CHECKLOCKSTEP algorithm is then called recursively on both *Terminated* and *Unfinished*, with its final result being the union of the two sets returned by these recursive calls.

The following theorem assumes that any relational invariant $\boldsymbol{I}(\vec{u}_1, \ldots, \vec{u}_k)$, generated externally and used by the algorithm, is stronger than any relational invariant $\boldsymbol{I}(\vec{u}_1, \ldots, \vec{u}_{i-1}, \vec{u}_{i+1}, \ldots, \vec{u}_k)$ that could be synthesized over the same set of k loops with the ith loop removed.

Theorem 1. *For any call to* CHECKLOCKSTEP, *it always partitions its set of input programs such that for all* $P_i \in$ *Terminated and* $P_j \in$ *Unfinished,* P_i *and* P_j *cannot be executed in lockstep.*

Proof. Assume that CHECKLOCKSTEP has partitioned its set of programs into the *Terminated* and *Unfinished* sets. Let $P_i \in$ *Terminated*, $P_j \in$ *Unfinished* be arbitrary programs. Based on how the partitioning is performed, we know that there is a model for Eq. 1 such that $Guard(\vec{u}_i)$ does not hold and $Guard(\vec{u}_j)$ does. We can thus conclude that the following formula is satisfiable:

$$\neg\Big(\boldsymbol{I}(\vec{u}_1, \ldots, \vec{u}_k) \wedge \neg Guard(\vec{u}_i) \implies \neg Guard(\vec{u}_j) \Big)$$

From the assumption on our invariant synthesizer, we conclude that the following is also satisfiable, indicating that P_i and P_j cannot be executed in lockstep:

$$\neg\Big(\boldsymbol{I}(\vec{u}_i, \vec{u}_j) \wedge \neg Guard(\vec{u}_i) \implies \neg Guard(\vec{u}_j) \Big)$$

where $\boldsymbol{I}(\vec{u}_i, \vec{u}_j)$ is the relational invariant for P_i and P_j that our invariant synthesizer infers. □

4.2 Synchronizing Conditionals

Let two programs have forms if Q_i then R_i else S_i, where $i \in \{1, 2\}$ and R_i and S_i are arbitrary blocks of code and could possibly have loops. Let them be a part of some RVP, which reduces to applying Propositions 1, 2, or 3, depending on the content of each block of code, to four pairs of programs. As we have seen in previous sections, each of the four verification tasks could be expensive. In order to reduce the number of verification tasks where possible, we use the relational preconditions to filter out pairs of programs for which verification conclusions can be derived trivially.

For k programs of the form if Q_i then R_i else S_i for $i \in \{1, \ldots, k\}$ and precondition $pre(\vec{x}_1, \ldots, \vec{x}_k)$, we can simultaneously generate all possible combinations of decisions by querying a solver for all truth assignments to the Q_is:

$$pre(\vec{x}_1, \ldots, \vec{x}_k) \wedge \bigwedge_{i=1}^{k} Q_i \tag{2}$$

We can then use the result of this All-SAT query to generate sets of programs in subtasks. For each assignment j, where each Q_i is assigned a Boolean value v_i, the following set is generated: {assume (V_1); U_1, ..., assume (V_k); U_k} where for each $i \in \{1, \ldots, k\}$, if $v_i = true$, then $V_i = Q_i$ and $U_i = R_i$, else $V_i = \neg Q_i$ and $U_i = S_i$. We need to apply our verification algorithm on only the resulting sets of programs. For example, in our above RVP, if Q_1 is equivalent to Q_2 in all solutions, then the RVP reduces to verification of just two pairs of programs:

assume (Q_1); R_1 and   assume (Q_2); R_2

assume ($\neg Q_1$); S_1 and   assume ($\neg Q_2$); S_2

Algorithm 1. Algorithm for constructing a graph to find symmetries.

1: **procedure** MAKEGRAPH(F)
2:      $(V, E) \leftarrow (\{v_1^{Id}, \ldots, v_k^{Id}\}, \varnothing)$ where each v_i^{Id} has $color(v_i^{Id}) = Id$
3:      **for** $d \in$ CLAUSES(F) **do** $(V, E) \leftarrow$ MAKECOLOREDAST(d) $\cup$ (V, E)

4:      **for** $v \in V$ with $x_i \in vars(color(v))$ **do**
5:          $V \leftarrow (V \setminus \{v\}) \cup \{\text{RECOLOR}(v, v[x_i \mapsto x])\}$
6:          $E \leftarrow E \cup \{(v, v_i^{Id})\}$

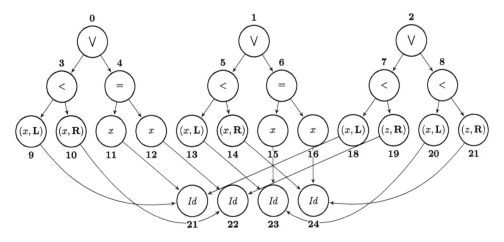

Fig. 2. Graph with vertex names (outside the vertices) and colors (inside the vertices).

4.3   Discovering and Exploiting Symmetries

Using the All-SAT query from Eq. 2 allows us to prune trivial RVPs. However, as we have seen in Sect. 2, some of the remaining RVPs could be regarded as equivalent due to symmetry. First, we discuss how to identify symmetries in formulas syntactically, and then we show how to use such symmetries.

4.3.1   Identifying Symmetries in Formulas

Formally, symmetries in formulas are defined as permutations. Note that any permutation π of set $\{1, \ldots, k\}$ can be lifted to be a permutation of set $\{\vec{x}_1, \ldots, \vec{x}_k\}$.

Definition 1 (Symmetry). *Let $\vec{x}_1, \ldots, \vec{x}_k$ be vectors of the same size over disjoint sets of variables. A symmetry π of a formula $F(\vec{x}_1, \ldots, \vec{x}_k)$ is a permutation of set $\{\vec{x}_i \mid 1 \leq i \leq k\}$ such that $F(\vec{x}_1, \ldots, \vec{x}_k) \iff F(\pi(\vec{x}_1), \ldots, \pi(\vec{x}_k))$.*

The task of finding symmetries within a set of formulas can be performed syntactically by first canonicalizing the formulas, converting the formulas into a graph representation of their syntax, and then using a graph automorphism algorithm to find the symmetries of the graph. We demonstrate how this can be done for a formula φ over Linear Integer Arithmetic with the following example.

Let $\varphi = (x_1 \leq x_2 \wedge x_3 \leq x_4) \wedge (x_1 < z_2 \vee x_3 < z_4)$. Note that this formula is symmetric under a permutation of the subscripts that simultaneously swaps

1 with 3 and 2 with 4. Let $\{(x_1, z_1), (x_2, z_2), (x_3, z_3), (x_4, z_4)\}$ be the vectors of variables. We identify a vector by its subscript (e.g., we identify (x_1, z_1) by 1).

Our algorithm starts with canonicalizing the formula: $\varphi = (x_1 < x_2 \vee x_1 = x_2) \wedge (x_3 < x_4 \vee x_3 = x_4) \wedge (x_1 < z_2 \vee x_3 < z_4)$. It then constructs a colored graph for the canonicalized formula with the procedure in Algorithm 1. The algorithm initializes a graph by the set of k vertices $v_1^{Id}, \ldots, v_k^{Id}$ with color Id (vertices 21–24 in Fig. 2), where k is the number of identifiers. It then (Line 3) adds to the graph the union of the abstract syntax trees (AST) for the formula's conjuncts, where each vertex has a color corresponding to the type of its AST node. If a parent vertex has a color of an ordering-sensitive operation or predicate, then the children should have colors that include a tag to indicate their ordering (e.g., vertices 9 and 10 in Fig. 2 have colors with tags because their parent has color $<$, but vertices 11 and 12 do not have tags because their parent has color $=$). Next (Line 4), the algorithm performs an appropriate renaming of vertex colors so that each indexed variable name x_i is replaced with a non-indexed version x, while simultaneously adding edges from each vertex with a renamed color to v_i^{Id}. The resulting graph for φ is shown in Fig. 2. Finally, the algorithm applies a graph automorphism finder to get the following automorphism (in addition to the identity automorphism), which is shown here in a cyclic notation where $(x \ y)$ means that $x \mapsto y$ and $y \mapsto x$ (vertices that map to themselves are omitted):

$$(0 \ 1)(3 \ 5)(4 \ 6)(7 \ 8)(9 \ 13)(10 \ 14)(11 \ 15)(12 \ 16)(17 \ 19)(18 \ 20)(21 \ 23)(22 \ 24)$$

We are only interested in permutations of the vectors, so we project out the relevant parts of the permutation $(21 \ 23)(22 \ 24)$ and map them back to our vector identifiers to get the following permutation on the identifiers:

$$\pi = \{1 \mapsto 3, 2 \mapsto 4, 3 \mapsto 1, 4 \mapsto 2\}$$

4.3.2 Exploiting Symmetries

We now define the notion of symmetric RVPs and application of symmetry-breaking to generate a single representative per equivalence class of RVPs.

Definition 2 (Symmetric RVPs). *Two RVPs:* $\langle Ps, pre(\vec{x}_1, \ldots, \vec{x}_k), post(\vec{y}_1, \ldots, \vec{y}_k) \rangle$ *and* $\langle Ps', pre(\vec{x}_1, \ldots, \vec{x}_k), post(\vec{y}_1, \ldots, \vec{y}_k) \rangle$, *where* $Ps = \{P_1, \ldots, P_k\}$, *and* $Ps' = \{P'_1, \ldots, P'_k\}$, *are called* symmetric *under a permutation* π *iff*

1. *π is a symmetry of formula $pre(\vec{x}_1, \ldots, \vec{x}_k) \wedge post(\vec{y}_1, \ldots, \vec{y}_k)$*
2. *for every $P_i \in Ps$ and $P_j \in Ps'$, if $\pi(i) = j$, then P_i and P_j have the same number of inputs and outputs and have logically equivalent encodings for the same set of input variables $\vec{x}_i$ and output variables $\vec{y}_i$*

As we have seen in Sect. 4.3.1, identification of symmetries could be made purely on the syntactic level of the relational preconditions and postconditions. For each detected symmetry, it remains to check equivalence between the corresponding programs' encodings, which can be formulated as an SMT problem.

To exploit symmetries, we propose a simple but intuitive approach. First, we identify the set of symmetries using $pre \wedge post$. Then, we solve the All-SAT query from Eq. 2 and get a *reduced* set R of RVPs (i.e., one without all trivial problems). For each $RVP_i \in R$, we perform the relational verification only if no symmetric $RVP_j \in R$ has already been verified. Thus, the most expensive part of the routine, checking equivalence of RVPs, is performed on demand and only on a subset of all possible pairs $\langle RVP_i, RVP_j \rangle$.

Alternatively, in some cases (e.g., for parallelizing the algorithm) it might help to identify all symmetric RVPs prior to solving the All-SAT query from Eq. 2. From this set, we can generate symmetry-breaking predicates (SBPs) [12] and conjoin them to Eq. 2. Constrained with SBPs, this query will have fewer models, and will contain a single representative per equivalence class of RVPs. We describe how to construct SBPs in more detail in the next section.

4.3.3 Generating Symmetry-Breaking Predicates (SBPs)

SBPs have previously been applied in pruning the search space explored by SAT solvers. Traditionally, techniques construct SBPs based on symmetries in truth assignments to the literals in the formula, but SBP-construction can be adapted to be based on symmetries in truth assignments to conditionals, allowing us to break symmetries in our setting.

We can construct an SBP by treating each condition the way a literal is treated in existing SBP constructions. In particular, we can construct the common Lex-Leader SBP used for predicate logic [12], which in our case will force a solver to choose the lexicographically least representative per equivalence class for a particular ordering of the conditions. For the ordering of conditions where $Q_i \leq Q_j$ iff $i \leq j$ and a set of symmetries S over $\{1, \dots, k\}$, we can construct a Lex-Leader SBP $SBP(S) = \bigwedge_{\pi \in S} PP(\pi)$ with the more efficient predicate chaining construction [2], where we have that

$$PP(\pi) = p_{\min(I)} \wedge \bigwedge_{i \in I} p_i \implies g_{prev(i,I)} \implies l_i \wedge p_{next(i,I)}$$

and that I is the support of π with the last condition for each cycle removed, $\min(I)$ is the minimal element of I, $prev(i, I)$ is the maximal element of I still less than i or 0 if there is none, $next(i, I)$ is the minimal element of I still greater than i or 0 if there is none, $p_0 = g_0 = true$, p_i is a fresh predicate for $i \neq 0$, $g_i = Q_{\pi(i)} \implies Q_i$ for $i \neq 0$, and $l_i = Q_i \implies Q_{\pi(i)}$.

After constructing the SBP, we conjoin it to the All-SAT query in Eq. 2. Our solver now generates sets of programs that, when combined with the relational precondition and postcondition, form a set of irredundant RVPs.

Example. Let us consider how SBPs can be applied to RVP_2 from Sect. 2 to avoid generating two of the eight RVPs we would otherwise generate.

First, we see that our three programs are all copies the same program and are at the same program point, so they will have the same encoding. Next, we find the set of permutations S over $\{1, 2, 3\}$ such that for each $\pi \in S$, we have that $i_1 > 0 \wedge i_2 \geq i_1 \wedge i_1 = i_3$ iff $i_{\pi(1)} > 0 \wedge i_{\pi(2)} \geq i_{\pi(1)} \wedge i_{\pi(1)} = i_{\pi(3)}$. In this case, we have that S is the set of permutations $\{\{1 \mapsto 1, 2 \mapsto 2, 3 \mapsto 3\}, \{1 \mapsto 3, 2 \mapsto 2, 3 \mapsto 3\}\}$. Now, we construct a Lex-Leader SBP (using the predicate chaining construction described above):

$$p_1 \wedge (p_1 \implies ((y_1 > 20) \implies (y_2 > 20)))$$

where p_1 is a fresh predicate. Conjoining this SBP to Eq. 2, leads to the RVPs arising from the control-flow decisions $y_1 > 20 \wedge y_2 > 20 \wedge y_3 \leq 20$ and $y_1 > 20 \wedge y_2 \leq 20 \wedge y_3 \leq 20$ no longer being generated.

5 Instantiation of Strategies in Forward Analysis

We now describe an instantiation of our proposed strategies in a verification algorithm based on forward analysis using a strongest-postcondition computation. Other instantiations, e.g., on top of a Horn solver based on Property-Directed Reachability [24] are possible, but outside the scope of this work.

1: **procedure** VERIFY(*pre, Current, Ifs, Loops, post*)
2:     **while** *Current* $\neq \varnothing$ **do**
3:         **if** PROCESSSTATEMENT(*pre, P_i, Ifs, Loops, post*) = safe **then return** safe
4:     **if** *Loops* $\neq \varnothing$ **then** HANDLELOOPS(*pre, Loops, post*)
5:     **else if** *Ifs* $\neq \varnothing$ **then** HANDLEIFS(*pre, Ifs, Loops, post*)
6:     **else return** unsafe

Given an RVP in the form of a Hoare triple $\{Pre\}\ P_1 || \cdots || P_k\ \{Post\}$, where $||$ denotes parallel composition, the top-level VERIFY procedure takes as input the relational specification *pre* = *Pre* and *post* = *Post*, the set of input programs *Current* = $\{P_1, \ldots, P_k\}$, and empty sets *Loops* and *Ifs*. It uses a strongest-postcondition computation to compute the next Hoare triple at each step until it can conclude the validity of the original Hoare triple.

Synchronization. Throughout verification, the algorithm maintains three disjoint sets of programs: one for programs that are currently being processed (*Current*), one for programs that have been processed up until a loop (*Loops*), and one for programs that have been processed up until a conditional statement (*Ifs*). The algorithm processes statements in each program independently, with PROCESSSTATEMENT choosing an arbitrary interleaving of statements from the programs in *Current*. When the algorithm encounters the end of a program in its call to PROCESSSTATEMENT, it removes this program from the *Current* set. At this point, the algorithm returns safe if the current Hoare triple is proven valid. When a program has reached a point of control-flow divergence and is processed by PROCESSSTATEMENT, it is removed from *Current* and added to the appropriate set (*Loops* or *Ifs*).

Handling Loops. Once all programs are in the *Loops* or *Ifs* sets (i.e. *Current* = ∅), the algorithm handles the programs in the *Loops* set if it is nonempty. HANDLELOOPS behaves like CHECKLOCKSTEP but computes postconditions where possible; when a set of loops are able to be executed in lockstep, HANDLELOOPS computes their postconditions before placing the programs into the *Terminated* set. After all loops have been placed in the *Terminated* set and a new precondition *pre'* has been computed, rather than returning *Terminated*, HANDLELOOPS invokes VERIFY(*pre'*, *Terminated*, *Ifs*, ∅, *post*).

Handling Conditionals. When *Current* = *Loops* = ∅, VERIFY handles conditional statements. HANDLEIFS exploits symmetries by using the All-SAT query with Lex-Leader SBPs as described in Sect. 4 and calls VERIFY on each generated verification problem.

6 Implementation and Evaluation

To evaluate the effectiveness of increased lockstep execution of loops and symmetry-breaking, we implemented our algorithm from Sect. 5 on top of the DESCARTES tool for verifying k-safety properties, i.e., RVPs over k identical Java programs. We implemented two variants: SYN uses only synchrony (i.e., no symmetry is used), while SYNONYM uses both. All implementations (including DESCARTES) use the same guess-and-check invariant generator (the same originally used by DESCARTES, but modified to generate more candidate invariants). In SYNONYM, we compute symmetries in preconditions and postconditions only when all program copies are the same. For our examples, it sufficed to compute symmetries simply by checking if each possible permutation leads to equivalent formulas[1]. We compare the performance of our prototype implementations to DESCARTES[2]. We use two metrics for comparison: the time taken and the number of Hoare triples processed by the verification procedure. All experiments were conducted on a MacBook Pro, with a 2.7 GHz Intel Core i5 processor and 8 GB RAM.

6.1 Stackoverflow Benchmarks

The first set of benchmarks we consider are the Stackoverflow benchmarks originally used to evaluate DESCARTES. These implement (correctly or incorrectly) the Java `Comparator` or `Comparable` interface, and check whether or not their *compare* functions satisfy the following properties:

---

[1] Our implementation includes the syntactic symmetry-finding algorithm from Sect. 4.3.1, though we do not use it for evaluation here due to its high overhead in using an external tool for finding graph automorphisms.

[2] While there are several tools for relational verification (e.g. ROSETTE/UNBOUND [25], VERIMAPREL [13], REVE [17], MOCHI [17], SYMDIFF [22]), most of these do not handle Java programs, and to the best of our knowledge, none of these tools has support for k-safety verification for k greater than 2.

P1: $\forall x, y. sgn(compare(x,y)) = -sgn(compare(y,x))$
P2: $\forall x, y, z. (compare(x,y) > 0 \wedge compare(y,z) > 0) \implies compare(x,z) > 0$
P3: $\forall x, y, z. (compare(x,y) = 0) \implies (sgn(compare(x,z)) = sgn(compare(y,z)))$

(One of the original 34 Stackoverflow examples is excluded from our evaluation here because of the inability of the invariant generator to produce a suitable invariant.) We compare the results of running SYN and SYNONYM vs. DESCARTES for each property in Table 1. (Expanded versions and plots of these results are available in an extended version of the paper [26].)

Because property P1 contains a symmetry, we notice an improvement in terms of number of Hoare triples with the use of symmetry for this property; however, the overhead of computing symmetries leads to SYNONYM performing more slowly than SYN even for some examples that exhibit reduced Hoare triple counts. Property P1 is also the easiest to prove (all implementations can verify each example in under 0.3 s), so the overheads contribute more significantly to the runtime. For examples on which our implementations do not perform as well as DESCARTES, we perform reasonably closely to DESCARTES. These examples are typically smaller, and again overheads play a larger role in our poorer performance.

Table 1. Stackoverflow Benchmarks. Total times (in seconds) and Hoare triple counts (HTC) for Stackoverflow benchmarks, where for each property, the results for SYN and SYNONYM are divided into those for examples where they exhibit a factor of improvement over DESCARTES that is greater or equal to 1 (top) and those for which they do not (bottom). *Improv* reports the factor of improvement over DESCARTES, where the number of examples is given in parentheses.

Prop	DESCARTES		SYN				SYNONYM			
	Time	HTC	Time	Improv	HTC	Improv	Time	Improv	HTC	Improv
P1	3.11	4422	1.91	1.39 (27)	2255	1.69 (27)	1.82	1.32 (25)	2401	1.82 (32)
			0.57	0.789 (6)	752	0.809 (6)	0.87	0.816 (8)	48	0.979 (1)
P2	24.6	13434	7.83	2.62 (20)	3285	3.081 (16)	7.31	2.80 (19)	3224	3.140 (16)
			4.98	0.823 (13)	4638	0.714 (17)	5.1	0.816 (14)	4638	0.714 (17)
P3	18.85	10938	5.22	2.92 (20)	1565	4.36 (16)	5.22	2.91 (19)	1537	4.74 (16)
			6.18	0.584 (13)	6600	0.623 (17)	6.16	0.594 (14)	6600	0.623 (17)

6.2 Modified Stackoverflow Benchmarks

The original Stackoverflow examples are fairly small, with all implementations taking under 6 s to verify any example. To assess how we perform on larger examples, we modified several of the larger Stackoverflow comparator examples to be longer, take more arguments, and contain more control-flow decisions. The resulting functions take three arguments and pick the "largest" object's id, where comparison among objects is performed based on the original Stackoverflow example code. (Ties are broken by choosing the least id.) We check whether these *pick* functions satisfy the following properties that allow reordering input arguments:

P13: $\forall x, y, z.pick(x, y, z) = pick(y, x, z)$
P14: $\forall x, y, z.pick(x, y, z) = pick(y, x, z) \wedge pick(x, y, z) = pick(z, y, x)$

Note that P13 allows swapping the first two input arguments, while P14 allows any permutation of inputs, a useful hyperproperty.

The results from running property P13 are shown in Table 2. We see here that for these larger examples, Hoare triple counts are more reliably correlated with the time taken to perform verification. SYN outperforms DESCARTES on 14 of the 16 examples, and SYNONYM outperforms both DESCARTES and SYN on all 16 examples.

The results from running property P14 are shown in Table 3. For this property, note thatDESCARTES is unable to verify any of the examples within a one-hour timeout. Meanwhile, SYN is able to verify 10 of the 16 examples without exceeding the timeout. Exploiting symmetries here exhibits an obvious improvement, with SYNONYM not only being able to verify the same examples as SYN, with consistently faster performance on the larger examples, but also being able to verify an additional example within an hour.

Table 2. Verifying P13 for modified Stackoverflow examples. Times (in seconds) and Hoare triple counts (HTC).

Example	DESCARTES		SYN		SYNONYM	
	Time	HTC	Time	HTC	Time	HTC
ArrayInt-pick3-false-simple	1.71	2573	1	1355	0.64	682
ArrayInt-pick3-false	1.55	2591	1.06	1439	0.8	724
ArrayInt-pick3-true-simple	1.71	2573	1.03	1355	0.65	682
ArrayInt-pick3-true	1.55	2591	1.08	1439	0.81	724
Chromosome-pick3-false-simple	0.9	1115	0.9	883	0.53	446
Chromosome-pick3-false	2.51	2891	2.94	3019	1.59	1514
Chromosome-pick3-true-simple	0.9	1115	0.9	883	0.53	446
Chromosome-pick3-true	2.51	2891	2.96	3019	1.59	1514
PokerHand-pick3-false-part1	5.87	5825	0.42	359	0.46	359
PokerHand-pick3-false-part2	9.74	10589	0.85	323	0.86	323
PokerHand-pick3-false	16.91	16475	0.73	159	0.79	159
PokerHand-pick3-true-part1	5.83	5825	3.98	3503	2.4	1756
PokerHand-pick3-true-part2	9.8	10565	7.36	5933	4.53	2971
PokerHand-pick3-true	17.25	16475	12.1	9293	7.34	4651
Solution-pick3-false	76.4	99910	25.05	20645	20.42	10327
Solution-pick3-true	64.5	99910	19.66	20645	15.21	10327
Total	219.64	283914	82.02	74252	59.15	37605
Improvement	1	1	2.68	3.8237	3.713	7.5499

Table 3. Verifying P14 for modified Stackoverflow examples. Times (in seconds) and Hoare triple counts (HTC). - indicates that no sufficient invariant could be inferred.

Example	DESCARTES		SYN		SYNONYM	
	Time	HTC	Time	HTC	Time	HTC
ArrayInt-pick3-false-simple	TO	TO	4.12	1938	4.66	1734
ArrayInt-pick3-false	TO	TO	4.92	2017	6.03	1500
ArrayInt-pick3-true-simple	TO	TO	321.15	140593	170.43	58586
ArrayInt-pick3-true	TO	TO	366.98	149125	240.25	62141
Chromosome-pick3-false-simple	TO	TO	47.8	14097	1.67	834
Chromosome-pick3-false	TO	TO	264.21	93052	4.91	3043
Chromosome-pick3-true-simple	TO	TO	299.51	79613	135.56	33179
Chromosome-pick3-true	TO	TO	TO	TO	848.22	225044
PokerHand-pick3-false-part1	TO	TO	0.57	391	0.73	391
PokerHand-pick3-false-part2	TO	TO	0.81	228	0.81	228
PokerHand-pick3-false	-	-	-	-	-	-
PokerHand-pick3-true-part1	TO	TO	2277.03	819553	1272.58	341486
PokerHand-pick3-true-part2	TO	TO	-	-	-	-
PokerHand-pick3-true	-	-	-	-	-	-
Solution-pick3-false	TO	TO	TO	TO	TO	TO
Solution-pick3-false	TO	TO	TO	TO	TO	TO

Summary of Experimental Results. Our experiments indicate that our performance improvements are consistent: on all DESCARTES benchmarks (in Table 1, which are all small) our techniques either have low overhead or show some improvement despite the overhead; and on modified (bigger) programs they lead to significant improvements. In particular, we report (Table 2) speedups up to 21.4x (on an example where the property doesn't hold) and 4.2x (on an example where it does). More importantly, we report (Table 3) that DESCARTES times out on 14 examples, where of these SYNONYM times out for 2 and cannot infer an invariant for one example.

7 Related Work

The work most closely related to ours is by Sousa and Dillig [27], which proposed Cartesian Hoare Logic (CHL) for proving k-safety properties and the tool DESCARTES for automated reasoning in CHL. In addition to the core program logic, CHL includes additional proof rules for loops, referred to as Cartesian Loop Logic (CLL). A generalization of CHL, called Quantitative Cartesian Hoare Logic was subsequently used by Chen et al. [10] to detect side-channel vulnerabilities in cryptographic implementations.

In terms of comparison, neither CHL nor CLL force alignment at conditional statements or take advantage of symmetries. We believe our algorithm for identifying a maximal set of lockstep loops is also novel and can be used in other methods that do not rely on CHL/CLL. On the other hand, CLL proof rules allow not only fully lockstep loops, but also *partially* lockstep loops. Although we did not consider it here, our maximal lockstep-loop detection algorithm can be combined with their partial lockstep execution to further improve the efficiency of verification. For example, applying the Fusion 2 rule from CLL to our example while loops generated from RVP_1 (Sect. 2) would result in *three* subproblems and require reasoning twice about the second copy's loop finishing later. When combined with maximal lockstep-loop detection, we could generate just *two* subproblems: one where the first and third loops terminate first, and another where the second loop terminates first.

Other automatic efforts for relational verification typically use some kind of product programs [6,13,17,21,22,24,28], with a possible reduction to Horn solving [13,17,21,24]. Similarly to our strategy for synchrony, most of them attempt to leverage similarity (structural or functional) in programs to ease verification. However, we have seen less focus on leveraging relational specifications themselves to simplify verification tasks, although this varies according to the verification method used. Some efforts do not reason over product programs at all, relying on techniques based on decomposition [3] or customized theories with theorem proving [4,30] instead. To the best of our knowledge, none of these efforts exploit symmetry in programs or in relational specifications.

On the other hand, symmetry has been used very successfully in model checking parametric finite state systems [11,15,20] and concurrent programs [14]. Our work differs from these efforts in two main respects. First, the parametric systems considered in these efforts have components that interact with each other or share variables. Second, the correctness specifications are also parametric, usually single-index or double-index properties in a propositional (temporal) logic. In contrast, in our RVPs, the individual programs are independent and do not share any common variables. The only interaction between them is via relational specifications. Furthermore, we discover symmetries in these relational specifications over multi-index variables, expressed as formulas in first-order theories (e.g., linear integer arithmetic). We then exploit these symmetries to prune redundant RVPs during verification.

There are also some similarities between relational verification and verification of concurrent/parallel programs. In the latter, a typical verifier [18] would use *visible* operations (i.e., synchronization operations or communication on shared state) as synchronizing points in the composed program. In our work, this selection is made based on the structure of the component programs and the ease of utilizing or deriving relational assertions for the code fragments. Furthermore, one does not need to consider different orderings in interleavings of programs in the RVPs. Since these fragments are independent, it suffices to explore any one ordering. Instead, we exploit symmetries in the relational assertions to prune away redundant RVPs.

Finally, specific applications may impose additional synchrony requirements pertaining to visibility. For example, one may want to check for information leaks from private inputs to public outputs not only at the end of a program but at other specified intermediate points, or information leakage models for side-channel attacks may check for leaks based on given observer models [1]. Such requirements can be viewed as relational specifications at selected synchronizing points in the composed program. Again, we can leverage these relational specifications to simplify the resulting verification subproblems.

8 Conclusions and Future Work

We have proposed novel techniques for improving relational verification, which has several applications including security verification, program equivalence checking, and regression verification. Our two key ideas are maximizing the amount of code that can be synchronized and identifying symmetries in relational specifications to avoid redundant subtasks. Our prototype implementation on top of the DESCARTES verification tool leads to consistent improvements on a range of benchmarks. In the future, we would be interested in implementing these ideas on top of a Horn-based relational verifier (e.g., [25]) and extending it to work with recursive data structures. We are also interested in developing an algorithm for finding symmetries in formulas that does not rely on an external graph automorphism tool.

Acknowledgements. We gratefully acknowledge the help from Marcelo Sousa and Işil Dillig on their DESCARTES tool, which provides the base for our prototype development and experimental comparison. This work was supported in part by NSF Grant 1525936.

References

1. Almeida, J.B., Barbosa, M., Barthe, G., Dupressoir, F., Emmi, M.: Verifying constant-time implementations. In: USENIX, pp. 53–70. USENIX Association (2016)
2. Aloul, F.A., Sakallah, K.A., Markov, I.L.: Efficient symmetry breaking for Boolean satisfiability. IEEE Trans. Comput. **55**(5), 549–558 (2006)
3. Antonopoulos, T., Gazzillo, P., Hicks, M., Koskinen, E., Terauchi, T., Wei, S.: Decomposition instead of self-composition for proving the absence of timing channels. In: PLDI, pp. 362–375 (2017)
4. Asada, K., Sato, R., Kobayashi, N.: Verifying relational properties of functional programs by first-order refinement. Sci. Comput. Program. **137**, 2–62 (2017)
5. Banerjee, A., Naumann, D.A., Nikouei, M.: Relational logic with framing and hypotheses. In: IARCS. LIPIcs, vol. 65, pp. 11:1–11:16. Schloss Dagstuhl - Leibniz-Zentrum fuer Informatik (2016)
6. Barthe, G., Crespo, J.M., Kunz, C.: Relational verification using product programs. In: Butler, M., Schulte, W. (eds.) FM 2011. LNCS, vol. 6664, pp. 200–214. Springer, Heidelberg (2011). https://doi.org/10.1007/978-3-642-21437-0_17
7. Barthe, G., D'Argenio, P.R., Rezk, T.: Secure information flow by self-composition. In: CSFW, pp. 100–114. IEEE (2004)
8. Benton, N.: Simple relational correctness proofs for static analyses and program transformations. In: POPL, pp. 14–25 (2004)

9. Beringer, L., Hofmann, M.: Secure information flow and program logics. In: CSF, pp. 233–248. IEEE Computer Society (2007)
10. Chen, J., Feng, Y., Dillig, I.: Precise detection of side-channel vulnerabilities using quantitative Cartesian hoare logic. In: Proceedings of the 2017 ACM SIGSAC Conference on Computer and Communications Security, CCS 2017, pp. 875–890 (2017)
11. Clarke, E.M., Filkorn, T., Jha, S.: Exploiting symmetry in temporal logic model checking. In: Courcoubetis, C. (ed.) CAV 1993. LNCS, vol. 697, pp. 450–462. Springer, Heidelberg (1993). https://doi.org/10.1007/3-540-56922-7_37
12. Crawford, J.M., Ginsberg, M.L., Luks, E.M., Roy, A.: Symmetry-breaking predicates for search problems. In: KR, pp. 148–159 (1996)
13. De Angelis, E., Fioravanti, F., Pettorossi, A., Proietti, M.: Relational verification through horn clause transformation. In: Rival, X. (ed.) SAS 2016. LNCS, vol. 9837, pp. 147–169. Springer, Heidelberg (2016). https://doi.org/10.1007/978-3-662-53413-7_8
14. Donaldson, A., Kaiser, A., Kroening, D., Wahl, T.: Symmetry-aware predicate abstraction for shared-variable concurrent programs. In: Gopalakrishnan, G., Qadeer, S. (eds.) CAV 2011. LNCS, vol. 6806, pp. 356–371. Springer, Heidelberg (2011). https://doi.org/10.1007/978-3-642-22110-1_28
15. Emerson, E.A., Sistla, A.P.: Symmetry and model checking. In: Courcoubetis, C. (ed.) CAV 1993. LNCS, vol. 697, pp. 463–478. Springer, Heidelberg (1993). https://doi.org/10.1007/3-540-56922-7_38
16. Fedyukovich, G., Gurfinkel, A., Sharygina, N.: Property directed equivalence via abstract simulation. In: Chaudhuri, S., Farzan, A. (eds.) CAV 2016. LNCS, vol. 9780, pp. 433–453. Springer, Cham (2016). https://doi.org/10.1007/978-3-319-41540-6_24
17. Felsing, D., Grebing, S., Klebanov, V., Rümmer, P., Ulbrich, M.: Automating regression verification. In: ASE, pp. 349–360. ACM (2014)
18. Godefroid, P.: VeriSoft: a tool for the automatic analysis of concurrent reactive software. In: Grumberg, O. (ed.) CAV 1997. LNCS, vol. 1254, pp. 476–479. Springer, Heidelberg (1997). https://doi.org/10.1007/3-540-63166-6_52
19. Godlin, B., Strichman, O.: Regression verification. In: DAC, pp. 466–471. ACM (2009)
20. Ip, C.N., Dill, D.L.: Verifying systems with replicated components in murφ. In: Alur, R., Henzinger, T.A. (eds.) CAV 1996. LNCS, vol. 1102, pp. 147–158. Springer, Heidelberg (1996). https://doi.org/10.1007/3-540-61474-5_65
21. Kiefer, M., Klebanov, V., Ulbrich, M.: Relational program reasoning using compiler IR. In: Blazy, S., Chechik, M. (eds.) VSTTE 2016. LNCS, vol. 9971, pp. 149–165. Springer, Cham (2016). https://doi.org/10.1007/978-3-319-48869-1_12
22. Lahiri, S.K., McMillan, K.L., Sharma, R., Hawblitzel, C.: Differential assertion checking. In: FSE, pp. 345–355. ACM (2013)
23. Logozzo, F., Lahiri, S.K., Fähndrich, M., Blackshear, S.: Verification modulo versions: towards usable verification. In: PLDI, p. 32. ACM (2014)
24. Mordvinov, D., Fedyukovich, G.: Synchronizing constrained horn clauses. In: LPAR. EPiC Series in Computing, vol. 46, pp. 338–355. EasyChair (2017)
25. Mordvinov, D., Fedyukovich, G.: Verifying safety of functional programs with rosette/unbound. CoRR, abs/1704.04558 (2017). https://github.com/dvvrd/rosette
26. Pick, L., Fedyukovich, G., Gupta, A.: Exploiting synchrony and symmetry in relational verification (extended version of CAV 2018 paper). https://cs.princeton.edu/%7Eaartig/papers/synonym-cav18.pdf

27. Sousa, M., Dillig, I.: Cartesian hoare logic for verifying k-safety properties. In: PLDI, pp. 57–69. ACM (2016)

28. Strichman, O., Veitsman, M.: Regression verification for unbalanced recursive functions. In: Fitzgerald, J., Heitmeyer, C., Gnesi, S., Philippou, A. (eds.) FM 2016. LNCS, vol. 9995, pp. 645–658. Springer, Cham (2016). https://doi.org/10.1007/978-3-319-48989-6_39

29. Terauchi, T., Aiken, A.: Secure information flow as a safety problem. In: Hankin, C., Siveroni, I. (eds.) SAS 2005. LNCS, vol. 3672, pp. 352–367. Springer, Heidelberg (2005). https://doi.org/10.1007/11547662_24

30. Unno, H., Torii, S., Sakamoto, H.: Automating induction for solving horn clauses. In: Majumdar, R., Kunčak, V. (eds.) CAV 2017. LNCS, vol. 10427, pp. 571–591. Springer, Cham (2017). https://doi.org/10.1007/978-3-319-63390-9_30

31. Yang, H.: Relational separation logic. Theoret. Comput. Sci. **375**(1–3), 308–334 (2007)

32. Zaks, A., Pnueli, A.: CoVaC: compiler validation by program analysis of the cross-product. In: Cuellar, J., Maibaum, T., Sere, K. (eds.) FM 2008. LNCS, vol. 5014, pp. 35–51. Springer, Heidelberg (2008). https://doi.org/10.1007/978-3-540-68237-0_5

4

Eager Abstraction for Symbolic Model Checking

Kenneth L. McMillan[✉]

Microsoft Research, Redmond, USA
kenmcmil@microsoft.com

Abstract. We introduce a method of abstraction from infinite-state to finite-state model checking based on eager theory explication and evaluate the method in a collection of case studies.

1 Introduction

In constructing decision procedures for arithmetic formulas and other theories, a successful approach has been to separate propositional reasoning and theory reasoning in a modular way. This approach is usually called Satisfiability Modulo Theories, or SMT [1]. There are two primary approaches to SMT: *eager* and *lazy* theory explication. Both approaches abstract the formula in question by constructing its propositional skeleton, that is, converting each atomic predicate to a corresponding free Boolean variable. Obviously, propositional abstraction loses a great deal of information. The eager approach compensates for this by conjoining tautologies of the theory to the formula before propositional abstraction. In abstract interpretation terms, we can think of this as a *semantic reduction*: it makes the formula more explicit without changing its semantics. The lazy approach, on the other hand, performs the propositional abstraction first, then retroactively adds tautologies of the theory to rule out infeasible propositional models.

In this paper, we will consider applying the same concepts to the symbolic model checking problem (SMC). In this problem, we are given a Kripke model M that is expressed implicitly using logical formulas, and a temporal formula ϕ, and we wish to determine whether $M \models \phi$. The states of the Kripke model are structures of a logic L over a given vocabulary, while the set of initial states I and the set of transitions T are expressed, respectively, by one- and two-vocabulary formulas. The atomic propositions in ϕ are also presumed to be expressed in L.

In the case where L is propositional logic, the Kripke model is finite-state, the SMC problem is PSPACE-complete, and many well-developed techniques are available to solve it in a heuristically efficient way. On the other hand, if L is a richer logic (say, Presburger arithmetic) SMC is usually undecidable. Here, we propose to solve instances of this problem by separating propositional reasoning and theory reasoning in a modular way, as in SMT. Given an SMC problem (I, T, ϕ), we will form its propositional abstraction by computing the propositional skeletons of I, T and ϕ. This abstraction is sound, and allows us to apply well-developed tools for propositional SMC, however it loses a great deal of information. To compensate for this loss, we will use incomplete eager theory explication. By controlling theory explication, the user controls the abstraction. We will call this general approach *eager symbolic model checking*, or ESMC.

Related Work. Because of the propositional abstraction, ESMC may at first seem to be a form of predicate abstraction [9]. This is not the case, however. Predicate abstraction uses a vocabulary of predicates to abstract the state, but does not abstract the theory itself. As a result, a decision procedure for the theory is needed to compute the best abstract transformer. This is problematic if the logic is undecidable, and in any event requires an exponential number of decision procedure calls in the worst case. In ESMC, the abstraction is performed in a purely syntactic way. One controls the abstraction by giving a set of axiom schemata to be instantiated and by introducing prophecy variables, as opposed to giving abstraction predicates. One effect of this is that the abstraction may depend on the precise syntactic expression of the transition relation.

The technique of "datatype reductions" [18] is also closely related. This method has been used to verify various parameterized protocols and microarchitectures using finite-state model checking [5,6,12,19,20]. The technique also abstracts an infinite-state SMC problem to a finite-state one syntactically. Though it does not do this by explicating the theory, we will see that the abstraction it produces can be simulated by ESMC. Compared to this method, ESMC is user-extensible and allows both a simpler theoretical account and a simpler implementation. Moreover, it uses a smaller trusted computing base, since the tautologies it introduces can be mechanically checked.

The methods of Invisible Invariants [25] and Indexed Predicate Abstraction [14] use different methods to compute the least fixed point in a finite abstract domain of quantified formulas. This requires decidability and incurs a relatively high cost for computing an extremal fixed point, limiting scalability (though IPA can approximate the best transformer in the undecidable case). The abstractions are also difficult to refine in practice.

Road Map. After preliminaries in the next section, we introduce our schema-based class of abstractions in Sect. 3. The next section gives some useful instantiations of this class. Section 5 describes a methodology for exploiting the abstraction in proofs of infinite-state systems, as implemented in the IVy tool. In Sect. 5, we evaluate the approach using case studies.

2   Preliminaries

Let $FO_=(\mathbb{S}, \Sigma)$ be standard sorted first-order logic with equality, where $\mathbb{S}$ is a collection of first-order sorts and Σ is a vocabulary of sorted non-logical symbols. We assume a special sort $\mathbb{B} \in \mathbb{S}$ that is the sort of propositions. Each symbol

$f^S \in \Sigma$ has an associated sort S of the form $D_1 \times \cdots \times D_n \rightarrow R$, where $D_i, R \in \mathbb{S}$ and $n \geq 0$ is the *arity* of the symbol. If $n = 0$, we say f^S is a *constant*, and if $R = \mathbb{B}$ it is a *relation*. We write $\mathrm{vocab}(t)$ for the set of non-logical symbols occurring in term t.

Given a set of sorts $\mathbb{S}$, a *universe* U maps each sort in $\mathbb{S}$ to a non-empty set (with $U(\mathbb{B}) = \{\top, \bot\}$). An *interpretation* of a vocabulary Σ over universe U maps each symbol $f^{D_1 \times \cdots \times D_n \rightarrow R}$ in Σ to a function in $U(D_1) \times \cdots \times U(D_n) \rightarrow U(R)$. A Σ-*structure* is a pair $\mathcal{M} = (U, \mathcal{I})$ where U is a universe and $\mathcal{I}$ is an interpretation of Σ over U. The structure is a *model* of a proposition ϕ in $FO_=(\mathbb{S}, \Sigma)$ if ϕ evaluates to $\top$ under $\mathcal{I}$ according to the standard semantics of first-order logic. In this case, we write $\mathcal{M} \models \phi$. Given an interpretation $\mathcal{J}$ with domain disjoint from $\mathcal{I}$, we write $\mathcal{M}, \mathcal{J}$ to abbreviate the structure $(U, \mathcal{I} \cup \mathcal{J})$.

In the sequel, we take the vocabulary Σ to be a disjoint union of four sets: Σ_S, the *state* symbols, Σ_S' the *primed* symbols, Σ_T the *temporary* symbols, and Σ_B, the *background* symbols. We take $(\cdot)'$ to be a bijection $\Sigma_S \rightarrow \Sigma_S'$ and extend it in the expected way to terms and interpretations. We write $\mathrm{unprime}(t)$ for the term u such that $u' = t$, if u exists.

A *transition system* is a pair (I, T) where I is a proposition over $\Sigma_S \cup \Sigma_B$ and T is a proposition over Σ. Let $\mathcal{M}_B = (U, \mathcal{I}_B)$ be a Σ_B-structure (that is, fix the universe and the interpretation of the background symbols). A U-*state* of the system is an interpretation of Σ_S (the state symbols) over U. A $\mathcal{M}_B$-*run* of the system is an infinite sequence $s_0, s_1, \ldots$ of U-states such that:

- $\mathcal{M}_B, s_0 \models I$, and
- for all $0 \leq i$, there exists and interpretation $\mathcal{I}_T$ of Σ_T over U such that $\mathcal{M}_B, s_i, \mathcal{I}_T, s_{i+1}' \models T$.

That is, under the background interpretation, the initial state must satisfy the initial condition, and for every successive pair of states, there must be an interpretation of the temporary symbols such that the transition condition is satisfied. The temporary symbols are used, for example, to model local variables of procedures, and may also be Skolem symbols. Because they can have second-order sort, we cannot existentially quantify them within the logic, so instead we quantify them implicitly in the transition system semantics. Given a background theory $\mathcal{T}$ over Σ_B, a $\mathcal{T}$-*run* is any $\mathcal{M}_B$-run such that $\mathcal{M}_B \models \mathcal{T}$.

A *linear temporal formula* over Σ applies the operators of $FO_=(\mathbb{S}, \Sigma)$ plus the standard strict until operator $\mathcal{U}$ and strict since operator $\mathcal{S}$. We define $\bigcirc \phi = \bot \mathcal{U} \phi$, $\square \phi = \phi \wedge \neg(\top \mathcal{U} \neg \phi)$ and also $\mathcal{H} \phi = \phi \mathcal{S} \bot$, meaning "always ϕ in the strict past". We fix $\mathcal{T}$ and say $(I, T) \models \phi$ if every $\mathcal{T}$-run of (I, T) satisfies ϕ under the standard LTL semantics. The symbolic model checking problem SMC is to determine whether $(I, T) \models \phi$.

3 A Schema-Based Abstraction Class

An *atom* is a proposition in which every instance of $\{\wedge, \vee, \neg, \mathcal{U}, \mathcal{S}\}$ occurs under a quantifier. The *propositional skeleton* of a proposition ϕ is obtained by replacing each atom in ϕ by a corresponding propositional constant. The propositional skeleton is an abstraction, in the sense that for every model M of ϕ we can construct a model of its propositional skeleton from the truth values of each atomic proposition in M. We will use propositional skeletons here to convert an infinite-state model checking problem to a finite-state one.

We assume that each vocabulary Σ_B, Σ_S and Σ_T contains a countably infinite set of propositional constants. This allows us to construct injections $\mathcal{A}_B$, $\mathcal{A}_S$, $\mathcal{A}_T$ from atomic propositions of the logic to propositional constants in Σ_B, Σ_S and Σ_T respectively.

In defining the propositional skeleton of a transition formula we must consider atomic propositions containing symbols from more than one vocabulary. To which vocabulary should we map such an atom in the propositional skeleton? Here, we take a simple solution that is sound, though it may lose some state information. That is, for any atomic proposition ϕ, we say

- if $\text{vocab}(\phi) \subseteq \Sigma_B$, then $\mathcal{A}(\phi) = \mathcal{A}_B(\phi)$,
- else if $\text{vocab}(\phi) \subseteq \Sigma_B \cup \Sigma_S$ then $\mathcal{A}(\phi) = \mathcal{A}_S(\phi)$
- else if $\text{vocab}(\phi) \subseteq \Sigma_B \cup \Sigma_S'$ then $\mathcal{A}(\phi) = \mathcal{A}_S(\text{unprime}(\phi))'$
- else $\mathcal{A}(\phi) = \mathcal{A}_T(\phi)$

That is, pure background propositions are abstracted to background symbols, state propositions are abstracted to state symbols and next-state propositions are abstracted to the primed version of the corresponding state proposition. Everything else is abstracted to a temporary symbol (which is existentially quantified in the abstract transition relation).

We then extend $\mathcal{A}$ to non-atomic formulas in the obvious way, such that $\mathcal{A}(\phi \wedge \psi) = \mathcal{A}(\phi) \wedge \mathcal{A}(\psi)$, $\mathcal{A}(\bigcirc\phi) = \bigcirc\mathcal{A}(\phi)$ and so on. The following theorem shows that we can use propositional skeletons to convert infinite-state to finite-state model checking problems in a sound (but incomplete) way:

Theorem 1. *For any symbolic transition system (I, T) and linear temporal formula ϕ, if $(\mathcal{A}(I), \mathcal{A}(T)) \models \mathcal{A}(\phi)$ then $(I, T) \models \phi$.*

Intuitively, this holds because we can convert every concrete counterexample to an abstract one by simply extracting the truth values of the atomic propositions.

Theory Explication. While propositional skeletons are sound, they lose a great deal of information. For example, suppose our transition relation is $y' = x$. Given a predicate p, we would like to infer that $p(x) \Rightarrow \bigcirc p(y)$. However, in the propositional skeleton, the transition relation $\mathcal{A}(T)$ is just $\mathcal{A}_T(y' = x)$. In other words, it is just a free propositional symbol with no relation to any other proposition. Thus, we cannot prove the abstracted property $\mathcal{A}(p(x)) \Rightarrow \bigcirc\mathcal{A}(p(y))$.

To mitigate this loss of information, we use *theory explication*. That is, before abstracting T, we conjoin to it tautologies of the logic or the background theory. This doesn't change the semantics of T, and thus the set of runs of the transition system remains unchanged. It does, however, change the propositional skeleton.

For example, $y' = x \wedge p(x) \Rightarrow p(y')$ is a tautology of the theory of equality. If we conjoin this formula to T in the above example, the abstract transition relation becomes $\mathcal{A}_T(y' = x) \wedge (\mathcal{A}_T(y' = x) \wedge \mathcal{A}_S(p(x)) \Rightarrow \mathcal{A}_S(p(y)))'$) which is strong enough to prove the abstracted property.

In general, theory explication adds predicates to the abstraction. This is the only mechanism we will use to add predicates; we will not supply them manually, or obtain them automatically from counterexamples. The following theorem justifies model checking with eager theory explication:

Theorem 2. *For any symbolic transition system* (I, T), *linear temporal formula* ϕ, $\Sigma_B \cup \Sigma_S$ *formula* ψ_I *and* Σ *formula* ψ_T, *if* $T \models \psi_I \wedge \psi_T$ *then* $(I \wedge \psi_I, T \wedge \psi_T) \models \phi$ *iff* $(I, T) \models \phi$.

The question, of course, is how to choose the tautologies in ψ_I and ψ_T. This is not just a question of capturing the transition relation semantics, since theory explication also determines the FO predicates representing state of the finite abstraction. Thus, complete theory explication is at least as hard as predicate discovery in predicate abstraction. Our goal is not to solve this problem, but to find an effective incomplete strategy that is useful in practice. It is important that the resulting finite-state model checking problems be easily resolved by a modern model checker, and that in case the strategy fails, a human can use the resulting counterexample and effectively refine the abstraction.

Schema-Based Theory Explication. The basic approach we will use to controlling theory explication is a restricted case of the pattern-based quantifier instantiation method introduced in the Simplify prover [8]. That is, we are given a set of axioms, and for each axiom a set of triggers. A trigger is a term (or terms) containing all of the free variables in the axiom. The trigger is matched against all ground subterms in the formula being explicated. Each match induces an instance of the axiom.

In our example above, suppose we have the axiom $Y = X \wedge p(X) \Rightarrow p(Y)$ with a trigger $Y = X$ (here and in the sequel, capital letters will stand for free variables). The trigger $Y = X$ matches the ground term $y' = x$ in T which generates the ground instance $y' = x \wedge p(x) \Rightarrow p(y')$. Since we match modulo the symmetry of equality, we also get $x = y' \wedge p(y') \Rightarrow p(x)$.

A risk of trigger-based instantiation is the matching loop. For example, if we have the axiom $f(X) > X + 1$ with a trigger $f(X)$, then we can generate an infinite sequence of instantiations: $f(y) > y + 1$, $f(f(y)) > f(y) + 1$ and so on. A simple approach to prevent this is to bound the number of generations of matching. In practice, we will use just one generation and expand the set axioms in cases where more than one generation is needed. This has the benefit of keeping the number of generated terms small, which limits the size of the SMC problem and also makes it easier for users to understand counterexamples.

To avoid having to write a large number of axioms, we specify the axioms using general schemata. A schema is a parameterized axiom. It takes a list of sorts and symbols as parameters and yields an axiom. In the sequel we will use s

and t to stand for sort parameters. As an example, here is a general congruence schema that can be used in place of our axiom above:

$$\frac{f : s \to t}{X = Y \Rightarrow f(X) = f(Y) \; \{X = Y\}}$$

The trigger is in curly braces. We first instantiate the axiom schemata for all possible parameter valuations using the sorts and symbols of the concrete system. Then we ground the resulting axioms using pattern-based instantiation.

One further technique is needed, however, to ground the quantifiers occurring in the formula being explicated. Quantifiers usually occur in the transition relations of parameterized systems either in the guards of guarded commands or in state updates. As an example, suppose a given command sets the state of process p to 'ready'. This would appear in the transition formula as a constraint such as the following:

$$\forall x. \; \text{state}'(x) = \text{ready if } x = p \text{ else state}(x)$$

If this quantifier is not instantiated, then all information about process state will be lost. To avoid this, we would like to apply the following schema:

$$\frac{y : s, \; p : s \to \mathbb{B}}{(\forall X. \; p(X)) \Rightarrow p(y) \; \{\forall X. \; p(X)\}}$$

Here we intend that p should match *any* predicate with one free variable and not just a predicate symbol (including non-temporal sub-formulas of the property to be proved). However, rather than implement a general second-order matching scheme, it is simpler to build this particular schema into the theory explication process. There is some question as to which ground terms to supply for the parameter y. As with other schemata, only constants are used in the current implementation. This appears to be adequate, but it might also be useful to allow the user to supply explicit triggers for quantifiers in the transition system or property.

The theory explication process thus has three steps:

1. Instantiate quantifiers in the formulas using the quantifier schema above.
2. Generate axioms from the user axiom schemata, supplying symbols from the formulas as parameters.
3. Instantiate the axioms using triggers for one generation.

Notice this is a slight departure from the policy of one generation of matching, since terms generated in step 1 can be used to match axioms in step 3. This is important in practice since without grounding the quantifiers there may be no ground terms to match in step 3.

4 Example Abstractions in the Class

A typical approach to verifying parameterized protocols with finite-state model checking is to track the state of a representative fixed collection of processes and abstract away the state of the remaining processes. In this approach, introduced in [17], a small collection background constants (typically two or three) is used to identify the tracked processes. For each process identifier in the system, the abstraction records whether it is equal to each of the tracked ids, but carries no further information. For each function f over process ids, the abstraction maintains the value of $f(x)$ only if x is equal to one of the background constants. This approach has been used, for example, to verify processor microarchitectures [12, 16, 17] and cache coherence protocols [5, 6, 19].

This abstraction can be implemented using schema-based instantiation. The high-level idea is to create a set of schemata that make it possible to abstractly evaluate terms in a bottom-up manner.

For example, consider an occurrence $t = u$ of the equality operator where t and u are terms of sort s. The abstract value of this term is $\top$ if t and u are both equal to some background constant c, $\bot$ if $t = c$ and $u \neq c$, and otherwise is unknown. To implement this abstraction, we use the following schemata:

$$\frac{c : s}{X = c \land Y = c \Rightarrow X = Y \ \{X = Y\}} \qquad \frac{c : s}{X = c \land Y \neq c \Rightarrow X \neq Y \ \{X = Y\}}$$

The triggers of these two schemata cause them to be applied to every occurrence of an equality operator in the formula being abstracted.

For an application $f(t)$ of a function symbol, the abstract value is the abstraction of $f(c)$ if t is equal to background constant c, and is otherwise unknown. This fact could be captured by chaining the congruence schema above with the above two equality schemata. That is, matching the congruence schema, we obtain $t = c \Rightarrow f(t) = f(c)$. Then matching the equality operator schemata with this result, we obtain (in the contrapositive) $f(t) = f(c) \land f(c) = d \Rightarrow f(t) = d$ and $f(t) = f(c) \land f(c) \neq d \Rightarrow f(t) \neq d$ (for any background constants c, d). Recall, however, that we allow only one generation of matching, so this second matching step will not occur. Instead, we write the above two facts explicitly as a schema:

$$\frac{c : s, \ d : t, \ f : s \to t}{X = c \Rightarrow (f(X) = d \Leftrightarrow f(c) = d) \ \{f(X)\}}$$

This schema is matched for every application of a symbol of arity one in the formula. We also specify similar schemata for arities greater than one. Notice that this schema also applies to relation symbols if we treat $\top$ and $\bot$ as background constants of sort $\mathbb{B}$. However, for relations and functions to finitely enumerated sorts, it is more efficient to use the congruence schema, since it produces fewer instances.

Finally, we need one additional schema to guarantee that the abstract values are consistent with the equality relation on the background constants:

$$\frac{c : s, \ d : s}{X = c \Rightarrow (X = d \Leftrightarrow c = d) \ \{X\}}$$

Notice that this axiom is instantiated for every term in the formula (though in practice not for propositions). Though it doesn't affect satisfiability of formulas, it is also helpful to add reflexivity, symmetry and transitivity over the background constants as it makes the resulting counterexamples easier to understand.

These schemata produce an abstraction of the formula that is at least as strong as the datatype reduction for scalarset types described in [18]. In fact, this is true if we restrict the application of the schemata to constants c and d in the set of background constants, which we do in practice. The cost of the abstraction is moderate, since the number of axiom instances is directly proportional to the size of the formula and to the number of background constants.

An advantage of the schema-based explication approach is that we can use it to construct abstractions for various datatypes and even use different abstractions of the same datatype for different applications. As an example, consider an abstraction for totally ordered datatypes such as the integers. We want the abstraction to track, for any term t of this sort, whether it is equal to, less than or greater than each background constant. The abstract value of a term t is captured by the values of the predicates $t < c$ and $t = c$ for background constants c. We begin with the abstract semantics of equality given above. The abstract semantics of the $<$ relation can be given by the following schemata (where $t \leq c$ is an abbreviation for $t < c \vee t = c$):

$$\frac{c : s}{X \leq c \wedge c < Y \Rightarrow X < Y \; \{X < Y\}} \qquad \frac{c : s}{X < c \wedge c \leq Y \Rightarrow X < Y \; \{X < Y\}}$$

$$\frac{c : s}{Y \leq c \wedge \neg(X < c) \Rightarrow \neg(X < Y) \; \{X < Y\}}$$

By chaining the congruence schema with these, we can obtain the abstract semantics of function application, but again we wish to limit the number of matching generations to one. Thus, as with equality, we write an explicit schema combining the two steps:

$$\frac{c : s, \; d : t, \; f : s \to t}{X = c \Rightarrow (f(X) < d \Leftrightarrow f(c) < d) \; \{f(X)\}}$$

We also require that the abstract value of every term be consistent with the interpretation of $=$ and $<$ over the background constants. This gives us:

$$\frac{c : s}{\neg(X = c \wedge X < c) \; \{X\}} \qquad \frac{c : s, \; d : t}{X \leq d \wedge \neg(X < c) \Rightarrow c \leq d \; \{X\}}$$

With the equality schemata, these imply that the background constants are totally ordered. As an extension, if the totally ordered sort has a least element 0, we can add it as a background constant along with the axiom $\neg(X < 0)$.

This abstraction is a bit weaker than the "ordset" abstraction used, for example, in [20]. We can simulate that abstraction by adding schemata that interpret the $+$ operator, and facts about numeric constants such as $0 < 1$. In general, for a given datatype, we can tailor an abstraction that captures just the properties of that type needed to prove a given system property. This extensibility makes the schema-based approach more flexible and possibly more efficient than the built-in abstractions of [18]. The above schemata have been verified by Z3.

5   Proof Methodology

In the previous sections, we developed an approach to produce a sound finite-state abstraction of an infinite-state system using eager theory explication and propositional skeletons. Now we consider how to construct proofs of systems using this approach. This section is essentially a summary of some results in [18].

The first question that arises is how to obtain the set of background constants that determine the abstraction. Generally speaking these arise as prophecy variables. For example, suppose we wish to prove a mutual exclusion property of the form $\Box \forall x, y. \ p(x) \wedge p(y) \Rightarrow x = y$. To do this, we replace the bound variables x and y with fresh background constants a and b, to obtain the quantifier-free property $\Box p(a) \wedge p(b) \Rightarrow a = b$. In effect a and b are immutable prophecy variables that predict the values of x and y for which the property will fail. By introducing prophecy variables, we refine the abstraction so that it tracks the state of the pair of processes that ostensibly cause the mutual exclusion property to fail. We hope, of course, to prove that there are no such processes. We apply the following theorem to introduce prophecy variables soundly:

Theorem 3. *Let (I, T) be a symbolic transition system, $x{:}s$ a variable, $\phi(x)$ a temporal formula and $v{:}s$ a background symbol not occurring in I, T, ϕ. Then $(I, T) \models \Box \forall x. \ \phi(x)$ iff $(I, T) \models \Box \phi(v)$.*

This theorem can be applied as many times as needed to eliminate universal quantifiers from an invariance property. Further refinement can be obtained if needed by manually adding prophesy variables. For example, suppose that each process x has a ticket number $t(x)$, and we wish to track the ticket number held by process a at the time of the failure. To do this, we replace our property with the property $\Box \ c = t(a) \Rightarrow (p(a) \wedge p(b) \Rightarrow a = b)$ where c is a fresh background constant. In general, we can introduce additional prophecy variables using this theorem:

Theorem 4. *Let (I, T) be a transition system, ϕ a temporal formula and t a term. Then $(I, T) \models \Box \phi$ iff $(I, T) \models \Box \forall x. \ x = t \Rightarrow \phi$, where x is not free in ϕ.*

The theorem can be applied repeatedly to introduce as many prophecy variables as needed to refine the abstraction. The introduced quantifiers can be converted to background symbols by the preceding theorem.

Since our abstraction tracks the state of only processes a and b, a protocol step in which an untracked process sends a message to a or b is likely to produce an incorrect result in the abstraction. To mitigate this problem, we assume by induction over time that our universally quantified invariant property ϕ has always held in the strict past. This makes use of the following theorem:

Theorem 5. *Let (I, T) be a symbolic transition system, and ϕ a temporal formula. Then $(I, T) \models \Box \phi$ iff $(I, T) \models \Box \ (\mathcal{H}\phi) \Rightarrow \phi$.*

The quantifiers in ϕ will be instantiated with ground terms in T. Thus, in our mutual exclusion example, we can rely on the fact that the sender of a past message (identified by some temporary symbol) is not in its critical section if either a or b are. Using induction in this way can mitigate the loss of information in the finite abstraction. Note we can pull quantifiers out of the above implication in order to apply Theorem 3. That is, $(\mathcal{H}\forall x.\ \phi) \Rightarrow \forall x.\phi$ is equivalent to $\forall x.\ (\mathcal{H}\forall x.\ \phi) \Rightarrow \phi$.

If the above tactics fail to prove an invariant property because the abstraction loses too much information, we can strengthen the invariant by adding conjuncts to it. These conjuncts have been called "non-interference lemmas", since they serve to reduce the interference with the tracked processes that is caused by loss of information about the untracked processes. We use the following theorem:

Theorem 6. *Let (I, T) be a symbolic transition system, and ϕ, ψ temporal formulas. Then if $(I, T) \models \Box\phi \wedge \psi$ then $(I, T) \models \Box\phi$.*

The general proof approach has the following steps:

1. Strengthen the invariant property (manually) with Theorem 6.
2. Apply temporal induction with Theorem 5.
3. Add quantifiers to the invariant with Theorem 4.
4. Convert the invariant quantifiers to background symbols with Theorem 3.
5. Add tautologies to the system using Theorem 2 and specified schemata.
6. Abstract to a finite-state SMC problem using Theorem 1.
7. Apply a finite-state symbolic model checker to check the property.

Implementation in IVy. This approach has been implemented in the IVy tool [15]. In IVy, the state of the model is expressed in terms of mutable functions and relations over primitive sorts. The language is procedural, and allows the expression of protocol models as interleavings of atomic guarded commands, the semantics of which is expressible in first-order logic.

To implement the approach, IVy's language was augmented with a syntax for expressing schemata. The schemata of Sect. 4 were added to the tool's standard library. Syntax is also provided to decorate invariant assertions with terms to be used as prophecy variables. IVy extends the above theory slightly by allowing invariant properties to be asserted not only between commands, but also in the middle of sequential commands. This can be convenient, since it allows invariants to reference local variables inside the commands.

With this input, the tool applies the six transformation steps detailed above to produce a purely propositional SMC problem. This problem is then converted to the AIGER format [2], a standard for hardware model checking. At present, the system only handles safety properties of the form $\Box(\mathcal{H}\phi) \Rightarrow \phi$, where ϕ is non-temporal. The AIGER format does support liveness, however, and this is planned as a future extension.

The resulting AIGER file is passed to the tool ABC [4] which uses its implementation of property driven reachability [10] to check the property. The counterexample, if any, is converted back to a run of the abstract transition system. The propositional symbols in this run are converted back to the corresponding atoms by inverting the abstraction mapping $\mathcal{A}$. This yields an *abstract counterexample*: a sequence of predicate valuations that correspond to both the state and temporary symbols in the abstraction.

The abstract counterexample may be spurious in the sense that it corresponds to no run of the concrete transition system. In this case, the user must analyze the trace to determine where necessary information was lost and either modify the invariant or refine the abstraction by adding a prophecy variable.

6 Case Studies

In this section, we consider the proof of safety properties of four parameterized algorithms and protocols. We wish to address three main questions. First, is the abstraction approach efficient? That is, if we construct an abstract model using schema-based theory explication, can the resulting finite-state problem be solved using a modern symbolic model checker? Second, is the methodology usable? That is, can a human user construct a proof using the methodology by analyzing the abstract counterexamples? Third, when is it more effective than the current best alternative, which is to write an inductive invariant manually and check it using an SMT solver, as in [11]? We will call this approach "invariant checking". We note that predicate abstraction is not suitable to these examples because the invariants require complex quantified formulas while current methods that synthesize quantified invariants for parameterized systems are unreliable in practice and do not scale well.

The last question in particular has not been well addressed in prior work on model checking approaches to parameterized verification. In most cases, either no comparison was made, or comparison was made to proofs using general-purpose proof assistants, which tend to be extremely laborious and do not make use of current state-of-the art proof automation techniques. To make a reasonably direct comparison, we construct proofs of each model using both methodologies, using the same language and tool, using the state-of-the art tools ABC [4] for model checking and Z3 [7] for invariant checking.

To apply the invariant checking method, some of the protocol models have been slightly re-encoded. In particular, it is helpful in some cases to use relations rather than functions in modeling the protocol state, as this can prevent the prover from diverging in a "matching loop" [8]. This re-encoding adds negligibly to the proof effort and is arguably harmless, since it does not appear in practice to affect the difficulty of refining the model to a concrete implementation.

Our four example models are:

1. **Tomasulo:** a parameterized model of Tomasulo's algorithm for out-or-order instruction execution, taken from [17].
2. **German:** a model of a simple directory-based cache coherence protocol from [6].
3. **FLASH:** a model of a more complex and realistic cache coherence protocol from [19,23], based on the Stanford FLASH multiprocessor [13].
4. **VS-Paxos:** a model of Virtually Synchronous Paxos [3], a distributed consensus algorithm, from [21].

Table 1. Comparison of proofs using two methodologies.

Model	Size	Model checking					Invariant checking			
		|Inv|	HVars	PVars	|Pf|	Time	|Inv|	HVars	|Pf|	Time
Tomasulo	1245	100	6	11	248	0.39	318	5	398	2.4
German	754	23	1	0	29	0.60	234	1	240	1.8
FLASH	2427	81	3	2	122	69	1235	1	1255	9.1
VS-Paxos	1442	224	8	34	512	23	1022	2	1101	59

A comparison of the proofs obtained using the two methodologies is shown in Table 1. The column "size" shows the textual size of the model plus property in lexical tokens. The columns labeled |Inv| give the size of the auxiliary invariants used in the proofs, expressed in the number of lexical tokens not including the property to be proved. Since both methods require the user to supply auxiliary invariants and discovering this invariant is the largest part of the effort in both cases, this number provides a fairly direct comparison of the complexity of the proofs. In both methodologies, the user also defines history or "ghost" variables that help in expressing the invariant. The number of these variables is shown in the columns labeled HVars. In the model checking approach, the user also refines the abstraction by defining prophecy variables. These were not used in the invariant checking proofs. The closest analogy in invariant checking proofs to this type of information would be quantifier instantiations or triggers provided by the user. This was not needed, however, since the methodology of [22] was applied to ensure that all verification conditions reside in a decidable fragment of the logic. For the model checking methodology, the number of distinct terms supplied by the user as prophecy variables is shown in the column labeled PVars. The time columns show the total time in seconds for model checking or invariant checking for the completed proofs on a 2.6 GHz Intel Xeon CPU using one core. Times to produce counterexamples were generally faster.

When measuring the overall complexity of the proofs, it is unclear how to weight the three kinds of information supplied by the user. In a sense, prophecy variables are the easiest to handle, since their behavior is monotone. That is, adding a prophecy variable only increases precision so it cannot cause passing invariants to fail. Ghost variables are more conceptually difficult to introduce, since the invariants depend on them. If a ghost variable definition is changed to repair a failing invariant, this may cause a different invariant to fail. Similarly if we strengthen a passing invariant, it may fail to be proved and if we weaken a failing one it may cause other formerly passing invariants to fail. This instability can cause the manual proof search to fail to converge and is the chief cause of conceptual difficulty in constructing proofs in both methodologies. Having said this, for lack of a principled way to weight the different aspects of the proof effort, we will measure the proof size as simply the sum of the number of lexical tokens in the auxiliary invariant, the history variable definitions, and all terms used as prophecy variables. The total proof size is shown in the columns labeled |Pf|.

These numbers should be taken as unreliable for several reasons that are
common to any attempt to measure the effectiveness of a proof methodology.
First, the size of the proof (or any other measure of the proof difficulty, such
as expended time) can depend on the proficiency of the user in the particular
methodology. Even if the same user produces both proofs, the user's proficiency
in the two methodologies may differ, and knowledge gained in the first proof
will effect the second one. Since resources were not available to train and test a
statistically significant population users in both methodologies (assuming such
could be found) the numbers presented here should not be considered a direct
comparison of the methods. Rather, they are presented to support some observations made below about the specific case studies and proofs.

Case Study: Tomasulo's Algorithm. This is a simple abstract model of a
processor microarchitecture that executes instructions concurrently out of order.
The model state consists of a register file, a set of reservation stations (RS) and
a set of execution units (EU) and is parameterized on the size of each of these,
as well as the data word size. The machine's instructions are register-to-register
and are modeled abstractly by an uninterpreted function. Each register has a
flag that records whether it is the destination of a pending instruction. If so, its
tag indicates which RS is holding that instruction. Each RS stores the tags of
its instruction arguments, and waits for these to be computed before issuing the
instruction to an EU.

Both proofs are based on history variables that record the correct values of
arguments and result for each RS. The principal invariant of both states that
the arguments obtained by all RS's are correct. In the model checking case, the
abstraction is refined by making the tags of these arguments and chosen EU into
prophecy variables. This allows the model checker to track enough state information to prove the main invariant, though one additional "non-interference"
lemma is needed to guarantee that other EU's do not interfere by producing an
incorrect tag. An interesting aspect of the invariant is that it does not refer to
the states of the register file or EU's. The necessary invariants of these structures
can be inferred by the model checker. On the other hand, this information must
be supplied explicitly in the manual invariant. As the table shows, the resulting
invariant is more complex.

Case Study: German's Cache Protocol. This simple distributed directory-
based cache coherence protocol allows the caches to communicate directly only
with the directory. The property proved is coherence, in effect that exclusive
copies are exclusive. In the model checking proof, there is one non-interference
lemma, stating that no cache produces a spurious invalidation acknowledgment
message. No extra prophecy variables are need, as tracking the state of just the
two caches that produce the coherence failure suffices. The manual invariant on
the other hand is much more detailed, in fact about an order of magnitude larger.
This is because it must relate the state of all the various types of messages in

the network to the cache and directory states. These relationships were inferred automatically by the model checker, resulting in a much simpler proof.

Case Study: FLASH Cache Coherence Protocol. This is a much more complex (and realistic) distributed cache coherence protocol model. The increased protocol complexity derives from the fact that information can be transferred directly from one cache to another. In a typical transaction, a cache sends a request to the directory for (say) an exclusive copy of a cache line. The directory forwards the request to the current owner of the line, which then sends a copy to the original requester, as well as a response to the directory confirming the ownership transfer. Handling various race conditions in this scheme makes both the protocol and its proof complex. Again the property proved is coherence. The model checking proof is similar to [19], though there data correctness and liveness were proved.

In this case, three non-interference lemmas are used in the model checking proof, ruling out three types of spurious messages. Also two additional prophecy variables are needed. For example, one of these identifies the cache that sent an exclusive copy. This allows the abstraction to track the state of the third participant in the triangular transaction described above. Generally, protocols with more complex communication patterns require more prophecy variables to refine the abstraction.

As with German's protocol, and for the same reason, the manual invariant is an order of magnitude larger. In this case, the additional protocol complexity makes it quite challenging to converge to an invariant and a large number of strengthenings and weakenings were needed.

Case Study: Virtually Synchronous Paxos. This is a high-level model of a distributed consensus protocol, designed to allow a collection of processes to agree on a sequence of decisions, despite process and network failures. This model was previous proved by a manual invariant to be consistent, meaning that two decisions for a given index never disagree [21].

The protocol operates in a sequence of epochs, each of which has a leader process. The leader proposes decision values and any proposal that receives votes of a majority of processes becomes a decision. When the leader fails the protocol must move on to a new epoch. For consistency, any decisions that are possibly made in the old epoch must be preserved in the new. This is accomplished by choosing a majority of processes to start the new epoch and preserving all of their votes. Any decision having a majority of votes in the old epoch must have one voter in the new epoch's starting majority and thus must be preserved. The choice of an epoch's starting majority is itself a single-decree consensus problem. This is solved in a sequence of rounds called "stakes". A stake can be created by a majority of processes and proposes the votes of some majority to be carried to the next epoch. Each process in the stake promises not accept any lesser stake with differing votes. If a majority accepts the stake, then the votes of that stake can be passed to the next epoch.

The important auxiliary invariants of the model checking proof are these:

- At each epoch, the votes of the majority that ends the epoch are known to the leaders of all future epochs, and
- When a stake is created, every lesser stake with different votes is "dead" in the sense that a majority of nodes has promised not to accept it, and
- In any epoch, any two accepted stakes agree on their votes.

Perhaps not surprisingly, the manual invariant is much larger. The model checking proof, however, requires many extra prophecy variables. This is mainly accounted for by the fact that the model has seven unbounded sorts: process id's, decision indices, decision values, epochs, stakes, vote sets and process sets. Typically each invariant (including the one to be proved) requires one or two prophecy variables of each sort to refine the abstraction (though some of these may not be unique).

An additional complication is dealing with sets and majorities. Sets of processes are represented by an abstract data type. This type provides a predicate called 'majority' that indicates that a set contains more than half of the process id's. A function 'common' returns a common element between two sets if both are majorities (and is otherwise undefined). For example, to prove that we cannot have two conflicting decisions, we use the majorities that voted for each decision and declare the common process between these majorities as a prophecy variable. It then suffices to show that this particular process cannot have voted for both decisions (which requires the auxiliary invariants above). Since majorities are used in several places in the protocol, this tactic is applied several times.

Because of the larger number of prophecy variables, our (admittedly arbitrary) measure of overall proof complexity does not show as much advantage for model checking in this protocol as it does for the cache protocols. In fact, getting the details right in this proof was much more difficult subjectively than for FLASH.

This difficulty may be related to the two sorts in the model that are totally ordered: epochs and stakes. For these sorts we use the schemata for totally ordered sets detailed in Sect. 4. The ordering of these sorts introduces some difficulty in the proof, requiring more detailed invariants. For example, suppose we want to show that the first invariant above holds at the moment when a given process leaves one epoch and enters the next. The votes received at the epoch depend on all the previous epochs. We cannot however, make all of the unboundedly many lesser epochs concrete by adding a finite number of prophecy variables. This means our property must be inductive over epochs, that is, it holds now if it held in the past at the start of some *particular* epoch we can identify (perhaps the previous one). The need to write invariants that are inductive over ordered datatypes may account for the fact that the VS-Paxos invariant is more complex than that of the more complex FLASH protocol.

Discussion. We can make several general observations about these case studies. First, the performance of the finite-state model checker was never problematic. It always produced results in a reasonable amount of time and was not the bottleneck in constructing any of the proofs. Rather the most time-consuming task was usually analyzing the abstract counterexamples. This task proved tractable in practice, allowing the proof search process to converge.

Second, the invariants used in the model checking approach are generally much smaller than the manual ones because of the model checker's ability to infer state invariants.

This advantage may be somewhat offset by the need to provide prophecy variables to refine the abstraction, especially in the case where there are many unbounded sorts. Moreover, the need to write properties that are inductive over ordered sorts may lessen the advantage of model checking in invariant complexity. This was evident in the case of VS-Paxos and to some extent in Tomasulo as well, because of the implicit induction over the instruction stream. These criteria may be helpful in deciding which approach to take to a given proof problem.

Finally, it is interesting to note that the schemata presented in Sect. 4 proved adequate in all cases. That is, in no case was it necessary to add a schema to refine the abstraction of the transition relation. This indicates there is no need in practice to restrict to decidable logics or pay the cost of computing best transformers.

7   Conclusion

We have presented a method of abstracting parameterized or infinite-state SMC problems to finite-state problems based on propositional skeletons and eager theory explication. The method is extensible in the sense that users can add abstractions (or refine existing abstractions) by providing axiom schemata. It generalizes the 'datatype reduction' approach of [18] while giving both a simpler theoretical account and allowing a simpler implementation. Compared to predicate abstraction, it has the advantage that it can be applied to undecidable logics and does not require a costly decision procedure in the loop. The approach has been implemented in the IVy tool. Based on some case studies, we found that the approach is practical and requires substantially less complex auxiliary invariants than inductive invariant checking. We identified some conditions under which the approach is likely to be most effective.

Conceivably some of the tasks performed here by a human could be automated. However, the resulting system would be liable to fail unpredictably and opaquely. The present approach is an attempt to create a usable trade-off between human input and reliability.

The next step is to implement liveness. Recent work has constructed liveness proofs in IVy by an infinite-state liveness-to-safety reduction, but the proofs are complex [21]. It would interesting to compare this to an approach that leverages a finite-state model checker's ability to prove liveness.

References

1. Barrett, C., Sebastiani, R., Seshia, S.A., Tinelli, C.: Satisfiability modulo theories. In: Biere, A., Heule, M., van Maaren, H., Walsch, T. (eds.) Handbook of Satisfiability, chap. 12, pp. 737–797. IOS Press (2008)
2. Biere, A., Heljanko, K., Wieringa, S.: AIGER 1.9 and beyond. Technical report 11/2, Institute for Formal Models and Verification, Johannes Kepler University, July 2011
3. Birman, K., Malkhi, D., van Renesse, R.: Virtually synchronous methodology for dynamic service replication. Technical report MSR-TR-2010-151, Microsoft Research, November 2010
4. Brayton, R., Mishchenko, A.: ABC: an academic industrial-strength verification tool. In: Touili, T., Cook, B., Jackson, P. (eds.) CAV 2010. LNCS, vol. 6174, pp. 24–40. Springer, Heidelberg (2010). https://doi.org/10.1007/978-3-642-14295-6_5
5. Chen, X., Yang, Y., Gopalakrishnan, G., Chou, C.-T.: Reducing verification complexity of a multicore coherence protocol using assume/guarantee. In: Proceedings of the 6th International Conference on Formal Methods in Computer-Aided Design, FMCAD 2006, San Jose, California, USA, 12–16 November 2006, pp. 81–88. IEEE Computer Society (2006)
6. Chou, C.-T., Mannava, P.K., Park, S.: A simple method for parameterized verification of cache coherence protocols. In: Hu, A.J., Martin, A.K. (eds.) FMCAD 2004. LNCS, vol. 3312, pp. 382–398. Springer, Heidelberg (2004). https://doi.org/10.1007/978-3-540-30494-4_27
7. de Moura, L., Bjørner, N.: Z3: an efficient SMT solver. In: Ramakrishnan, C.R., Rehof, J. (eds.) TACAS 2008. LNCS, vol. 4963, pp. 337–340. Springer, Heidelberg (2008). https://doi.org/10.1007/978-3-540-78800-3_24
8. Detlefs, D., Nelson, G., Saxe, J.B.: Simplify: a theorem prover for program checking. J. ACM **52**(3), 365–473 (2005)
9. Graf, S., Saidi, H.: Construction of abstract state graphs with PVS. In: Grumberg, O. (ed.) CAV 1997. LNCS, vol. 1254, pp. 72–83. Springer, Heidelberg (1997). https://doi.org/10.1007/3-540-63166-6_10
10. Hassan, Z., Bradley, A.R., Somenzi, F.: Better generalization in IC3. In: Formal Methods in Computer-Aided Design, FMCAD 2013, Portland, OR, USA, 20–23 October 2013, pp. 157–164. IEEE (2013)
11. Hawblitzel, C., Howell, J., Kapritsos, M., Lorch, J.R., Parno, B., Roberts, M.L., Setty, S.T.V., Zill, B.: IronFleet: proving practical distributed systems correct. In: Miller, E.L., Hand, S. (eds.) Proceedings of the 25th Symposium on Operating Systems Principles, SOSP 2015, Monterey, CA, USA, 4–7 October 2015, pp. 1–17. ACM (2015)
12. Jhala, R., McMillan, K.L.: Microarchitecture verification by compositional model checking. In: Berry, G., Comon, H., Finkel, A. (eds.) CAV 2001. LNCS, vol. 2102, pp. 396–410. Springer, Heidelberg (2001). https://doi.org/10.1007/3-540-44585-4_40
13. Kuskin, J., Ofelt, D., Heinrich, M., Heinlein, J., Simoni, R., Gharachorloo, K., Chapin, J., Nakahira, D., Baxter, J., Horowitz, M., Gupta, A., Rosenblum, M., Hennessy, J.L.: The stanford FLASH multiprocessor. In: Patterson, D.A. (ed.) Proceedings of the 21st Annual International Symposium on Computer Architecture, Chicago, IL, USA, April 1994, pp. 302–313. IEEE Computer Society (1994)
14. Lahiri, S.K., Bryant, R.E.: Constructing quantified invariants via predicate abstraction. In: Steffen, B., Levi, G. (eds.) VMCAI 2004. LNCS, vol. 2937, pp. 267–281. Springer, Heidelberg (2004). https://doi.org/10.1007/978-3-540-24622-0_22

15. McMillan, K.L.: IVy. http://microsoft.github.io/ivy/. Accessed 28 Jan 2018
16. McMillan, K.L.: Circular compositional reasoning about liveness. In: Pierre and Kropf [24], pp. 342–345
17. McMillan, K.L.: Verification of infinite state systems by compositional model checking. In: Pierre and Kropf [24], pp. 219–234
18. McMillan, K.L.: A methodology for hardware verification using compositional model checking. Sci. Comput. Program. **37**(1–3), 279–309 (2000)
19. McMillan, K.L.: Parameterized verification of the FLASH cache coherence protocol by compositional model checking. In: Margaria, T., Melham, T. (eds.) CHARME 2001. LNCS, vol. 2144, pp. 179–195. Springer, Heidelberg (2001). https://doi.org/10.1007/3-540-44798-9_17
20. McMillan, K.L., Qadeer, S., Saxe, J.B.: Induction in compositional model checking. In: Emerson, E.A., Sistla, A.P. (eds.) CAV 2000. LNCS, vol. 1855, pp. 312–327. Springer, Heidelberg (2000). https://doi.org/10.1007/10722167_25
21. Padon, O., Losa, G., Sagiv, M., Shoham, S.: Paxos made EPR: decidable reasoning about distributed protocols. PACMPL **1**(OOPSLA), 108:1–108:31 (2017)
22. Padon, O., McMillan, K.L., Panda, A., Sagiv, M., Shoham, S.: Ivy: safety verification by interactive generalization. In: Krintz, C., Berger, E. (eds.) Proceedings of the 37th ACM SIGPLAN Conference on Programming Language Design and Implementation, PLDI 2016, Santa Barbara, CA, USA, 13–17 June 2016, pp. 614–630. ACM (2016)
23. Park, S., Dill, D.L.: Verification of FLASH cache coherence protocol by aggregation of distributed transactions. In: SPAA, pp. 288–296 (1996)
24. Pierre, L., Kropf, T. (eds.): CHARME 1999. LNCS, vol. 1703. Springer, Heidelberg (1999). https://doi.org/10.1007/3-540-48153-2
25. Pnueli, A., Ruah, S., Zuck, L.: Automatic deductive verification with invisible invariants. In: Margaria, T., Yi, W. (eds.) TACAS 2001. LNCS, vol. 2031, pp. 82–97. Springer, Heidelberg (2001). https://doi.org/10.1007/3-540-45319-9_7

5

Counterexample Guided Inductive Synthesis Modulo Theories

Alessandro Abate[1]⬚, Cristina David[2,3](✉)⬚, Pascal Kesseli[3]⬚,
Daniel Kroening[1,3]⬚, and Elizabeth Polgreen[1]

[1] University of Oxford, Oxford, UK
[2] University of Cambridge, Cambridge, UK
cd652@cam.ac.uk
[3] Diffblue Ltd., Oxford, UK

Abstract. Program synthesis is the mechanised construction of software. One of the main difficulties is the efficient exploration of the very large solution space, and tools often require a user-provided syntactic restriction of the search space. We propose a new approach to program synthesis that combines the strengths of a counterexample-guided inductive synthesizer with those of a theory solver, exploring the solution space more efficiently without relying on user guidance. We call this approach CEGIS($\mathcal{T}$), where $\mathcal{T}$ is a first-order theory. In this paper, we focus on one particular challenge for program synthesizers, namely the generation of programs that require non-trivial constants. This is a fundamentally difficult task for state-of-the-art synthesizers. We present two exemplars, one based on Fourier-Motzkin (FM) variable elimination and one based on first-order satisfiability. We demonstrate the practical value of CEGIS($\mathcal{T}$) by automatically synthesizing programs for a set of intricate benchmarks.

1 Introduction

Program synthesis is the problem of finding a program that meets a correctness specification given as a logical formula. This is an active area of research in which substantial progress has been made in recent years.

In full generality, program synthesis is an exceptionally difficult problem, and thus, the research community has explored pragmatic restrictions. One particularly successful direction is *Syntax-Guided Program Synthesis* (SyGuS) [2]. The key idea of SyGuS is that the user supplements the logical specification with a syntactic template for the solution. Leveraging the user's intuition, SyGuS reduces the solution space size substantially, resulting in significant speed-ups.

Unfortunately, it is difficult to provide the syntactic template in many practical applications. A very obvious exemplar of the limits of the syntax-guided approach are programs that require non-trivial constants. In such a scenario, the syntax-guided approach requires that the user provides the exact value of the constants in the solution.

For illustration, let's consider a user who wants to synthesize a program that rounds up a given 32-bit unsigned number x to the next highest power of two. If we denote the function computed by the program by $f(x)$, then the specification can be written as $x < 2^{31} \Rightarrow f(x)\&(-f(x)) = f(x) \wedge f(x) \geq x \wedge 2x \geq f(x)$. The first conjunct forces $f(x)$ to be a power of two, the other requires it to be the next highest. A possible solution for this is given by the following C program:

```
1   x=x−1;
2   x |= x >> 1;
3   x |= x >> 2;
4   x |= x >> 4;
5   x |= x >> 8;
6   x |= x >> 16;
7   x=x+1;
```

It is improbable that the user knows that the constants in the solution are exactly 1, 2, 4, 8, 16, and thus, she will be unable to explicitly restrict the solution space. As a result, synthesizers are very likely to enumerate possible combinations of constants, which is highly inefficient.

In this paper we propose a new approach to program synthesis that combines the strengths of a counterexample-guided inductive synthesizer with those of a solver for a first-order theory in order to perform a more efficient exploration of the solution space, without relying on user guidance. Our inspiration for this proposal is DPLL($\mathcal{T}$), which has boosted the performance of solvers for many fragments of quantifier-free first-order logic [16, 23]. DPLL($\mathcal{T}$) combines reasoning about the Boolean structure of a formula with reasoning about theory facts to decide satisfiability of a given formula.

In an attempt to generate similar technological advancements in program synthesis, we propose a new algorithm for program synthesis called CounterExample-Guided Inductive Synthesis($\mathcal{T}$), where $\mathcal{T}$ is a given first-order theory for which we have a specialised solver. Similar to its counterpart DPLL($\mathcal{T}$), the CEGIS($\mathcal{T}$) architecture features communication between a synthesizer and a theory solver, which results in a much more efficient exploration of the search space.

While standard CEGIS architectures [19, 30] already make use of SMT solvers, the typical role of such a solver is restricted to validating candidate solutions and providing concrete counterexamples that direct subsequent search. By contrast, CEGIS($\mathcal{T}$) allows the theory solver to communicate generalised constraints back to the synthesizer, thus enabling more significant pruning of the search space.

There are instances of more sophisticated collaboration between a program synthesizer and theory solvers. The most obvious such instance is the program synthesizer inside the CVC4 SMT solver [27]. This approach features a very tight coupling between the two components (i.e., the synthesizer and the theory solvers) that takes advantage of the particular strengths of the SMT solver by reformulating the synthesis problem as the problem of refuting a universally quantified formula (SMT solvers are better at refuting universally quantified formulae than at proving them). Conversely, in our approach we maintain a clear separation between the synthesizer and the theory solver while performing comprehensive and well-defined communication between the two components. This enables the flexible combination of CEGIS with a variety of theory solvers, which excel at exploring different solution spaces.

Contributions

- We propose CEGIS($\mathcal{T}$), a program synthesis architecture that facilitates the communication between an inductive synthesizer and a solver for a first-order theory, resulting in an efficient exploration of the search space.
- We present two exemplars of this architecture, one based on Fourier-Motzkin (FM) variable elimination [7] and one using an off-the-shelf SMT solver.
- We have implemented CEGIS($\mathcal{T}$) and compared it against state-of-the-art program synthesizers on benchmarks that require intricate constants in the solution.

2   Preliminaries

2.1   The Program Synthesis Problem

Program synthesis is the task of automatically generating programs that satisfy a given logical specification. A program synthesizer can be viewed as a solver for existential second-order logic. An existential second-order logic formula allows quantification over functions as well as ground terms [28].

The input specification provided to a program synthesizer is of the form $\exists P.\, \forall \boldsymbol{x}.\, \sigma(P, \boldsymbol{x})$, where P ranges over functions (where a function is represented by the program computing it), $\boldsymbol{x}$ ranges over ground terms, and σ is a quantifier-free formula.

2.2   CounterExample Guided Inductive Synthesis

CounterExample-Guided Inductive Synthesis (CEGIS) is a popular approach to program synthesis, and is an iterative process. Each iteration performs inductive generalisation based on counterexamples provided by a verification oracle. Essentially, the inductive generalisation uses information about a limited number of inputs to make claims about all the possible inputs in the form of candidate solutions.

The CEGIS framework is illustrated in Fig. 1 and consists of two phases: the synthesis phase and the verification phase. Given the specification of the desired program, σ, the inductive synthesis procedure generates a candidate program P^* that satisfies $\sigma(P^*, \boldsymbol{x})$ for a subset $\boldsymbol{x}_{inputs}$ of all possible inputs. The candidate program P^* is passed to the verification phase, which checks whether

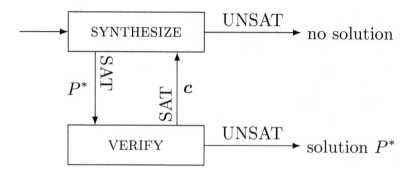

Fig. 1. CEGIS block diagram

it satisfies the specification $\sigma(P^*, \boldsymbol{x})$ for all possible inputs. This is done by checking whether $\neg\sigma(P^*, \boldsymbol{x})$ is unsatisfiable. If so, $\forall x.\neg\sigma(P^*, \boldsymbol{x})$ is valid, and we have successfully synthesized a solution and the algorithm terminates. Otherwise, the verifier produces a counterexample $\boldsymbol{c}$ from the satisfying assignment, which is then added to the set of inputs passed to the synthesizer, and the loop repeats.

The method used in the synthesis and verification blocks varies in different CEGIS implementations; our CEGIS implementation uses Bounded Model Checking [8].

2.3 DPLL($\mathcal{T}$)

DPLL($\mathcal{T}$) is an extension of the DPLL algorithm, used by most propositional SAT solvers, by a theory $\mathcal{T}$. We give a brief overview of DPLL($\mathcal{T}$) and compare DPLL($\mathcal{T}$) with CEGIS($\mathcal{T}$).

Given a formula F from a theory $\mathcal{T}$, a propositional formula F_p is created from F in which the theory atoms are replaced by Boolean variables (the "propositional skeleton"). The standard DPLL algorithm, comprising DECIDE, Boolean Constraint Propagation (BCP), ANALYZE-CONFLICT and BACKTRACK, generates an assignment to the Boolean variables in F_p, as illustrated in Fig. 2. The theory solver then checks whether this assignment is still consistent when the Boolean variables are replaced by their original atoms. If so, a satisfying assignment for F has been found. Otherwise, a constraint over the Boolean variables in F_p is passed back to DECIDE, and the process repeats.

In the very first SMT solvers, a full assignment to the Boolean variables was obtained, and then the theory solver returned only a single counterexample, similar to the implementations of CEGIS that are standard now. Such SMT solvers are prone to enumerating all possible counterexamples, and so the key improvement in DPLL($\mathcal{T}$) was the ability to pass back a more general constraint over the variables in the formula as a counterexample [16]. Furthermore, modern variants of DPLL($\mathcal{T}$) call the theory solver on partial assignments to the variables in F_p. Our proposed, new synthesis algorithm offers equivalents of both of these ideas that have improved DPLL($\mathcal{T}$).

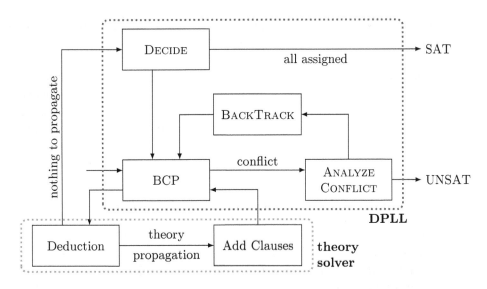

Fig. 2. DPLL($\mathcal{T}$) with theory propagation

3 Motivating Example

In each iteration of a standard CEGIS loop, the communication from the verification phase back to the synthesis phase is restricted to concrete counterexamples. This is particularly detrimental when synthesizing programs that require non-trivial constants. In such a setting, it is typical that a counterexample provided by the verification phase only eliminates a single candidate solution and, consequently, the synthesizer ends up enumerating possible constants.

For illustration, let's consider the trivial problem of synthesizing a function $f(x)$ where $f(x) < 0$ if $x < 334455$ and $f(x) = 0$, otherwise. One possible solution is $f(x) = ite\ (x < 334455) - 10$, where *ite* stands for *if then else*.

In order to make the synthesis task even simpler, we are going to assume that we know a part of this solution, namely we know that it must be of the form $f(x) = ite\ (x < ?) -1\ 0$, where "?" is a placeholder for the missing constant that we must synthesize. A plausible scenario for a run of CEGIS is presented next: the synthesis phase guesses $f(x) = ite\ (x < 0) -1\ 0$, for which the verification phase returns $x = 0$ as a counterexample. In the next iteration of the CEGIS loop, the synthesis phase guesses $f(x) = ite(x < 1)-1\ 0$ (which works for $x = 0$) and the verifier produces $x = 1$ as a counterexample. Following the same pattern, the synthesis phase will enumerate all the candidates

$$f(x) = ite\ (x < 2) -1\ 0$$

$$\cdots$$

$$f(x) = ite\ (x < 334454) -1\ 0$$

before finding the solution. This is caused by the fact that each of the concrete counterexamples $0, \ldots, 334454$ eliminate one candidate only from the solution space. Consequently, we need to propagate more information from the verifier to the synthesis phase in each iteration of the CEGIS loop.

Proving Properties of Programs. Synthesis engines can be used as reasoning engines in program analysers, and constants are important for this application. For illustration, let's consider the very simple program below, which increments a variable x from 0 to 100000 and asserts that its value is less than 100005 on exit from the loop.

```
1  int x=0;
2  while (x<=100000) x++;
3  assert(x<100005);
```

Proving the safety of such a program, i.e., that the assertion at line 3 is not violated in any execution of the program, is a task well-suited for synthesis (the Syntax Guided Synthesis Competition [5] has a track dedicated to synthesizing safety invariants). For this example, a safety invariant is $x < 100002$, which holds on entrance to the loop, is inductive with respect to the loop's body, and implies the assertion on exit from the loop.

While it is very easy for a human to deduce this invariant, the need for a non-trivial constant makes it surprisingly difficult for state-of-the-art synthesizers: both CVC4 (version 1.5) [27] and EUSolver (version 2017-06-15) [3] fail to find a solution in an hour.

4   CEGIS($\mathcal{T}$)

4.1   Overview

In this section, we describe the architecture of CEGIS($\mathcal{T}$), which is obtained by augmenting the standard CEGIS loop with a theory solver. As we are particularly interested in the synthesis of programs with constants, we present CEGIS($\mathcal{T}$) from this particular perspective. In such a setting, CEGIS is responsible for synthesizing program skeletons, whereas the theory solver generates constraints over the literals that denote constants. These constraints are then propagated back to the synthesizer.

In order to explain the main ideas behind CEGIS($\mathcal{T}$) in more detail, we first differentiate between a candidate solution, a candidate solution skeleton, a generalised candidate solution and a final solution.

Definition 1 (Candidate solution). *Using the notation in Sect. 2.2, a program P is a* candidate solution *if $\forall \boldsymbol{x}_{inputs}.\sigma(P, \boldsymbol{x}_{inputs})$ is true for some subset $\boldsymbol{x}_{inputs}$ of all possible $\boldsymbol{x}$.*

Definition 2 (Candidate solution skeleton). *Given a candidate solution P, the* skeleton *of P, denoted by $P[?]$, is obtained by replacing each constant in P with a hole.*

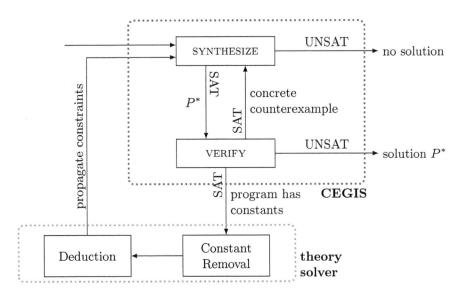

Fig. 3. CEGIS($\mathcal{T}$)

Definition 3 (Generalised candidate solution). *Given a candidate solution skeleton $P[?]$, we obtain a* generalised candidate $P[\boldsymbol{v}]$ *by filling each hole in $P[?]$ with a distinct symbolic variable, i.e., variable v_i will correspond to the i-th hole. Then $\boldsymbol{v} = [v_1, \ldots, v_n]$, where n denotes the number of holes in $P[?]$.*

Definition 4 (Final solution). *A candidate solution P is a* final solution *if the formula $\forall \boldsymbol{x}.\sigma(P, \boldsymbol{x})$ is valid.*

Example 1 (Candidate solution, candidate solution skeleton, generalised candidate solution, final solution). Given the example in Sect. 3, if $\boldsymbol{x}_{inputs} = \{0\}$, then $f(x) = -2$ is a candidate solution. The corresponding candidate skeleton is $f[?](x) = ?$ and the generalised candidate is $f[v_1](x) = v_1$. A final solution for this example is $f(x) = ite\ (x < 334455)\ -1\ 0$.

The communication between the synthesizer and the theory solver in CEGIS($\mathcal{T}$) is illustrated in Fig. 3 and can be described as follows:

- The CEGIS architecture (enclosed in a red rectangle) deduces the candidate solution P^*, which is provided to the theory solver.
- The theory solver (enclosed in a blue rectangle) obtains the skeleton $P^*[?]$ of P^* and generalises it to $P^*[\boldsymbol{v}]$ in the box marked CONSTANT REMOVAL. Subsequently, DEDUCTION attempts to find a constraint over $\boldsymbol{v}$ describing those values for which $P^*[\boldsymbol{v}]$ is a final solution. This constraint is propagated back to CEGIS. Whenever there is no valuation of $\boldsymbol{v}$ for which $P^*[\boldsymbol{v}]$ becomes a final solution, the constraint needs to block the current skeleton $P^*[?]$.

The CEGIS($\mathcal{T}$) algorithm is given as Algorithm 1 and proceeds as follows:

- **CEGIS synthesis phase:** checks the satisfiability of $\forall \boldsymbol{x}_{inputs} \cdot \sigma(P, \boldsymbol{x}_{inputs})$ where $\boldsymbol{x}_{inputs}$ is a subset of all possible $\boldsymbol{x}$ and obtains a candidate solution P^*. If this formula is unsatisfiable, then the synthesis problem has no solution.
- **CEGIS verification phase:** checks whether there exists a concrete counterexample for the current candidate solution by checking the satisfiability of the formula $\neg\sigma(P^*, \boldsymbol{x})$. If the result is UNSAT, then P^* is a final solution to the synthesis problem. If the result is SAT, a concrete counterexample $\boldsymbol{cex}$ can be extracted from the satisfying assignment.
- **Theory solver:** if P^* contains constants, then they are eliminated, resulting in the $P^*[?]$ skeleton, which is afterwards generalised to $P^*[\boldsymbol{v}]$. The goal of the theory solver is to find $\mathcal{T}$-implied literals and communicate them back to the CEGIS part in the form of a constraint, $C(P, P^*, \boldsymbol{v})$. In Algorithm 1, this is done by $Deduction(\sigma, P^*[\boldsymbol{v}])$. The result of $Deduction(\sigma, P^*[\boldsymbol{v}])$ is of the following form: whenever there exists a valuation of $\boldsymbol{v}$ for which the current skeleton $P^*[?]$ is a final solution, $res = true$ and $C(P, P^*, \boldsymbol{v}) = \bigwedge_{i=1 \cdot n} v_i = c_i$, where c_i are constants; otherwise, $res = false$ and $C(P, P^*, \boldsymbol{v})$ needs to block the current skeleton $P^*[?]$, i.e., $C(P, P^*, \boldsymbol{v}) = P[?] \neq P^*[?]$.
- **CEGIS learning phase:** adds new information to the problem specification. If we did not use the theory solver (i.e., the candidate P^* found by the synthesizer did not contain constants or the problem specification was out of the theory solver's scope), then the learning would be limited to adding the concrete counterexample $\boldsymbol{cex}$ obtained from the verification phase to the set $\boldsymbol{x}_{inputs}$. However, if the theory solver is used and returns $res = true$, then the second element in the tuple contains valuations for $\boldsymbol{v}$ such that $P^*[\boldsymbol{v}]$ is a final solution. If $res = false$, then the second element blocks the current skeleton and needs to be added to σ.

4.2 CEGIS($\mathcal{T}$) with a Theory Solver Based on FM Elimination

In this section we describe a theory solver based on FM variable elimination. Other techniques for eliminating existentially quantified variables can be used. For instance, one might use cylindrical algebraic decomposition [9] for specifications with non-linear arithmetic. In our case, whenever the specification σ does not belong to linear arithmetic, the FM theory solver is not called.

As mentioned above, we need to produce a constraint over variables $\boldsymbol{v}$ describing the situation when $P^*[\boldsymbol{v}]$ is a final solution. For this purpose, we consider the formula $\exists \boldsymbol{x}. \neg\sigma(P^*[\boldsymbol{v}], \boldsymbol{x})$, where $\boldsymbol{v}$ is a satisfiability witness if the specification σ admits a counterexample $\boldsymbol{x}$ for P^*. Let $E(\boldsymbol{v})$ be the formula obtained by eliminating $\boldsymbol{x}$ from $\exists \boldsymbol{x}. \neg\sigma(P^*[\boldsymbol{v}], \boldsymbol{x})$. If $\neg E(\boldsymbol{v})$ is satisfiable, any satisfiability witness gives us the necessary valuation for $\boldsymbol{v}$:

$$C(P, P^*, \boldsymbol{v}) = \bigwedge_{i=1 \cdot n} v_i = c_i.$$

Algorithm 1. CEGIS($\mathcal{T}$)

1: **function** $CEGIS(\mathcal{T})$(specification σ)
2:     **while** *true* **do**
3:         /* **CEGIS synthesis phase** */
4:         **if** $\forall \boldsymbol{x}_{inputs}.\sigma(P, \boldsymbol{x}_{inputs})$ is UNSAT **then return** Failure;
5:         **else**
6:             $P^* =$ satisfiability witness for $\forall \boldsymbol{x}_{inputs}.\sigma(P, \boldsymbol{x}_{inputs})$;
7:             /* **CEGIS verification phase** */
8:             **if** $\neg(\sigma(P^*, \boldsymbol{x}))$ is UNSAT **then return** Final solution P^*;
9:             **else**
10:                 $\boldsymbol{cex} =$ satisfiability witness for $\neg(\sigma(P^*, \boldsymbol{x}))$;
11:                 /* **Theory solver** */
12:                 **if** P^* contains constants **then**
13:                     Obtain $P^*[?]$ from P^*;
14:                     Generalise $P^*[?]$ to $P^*[\boldsymbol{v}]$;
15:                     $(res, C(P, P^*, \boldsymbol{v})) = Deduction(\sigma, P^*[\boldsymbol{v}])$;
16:                 **end if**
17:             **end if**
18:         **end if**
19:         /* **CEGIS learning phase** */
20:         **if** res **then**
21:             $C(P, P^*, \boldsymbol{v})$ is of the form $\bigwedge_{i=1 \cdot n} v_i = c_i$.
22:             **return** Final solution $P^*[\boldsymbol{c}]$;
23:         **else**
24:             $\sigma(P, \boldsymbol{x}) = \sigma(P, \boldsymbol{x}) \wedge C(P, P^*, \boldsymbol{v})$;
25:             $\boldsymbol{x}_{inputs} = \boldsymbol{x}_{inputs} \cup \{\boldsymbol{cex}\}$;
26:         **end if**
27:     **end while**
28: **end function**

If $\neg E(\boldsymbol{v})$ is UNSAT, then the current skeleton $P^*[?]$ needs to be blocked. This reasoning is supported by Lemma 1 and Corollary 1.

Lemma 1. *Let $E(\boldsymbol{v})$ be the formula that is obtained by eliminating $\boldsymbol{x}$ from $\exists \boldsymbol{x}. \neg\sigma(P^*[\boldsymbol{v}], \boldsymbol{x})$. Then, any witness $\boldsymbol{v}^{\#}$ to the satisfiability of $\neg E(\boldsymbol{v})$ gives us a final solution $P^*[\boldsymbol{v}^{\#}]$ to the synthesis problem.*

Proof. From the fact that $E(\boldsymbol{v})$ is obtained by eliminating $\boldsymbol{x}$ from $\exists \boldsymbol{x}. \neg\sigma(P^*[\boldsymbol{v}], \boldsymbol{x})$, we get that $E(\boldsymbol{v})$ is equivalent with $\exists \boldsymbol{x}. \neg\sigma(P^*[\boldsymbol{v}], \boldsymbol{x})$ (we use $\equiv$ to denote equivalence):

$$E(\boldsymbol{v}) \equiv \exists \boldsymbol{x}. \neg\sigma(P^*[\boldsymbol{v}], \boldsymbol{x}).$$

Then:

$$\neg E(\boldsymbol{v}) \equiv \forall \boldsymbol{x}. \sigma(P^*[\boldsymbol{v}], \boldsymbol{x}).$$

Consequently, any $\boldsymbol{v}^{\#}$ satisfying $\neg E(\boldsymbol{v})$ also satisfies $\forall \boldsymbol{x}. \sigma(P^*[\boldsymbol{v}], \boldsymbol{x})$. From $\forall \boldsymbol{x}. \sigma(P^*[\boldsymbol{v}^{\#}], \boldsymbol{x})$ and Definition 4 we get that $P^*[\boldsymbol{v}^{\#}]$ is a final solution.

Corollary 1. *Let* $E(v)$ *be the formula that is obtained by eliminating* x *from* $\exists x. \neg\sigma(P^*[v], x)$. *If* $\neg E(v)$ *is unsatisfiable, then the corresponding synthesis problem does not admit a solution for the skeleton* $P^*[?]$.

Proof. Given that $\neg E(v) \equiv \forall x. \sigma(P^*[v], x)$, if $\neg E(v)$ is unsatisfiable, so is $\forall x. \sigma(P^*[v], x)$, meaning that there is no valuation for v such that the specification σ is obeyed for all inputs x.

For the current skeleton $P^*[?]$, the constraint $E(v)$ generalises the concrete counterexample cex (found during the CEGIS verification phase) in the sense that the instantiation $v^\#$ of v for which cex failed the specification, i.e., $\neg\sigma(P^*[v^\#], cex)$, is a satisfiability witness for $E(v)$. This is true as $E(v) \equiv \exists x. \neg\sigma(P^*[v], x)$, which means that the satisfiability witness $(v^\#, cex)$ for $\neg\sigma(P^*[v], x)$ projected on v is a satisfiability witness for $E(v)$.

Disjunction. The specification σ and the candidate solution may contain disjunctions. However, most theory solvers (and in particular the FM variable elimination [7]) work on conjunctive fragments only. A naïve approach could use case-splitting, i.e., transforming the formula into Disjunctive Normal Form (DNF) and then solving each clause separately. This can result in a number of clauses exponential in the size of the original formula. Instead, we handle disjunction using the Boolean Fourier Motzkin procedure [20,32]. As a result, the constraints we generate may be non-clausal.

Applying CEGIS($\mathcal{T}$) with FM to the Motivational Example. We recall the example in Sect. 3 and apply CEGIS($\mathcal{T}$). The problem is

$$\exists f. \forall x. x < 334455 \rightarrow f(x) < 0 \wedge x \geq 334455 \rightarrow f(x) = 0$$

which gives us the following specification:

$$\sigma(f, x) = (x \geq 334455 \vee f(x) < 0) \wedge (x < 334455 \vee f(x) = 0).$$

The first synthesis phase generates the candidate $f^*(x) = 0$ for which the verification phase returns the concrete counterexample $x = 0$. As this candidate contains the constant 0, we generalise it to $f^*[v_1](x) = v_1$, for which we get

$$\sigma(f^*[v_1], x) = (x \geq 334455 \vee v_1 < 0) \wedge (x < 334455 \vee v_1 = 0).$$

Next, we use FM to eliminate x from

$$\exists x. \neg(\sigma(f^*[v_1], x)) = \exists x. (x < 334455 \wedge v_1 \geq 0) \vee (x \geq 334455 \wedge v_1 \neq 0).$$

Note that, given that formula $\neg\sigma(f^*[v_1], x)$ is in DNF, for convenience we directly apply FM to each disjunct and obtain $E(v_1) = v_1 \geq 0 \vee v_1 \neq 0$, which characterises all the values of v_1 for which there exists a counterexample. When negating $E(v_1)$ we get $v_1 < 0 \wedge v_1 = 0$, which is UNSAT. As there is no valuation of

v_1 for which the current f^* is a final solution, the result returned by the theory solver is $(false, f[?] \neq f^*[?])$, which is used to augment the specification. Subsequently, a new CEGIS($\mathcal{T}$) iteration starts. The learning phase has changed the specification σ to

$$\sigma(f, x) = (x \geq 334455 \vee f(x) < 0) \wedge (x < 334455 \vee f(x) = 0) \wedge f[?] \neq ?.$$

This forces the synthesis phase to pick a new candidate solution with a different skeleton. The new candidate solution we get is $f^*(x) = ite\ (x < 100)\ -3\ 1$, which works for the previous counterexample $x = 0$. However, the verification phase returns the counterexample $x = 100$. Again, this candidate contains constants which we replace by symbolic variables, obtaining

$$f^*[v_1, v_2, v_3](x) = ite\ (x < v_1)\ v_2\ v_3.$$

Next, we use FM to eliminate x from

$$
\begin{aligned}
&\exists x. \neg(\sigma(f^*[v_1, v_2, v_3], x)) = \\
&\exists x. \neg(x \geq 334455 \vee (x < v_1 \to v_2 < 0 \wedge x \geq v_1 \to v_3 < 0) \wedge \\
&\quad x < 334455 \vee (x < v_1 \to v_2 = 0 \wedge x \geq v_1 \to v_3 = 0)) = \\
&\exists x. \neg((x \geq 334455 \vee x \geq v_1 \vee v_2 < 0) \wedge (x \geq 334455 \vee x < v_1 \vee v_3 < 0) \wedge \\
&\quad (x < 334455 \vee x \geq v_1 \vee v_2 = 0) \wedge (x < 334455 \vee x < v_1 \vee v_3 = 0)) = \\
&\exists x. (x < 334455 \wedge x < v_1 \wedge v_2 \geq 0) \vee (x < 334455 \wedge x \geq v_1 \wedge v_3 \geq 0) \vee \\
&\quad (x \geq 334455 \wedge x < v_1 \wedge v_2 \neq 0) \vee (x \geq 334455 \wedge x \geq v_1 \wedge v_3 \neq 0).
\end{aligned}
$$

As we work with integers, we can rewrite $x < 334455$ to $x \leq 334454$ and $x < v_1$ to $x \leq v_1 - 1$. Then, we obtain the following constraint $E(v_1, v_2, v_3)$ (as aforementioned, we applied FM to each disjunct in $\neg\sigma(f^*[v_1, v_2, v_3], x)$)

$$E(v_1, v_2, v_3) = v_2{\geq}0 \vee (v_1 \leq 334454 \wedge v_3 \geq 0) \vee (v_1 \geq 334456 \wedge v_2 \neq 0) \vee v_3 \neq 0$$

whose negation is

$$\neg E(v_1, v_2, v_3) = v_2 < 0 \wedge (v_1 > 334454 \vee v_3 < 0) \wedge (v_1 < 334456 \vee v_2 = 0) \wedge v_3 = 0$$

A satisfiability witness is $v_1 = 334455$, $v_2 = -1$ and $v_3 = 0$. Thus, the result returned by the theory solver is $(true, v_1 = 334455 \wedge v_2 = -1 \wedge v_3 = 0)$, which is used by CEGIS to obtain the final solution

$$f^*(x) = ite\ (x < 334455)\ -1\ 0\ .$$

4.3 CEGIS($\mathcal{T}$) with an SMT-based Theory Solver

For our second variant of a theory solver, we make use of an off-the-shelf SMT solver that supports quantified first-order formulae. This approach is more generic than the one described in Sect. 4.2, as there are solvers for a broad range of theories.

Recall that our goal is to obtain a constraint $C(P, P^*, \boldsymbol{v})$ that either characterises the valuations of $\boldsymbol{v}$ for which $P^*[\boldsymbol{v}]$ is a final solution or blocks $P^*[?]$ whenever no such valuation exists. Consequently, we use the SMT solver to check the satisfiability of the formula

$$\Phi = \forall \boldsymbol{x}.\, \sigma(P^*[\boldsymbol{v}], \boldsymbol{x}).$$

If Φ is satisfiable, then any satisfiability witness $\boldsymbol{c}$ gives us a valuation for $\boldsymbol{v}$ such that P^* is a final solution: $C(P, P^*, \boldsymbol{v}) = \bigwedge_{i=1 \cdot n} v_i = c_i$. Conversely, if Φ is unsatisfiable then $C(P, P^*, \boldsymbol{v})$ must block the current skeleton $P^*[?]$: $C(P, P^*, \boldsymbol{v}) = P[?] \neq P^*[?]$.

Applying SMT-based CEGIS($\mathcal{T}$) to the Motivational Example. Again, we recall the example in Sect. 3. We will solve it by using SMT-based CEGIS($\mathcal{T}$) for the theory of linear arithmetic. For this purpose, we assume that the synthesis phase finds the same sequence of candidate solutions as in Sect. 3. Namely, the first candidate is $f^*(x) = 0$, which gets generalised to $f^*[v_1](x) = v_1$. Then, the first SMT call is for $\forall x.\, \sigma(v_1, x)$, where

$$\sigma(v_1, x) = (x \geq 334455 \vee v_1 < 0) \wedge (x < 334455 \vee v_1 = 0).$$

The SMT solver returns UNSAT, which means that $C(f, f^*, v_1) = f[?] \neq ?$. The second candidate is $f^*(x) = ite\ (x < 100)\ -3\ 1$, which generalises to $f^*[v_1, v_2, v_3](x) = ite\ (x < v_1)\ v_2\ v_3$. The corresponding call to the SMT solver is for $\forall x.\, \sigma((ite\ (x < v_1)\ v_2\ v_3), x)$, for which we obtain the satisfiability witness $v_1 = 334455$, $v_2 = -1$ and $v_3 = 0$. Then $C(f, f^*, v_1, v_2, v_3) = v_1 = 334455 \wedge v_2 = -1 \wedge v_3 = 0$, which gives us the same final solution we obtained when using FM in Sect. 3.

5   Experimental Evaluation

5.1   Implementation

Incremental Satisfiability Solving. Our implementation of CEGIS may sometimes perform hundreds of loop iterations before finding the correct solution. Recall that the synthesis block of CEGIS is based on Bounded Model Checking (BMC). Ultimately, this BMC module performs calls to a SAT solver. Consequently, we may have hundreds of calls to this SAT solver, which are all very similar (the same base specification with some extra constraints added in each iteration). This makes CEGIS a prime candidate for incremental SAT solving. We implemented incremental solving in the synthesis block of CEGIS.

5.2   Benchmarks

We have selected a set of bitvector benchmarks from the Syntax-Guided Synthesis (SyGuS) competition [4] and a set of benchmarks synthesizing safety invariants and danger invariants for C programs [10]. All benchmarks are written in SyGuS-IF [26], a variant of SMT-LIB2.

Given that the syntactic restrictions (called the *grammar* or the *template*) provided in the SyGuS benchmarks contain all the necessary non-trivial constants, we removed them completely from these benchmarks. Removing just the non-trivial constants and keeping the rest of the grammar (with the only constants being 0 and 1) would have made the problem much more difficult, as the constants would have had to be incrementally constructed by applying the operators available to 0 and 1.

We group the benchmarks into three categories: invariant generation, which covers danger invariants, safety invariants and the class of invariant generation benchmarks from the SyGuS competition; hackers/crypto, which includes benchmarks from hackers-delight and cryptographic circuits; and comparisons, composed of benchmarks that require synthesizing longer programs with comparisons, e.g., finding the maximum value of 10 variables.

5.3 Experimental Setup

We conduct the experimental evaluation on a 12-core 2.40 GHz Intel Xeon E5-2440 with 96 GB of RAM and Linux OS. We use the Linux *times* command to measure CPU time used for each benchmark. The runtime is limited to 600 s per benchmark. We use MiniSat [12] as the SAT solver, and Z3 v4.5.1 [22] as the SMT-solver in CEGIS(T) with SMT-based theory solver. The SAT solver could, in principle, be replaced with Z3 to solve benchmarks over a broader range of theories.

We present results for four different configurations of CEGIS:

- CEGIS(T)-FM: CEGIS(T) with Fourier Motzkin as the theory solver;
- CEGIS(T)-SMT: CEGIS(T) with Z3 as the theory solver;
- CEGIS: basic CEGIS as described in Sect. 2.2;
- CEGIS-Inc: basic CEGIS with incremental SAT solving.

We compare our results against the latest release of CVC4, version 1.5. As we are interested in running our benchmarks without any syntactic template, the first reason for choosing CVC4 [6] as our comparison point is the fact that it performs well when no such templates are provided. This is illustrated by the fact that it won the Conditional Linear Integer Arithmetic track of the SyGuS competition 2017 [4], one of two tracks where a syntactic template was not used. The other track without syntactic templates is the invariant generation track, in which CVC4 was close second to LoopInvGen [24]. A second reason for picking CVC4 is its overall good performance on all benchmarks, whereas LoopInvGen is a solver specialised to invariant generation.

We also give a row of results for a hypothetical 4-core implementation, as would be allowed in the SyGuS Competition, running 4 configurations in parallel: CEGIS(T)-FM, CEGIS(T)-SMT, CEGIS, and CEGIS-Inc. A link to the full experimental environment, including scripts to reproduce the results, all benchmarks and the tool, is provided in the footnote as an Open Virtual Appliance (OVA)[1].

---

[1] www.cprover.org/synthesis.

Table 1. Experimental results – for every set of benchmarks, we give the number of benchmarks solved by each configuration within the timeout and the average time taken per solved benchmark

Configuration	inv		hackers		comparisons		other		total	
	#	s	#	s	#	s	#	s	#	s
CEGIS($\mathcal{T}$)-SMT	33	33.1	4	2.5	3	195.5	16	14.0	56	34.1
CEGIS($\mathcal{T}$)-FM	16	93.1	4	52.8	1	0.06	12	0.7	33	51.8
CEGIS	16	31.3	4	52.0	1	0.03	14	5.3	35	22.4
CEGIS-Inc	16	39.4	5	167.4	1	0.03	14	4.2	36	42.4
Multi-core	33	32.5	5	92.2	3	194.7	16	3.8	57	38.3
CVC4	6	6.5	6	0.002	7	0.006	11	0.003	30	1.3
# benchmarks	48		6		7		19		80	
CVC4 with grammar	4	45.8	0		0		6	2.4	10	19.8
# benchmarks with grammar	8		3		7		16		34	

5.4 Results

The results are given in Table 1. In combination, our CEGIS combination (i.e., CEGIS multi-core) solves 27 more benchmarks than CVC4, but the average time per benchmark is significantly higher.

As expected, both CEGIS($\mathcal{T}$)-SMT and CEGIS($\mathcal{T}$)-FM solve more of the invariant generation benchmarks which require synthesizing arbitrary constants than CVC4. Conversely, CVC4 performs better on benchmarks that require synthesizing long programs with many comparison operations, e.g., finding the maximum value in a series of numbers. CVC4 solves more of the hackers-delight and cryptographic circuit benchmarks, none of which require constants.

Our implementation of basic CEGIS (and consequently of all configurations built on top of this) only increases the length of the synthesized program when no program of a shorter length exists. Thus, it is expensive to synthesize longer programs. However, a benefit of this architecture is that the programs we synthesize are the minimum possible length. Many of the expressions synthesized by CVC4 are very large. This has been noted previously in the Syntax-Guided Synthesis Competition [5], and synthesizing without the syntactic template causes the expressions synthesized to be even longer.

Although CEGIS-Inc is quicker per iteration of the CEGIS loop than basic CEGIS, the average time per benchmark is not significantly better because of the variation in times produced by CEGIS. We hypothesise that the use of incremental solving makes CEGIS-Inc more prone to getting stuck exploring "bad" areas of the solution space than basic CEGIS, and so it requires more iterations than basic CEGIS for some benchmarks. The incremental solving preserves clauses learnt from any conflicts in previous iterations, which means that each SAT solving iteration will begin from exactly the same state as the previous one. The basic implementation doesn't preserve these clauses and so is free to start exploring a new part of the search space each iteration. These effects could be mitigated by running multiple incremental solving instances in parallel.

In order to validate the assumption that CVC4 works better without a template than with one where the non-trivial constants were removed (see Sect. 5.2), we also ran CVC4 on a subset of the benchmarks with a syntactic template comprising the full instruction set we give to CEGIS, plus the constants 0 and 1. Note for some benchmarks it is not possible to add a grammar because the SYGUS-IF language does not allow syntactic templates for benchmarks that use the loop invariant syntax. With a grammar, CVC4 solves fewer of the benchmarks, and takes longer per benchmark. The syntactic template is helpful only in cases where non-trivial constants are needed and the non-trivial constants are contained within the template.

We ran EUSolver on the benchmarks with the syntactic templates, but the bitvector support is incomplete and missing some key operations. As a result EUSolver was unable to solve any benchmarks in the set, and so we have not included the results in the table.

Benefit of Literal Constants. We have investigated how useful the constants in the problem specification are, and have tried a configuration that seeds all constants in the problem specification as hints into the synthesis engine. This proved helpful for basic CEGIS only but not for the CEGIS(T) configurations. Our hypothesis is that the latter do not benefit from this because they already have good support for computing constants. We dropped this option in the results presented in this section.

5.5 Threats to Validity

Benchmark Selection: We report an assessment of our approach on a diverse selection of benchmarks. Nevertheless, the set of benchmarks is limited within the scope of this paper, and the performance may not generalise to other benchmarks.

Comparison with State of the Art: CVC4 has not, as far as we are aware, been used for synthesis of bitvector functions without syntactic templates, and so this unanticipated use case may not have been fully tested. We are unable to compare all results to other solvers from the SyGuS Competition because EUSolver and EUPhony do not support synthesizing bitvector programs without a syntactic template, EUSolver's support for bitvectors is incomplete even when used with a template, LoopInvGen and DryadSynth do not support bitvectors, and E3Solver tackles only Programming By Example benchmarks [5].

Choice of Theories: We evaluated the benefits of CEGIS(T) in the context of two specific theory instances. While the improvements in our experiments are significant, it is uncertain whether this will generalise to other theories.

6   Related Work

The traditional view of program synthesis is that of synthesis from complete specifications [21]. Such specifications are often unavailable, difficult to write, or expensive to check against using automated verification techniques. This has led to the proposal of inductive synthesis and, more recently, of oracle-based inductive synthesis, in which the complete specification is not available and oracles are queried to choose programs [19].

A well-known application of CEGIS is program sketching [29,31], where the programmer uses a partial program, called a *sketch*, to describe the desired implementation strategy, and leaves the low-level details of the implementation to an automated synthesis procedure. Inspired by sketching, Syntax-Guided Program Synthesis (SyGuS) [2] requires the user to supplement the logical specification provided to the program synthesizer with a syntactic template that constrains the space of solutions. In contrast to SyGuS, our aim is to improve the efficiency of the exploration to the point that user guidance is no longer required.

Another very active area of program synthesis is denoted by component-based approaches [1,13–15,17,18,25]. Such approaches are concerned with assembling programs from a database of existing components and make use of various techniques, from counterexample-guided synthesis [17] to type-directed search with lightweight SMT-based deduction and partial evaluation [14] and Petri-nets [15]. The techniques developed in the current paper are applicable to any component-based synthesis approach that relies on counterexample-guided inductive synthesis.

Heuristics for constant synthesis are presented in [11], where the solution language is parameterised, inducing a lattice of progressively more expressive languages. One of the parameters is word width, which allows synthesizing programs with constants that satisfy the specification for smaller word widths. Subsequently, heuristics extend the program (including the constants) to the required word width. As opposed to this work, CEGIS($\mathcal{T}$) denotes a systematic approach that does not rely on ad-hoc heuristics.

Regarding the use of SMT solvers in program synthesis, they are frequently employed as oracles. By contrast, Reynolds et al. [27] present an efficient encoding able to solve program synthesis constraints directly within an SMT solver. Their approach relies on rephrasing the synthesis constraint as the problem of refuting a universally quantified formula, which can be solved using first-order quantifier instantiation. Conversely, in our approach we maintain a clear separation between the synthesizer and the theory solver, which communicate in a well-defined manner. In Sect. 5, we provide a comprehensive experimental comparison with the synthesizer described in [27].

7   Conclusion

We proposed CEGIS($\mathcal{T}$), a new approach to program synthesis that combines the strengths of a counterexample-guided inductive synthesizer with those of a theory solver to provide a more efficient exploration of the solution space. We discussed two options for the theory solver, one based on FM variable elimination and one relying on an off-the-shelf SMT solver. Our experiments results showed that, although slower than CVC4, CEGIS($\mathcal{T}$) can solve more benchmarks within a reasonable time that require synthesizing arbitrary constants, where CVC4 fails.

References

1. Albarghouthi, A., Gulwani, S., Kincaid, Z.: Recursive program synthesis. In: Sharygina, N., Veith, H. (eds.) CAV 2013. LNCS, vol. 8044, pp. 934–950. Springer, Heidelberg (2013). https://doi.org/10.1007/978-3-642-39799-8_67
2. Alur, R., Bodík, R., Juniwal, G., Martin, M.M.K., Raghothaman, M., Seshia, S.A., Singh, R., Solar-Lezama, A., Torlak, E., Udupa, A.: Syntax-guided synthesis. In: FMCAD, pp. 1–8. IEEE (2013)
3. Alur, R., Černý, P., Radhakrishna, A.: Synthesis through unification. In: Kroening, D., Păsăreanu, C.S. (eds.) CAV 2015. LNCS, vol. 9207, pp. 163–179. Springer, Cham (2015). https://doi.org/10.1007/978-3-319-21668-3_10
4. Alur, R., Fisman, D., Singh, R., Solar-Lezama, A.: SyGuS-Comp 2017: results and analysis. CoRR abs/1711.11438 (2017)
5. Alur, R., Fisman, D., Singh, R., Udupa, A.: Syntax guided synthesis competition (2017). http://sygus.seas.upenn.edu/SyGuS-COMP2017.html
6. Barrett, C., Conway, C.L., Deters, M., Hadarean, L., Jovanović, D., King, T., Reynolds, A., Tinelli, C.: CVC4. In: Gopalakrishnan, G., Qadeer, S. (eds.) CAV 2011. LNCS, vol. 6806, pp. 171–177. Springer, Heidelberg (2011). https://doi.org/10.1007/978-3-642-22110-1_14
7. Bik, A.J.C., Wijshoff, H.A.G.: Implementation of Fourier-Motzkin elimination. Technical report, Rijksuniversiteit Leiden (1994)
8. Clarke, E., Kroening, D., Lerda, F.: A tool for checking ANSI-C programs. In: Jensen, K., Podelski, A. (eds.) TACAS 2004. LNCS, vol. 2988, pp. 168–176. Springer, Heidelberg (2004). https://doi.org/10.1007/978-3-540-24730-2_15
9. Collins, G.E.: Hauptvortrag: quantifier elimination for real closed fields by cylindrical algebraic decompostion. In: Brakhage, H. (ed.) GI-Fachtagung 1975. LNCS, vol. 33, pp. 134–183. Springer, Heidelberg (1975). https://doi.org/10.1007/3-540-07407-4_17
10. David, C., Kesseli, P., Kroening, D., Lewis, M.: Danger invariants. In: Fitzgerald, J., Heitmeyer, C., Gnesi, S., Philippou, A. (eds.) FM 2016. LNCS, vol. 9995, pp. 182–198. Springer, Cham (2016). https://doi.org/10.1007/978-3-319-48989-6_12
11. David, C., Kroening, D., Lewis, M.: Using program synthesis for program analysis. In: Davis, M., Fehnker, A., McIver, A., Voronkov, A. (eds.) LPAR 2015. LNCS, vol. 9450, pp. 483–498. Springer, Heidelberg (2015). https://doi.org/10.1007/978-3-662-48899-7_34
12. Eén, N., Sörensson, N.: An extensible SAT-solver. In: Giunchiglia, E., Tacchella, A. (eds.) SAT 2003. LNCS, vol. 2919, pp. 502–518. Springer, Heidelberg (2004). https://doi.org/10.1007/978-3-540-24605-3_37
13. Feng, Y., Bastani, O., Martins, R., Dillig, I., Anand, S.: Automated synthesis of semantic malware signatures using maximum satisfiability. In: NDSS. The Internet Society (2017)

14. Feng, Y., Martins, R., Geffen, J.V., Dillig, I., Chaudhuri, S.: Component-based synthesis of table consolidation and transformation tasks from examples. In: PLDI, pp. 422–436. ACM (2017)

15. Feng, Y., Martins, R., Wang, Y., Dillig, I., Reps, T.W.: Component-based synthesis for complex APIs. In: POPL, pp. 599–612. ACM (2017)

16. Ganzinger, H., Hagen, G., Nieuwenhuis, R., Oliveras, A., Tinelli, C.: DPLL(T): fast decision procedures. In: Alur, R., Peled, D.A. (eds.) CAV 2004. LNCS, vol. 3114, pp. 175–188. Springer, Heidelberg (2004). https://doi.org/10.1007/978-3-540-27813-9_14

17. Gulwani, S., Jha, S., Tiwari, A., Venkatesan, R.: Synthesis of loop-free programs. In: PLDI, pp. 62–73. ACM (2011)

18. Gulwani, S., Korthikanti, V.A., Tiwari, A.: Synthesizing geometry constructions. In: PLDI, pp. 50–61. ACM (2011)

19. Jha, S., Gulwani, S., Seshia, S.A., Tiwari, A.: Oracle-guided component-based program synthesis. In: ICSE, no. 1, pp. 215–224. ACM (2010)

20. Kroening, D., Strichman, O.: Decision Procedures: An Algorithmic Point of View, 1st edn. Springer, Heidelberg (2008). https://doi.org/10.1007/978-3-540-74105-3

21. Manna, Z., Waldinger, R.: A deductive approach to program synthesis. In: IJCAI. pp. 542–551. William Kaufmann (1979)

22. de Moura, L., Bjørner, N.: Z3: an efficient SMT solver. In: Ramakrishnan, C.R., Rehof, J. (eds.) TACAS 2008. LNCS, vol. 4963, pp. 337–340. Springer, Heidelberg (2008). https://doi.org/10.1007/978-3-540-78800-3_24

23. Nieuwenhuis, R., Oliveras, A., Tinelli, C.: Solving SAT and SAT modulo theories: From an abstract Davis-Putnam-Logemann-Loveland procedure to DPLL(T). J. ACM **53**(6), 937–977 (2006)

24. Padhi, S., Millstein, T.D.: Data-driven loop invariant inference with automatic feature synthesis. CoRR abs/1707.02029 (2017)

25. Perelman, D., Gulwani, S., Grossman, D., Provost, P.: Test-driven synthesis. In: PLDI, pp. 408–418. ACM (2014)

26. Raghothaman, M., Udupa, A.: Language to specify syntax-guided synthesis problems. CoRR abs/1405.5590 (2014)

27. Reynolds, A., Deters, M., Kuncak, V., Tinelli, C., Barrett, C.: Counterexample-guided quantifier instantiation for synthesis in SMT. In: Kroening, D., Păsăreanu, C.S. (eds.) CAV 2015. LNCS, vol. 9207, pp. 198–216. Springer, Cham (2015). https://doi.org/10.1007/978-3-319-21668-3_12

28. Rosen, E.: An existential fragment of second order logic. Arch. Math. Log. **38**(4–5), 217–234 (1999)

29. Solar-Lezama, A.: Program sketching. STTT **15**(5–6), 475–495 (2013)

30. Solar-Lezama, A., Rabbah, R.M., Bodík, R., Ebcioglu, K.: Programming by sketching for bit-streaming programs. In: PLDI, pp. 281–294. ACM (2005)

31. Solar-Lezama, A., Tancau, L., Bodík, R., Seshia, S.A., Saraswat, V.A.: Combinatorial sketching for finite programs. In: ASPLOS, pp. 404–415. ACM (2006)

32. Strichman, O.: On solving Presburger and linear arithmetic with SAT. In: Aagaard, M.D., O'Leary, J.W. (eds.) FMCAD 2002. LNCS, vol. 2517, pp. 160–170. Springer, Heidelberg (2002). https://doi.org/10.1007/3-540-36126-X_10

6

Constraint-Based Synthesis of Coupling Proofs

Aws Albarghouthi[1] and Justin Hsu[2,3]([envelope])

[1] University of Wisconsin–Madison, Madison, WI, USA
[2] University College London, London, UK
[3] Cornell University, Ithaca, NY, USA
email@justinh.su

Abstract. *Proof by coupling* is a classical technique for proving properties about pairs of randomized algorithms by carefully *relating* (or *coupling*) two probabilistic executions. In this paper, we show how to automatically construct such proofs for probabilistic programs. First, we present *f-coupled postconditions*, an abstraction describing two correlated program executions. Second, we show how properties of *f*-coupled postconditions can imply various probabilistic properties of the original programs. Third, we demonstrate how to reduce the proof-search problem to a purely logical *synthesis problem* of the form $\exists f. \forall X. \varphi$, making probabilistic reasoning unnecessary. We develop a prototype implementation to automatically build coupling proofs for probabilistic properties, including uniformity and independence of program expressions.

1 Introduction

In this paper, we aim to automatically synthesize *coupling proofs* for probabilistic programs and properties. Originally designed for proving properties comparing two probabilistic programs—so-called *relational properties*—a coupling proof describes how to correlate two executions of the given programs, simulating both programs with a single probabilistic program. By reasoning about this combined, *coupled* process, we can often give simpler proofs of probabilistic properties for the original pair of programs.

A number of recent works have leveraged this idea to verify relational properties of randomized algorithms, including differential privacy [8,10,12], security of cryptographic protocols [9], convergence of Markov chains [11], robustness of machine learning algorithms [7], and more. Recently, Barthe et al. [6] showed how to reduce certain *non-relational* properties—which describe a single probabilistic program—to relational properties of two programs, by duplicating the original program or by sequentially composing it with itself.

While coupling proofs can simplify reasoning about probabilistic properties, they are not so easy to use; most existing proofs are carried out manually in relational program logics using interactive theorem provers. In a nutshell, the main challenge in a coupling proof is to select a correlation for each pair of corresponding sampling instructions, aiming to induce a particular relation between the outputs of the coupled process; this relation then implies the desired relational property. Just like finding inductive invariants in proofs for deterministic programs, picking suitable couplings in proofs can require substantial ingenuity.

To ease this task, we recently showed how to cast the search for coupling proofs as a program synthesis problem [1], giving a way to automatically find sophisticated proofs of differential privacy previously beyond the reach of automated verification. In the present paper, we build on this idea and present a general technique for constructing coupling proofs, targeting *uniformity* and *probabilistic independence* properties. Both are fundamental properties in the analysis of randomized algorithms, either in their own right or as prerequisites to proving more sophisticated guarantees; uniformity states that a randomized expression takes on all values in a finite range with equal probability, while probabilistic independence states that two probabilistic expressions are somehow uncorrelated—learning the value of one reveals no additional information about the value of the other.

Our techniques are inspired by the automated proofs of differential privacy we considered previously [1], but the present setting raises new technical challenges.

Non-lockstep execution. To prove differential privacy, the behavior of a single program is compared on two related inputs. To take advantage of the identical program structure, previous work restricted attention to *synchronizing* proofs, where the two executions can be analyzed assuming they follow the same control flow path. In contrast, coupling proofs for uniformity and independence often require relating two programs with different shapes, possibly following completely different control flows [6].

To overcome this challenge, we take a different approach. Instead of incrementally finding couplings for corresponding pairs of sampling instructions—requiring the executions to be tightly synchronized—we first lift all sampling instructions to the front of the program and pick a coupling once and for all. The remaining execution of both programs can then be encoded separately, with no need for lockstep synchronization (at least for loop-free programs—looping programs require a more careful treatment).

Richer space of couplings. The heart of a coupling proof is selecting—among multiple possible options—a particular correlation for each pair of random sampling instructions. Random sampling in differentially private programs typically use highly domain-specific distributions, like the Laplace distribution, which support a small number of useful couplings. Our prior work leveraged this feature to encode a collection of primitive couplings into the synthesis system. However, this is no longer possible when programs sample from distributions supporting richer couplings, like the uniform distribution. Since our approach coalesces all sampling instructions at the beginning of the program (more generally, at the head of the loop), we also need to find couplings for products of distributions.

We address this problem in two ways. First, we allow couplings of two sampling instructions to be specified by an injective function f from one range to another. Then, we impose requirements—encoded as standard logical constraints—to ensure that f indeed represents a coupling; we call such couplings f-*couplings*.

More general class of properties. Finally, we consider a broad class of properties rather than just differential privacy. While we focus on uniformity and independence for concreteness, our approach can establish general equalities between products of probabilities, i.e., probabilistic properties of the form

$$\prod_{i=1}^{m} \Pr[e_i \in E_i] = \prod_{j=1}^{n} \Pr[e'_j \in E'_j],$$

where e_i and e'_j are program expressions in the first and second programs respectively, and E_i and E'_j are predicates. As an example, we automatically establish a key step in the proof of Bertrand's Ballot theorem [20].

Paper Outline. After overviewing our technique on a motivating example (Sect. 2), we detail our main contributions.

- **Proof technique:** We introduce f-*coupled postconditions*, a form of postcondition for two probabilistic programs where random sampling instructions in the two programs are correlated by a function f. Using f-coupled postconditions, we present proof rules for establishing uniformity and independence of program variables, fundamental properties in the analysis of randomized algorithms (Sect. 3).
- **Reduction to constraint-based synthesis:** We demonstrate how to automatically find coupling proofs by transforming our proof rules into logical constraints of the form $\exists f. \forall X. \varphi$—a synthesis problem. A satisfiable constraint shows the existence of a function f—essentially, a compact encoding of a coupling proof—implying the target property (Sect. 4).
- **Extension to looping programs:** We extend our technique to reason about loops, by requiring synchronization at the loop head and finding a coupled invariant (Sect. 5).
- **Implementation and evaluation:** We implement our technique and evaluate it on several case studies, automatically constructing coupling proofs for interesting properties of a variety of algorithms (Sect. 6).

We conclude by comparing our technique with related approaches (Sect. 7).

2 Overview and Illustration

2.1 Introducing f-Couplings

A Simple Example. We begin by illustrating f-couplings over two identical Bernoulli distributions, denoted by the following *probability mass functions*:

$\mu_1(x) = \mu_2(x) = 0.5$ for all $x \in \mathbb{B}$ (where $\mathbb{B} = \{true, false\}$). In other words, the distribution μ_i returns $true$ with probability 0.5, and $false$ with probability 0.5.

An f-*coupling* for μ_1, μ_2 is a function $f : \mathbb{B} \to \mathbb{B}$ from the domain of the first distribution ($\mathbb{B}$) to the domain of the second (also $\mathbb{B}$); f should be injective and satisfy the *monotonicity property*: $\mu_1(x) \le \mu_2(f(x))$ for all $x \in \mathbb{B}$. In other words, f relates each element $x \in \mathbb{B}$ with an element $f(x)$ that has an equal or larger probability in μ_2. For example, consider the function $f_\neg$ defined as

$$f_\neg(x) = \neg x.$$

This function relates $true$ in μ_1 with $false$ in μ_2, and vice versa. Observe that $\mu_1(x) \le \mu_2(f_\neg(x))$ for all $x \in \mathbb{B}$, satisfying the definition of an $f_\neg$-coupling. We write $\mu_1 \leftrightsquigarrow^{f_\neg} \mu_2$ when there is an $f_\neg$-coupling for μ_1 and μ_2.

Using f-Couplings. An f-coupling can imply useful properties about the distributions μ_1 and μ_2. For example, suppose we want to prove that $\mu_1(true) = \mu_2(false)$. The fact that there is an $f_\neg$-coupling of μ_1 and μ_2 immediately implies the equality: by the monotonicity property,

$$\mu_1(true) \le \mu_2(f_\neg(true)) = \mu_2(false)$$
$$\mu_1(false) \le \mu_2(f_\neg(false)) = \mu_2(true)$$

and therefore $\mu_1(true) = \mu_2(false)$. More generally, it suffices to find an f-coupling of μ_1 and μ_2 such that

$$\underbrace{\{(x, f(x)) \mid x \in \mathbb{B}\}}_{\Psi_f} \subseteq \{(z_1, z_2) \mid z_1 = true \iff z_2 = false\},$$

where Ψ_f is induced by f; in particular, the $f_\neg$-coupling satisfies this property.

2.2 Simulating a Fair Coin

Now, let's use f-couplings to prove more interesting properties. Consider the program fairCoin in Fig. 1; the program simulates a fair coin by flipping a possibly biased coin that returns $true$ with probability $p \in (0, 1)$, where p is a program parameter. Our goal is to prove that for any p, the output of the program is a uniform distribution—it simulates a fair coin. We consider two separate copies of fairCoin generating distributions μ_1 and μ_2 over the returned value x for the same bias p, and we construct a coupling showing $\mu_1(true) = \mu_2(false)$, that is, heads and tails have equal probability.

```
fun fairCoin(p ∈ (0, 1))
    x ← false
    y ← false
    while x = y do
        x ~ bern(p)
        y ~ bern(p)
    return x
```

Fig. 1. Simulating a fair coin using an unfair one

Constructing f-Couplings. At first glance, it is unclear how to construct an f-coupling; unlike the distributions in our simple example, we do not have a concrete description of μ_1 and μ_2 as uniform distributions (indeed, this is what we are trying to establish). The key insight is that we do not need to construct our coupling in one shot. Instead, we can specify a coupling for the concrete, primitive sampling instructions in the body of the loop—which we know sample from $\mathsf{bern}(p)$—and then extend to a f-coupling for the whole loop and μ_1, μ_2.

For each copy of $\mathsf{fairCoin}$, we coalesce the two sampling statements inside the loop into a single sampling statement from the product distribution:

$$x, y \sim \mathsf{bern}(p) \times \mathsf{bern}(p)$$

We have two such joint distributions $\mathsf{bern}(p) \times \mathsf{bern}(p)$ to couple, one from each copy of $\mathsf{fairCoin}$. We use the following function $f_{swap} : \mathbb{B}^2 \to \mathbb{B}^2$:

$$f_{swap}(x, y) = (y, x)$$

which exchanges the values of x and y. Since this is an injective function satisfying the monotonicity property

$$(\mathsf{bern}(p) \times \mathsf{bern}(p))(x, y) \leqslant (\mathsf{bern}(p) \times \mathsf{bern}(p))(f_{swap}(x, y))$$

for all $(x, y) \in \mathbb{B} \times \mathbb{B}$ and $p \in (0, 1)$, we have an f_{swap}-coupling for the two copies of $\mathsf{bern}(p) \times \mathsf{bern}(p)$.

Analyzing the Loop. To extend a f_{body}-coupling on loop bodies to the entire loop, it suffices to check a synchronization condition: the coupling from f_{body} must ensure that the loop guards are equal so the two executions synchronize at the loop head. This holds in our case: every time the first program executes the statement $x, y \sim \mathsf{bern}(p) \times \mathsf{bern}(p)$, we can think of x, y as non-deterministically set to some values (a, b), and the corresponding variables in the second program as set to $f_{swap}(a, b) = (b, a)$. The loop guards in the two programs are equivalent under this choice, since $a = b$ is equivalent to $b = a$, hence we can analyze the loops in lockstep. In general, couplings enable us to relate samples from a pair of probabilistic assignments as if they were selected non-deterministically, often avoiding quantitative reasoning about probabilities.

Our constructed coupling for the loop guarantees that (i) both programs exit the loop at the same time, and (ii) when the two programs exit the loop, x takes opposite values in the two programs. In other words, there is an f_{loop}-coupling of μ_1 and μ_2 for some function f_{loop} such that

$$\Psi_{f_{loop}} \subseteq \{(z_1, z_2) \mid z_1 = true \iff z_2 = false\}, \tag{1}$$

implying $\mu_1(true) = \mu_2(false)$. Since both distributions are output distributions of $\mathsf{fairCoin}$—hence $\mu_1 = \mu_2$—we conclude that $\mathsf{fairCoin}$ simulates a fair coin.

Note that our approach does not need to construct f_{loop} concretely—this function may be highly complex. Instead, we only need to show that $\Psi_{f_{loop}}$ (or some over-approximation) lies inside the target relation in Formula 1.

Achieving Automation. Observe that once we have fixed an f_{body}-coupling for the sampling instructions inside the loop body, checking that the f_{loop}-coupling

satisfies the conditions for uniformity (Formula 1) is essentially a program verification problem. Therefore, we can cast the problem of constructing a coupling
proof as a logical problem of the form $\exists f. \forall X. \varphi$, where f is the f-coupling we
need to discover and $\forall X. \varphi$ is a constraint ensuring that (i) f indeed represents an f-coupling, and (ii) the f-coupling implies uniformity. Thus, we can
use established synthesis-verification techniques to solve the resulting constraints
(see, e.g., [2,13,27]).

3   A Proof Rule for Coupling Proofs

In this section, we develop a technique for constructing couplings and formalize
proof rules for establishing uniformity and independence properties over program
variables. We begin with background on probability distributions and couplings.

3.1   Distributions and Couplings

Distributions. A function $\mu : B \to [0,1]$ defines a *distribution* over a countable
set B if $\sum_{b \in B} \mu(b) = 1$. We will often write $\mu(A)$ for a subset $A \subseteq B$ to mean
$\sum_{x \in A} \mu(x)$. We write $dist(B)$ for the set of all distributions over B.

We will need a few standard constructions on distributions. First, the *support*
of a distribution μ is defined as $supp(\mu) = \{b \in B \mid \mu(b) > 0\}$. Second, for a
distribution on pairs $\mu \in dist(B_1 \times B_2)$, the first and second *marginals* of μ,
denoted $\pi_1(\mu)$ and $\pi_2(\mu)$ respectively, are distributions over B_1 and B_2:

$$\pi_1(\mu)(b_1) \triangleq \sum_{b_2 \in B_2} \mu(b_1, b_2) \qquad \pi_2(\mu)(b_2) \triangleq \sum_{b_1 \in B_1} \mu(b_1, b_2).$$

Couplings. Let $\Psi \subseteq B_1 \times B_2$ be a binary relation. A Ψ-*coupling* for distributions
μ_1 and μ_2 over B_1 and B_2 is a distribution $\mu \in dist(B_1 \times B_2)$ with (i) $\pi_1(\mu) = \mu_1$
and $\pi_2(\mu) = \mu_2$; and (ii) $supp(\mu) \subseteq \Psi$. We write $\mu_1 \leftrightsquigarrow^{\Psi} \mu_2$ when there exists a
Ψ-coupling between μ_1 and μ_2.

An important fact is that an injective function $f : B_1 \to B_2$ where $\mu_1(b) \leqslant$
$\mu_2(f(b))$ for all $b \in B_1$ induces a coupling between μ_1 and μ_2; this follows
from a general theorem by Strassen [28], see also [23]. We write $\mu_1 \leftrightsquigarrow^{f} \mu_2$ for
$\mu_1 \leftrightsquigarrow^{\Psi_f} \mu_2$, where $\Psi_f = \{(b_1, f(b_1)) \mid b_1 \in B_1\}$. The existence of a coupling
can imply various useful properties about the two distributions. The following
general fact will be the most important for our purposes—couplings can prove
equalities between probabilities.

Proposition 1. *Let $E_1 \subseteq B_1$ and $E_2 \subseteq B_2$ be two events, and let $\Psi_= \triangleq$
$\{(b_1, b_2) \mid b_1 \in E_1 \iff b_2 \in E_2\}$. If $\mu_1 \leftrightsquigarrow^{\Psi_=} \mu_2$, then $\mu_1(E_1) = \mu_2(E_2)$.*

3.2 Program Model

Our program model uses an imperative language with probabilistic assignments, where we can draw a random value from primitive distributions. We consider the easier case of loop-free programs first; we consider looping programs in Sect. 5.

Syntax. A (loop-free) program P is defined using the following grammar:

$$
\begin{aligned}
P := \ & V \leftarrow exp & \text{(assignment)} \\
& |\ V \sim dexp & \text{(probabilistic assignment)} \\
& |\ \texttt{if } bexp \texttt{ then } P \texttt{ else } P & \text{(conditional)} \\
& |\ P; P & \text{(sequential composition)}
\end{aligned}
$$

where V is the set of variables that can appear in P, exp is an expression over V, and $bexp$ is a Boolean expression over V. A probabilistic assignment samples from a probability distribution defined by expression $dexp$; for instance, $dexp$ might be $\mathsf{bern}(p)$, the Bernoulli distribution with probability p of returning $true$. We use $V^I \subseteq V$ to denote the set of input program variables, which are never assigned to. All other variables are assumed to be defined before use.

We make a few simplifying assumptions. First, distribution expressions only mention input variables V^I, e.g., in the example above, $\mathsf{bern}(p)$, we have $p \in V^I$. Also, all programs are in *static single assignment* (SSA) form, where each variable is assigned to only once and are well-typed. These assumptions are relatively minor; they can can be verified using existing tools, or lifted entirely at the cost of slightly more complexity in our encoding.

Semantics. A state s of a program P is a valuation of all of its variables, represented as a map from variables to values, e.g., $s(x)$ is the value of $x \in V$ in s. We extend this mapping to expressions: $s(exp)$ is the valuation of exp in s, and $s(dexp)$ is the probability distribution defined by $dexp$ in s.

We use S to denote the set of all possible program states. As is standard [24], we can give a semantics of P as a function $[\![P]\!] : S \to dist(S)$ from states to distributions over states. For an output distribution $\mu = [\![P]\!](s)$, we will abuse notation and write, e.g., $\mu(x = y)$ to denote the probability of the event that the program returns a state s where $s(x = y) = true$.

Self-Composition. We will sometimes need to simulate two separate executions of a program with a single probabilistic program. Given a program P, we use P_i to denote a program identical to P but with all variables *tagged* with the subscript i. We can then define the *self-composition*: given a program P, the program $P_1; P_2$ first executes P_1, and then executes the (separate) copy P_2.

3.3 Coupled Postconditions

We are now ready to present the *f-coupled postcondition*, an operator for approximating the outputs of two coupled programs.

Strongest Postcondition. We begin by defining a standard strongest post-condition operator over single programs, treating probabilistic assignments as no-ops. Given a set of states $Q \subseteq S$, we define post as follows:

$$\mathsf{post}(v \leftarrow exp, Q) = \{s[v \mapsto s(exp)] \mid s \in Q\}$$
$$\mathsf{post}(v \sim dexp, Q) = Q$$
$$\mathsf{post}(\mathtt{if}\ \ bexp\ \ \mathtt{then}\ \ P\ \ \mathtt{else}\ \ P',\ Q) = \{s' \mid s \in Q, s' \in \mathsf{post}(P, s), s(bexp) = true\}$$
$$\cup\ \{s' \mid s \in Q, s' \in \mathsf{post}(P', s), s(bexp) = false\}$$
$$\mathsf{post}(P; P', Q) = \mathsf{post}(P', \mathsf{post}(P, Q))$$

where $s[v \mapsto c]$ is state s with variable v mapped to the value c.

f-Coupled Postcondition. We rewrite programs so that all probabilistic assignments are combined into a single probabilistic assignment to a vector of variables appearing at the beginning of the program, i.e., an assignment of the form $\boldsymbol{v} \sim dexp$ in P and $\boldsymbol{v}' \sim dexp'$ in P', where $\boldsymbol{v}, \boldsymbol{v}'$ are vectors of variables. For instance, we can combine $x \sim \mathsf{bern}(0.5); y \sim \mathsf{bern}(0.5)$ into the single statement $x, y \sim \mathsf{bern}(0.5) \times \mathsf{bern}(0.5)$.

Let B, B' be the domains of $\boldsymbol{v}$ and $\boldsymbol{v}'$, $f : B \to B'$ be a function, and $Q \subseteq S \times S'$ be a set of pairs of input states, where S and S' are the states of P and P', respectively. We define the f-coupled postcondition operator cpost as

$$\mathsf{cpost}(P, P', Q, f) = \{(\mathsf{post}(P, s), \mathsf{post}(P', s')) \mid (s, s') \in Q'\}$$
$$\text{where } Q' = \{(s[\boldsymbol{v} \mapsto \boldsymbol{b}], s'[\boldsymbol{v}' \mapsto f(\boldsymbol{b})]) \mid (s, s') \in Q, \boldsymbol{b} \in B\},$$
$$\text{assuming that} \quad \forall (s, s') \in Q.\, s(dexp) \leftrightsquigarrow^f s'(dexp'). \tag{2}$$

The intuition is that the values drawn from sampling assignments in both programs are coupled using the function f. Note that this operation non-deterministically assigns $\boldsymbol{v}$ from P with some values $\boldsymbol{b}$, and $\boldsymbol{v}'$ with $f(\boldsymbol{b})$. Then, the operation simulates the executions of the two programs. Formula 2 states that there is an f-coupling for every instantiation of the two distributions used in probabilistic assignments in both programs.

Example 1. Consider the simple program P defined as $x \sim \mathsf{bern}(0.5); x = \neg x$ and let $f_\neg(x) = \neg x$. Then, $\mathsf{cpost}(P, P, Q, f_\neg)$ is $\{(s, s') \mid s(x) = \neg s'(x)\}$.

The main soundness theorem shows there is a probabilistic coupling of the output distributions with support contained in the coupled postcondition (we defer all proofs to the full version of this paper).

Theorem 1. *Let programs P and P' be of the form $\boldsymbol{v} \sim dexp; P_D$ and $\boldsymbol{v}' \sim dexp'; P'_D$, for deterministic programs P_D, P'_D. Given a function $f : B \to B'$ satisfying Formula 2, for every $(s, s') \in S \times S'$ we have $[\![P]\!](s) \leftrightsquigarrow^\Psi [\![P']\!](s')$, where $\Psi = \mathsf{cpost}(P, P', (s, s'), f)$.*

3.4   Proof Rules for Uniformity and Independence

We are now ready to demonstrate how to establish uniformity and independence of program variables using f-coupled postconditions. We will continue to assume that random sampling commands have been lifted to the front of each program, and that f satisfies Formula 2.

Uniformity. Consider a program P and a variable $v^* \in V$ of finite, non-empty domain B. Let $\mu = [\![P]\!](s)$ for some state $s \in S$. We say that variable v^* is *uniformly distributed* in μ if $\mu(v^* = b) = \frac{1}{|B|}$ for every $b \in B$.

The following theorem connects uniformity with f-coupled postconditions.

Theorem 2 (Uniformity). *Consider a program P with $v \sim dexp$ as its first statement and a designated return variable $v^* \in V$ with domain B. Let $Q = \{(s, s) \mid s \in S\}$ be the input relation. If we have*

$$\exists f.\, \mathsf{cpost}(P, P, Q, f) \subseteq \{(s, s') \in S \times S \mid s(v^*) = b \iff s'(v^*) = b'\}$$

for all $b, b' \in B$, then for any input $s \in S$ the final value of v^* is uniformly distributed over B in $[\![P]\!](s)$.

The intuition is that in the two f-coupled copies of P, the first v^* is equal to b exactly when the second v^* is equal to b'. Hence, the probability of returning b in the first copy and b' in the second copy are the same. Repeating for every pair of values b, b', we conclude that v^* is uniformly distributed.

Example 2. Recall Example 1 and let $b = true$ and $b' = false$. We have

$$\mathsf{cpost}(P, P, Q, f_\neg) \subseteq \{(s, s') \in S \times S \mid s(x) = b \iff s'(x) = b'\}.$$

This is sufficient to prove uniformity (the case with $b = b'$ is trivial).

Independence. We now present a proof rule for independence. Consider a program P and two variables $v^*, w^* \in V$ with domains B and B', respectively. Let $\mu = [\![P]\!](s)$ for some state $s \in S$. We say that v^*, w^* are *probabilistically independent* in μ if $\mu(v^* = b \wedge w^* = b') = \mu(v^* = b) \cdot \mu(w^* = b')$ for every $b \in B$ and $b' \in B'$.

The following theorem connects independence with f-coupled postconditions. We will self-compose two tagged copies of P, called P_1 and P_2.

Theorem 3 (Independence). *Assume a program P and define the relation*

$$Q = \{(s, s_1 \oplus s_2) \mid s \in S, s_i \in S_i, s(v) = s_i(v_i), \;\; for \;\, all \;\; v \in V^I\},$$

where $\oplus$ takes the union of two maps with disjoint domains. Fix some $w^*, v^* \in V$ with domains B, B', and assume that for all $b \in B$, $b' \in B'$, there exists a function f such that $\mathsf{cpost}(P, (P_1; P_2), Q, f)$ is contained in

$$\{(s', s_1' \oplus s_2') \mid s'(v^*) = b \wedge s'(w^*) = b' \iff s_1'(v_1^*) = b \wedge s_2'(w_2^*) = b'\}.$$

Then, w^*, v^* are independently distributed in $[\![P]\!](s)$ for all inputs $s \in S$.

The idea is that under the coupling, the probability of P returning $v^* = b \wedge w^* = b'$ is the same as the probability of P_1 returning $v^* = b$ and P_2 returning $w^* = b'$, for all values b, b'. Since P_1 and P_2 are two independent executions of P by construction, this establishes independence of v^* and w^*.

4 Constraint-Based Formulation of Proof Rules

In Sect. 3, we formalized the problem of constructing a coupling proof using f-coupled postconditions. We now automatically find such proofs by posing the problem as a constraint, where a solution gives a function f establishing our desired property.

4.1 Generating Logical and Probabilistic Constraints

Logical Encoding. We first encode program executions as formulas in first-order logic, using the following encoding function:

$$\mathsf{enc}(v \leftarrow exp) \triangleq v = exp$$

$$\mathsf{enc}(v \sim dexp) \triangleq true$$

$$\mathsf{enc}(\text{if} \quad bexp \quad \text{then} \quad P \quad \text{else} \quad P') \triangleq (bexp \Rightarrow \mathsf{enc}(P)) \wedge (\neg bexp \Rightarrow \mathsf{enc}(P'))$$

$$\mathsf{enc}(P; P') \triangleq \mathsf{enc}(P) \wedge \mathsf{enc}(P')$$

We assume a direct correspondence between expressions in our language and the first-order theory used for our encoding, e.g., linear arithmetic. Note that the encoding disregards probabilistic assignments, encoding them as $true$; this mimics the semantics of our strongest postcondition operator post. Probabilistic assignments will be handled via a separate encoding of f-couplings.

As expected, enc reflects the strongest postcondition post.

Lemma 1. *Let P be a program and let ρ be any assignment of the variables. An assignment ρ' agreeing with ρ on all input variables V^I satisfies the constraint $\mathsf{enc}(P)[\rho'/V]$ precisely when $\mathsf{post}(P, \{\rho\}) = \{\rho'\}$, treating ρ, ρ' as program states.*

Uniformity Constraints. We can encode the conditions in Theorem 2 for showing uniformity as a logical constraint. For a program P and a copy P_1, with first statements $\boldsymbol{v} \sim dexp$ and $\boldsymbol{v}_1 \sim dexp_1$, we define the constraints:

$$\forall a, a'. \exists f. \forall V, V_1.$$
$$(V^I = V_1^I \wedge \boldsymbol{v}_1 = f(\boldsymbol{v}) \wedge \mathsf{enc}(P) \wedge \mathsf{enc}(P_1)) \tag{3}$$
$$\implies (v^* = a \iff v_1^* = a')$$
$$V^I = V_1^I \implies dexp \leadsto^f dexp_1 \tag{4}$$

Note that this is a second-order formula, as it quantifies over the *uninterpreted function* f. The left side of the implication in Formula 3 encodes an f-coupled execution of P and P_1, starting from equal initial states. The right side of this implication encodes the conditions for uniformity, as in Theorem 2.

Formula 4 ensures that there is an f-coupling between $dexp$ and $dexp_1$ for any initial state; recall that $dexp$ may mention input variables V^I. The constraint $dexp \leadsto^f dexp_1$ is not a standard logical constraint—intuitively, it is satisfied if $dexp \leadsto^f dexp_1$ holds for some interpretation of f, $dexp$, and $dexp_1$.

Example 3. The constraint

$$\exists f. \forall p, p'. p = p' \Rightarrow \mathsf{bern}(p) \leadsto^f \mathsf{bern}(p')$$

holds by setting f to the identity function id, since for any $p = p'$ we have an f-coupling $\mathsf{bern}(p) \leadsto^{\mathrm{id}} \mathsf{bern}(p')$.

Example 4. Consider the program $x \sim \mathsf{bern}(0.5); y = \neg x$. The constraints for uniformity of y are

$$\forall a, a'. \exists f. \forall V, V_1. (x_1 = f(x) \wedge y = \neg x \wedge y_1 = \neg x_1) \Longrightarrow (y = a \iff y_1 = a')$$
$$\mathsf{bern}(0.5) \leadsto^f \mathsf{bern}(0.5).$$

Since there are no input variables, $V^I = V_1^I$ is equivalent to *true*.

Theorem 4 (Uniformity constraints). *Fix a program P and variable $v^* \in V$. Let φ be the uniformity constraints in Formulas 3 and 4. If φ is valid, then v^* is uniformly distributed in $[\![P]\!](s)$ for all $s \in S$.*

Independence Constraints. Similarly, we can characterize independence constraints using the conditions in Theorem 3. After transforming the program $P_1; P_2$ to start with the single probabilistic assignment statement $\boldsymbol{v}_{1,2} \sim dexp_{1,2}$, combining probabilistic assignments in P_1 and P_2, we define the constraints:

$$\forall a, a'. \exists f. \forall V, V_1, V_2.$$
$$(V^I = V_1^I = V_2^I \wedge \boldsymbol{v}_{1,2} = f(\boldsymbol{v}) \wedge \mathsf{enc}(P) \wedge \mathsf{enc}(P_1; P_2)) \tag{5}$$
$$\Longrightarrow (v^* = a \wedge w^* = a' \iff v_1^* = a \wedge w_2^* = a')$$
$$V^I = V_1^I = V_2^I \Longrightarrow dexp \leadsto^f dexp_{1,2} \tag{6}$$

Theorem 5 (Independence constraints). *Fix a program P and two variables $v^*, w^* \in V$. Let φ be the independence constraints from Formulas 5 and 6. If φ is valid, then v^*, w^* are independent in $[\![P]\!](s)$ for all $s \in S$.*

4.2 Constraint Transformation

To solve our constraints, we transform our constraints into the form $\exists f. \forall X. \varphi$, where φ is a first-order formula. Such formulas can be viewed as *synthesis problems*, and are often solvable automatically using standard techniques.

We perform our transformation in two steps. First, we transform our constraint into the form $\exists f. \forall X. \varphi_p$, where φ_p still contains the coupling constraint. Then, we replace the coupling constraint with a first-order formula by logically encoding primitive distributions as uninterpreted functions.

Quantifier Reordering. Our constraints are of the form $\forall a, a'. \exists f. \forall X. \varphi$. Intuitively, this means that for *every* possible value of a, a', we want *one* function f satisfying $\forall X. \varphi$. We can pull the existential quantifier $\exists f$ to the outermost level by extending the function with additional parameters for a, a', thus defining a different function for every interpretation of a, a'. For the uniformity constraints this transformation yields the following formulas:

$$\exists g. \forall a, a'. \forall V, V_1.$$
$$(V^I = V_1^I \wedge \boldsymbol{v}_1 = g(a, a', \boldsymbol{v}) \wedge \mathsf{enc}(P) \wedge \mathsf{enc}(P_1)) \tag{7}$$
$$\implies (v^* = a \iff v_1^* = a')$$
$$V^I = V_1^I \implies dexp \leadsto^{g(a,a',-)} dexp_1 \tag{8}$$

where $g(a, a', -)$ is the function after partially applying g.

Transforming Coupling Constraints. Our next step is to eliminate coupling constraints. To do so, we use the definition of f-coupling, which states that $\mu_1 \leadsto^f \mu_2$ if (i) f is injective and (ii) $\forall x. \mu_1(x) \leqslant \mu_2(f(x))$. The first constraint (injectivity) is straightforward. For the second point (monotonicity), we can encode distribution expressions—which represent functions to reals—as uninterpreted functions, which we then further constrain. For instance, the coupling constraint $\mathsf{bern}(p) \leadsto^f \mathsf{bern}(p')$ can be encoded as

$$\forall x, y. x \neq y \Rightarrow f(x) \neq f(y) \qquad \text{(injectivity)}$$
$$\forall x. h(x) \leqslant h'(f(x)) \qquad \text{(monotonicity)}$$
$$\forall x. ite(x = true, h(x) = p, h(x) = 1 - p) \qquad (\mathsf{bern}(p) \text{ encoding})$$
$$\forall x. ite(x = true, h'(x) = p', h'(x) = 1 - p') \qquad (\mathsf{bern}(p') \text{ encoding})$$

where $h, h' : \mathbb{B} \to \mathbb{R}^{\geq 0}$ are uninterpreted functions representing the probability mass functions of $\mathsf{bern}(p)$ and $\mathsf{bern}(p')$; note that the third constraint encodes the distribution $\mathsf{bern}(p)$, which returns *true* with probability p and false with probability $1 - p$, and the fourth constraint encodes $\mathsf{bern}(p')$.

Note that if we cannot encode the definition of the distribution in our first-order theory (e.g., if it requires non-linear constraints), or if we do not have a concrete description of the distribution, we can simply elide the last two constraints and under-constrain h and h'. In Sect. 6 we use this feature to prove properties of a program encoding a Bayesian network, where the primitive distributions are unknown program parameters.

Theorem 6 (Transformation soundness). *Let φ be the constraints generated for some program P. Let φ' be the result of applying the above transformations to φ. If φ' is valid, then φ is valid.*

Constraint Solving. After performing these transformations, we finally arrive at constraints of the form $\exists g. \forall a, a'. \forall V. \varphi$, where φ is a first-order formula. These exactly match constraint-based program synthesis problems. In Sect. 6, we use SMT solvers and enumerative synthesis to handle these constraints.

5 Dealing with Loops

So far, we have only considered loop-free programs. In this section, we our approach to programs with loops.

f-Coupled Postconditions and Loops. We consider programs of the form

$$\textbf{while}\ \ bexp\ P^b$$

where P^b is a loop-free program that begins with the statement $\boldsymbol{v} \sim dexp$; our technique can also be extended to handle nested loops. We assume all programs terminate with probability 1 for any initial state; there are numerous systems for verifying this basic property automatically (see, e.g., [15–17]). To extend our f-coupled postconditions, we let $\mathsf{cpost}(P, P', Q, f)$ be the smallest set I satisfying:

$$Q \subseteq I \qquad\qquad\qquad\qquad\qquad\qquad\text{(initiation)}$$

$$\mathsf{cpost}(P^b, P^{b'}, I_{en}, f) \subseteq I \qquad\qquad\qquad\text{(consecution)}$$

$$I \subseteq \{s(bexp) = s'(bexp') \mid s \in S, s' \in S'\} \qquad\text{(synchronization)}$$

where $I_{en} \triangleq \{(s, s') \in I \mid s(bexp) = true\}$.

Intuitively, the set I is the least inductive invariant for the two coupled programs running with synchronized loops. Theorem 1, which establishes that f-coupled postconditions result in couplings over output distributions, naturally extends to a setting with loops.

Constraint Generation. To prove uniformity, we generate constraints much like the loop-free case except that we capture the invariant I, modeled as a relation over the variables of both programs, using a *Constrained Horn-Clause* (CHC) encoding. As is standard, we use V', V_1' to denote primed copies of program variables denoting their value after executing the body, and we assume that $\mathsf{enc}(P^b)$ encodes a loop-free program as a transition relation from states over V to states over V'.

$$\forall a, a'. \exists f, I. \forall V, V_1, V', V_1'.$$

$$V^I = V_1^I \implies I(V, V_1) \qquad\qquad\qquad\qquad\qquad\qquad\text{(initiation)}$$

$$I(V, V_1) \wedge bexp \wedge v_1' = f(v') \wedge \mathsf{enc}(P^b) \wedge \mathsf{enc}(P_1^b) \implies I(V', V_1') \qquad\text{(consecution)}$$

$$I(V, V_1) \implies bexp = bexp_1 \qquad\qquad\qquad\qquad\qquad\text{(synchronization)}$$

$$I(V, V_1) \implies dexp \leadsto^f dexp_1 \qquad\qquad\qquad\qquad\text{(coupling)}$$

$$I(V, V_1) \wedge \neg bexp \implies (v^* = a \iff v_1^* = a') \qquad\text{(uniformity)}$$

The first three constraints encode the definition of cpost; the last two ensure that f constructs a coupling and that the invariant implies the uniformity condition when the loop terminates. Using the technique presented in Sect. 4.2, we can transform these constraints into the form $\exists f, I. \forall X. \varphi$. That is, in addition to discovering the function f, we need to discover the invariant I.

Proving independence in looping programs poses additional challenges, as directly applying the self-composition construction from Sect. 3 requires relating a single loop with two loops. When the number of loop iterations is deterministic, however, we may simulate two sequentially composed loops with a single loop that interleaves the iterations (known as *synchronized* or *cross* product [4,29]) so that we reduce the synthesis problem to finding a coupling for two loops.

6   Implementation and Evaluation

We now discuss our implementation and five case studies used for evaluation.

```
fun fairCoin(p ∈ (0,1))          fun noisySum(n, p ∈ (0,1))
    x ← false                        sum ← 0                        fun ballot(n)
    y ← false                        for i = 1,...,n do                 tie ← false
    while x = y do                       noise[i] ~ bern(p)            xA ← 0
        x ~ bern(p)                      sum ← sum + noise[i]          xB ← 0
        y ~ bern(p)                  return sum                        for i = 1,...,n do
    return x                                                               r ~ bern(0.5)
                                                                           if r = 0 then
                                                                               xA ← xA + 1
fun fairDie                                                                else
    x ← false                    fun bayes(μ, μ', μ'')                          xB ← xB + 1
    y ← false                        x ~ μ                                 if i = 1 then
    z ← false                        y ~ μ'                                    first ← r
    while x = y = z do               z ~ μ''                            if xA = xB then
        x ~ bern(0.5)                w ← f(x, y)                             tie ← true
        y ~ bern(0.5)                w' ← g(y, z)                       return (first, tie)
        z ~ bern(0.5)                return (w, w')
    return (x, y, z)
```

Fig. 2. Case study programs

Implementation. To solve formulas of the form $\exists f. \forall X. \varphi$, we implemented a simple solver using a *guess-and-check* loop: We iterate through various interpretations of f, insert them into the formula, and check whether the resulting formula is valid. In the simplest case, we are searching for a function f from n-tuples to n-tuples. For instance, in Sect. 2.2, we discovered the function $f(x, y) = (y, x)$. Our implementation is parameterized by a grammar defining an infinite set of interpretations of f, which involves permuting the arguments (as above), conditionals, and other basic operations (e.g., negation for Boolean variables). For checking validity of $\forall X. \varphi$ given f, we use the Z3 SMT solver [19] for loop-free programs. For loops, we use an existing constrained-Horn-clause solver based on the MathSAT SMT solver [18].

Benchmarks and Results. As a set of case studies for our approach, we use 5 different programs collected from the literature and presented in Fig. 2. For these programs, we prove uniformity, (conditional) independence properties, and other probabilistic equalities. For instance, we use our implementation to prove a main lemma for the Ballot theorem [20], encoded as the program ballot.

Figure 3 shows the time and number of loop iterations required by our implementation to discover a coupling proof. The small number of iterations and time needed demonstrates the simplicity of the discovered proofs. For instance, the ballot theorem was proved in 3 s and only 4 iterations, while the fairCoin example (illustrated in Sect. 2.2) required only two iterations and 1.4 s. In all cases, the size of the synthesize function f in terms of depth of its AST is no more than 4. We describe these programs and properties in a bit more detail.

Case Studies: Uniformity (fairCoin, fairDie). The first two programs produce uniformly random values. Our approach synthesizes a coupling proof certifying uniformity for both of these programs. The first program fairCoin, which we saw in Sect. 2.2, produces a fair coin flip given access to biased coin flips by repeatedly flipping two coins while they are equal, and returning the result of the first coin as soon as the flips differ. Note that the bias of the coin flip is a program parameter, and not fixed statically. The synthesized coupling swaps the result of the two samples, mapping the values of (x, y) to (y, x).

The second program fairDie gives a different construction for simulating a roll of a fair die given fair coin flips. Three fair coins are repeatedly flipped as long as they are all equal; the returned triple is the binary representation of a number in $\{1, \ldots, 6\}$, the result of the simulated roll. The synthesized coupling is a bijection on triples of booleans $\mathbb{B} \times \mathbb{B} \times \mathbb{B}$; fixing any two possible output triples (b_1, b_2, b_3) and (b'_1, b'_2, b'_3) of distinct booleans, the coupling maps $(b_1, b_2, b_3) \mapsto (b'_1, b'_2, b'_3)$ and vice versa, leaving all other triples unchanged.

Program	Iters.	Time(s)
fairCoin	2	1.4
fairDie	9	6.1
noisySum	4	0.2
bayes	5	0.4
ballot	4	3.0

Fig. 3. Statistics

Case Studies: Independence (noisySum, bayes). In the next two programs, our approach synthesizes coupling proofs of independence and conditional independence of program variables in the output distribution. The first program, noisySum, is a stylized program inspired from privacy-preserving algorithms that sum a series of noisy samples; for giving accuracy guarantees, it is often important to show that the noisy draws are probabilistically independent. We show that any pair of samples are independent.

The second program, bayes, models a simple Bayesian network with three independent variables x, y, z and two dependent variables w and w', computed from (x, y) and (y, z) respectively. We want to show that w and w' are independent conditioned on any value of y; intuitively, w and w' only depend on each other through the value of y, and are independent otherwise. We use a constraint encoding similar to the encoding for showing independence to find a coupling proof of this fact. Note that the distributions μ, μ', μ'' of x, y, z are unknown parameters, and the functions f and g are also uninterpreted. This illustrates the advantage of using a constraint-based technique—we can encode unknown distributions and operations as uninterpreted functions.

Case Studies: Probabilistic Equalities (ballot). As we mentioned in Sect. 1, our approach extends naturally to proving general probabilistic equalities beyond uniformity and independence. To illustrate, we consider a lemma used to prove Bertrand's Ballot theorem [20]. Roughly speaking, this theorem considers counting ballots one-by-one in an election where there are n_A votes cast for candidate A and n_B votes cast for candidate B, where n_A, n_B are parameters. If $n_A > n_B$ (so A is the winner) and votes are counted in a uniformly random order, the Ballot theorem states that the probability that A leads throughout the whole counting process—without any ties—is precisely $(n_A - n_B)/(n_A + n_B)$.

One way of proving this theorem, sometimes called André's reflection principle, is to show that the probability of counting the first vote for A and reaching a tie is equal to the probability of counting the first vote for B and reaching a tie. We simulate the counting process slightly differently—instead of drawing a uniform order to count the votes, our program draws uniform samples for votes—but the original target property is equivalent to the equality

$$\Pr[\mathit{first}_1 = 0 \wedge \mathit{tie}_1 \wedge \psi(x_{A1}, x_{B1})] = \Pr[\mathit{first}_2 = 1 \wedge \mathit{tie}_2 \wedge \psi(x_{A2}, x_{B2})] \quad (9)$$

with $\psi(x_{Ai}, x_{Bi})$ is $x_{Ai} = n_A \wedge x_{Bi} = n_B$. Our approach synthesizes a coupling and loop invariant showing that the coupled post-condition is contained in

$$\{(s_1, s_2) \mid s_1(\mathit{first} = 0 \wedge \mathit{tie} \wedge \psi(x_A, x_B)) \iff s_2(\mathit{first} = 0 \wedge \mathit{tie} \wedge \psi(x_A, x_B))\},$$

giving Formula (9) by Proposition 1 (see Barthe et al. [6] for more details).

7   Related Work

Probabilistic programs have been a long-standing target of formal verification. We compare with two of the most well-developed lines of research: probabilistic model checking and deductive verification via program logics or expectations.

Probabilistic Model Checking. Model checking has proven to be a powerful tool for verifying probabilistic programs, capable of automated proofs for various probabilistic properties (typically encoded in probabilistic temporal logics); there are now numerous mature implementations (see, e.g., [21] or [3, Chap. 10] for more details). In comparison, our approach has the advantage of being fully constraint-based. This gives it a number of unique features: (i) it applies to programs with unknown inputs and variables over infinite domains; (ii) it applies to programs sampling from distributions with parameters, or even ones sampling from unknown distributions modeled as uninterpreted functions in first-order logic; (iii) it applies to distributions over infinite domains; and (iv) the generated coupling proofs are compact. At the same time, our approach is specialized to the coupling proof technique and is likely to be more incomplete.

Deductive Verification. Compared to general deductive verification systems for probabilistic programs, like program logics [5, 14, 22, 26] or techniques reasoning by pre-expectations [25], the main benefit of our technique is automation—deductive verification typically requires an interactive theorem prover to manipulate complex probabilistic invariants. In general, the coupling proof method limits reasoning about probabilities and distributions to just the random sampling commands; in the rest of the program, the proof can avoid quantitative reasoning entirely. As a result, our system can work with non-probabilistic invariants and achieve full automation. Our approach also smoothly handles properties involving the probabilities of multiple events, like probabilistic independence, unlike techniques that analyze probabilistic events one-by-one.

Acknowledgements. We thank Samuel Drews, Calvin Smith, and the anonymous reviewers for their helpful comments. Justin Hsu was partially supported by ERC grant #679127 and NSF grant #1637532. Aws Albarghouthi was supported by NSF grants #1566015, #1704117, and #1652140.

References

1. Albarghouthi, A., Hsu, J.: Synthesizing coupling proofs of differential privacy. Proc. ACM Programm. Lang. **2**(POPL), 58:1–58:30 (2018). http://doi.acm.org/10.1145/3158146
2. Alur, R., Bodik, R., Juniwal, G., Martin, M.M., Raghothaman, M., Seshia, S.A., Singh, R., Solar-Lezama, A., Torlak, E., Udupa, A.: Syntax-guided synthesis. In: Formal Methods in Computer-Aided Design (FMCAD), Portland, Oregon, pp. 1–8. IEEE (2013)
3. Baier, C., Katoen, J.P., Larsen, K.G.: Principles of Model Checking. MIT Press, Cambridge (2008)
4. Barthe, G., Crespo, J.M., Kunz, C.: Relational verification using product programs. In: Butler, M., Schulte, W. (eds.) FM 2011. LNCS, vol. 6664, pp. 200–214. Springer, Heidelberg (2011). https://doi.org/10.1007/978-3-642-21437-0_17
5. Barthe, G., Espitau, T., Gaboardi, M., Grégoire, B., Hsu, J., Strub, P.Y.: A program logic for probabilistic programs. In: European Symposium on Programming (ESOP), Thessaloniki, Greece (2018, to appear). https://justinh.su/files/papers/ellora.pdf
6. Barthe, G., Espitau, T., Grégoire, B., Hsu, J., Strub, P.Y.: Proving uniformity and independence by self-composition and coupling. In: International Conference on Logic for Programming, Artificial Intelligence and Reasoning (LPAR), Maun, Botswana. EPiC Series in Computing, vol. 46, pp. 385–403 (2017). https://arxiv.org/abs/1701.06477
7. Barthe, G., Espitau, T., Grégoire, B., Hsu, J., Strub, P.: Proving expected sensitivity of probabilistic programs. Proc. ACM Programm. Lang. **2**(POPL), 57:1–57:29 (2018). http://doi.acm.org/10.1145/3158145
8. Barthe, G., Fong, N., Gaboardi, M., Grégoire, B., Hsu, J., Strub, P.Y.: Advanced probabilistic couplings for differential privacy. In: ACM SIGSAC Conference on Computer and Communications Security (CCS), Vienna, Austria (2016). https://arxiv.org/abs/1606.07143
9. Barthe, G., Fournet, C., Grégoire, B., Strub, P.Y., Swamy, N., Zanella-Béguelin, S.: Probabilistic relational verification for cryptographic implementations. In: ACM SIGPLAN-SIGACT Symposium on Principles of Programming Languages (POPL), San Diego, California, pp. 193–206 (2014). https://research.microsoft.com/en-us/um/people/nswamy/papers/rfstar.pdf
10. Barthe, G., Gaboardi, M., Grégoire, B., Hsu, J., Strub, P.Y.: Proving differential privacy via probabilistic couplings. In: IEEE Symposium on Logic in Computer Science (LICS), New York, pp. 749–758 (2016), http://arxiv.org/abs/1601.05047

11. Barthe, G., Grégoire, B., Hsu, J., Strub, P.Y.: Coupling proofs are probabilistic product programs. In: ACM SIGPLAN-SIGACT Symposium on Principles of Programming Languages (POPL), Paris, France, pp. 161–174 (2017). http://arxiv.org/abs/1607.03455

12. Barthe, G., Köpf, B., Olmedo, F., Zanella-Béguelin, S.: Probabilistic relational reasoning for differential privacy. ACM Trans. Programm. Lang. Syst. **35**(3), 9 (2013). http://software.imdea.org/ bkoepf/papers/toplas13.pdf

13. Beyene, T., Chaudhuri, S., Popeea, C., Rybalchenko, A.: A constraint-based approach to solving games on infinite graphs. In: ACM SIGPLAN-SIGACT Symposium on Principles of Programming Languages (POPL), San Diego, California, pp. 221–233 (2014)

14. Chadha, R., Cruz-Filipe, L., Mateus, P., Sernadas, A.: Reasoning about probabilistic sequential programs. Theor. Comput. Sci. **379**(1), 142–165 (2007)

15. Chatterjee, K., Fu, H., Goharshady, A.K.: Termination analysis of probabilistic programs through Positivstellensatz's. In: Chaudhuri, S., Farzan, A. (eds.) CAV 2016. LNCS, vol. 9779, pp. 3–22. Springer, Cham (2016). https://doi.org/10.1007/978-3-319-41528-4_1

16. Chatterjee, K., Fu, H., Novotný, P., Hasheminezhad, R.: Algorithmic analysis of qualitative and quantitative termination problems for affine probabilistic programs. In: ACM SIGPLAN-SIGACT Symposium on Principles of Programming Languages (POPL), Saint Petersburg, Florida, pp. 327–342 (2016). https://doi.acm.org/10.1145/2837614.2837639

17. Chatterjee, K., Novotný, P., Žikelić, Đ.: Stochastic invariants for probabilistic termination. In: ACM SIGPLAN-SIGACT Symposium on Principles of Programming Languages (POPL), Paris, France, pp. 145–160 (2017). https://doi.acm.org/10.1145/3009837.3009873

18. Cimatti, A., Griggio, A., Schaafsma, B.J., Sebastiani, R.: The MathSAT5 SMT solver. In: Piterman, N., Smolka, S.A. (eds.) TACAS 2013. LNCS, vol. 7795, pp. 93–107. Springer, Heidelberg (2013). https://doi.org/10.1007/978-3-642-36742-7_7

19. de Moura, L., Bjørner, N.: Z3: an efficient SMT solver. In: Ramakrishnan, C.R., Rehof, J. (eds.) TACAS 2008. LNCS, vol. 4963, pp. 337–340. Springer, Heidelberg (2008). https://doi.org/10.1007/978-3-540-78800-3_24

20. Feller, W.: An Introduction to Probability Theory and Its Applications, vol. 1, 3rd edn. Wiley, Hoboken (1968)

21. Forejt, V., Kwiatkowska, M., Norman, G., Parker, D.: Automated verification techniques for probabilistic systems. In: Bernardo, M., Issarny, V. (eds.) SFM 2011. LNCS, vol. 6659, pp. 53–113. Springer, Heidelberg (2011). https://doi.org/10.1007/978-3-642-21455-4_3

22. den Hartog, J.: Probabilistic extensions of semantical models. Ph.D. thesis, Vrije Universiteit Amsterdam (2002)

23. Hsu, J.: Probabilistic Couplings for Probabilistic Reasoning. Ph.D. thesis, University of Pennsylvania (2017). https://arxiv.org/abs/1710.09951

24. Kozen, D.: Semantics of probabilistic programs. J. Comput. Syst. Sci. **22**(3), 328–350 (1981). https://www.sciencedirect.com/science/article/pii/0022000081900362

25. Morgan, C., McIver, A., Seidel, K.: Probabilistic predicate transformers. ACM Trans. Programm. Lang. Syst. **18**(3), 325–353 (1996). dl.acm.org/ft_gateway.cfm?id=229547

26. Rand, R., Zdancewic, S.: VPHL: a verified partial-correctness logic for probabilistic programs. In: Conference on the Mathematical Foundations of Programming Semantics (MFPS), Nijmegen, The Netherlands (2015)

27. Solar-Lezama, A., Tancau, L., Bodík, R., Seshia, S.A., Saraswat, V.A.: Combinatorial sketching for finite programs. In: International Conference on Architectural Support for Programming Langauages and Operating Systems (ASPLOS), San Jose, California, pp. 404–415 (2006). http://doi.acm.org/10.1145/1168857.1168907
28. Strassen, V.: The existence of probability measures with given marginals. Annals Math. Stat. 423–439 (1965). https://projecteuclid.org/euclid.aoms/1177700153
29. Zaks, A., Pnueli, A.: CoVaC: compiler validation by program analysis of the cross-product. In: Cuellar, J., Maibaum, T., Sere, K. (eds.) FM 2008. LNCS, vol. 5014, pp. 35–51. Springer, Heidelberg (2008). https://doi.org/10.1007/978-3-540-68237-0_5

7

Synthesis of Asynchronous Reactive Programs from Temporal Specifications

Suguman Bansal[1]([⊠]), Kedar S. Namjoshi[2]([⊠]), and Yaniv Sa'ar[3]([⊠])

[1] Rice University, Houston, TX, USA
suguman@rice.edu
[2] Bell Labs, Nokia, Murray Hill, NJ, USA
kedar.namjoshi@nokia-bell-labs.com
[3] Bell Labs, Nokia, Kfar Saba, Israel
yaniv.saar@nokia.bell-labs.com

Abstract. Asynchronous interactions are ubiquitous in computing systems and complicate design and programming. Automatic construction of asynchronous programs from specifications ("synthesis") could ease the difficulty, but known methods are complex, and intractable in practice. This work develops substantially simpler synthesis methods. A direct, exponentially more compact automaton construction is formulated for the reduction of asynchronous to synchronous synthesis. Experiments with a prototype implementation of the new method demonstrate feasibility. Furthermore, it is shown that for several useful classes of temporal properties, automaton-based methods can be avoided altogether and replaced with simpler Boolean constraint solving.

1 Introduction

Modern software and hardware systems harness asynchronous interactions to improve speed, responsiveness, and power consumption: delay-insensitive circuits, networks of sensors, multi-threaded programs and interacting web services are all asynchronous in nature. Various factors contribute to asynchrony, such as unpredictable transmission delays, concurrency, distributed execution, and parallelism. The common result is that each component of a system operates with partial, out-of-date knowledge of the state of the others, which considerably complicates system design and programming. Yet, it is often easier to state the desired behavior of an asynchronous program. We therefore consider the question of automatically constructing (i.e., synthesizing) a correct reactive asynchronous program directly from its temporal specification.

The *asynchronous synthesis problem* was originally formulated by Pnueli and Rosner in 1989 on the heels of their work on synchronous synthesis [31,32]. The task is that of constructing a (finite-state) program which interacts asynchronously with its environment while meeting a temporal specification on the actions at the interface between program and environment. Given a linear temporal specification φ, Pnueli-Rosner show that *asynchronous* synthesis can be reduced to checking whether a derived specification φ', specifying the required behavior of the scheduler, is *synchronously* synthesizable. That is, an asynchronous program can implement φ iff a synchronous program can implement φ'.

It may then appear straightforward to construct asynchronous programs using one of the many tools that exist for synchronous synthesis. However, the derived formula φ' embeds a nontrivial stutter quantification, which requires a complex intermediate automaton construction; it has not, to the authors' knowledge, ever been implemented. This situation is in stark contrast to that of synchronous synthesis, for which multiple tools and algorithms have been created.

Alternative methods have been proposed for asynchronous synthesis: Finkbeiner and Schewe reduce a bounded form of the problem to a SAT/SMT query [35], and Klein, Piterman and Pnueli show that some GR(1) specifications[1] can be transformed as above to an approximate synchronous GR(1) property [21,22]. These alternatives, however, have drawbacks of their own. The SAT/SMT reduction is exponential in the number of interface (input and output) bits, an important parameter; the GR(1) specifications amenable to transformation are limited and are characterized by semantic conditions that are not easily checked.

This work presents two key simplifications. First, we define a new property, $\mathsf{PR}(\varphi)$ (named in honor of Pnueli-Rosner's pioneering work) which, like φ', is synchronously realizable if, and only if, φ is asynchronously realizable. We then present an automaton construction for $\mathsf{PR}(\varphi)$ that is direct and simpler, and results in an exponentially smaller automaton than the one for φ'. In particular, the automaton for $\mathsf{PR}(\varphi)$ has only at most *twice* the states of the automaton for φ, as opposed to the *exponential blowup* of the state space (in the number of interface bits) incurred in the construction of the automaton for φ'. As almost all synchronous automaton-based synthesis tools use an explicit encoding for automaton states, this reduction is vital in practice.

We show how to implement the transformation PR symbolically (with BDDs), so that interface bits are always represented in symbolic form. One can then apply the modular strategy of Pnueli-Rosner: a symbolic automaton for φ is transformed to a symbolic automaton for $\mathsf{PR}(\varphi)$ (instead of φ'), which is analyzed with a synchronous synthesis tool. We establish that PR is conjunctive and preserves safety[2]. These are important properties, used by tools such as Acacia+ [8] and Unbeast [11] to optimize the synchronous synthesis task. The new construction has been implemented in a prototype tool, BAS, and experiments demonstrate feasibility in practice.

In addition, we establish that for several classes of temporal properties, which are easily characterized by syntax, the automaton-based method can be avoided entirely and replaced with Boolean constraint solving. The constraints are quantified Boolean formulae, with prefix $\exists\forall$ and a kernel that is derived from the original specification. This surprising reduction, which resolves a temporal prob-

---

[1] The GR(1) ("General Reactivity (1)") subclass has an efficient symbolic procedure for synchronous synthesis, formulated in [28] and implemented in several tools.

[2] I.e., $\mathsf{PR}(\bigwedge_i f_i) = \bigwedge_i \mathsf{PR}(f_i)$, and $\mathsf{PR}(f)$ is a safety property if f is a safety property.

lem with Boolean reasoning, is a consequence of the highly adversarial role of the environment in the asynchronous setting.

These contributions turn a seemingly intractable synthesis task into one that is feasible in practice.

2   Preliminaries

Temporal Specifications. Linear Temporal Logic (LTL) [29] extends propositional logic with temporal operators. LTL formulae are defined as $\varphi :: =$ True | False | p | $\neg\varphi$ | $\varphi_1 \wedge \varphi_2$ | $X\varphi$ | $\varphi_1 U \varphi_2$| $\Diamond\varphi$ | $\Box\varphi$ | $\boxminus\varphi$. Here p is a proposition, and X(Next), U (Until), $\Diamond$ (Eventually), $\Box$ (Always), and $\boxminus$(Always in the past) are temporal operators. The LTL semantics is standard, and is in the full version of the paper. For an LTL formula φ, let $\mathcal{L}(\varphi)$ denote the set of words (over subsets of propositions) that satisfy φ.

GR(1) is a useful fragment of LTL, where formulae are of the form $(\Box S_e \wedge \bigwedge_{i=0}^{m} \Box\Diamond P_i) \Rightarrow (\Box S_s \wedge \bigwedge_{i=0}^{n} \Box\Diamond Q_i)$, for propositional formulae S_e, S_s, P_i, Q_i. Typically, the left-hand side of the implication is used to restrict the environment, by requiring safety and liveness assumptions to hold, while the right-hand side is used to define the safety and liveness guarantees required of the system.

LTL specifications can be turned into equivalent Büchi automata, using standard constructions. A Büchi automaton, A, is specified by the tuple $(Q, Q_0, \Sigma, \delta, G)$, where Q is a set of states, $Q_0 \subseteq Q$ defines the initial states, Σ is the alphabet, $\delta \subseteq Q \times \Sigma \times Q$ is the transition relation, and $G \subseteq Q$ defines the "green" (also known as "accepting" or "final") states. A *run* r of the automaton on an infinite word $\sigma = a_0, a_1, \ldots$ over Σ is an infinite sequence $r = q_0, a_0, q_1, a_1, \ldots$ such that q_0 is an initial state, and for each k, (q_k, a_k, q_{k+1}) is in the transition relation. Run r is accepting if a green state appears on it infinitely often; the language of A, denoted $\mathcal{L}(A)$, is the set of words that have an accepting run.

The Asynchronous Synthesis Model. The goal of synthesis is to construct an "open" program M meeting a specification at its interface. In the asynchronous setting, the program M interacts in a fair interleaved manner with its environment E. The fairness restriction requires that E and M are each scheduled infinitely often in all infinite executions. Let $E//M$ denote this composition. The interface between E and M is formed by the variables x and y. Variable x is written by E and is read-only for M, while y is written by M and is read-only for E. One can consider x (resp., y) to represent a vector of variables, i.e., $x = (x_1, \ldots, x_n)$ (resp., $y = (y_1, \ldots, y_m)$) which is read (resp., written) atomically. Many of our results also extend to non-atomic reads and writes, and are discussed in the full version of the paper.

The synthesis task is to construct a program M which satisfies a temporal property $\varphi(x, y)$ over the interface variables in the composition $E//M$, for *any* environment E. The most adversarial environment is the one which sets x to an arbitrary value at each scheduled step, we denote it by CHAOS(x). The behaviors of the composition $\mathsf{CHAOS}(x)//M$ simulate those of $E//M$ for all E. Hence, it suffices to produce M which satisfies φ in the composition $\mathsf{CHAOS}(x)//M$. One can limit the set of environments through an assumption in the specification.

This leads to the formal definition of an *asynchronous schedule*, given by a pair of functions, $r, w : \mathbb{N} \rightarrow \mathbb{N}$, which represent read and write points, respectively. The initial write point, $w(0) = 0$, and represents the choice of initial value for the variable y. Without loss of generality, the read-write points alternate, i.e., for all $i \geq 0$, $w(i) \leq r(i) < w(i+1)$ and $r(i) < w(i+1) \leq r(i+1)$. A *strict* asynchronous schedule does not allow read and write points to overlap, i.e., the constraints are strengthened to $w(i) < r(i) < w(i+1)$ and $r(i) < w(i+1) < r(i+1)$. A *tight* asynchronous schedule is the strict schedule without any non-read-write gaps, i.e., $r(k) = 2k + 1$ and $w(k) = 2k$, for all k. A *synchronous* schedule is the special non-strict schedule where $r(i) = i$ and $w(i) = i$, for all i.

Let D^v denote the binary domain $\{\mathsf{True}, \mathsf{False}\}$ for a variable v. A program M can be represented semantically as a function $f : (D^x)^* \rightarrow D^y$. For an asynchronous schedule (r, w), a sequence $\sigma = (D^x \times D^y)^\omega$ is said to be an *asynchronous execution of f over (r, w)* if the value of y is changed only at writing points, in a manner that depends only on the values of x at prior reading points. Formally, for all $i \geq 0$, $y_{w(i+1)} = f(x_{r(0)} \ldots x_{r(i)})$, and for all j such that $w(i) \leq j < w(i+1)$, $y_j = y_{w(i)}$. The initial value of y is the value it has at point $w(0) = 0$. The set of such sequences is denoted as $\mathsf{asynch}(f)$. Over synchronous schedules, the set of such sequences is denoted by $\mathsf{synch}(f)$. Function f is an asynchronous implementation of φ if all asynchronous executions of f over all possible schedules satisfy φ, i.e., if $\mathsf{asynch}(f) \subseteq \mathcal{L}(\varphi)$.

This formulation agrees with that given by Pnueli and Rosner for strict schedules. For synchronous schedules (and other non-strict schedules), our formulation has a Moore-style semantics – the output depends on strictly earlier inputs – while Pnueli and Rosner formulate a Mealy semantics. A Moore semantics is more appropriate for modeling software programs, where the output variable is part of the state, and fits well with the theoretical constructions that follow.

Definition 1 (Asynchronous LTL Realizability). *Given an LTL property $\varphi(x, y)$ over the input variable x and output variable y, the asynchronous LTL realizability problem is to determine whether there is an asynchronous implementation for φ.*

Definition 2 (Asynchronous LTL Synthesis). *Given a realizable LTL-formula φ, the asynchronous LTL synthesis problem is to construct an asynchronous implementation of φ.*

Examples. Pnueli and Rosner give a number of interesting specifications. The specification $\square (y \equiv X x)$ ("the current output equals the next input") is satisfiable but not realizable, as any implementation would have to be clairvoyant. On the other hand, the flipped specification $\square (x \equiv X y)$ ("the next output equals the current input") is synchronously realizable by a Moore machine which replays the current input as the next output. The specification $\Diamond \Box x \equiv \Diamond \Box y$ is synchronously realizable by the same machine, but is asynchronously unrealizable, as shown next. Consider two input (x) sequences, under a schedule where reads happen only at odd positions. In both, let x=true at all reading points. Then any program must respond to both inputs with the same output sequence for y. Now suppose that in the first sequence x is false at all non-read positions, while in the second, x is true at all non-read positions. In the first case, the specification forces the output y-sequence to be false infinitely often; in the second, y is forced to be true from some point on, a contradiction.

The negated specification $\Diamond \Box x \not\equiv \Diamond \Box y$ is also asynchronously unrealizable, for the same reason. This "gap" illustrates an intriguing difference from the synchronous case, where either a specification is realizable for the system, or its negation is realizable for the environment. The two halves of the equivalence, i.e., $\Diamond \Box x \Rightarrow \Diamond \Box y$ and $\Diamond \Box y \Rightarrow \Diamond \Box x$ are individually asynchronously realizable, by strategies that fix the output to y=true and to y=false, respectively.

From Asynchronous to Synchronous Synthesis. Pnueli and Rosner reduced asynchronous LTL synthesis to synchronous synthesis of Büchi objectives. Their reduction applied to LTL formulas with a single input and output variable [32]; it was later extended to the non-atomic case [30]. The original Rosner-Pnueli reduction deals exclusively with strict schedules, since they showed that it is sufficient to consider only strict schedules.

Two infinite sequences are said to be *stuttering equivalent* if one sequence can be obtained from the other by a finite duplication ("stretching") of a given state or by deletion ("compressing") of finitely many contiguous identical states retaining at least one of them. The *stuttering quantification* $\exists^{\approx}$ is defined as follows: $\exists^{\approx} x.\varphi$ holds for sequence π if $\exists x.\varphi$ holds for a sequence π' that is stuttering equivalent to π. Pnueli-Rosner showed that an **LTL-formula** $\varphi(x, y)$ over input x and output y is asynchronously realizable iff a "kernel" formula (this is the precise formula referred to as φ' in the Introduction) $\mathcal{K}(r, w, x, y) = \alpha(r, w) \rightarrow \beta(r, w, x, y)$ over read sequence r, write sequence w, input sequence x and output sequence y is synchronously realizable:

$$\alpha(r, w) = \quad (\neg r \wedge \neg w \, \mathsf{U} \, r) \wedge \Box \neg (r \wedge w) \wedge \Box \, (r \Rightarrow (r \, \mathsf{U} \, (\neg r) \, \mathsf{U} \, w))$$
$$\wedge \Box \, (w \Rightarrow (w \, \mathsf{U} \, (\neg w) \, \mathsf{U} \, r))$$
$$\beta(r, w, x, y) = \quad \varphi(x, y) \wedge \forall a. \Box \, ((y = a) \Rightarrow ((y = a) \, \mathsf{U} \, (\neg w \wedge (y = a) \, \mathsf{U} \, w)))$$
$$\wedge \forall^{\approx} x'. (\Box \, (\neg r \Rightarrow \neg r \, \mathsf{U} \, (x = x')) \Rightarrow \varphi(x', y))$$

Here, α encodes the strict scheduling constraints on read and write points, while β encodes conditions which assure a correct asynchronous execution over (r, w). The $\forall^{\approx}$ quantification, intuitively, quantifies over all adversarial schedules similar to the current (r, w): it requires φ to hold over all sequences obtained from the current sequence σ by stretching or compressing the segments between read and write points, and choosing different values for x on those segments.

3   Symbolic Asynchronous Synthesis

Pnueli and Rosner's procedure for asynchronous synthesis [32] is as follows: first, a Büchi automaton is built for the kernel formula $\neg\mathcal{K}$. This automaton is then determinized and complemented to form a deterministic word automaton for $\mathcal{K}$, which is then re-interpreted as a tree automaton and tested for non-emptiness. The transformations use standard constructions, except for the interpretation of the $\exists^{\approx}$ operator in the formation of the Büchi automaton for $\neg\mathcal{K}$. For a Büchi automaton A, an automaton for $\exists^{\approx}\mathcal{L}(A)$ is constructed in two steps: first applying a "stretching" transformation on A, followed by a "compressing" transformation. Stretching introduces new automaton states of the form (q, a), for each state q of A and each letter a.

When this general construction is applied to the formula $\neg\mathcal{K}$, the alphabet of the automaton A is formed of all possible valuations of the pair of variables (x, y), which has size *exponential* in the number of interface bits. The stretching step introduces a copy of an automaton state for each letter, which results in an exponential blow-up of the state space of the constructed automaton. As all current tools for synchronous synthesis represent automaton states explicitly[3], the exponential blowup introduced by the stuttering quantification is a significant obstacle to implementation.

In Pnueli-Rosner's construction, the determinization and complementation steps are also complex, utilizing Safra's construction. These steps are simplified by the "Safraless" procedure adopted in current tools for synchronous synthesis.

The other major issue with the Pnueli-Rosner construction is that the kernel formula $\mathcal{K}$ introduces the scheduling variables r, w as input variables. However, the actions of a synthesized program should not rely on the values of these variables. Pnueli-Rosner ensure this by checking satisfiability over "canonical" tree models; it is unclear, however, how to realize this effect using a synchronous synthesis tool as a black box.

We define a new property, $\mathsf{PR}(\varphi)$, that differs from $\mathcal{K}$ but, similarly, is synchronously realizable if, and only if, φ is asynchronously realizable. We then present an automaton construction for $\mathsf{PR}(\varphi)$ that bypasses the general construction for $\exists^{\approx}$, avoiding the exponential blowup and resulting in an automaton with *at most twice* the states of the original. Moreover, this construction refers only to x and y, avoiding the second issue as well. We then show that this construction can be implemented fully symbolically.

3.1   Basic Formulations and Properties

As formulated in Sect. 2, an asynchronous execution of f is determined by the schedule (r, w). For a strict schedule, any infinite sequence representing an asynchronous behavior of f over (r, w) may be partitioned into a sequence of *blocks*, as follows. The start of the i'th block is at the i'th writing point, $w(i)$, and it

---

[3] With one exception. BoSy's DQBF procedure is fully symbolic but does not work as well as the default QBF procedure [12].

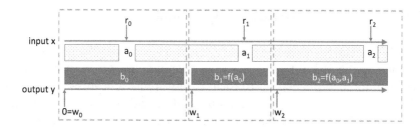

Fig. 1. A strict asynchronous computation for f. Values of x at non-reading points are shown as dotted. The y-value is constant between writing points, illustrated by a solid rectangle. Blocks are shown as dashed rectangles.

ends just before the $i + 1$'st writing point, $w(i+1)$. The schedule ensures the i'th block includes the i'th reading point, $r(i)$, associated with the input-output value (x_i, y_i). As the value of y changes only at writing points, y_i is constant in the i'th block. Thus, the i'th block follows the pattern $(\bot, y_i)^*(x_i, y_i)(\bot, y_i)^*$, where $\bot$ denotes an arbitrary choice of x-value. Figure 1 illustrates a strict asynchronous computation and its decomposition into blocks.

Expansions. The set of *expansions* of sequence $\delta = (x_0, y_0)(x_1, y_1) \ldots$ consists of all sequences obtained by simultaneously replacing each (x_i, y_i) in δ by a block with the pattern $(\bot, y_i)^*(x_i, y_i)(\bot, y_i)^*$. Formally, given sequences $\delta = (x_0, y_0)(x_1, y_1) \ldots$ and $\sigma = (\bar{x}_0, \bar{y}_0)(\bar{x}_1, \bar{y}_1) \ldots$, δ *expands to* σ, denoted as $\delta \exp \sigma$, if there exists an asynchronous schedule $(\hat{r}, \hat{w})$ for which σ is an execution that is a block pattern of δ, i.e., for all i, $x_i = \bar{x}_{\hat{r}(i)}$ and $y_i = \bar{y}_{\hat{w}(i)}$ and for all j, $\hat{w}(i) \leq j < \hat{w}(i+1)$ it is the case that $\bar{y}_j = \bar{y}_{\hat{w}(i)}$. The inverse relation (read as *contracts to*) is denoted by $\exp^{-1}$. Figure 2 shows the synchronous computation that contracts the computation shown in Fig. 1.

Relational Operators. For a relation R, the modal operators $\langle R \rangle$ and $[R]$ are defined as follows. For any set S,

$$u \in \langle R \rangle S = (\exists v : uRv \land v \in S) \qquad u \in [R]S = (\forall v : uRv \Rightarrow v \in S)$$

By definition, the operators are negation duals, i.e., $\neg \langle R \rangle (\neg S) = [R](S)$ for any R and any S. For an LTL formula φ and a relation R over infinite sequences, we let $\langle R \rangle \varphi$ abbreviate $\langle R \rangle (\mathcal{L}(\varphi))$, and similarly, let $[R]\varphi$ abbreviate $[R](\mathcal{L}(\varphi))$.

Galois Connections. Given partial orders $(A, \preceq_A)$ and $(B, \preceq_B)$, a pair of functions $g : A \to B$ and $h : B \to A$ form a Galois connection if, for all $a \in A, b \in B$: $g(a) \preceq_B b$ is equivalent to $a \preceq_A h(b)$. From the definitions, it is clear that the operators $(\langle R^{-1} \rangle, [R])$ form a Galois connection over the partial orders defined by the subset relation. I.e., for any sets S and T: $\langle R^{-1} \rangle S \subseteq T$ iff, $S \subseteq [R]T$.

   We first establish that the asynchronous executions of f are precisely the synchronous executions of f under an inverse expansion.

Theorem 1. *For an implementation f,* $\mathsf{asynch}(f) = \langle \exp^{-1} \rangle \mathsf{synch}(f)$.

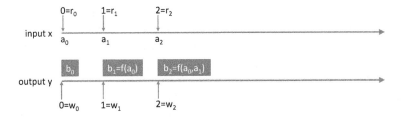

Fig. 2. The contracted synchronous (Moore) computation

Proof. (ping) Let σ be an execution in $\mathsf{asynch}(f)$, generated for some schedule (r, w). For any k, consider the k'th block of σ. This is the set of positions from $w(k)$ to $w(k+1) - 1$, which includes the k'th reading point $r(k)$, say with the value (x_k, y_k). Then the block follows the pattern $(\bot, y_k)^*(x_k, y_k)(\bot, y_k)^*$. So σ is an expansion of the sequence $\delta = (x_0, y_0)(x_1, y_1)\ldots$. By the definition of an asynchronous execution, the value $y_{k+1} = f(x_0, \ldots, x_k)$. This is precisely the requirement for δ to be a synchronous execution of f. Hence, we have that there is a δ such that $\delta \exp \sigma$ and $\delta \in \mathsf{synch}(f)$. Therefore, $\sigma \in \langle \exp^{-1} \rangle \mathsf{synch}(f)$.

(pong) Let σ be in $\langle \exp^{-1} \rangle \mathsf{synch}(f)$. By definition, there is a $\mathsf{synch}(f)$ execution $\delta = (x_0, y_0)(x_1, y_1)\ldots$ such that $\delta \exp \sigma$. As δ is a synchronous execution of f, the value $y_{k+1} = f(x_0, x_1, \ldots, x_k)$, for all k. Then σ is an asynchronous execution of f under the schedule where the k-th reading point is the point that the k'th entry, (x_k, y_k), from δ is mapped to in σ, and the $(k+1)$-th writing point is the first point of the $(k+1)$'st block in the expansion. $\qquad \square$

We now use the Galois connection to show how asynchronous synthesis can be reduced to an equivalent synchronous synthesis task. Consider a property φ that must hold asynchronously for an implementation f.

Theorem 2. *Let f be an implementation function, and φ a property. Then* $\mathsf{asynch}(f) \subseteq \mathcal{L}(\varphi)$ *if, and only if,* $\mathsf{synch}(f) \subseteq [\exp]\varphi$.

Proof. From Theorem 1, $\mathsf{asynch}(f) \subseteq \mathcal{L}(\varphi)$ holds iff $\langle \exp^{-1} \rangle \mathsf{synch}(f) \subseteq \mathcal{L}(\varphi)$ does. By the Galois connection, this is equivalent to $\mathsf{synch}(f) \subseteq [\exp]\varphi$. $\qquad \square$

3.2 The Pnueli-Rosner Closure

We refer to the property $[\exp]\varphi$ as the Pnueli-Rosner closure of φ, in honor of their pioneering work on this problem, and denote it by $\mathsf{PR}(\varphi)$. This has interesting mathematical properties, which are useful in practice.

Theorem 3. $\mathsf{PR}(\varphi) = [\exp]\varphi$ *has the following properties.*

1. *(Closure)* PR *is monotonic and a downward closure, i.e.,* $\mathsf{PR}(\varphi) \subseteq \mathcal{L}(\varphi)$
2. *(Conjunctivity)* PR *is conjunctive, i.e.,* $\mathsf{PR}(\bigwedge_i \varphi_i) = \bigcap_i \mathsf{PR}(\varphi_i)$
3. *(Safety Preservation)* *If φ is a safety property, so is* $\mathsf{PR}(\varphi)$

The closure property relies on the reflexivity and transitivity of exp , and that $[R]$ is monotonic for every R. Conjunctivity follows from the conjunctivity of $[R]$ for any R. Safety preservation is based on the Alpern-Schneider [4] formulation of safety over infinite words. Proofs are in the full version of the paper.

Conjunctivity is exploited by the tools Acacia+ [8] and Unbeast [11] to optimize the synchronous synthesis procedure. The Unbeast tool also separates out safety from non-safety sub-properties to optimize the synthesis procedure. Thus, if a specification φ has the form $\varphi_1 \wedge \varphi_2$, where φ_1 is a safety property, then $PR(\varphi) = PR(\varphi_1) \cap PR(\varphi_2)$ also denotes the intersection of the safety property $PR(\varphi_1)$ with another property.

3.3   The Closure Automaton Construction

By negation duality, $PR(\varphi)$ equals $\neg\langle\,exp\,\rangle(\neg\varphi)$. We use this property to reduce asynchronous to synchronous synthesis, as follows.

1. Construct a non-deterministic Büchi automaton A for $\neg\varphi$,
2. Transform A to a non-deterministic Büchi automaton B for the negated Pnueli-Rosner closure of φ, i.e., the language of B is $\langle\,exp\,\rangle\mathcal{L}(A) = \langle\,exp\,\rangle(\neg\varphi)$,
3. Consider the structure of B as that of a *universal* co-Büchi automaton, which has language $\neg\mathcal{L}(B)$,
4. Synthesize an implementation f in the synchronous model which satisfies $\neg\mathcal{L}(B) = \neg\langle\,exp\,\rangle\mathcal{L}(A) = \neg\langle\,exp\,\rangle(\neg\varphi) = [\,exp\,]\varphi = PR(\varphi)$.

The new step is the second one, which constructs B from A; the others use standard constructions and tools. This construction is as follows.

- The states and alphabet of B are the states and alphabet of A.
- The transitions of B are determined by a saturation procedure. For every pair of states q, q', and letter (x, y), let $\Pi(q, (x, y), q')$ be the set of paths in A from q to q' where the sequence of letters on the path matches the expansion pattern $(\bot, y)^*(x, y)(\bot, y)^*$. The transition $(q, (x, y), q')$ is in B if, and only if, this set is non-empty,
- If some path in $\Pi(q, (x, y), q')$ passes through a green (accepting) state of A, the transition $(q, (x, y), q')$ in B is colored "green" and that path is assigned as the witness to the transition in B. On the other hand, if none of the paths in $\Pi(q, (x, y), q')$ pass through a green state, this transition is not colored in B, and one of the paths in the set is chosen as the witness for this transition,
- The automaton B inherits the accepting ("green") states of A and it may have, in addition, green transitions introduced as defined above,
- A sequence is accepted by B if there is a run of B on the sequence such that either there are infinitely many green states, or infinitely many green transitions on that run.

We establish that $\mathcal{L}(B) = \langle\,exp\,\rangle\mathcal{L}(A)$ through the following two lemmas.

Lemma 1. $\langle\,exp\,\rangle\mathcal{L}(A) \subseteq \mathcal{L}(B)$.

Proof. Let $\delta = (x_0, y_0)(x_1, y_1) \ldots$ be a sequence in $\langle \exp \rangle \mathcal{L}(A)$. By definition, there exists a sequence σ in $\mathcal{L}(A)$ such that $\delta \exp \sigma$. The expansion σ follows the pattern $[(\perp, y_0)^*(x_0, y_0)(\perp, y_0)^*][(\perp, y_1)^*(x_1, y_1)(\perp, y_1)^*] \ldots$, where $[\ldots]$ are used merely to indicate the boundaries of a block. An accepting run of A on σ has the form $q_0[(\perp, y_0)^*(x_0, y_0)(\perp, y_0)^*]q_1[(\perp, y_1)^*(x_1, y_1)(\perp, y_1)^*]q_2 \ldots$, where the states on the run inside a block have been elided. By the definition of B, the segment $q_0(\perp, y_0)^*(x_0, y_0)(\perp, y_0)^*q_1$ induces a transition from q_0 to q_1 in B on the letter (x_0, y_0). Similarly, the following segment induces a transition from q_1 to q_2 on letter (x_1, y_1), and so forth. These transitions together form a run $q_0(x_0, y_0)q_1(x_1, y_1)q_2 \ldots$ of B on δ.

If one of the $\{q_i\}$ is green and appears infinitely often on the run on σ, the induced run on δ is accepting. Otherwise, as the run on σ is accepting, some green state of A occurs in the interior of infinitely many segments of that run. The transitions of B induced by those segments must be green, so the corresponding run on δ has infinitely many green edges, and is accepting for B.   □

Lemma 2. $\mathcal{L}(B) \subseteq \langle \exp \rangle \mathcal{L}(A)$.

Proof. Let δ be accepted by B. We show that there is σ such that $\delta \exp \sigma$ and σ is accepted by A. Let δ have the form $(x_0, y_0)(x_1, y_1) \ldots,$. Denote the accepting run of B on δ by $r = q_0(x_0, y_0)q_1(x_1, y_1) \ldots$. From the construction of B, the transition from q_0 to q_1 on (x_0, y_0) has an associated witness path through A from q_0 to q_1, which follows the expansion pattern $(\perp, y_0)^*(x_0, y_0)(\perp, y_0)^*$ on its edge labels. Stitching together the witness paths for each transition of r, we obtain both a sequence σ that is an expansion of δ and a run r' of A on σ.

As r is accepting for B, it must enter infinitely often either a green state or a green edge. If it enters a green state infinitely often, that state appears infinitely often on r'. If r enters a green edge infinitely often, the witness path for that edge contains a green state of A, say q; as this path is repeated infinitely often on σ, q appears infinitely often on r'. In either case, a green state of A appears infinitely often on r', which is therefore, an accepting run of A on σ.   □

Automaton B can be placed in standard form by converting its green edges to green states as follows, forming a new automaton, $\hat{B}$. Form a green copy of the state space, i.e., for each state q, form a green variant, $G(q)$, which is marked as an accepting state. Set up transitions as follows. If (q, a, q') is an original non-green transition, then (q, a, q') and $(G(q), a, q')$ are new transitions. If (q, a, q') is an original green transition, then $(q, a, G(q'))$ and $(G(q), a, G(q'))$ are new transitions. This at most doubles the size of the automaton. It is straightforward to establish that $\mathcal{L}(B) = \mathcal{L}(\hat{B})$.

3.4   Symbolic Construction

The symbolic construction of $\hat{B}$ closely follows the definitions above. It is easily implemented with BDDs representing predicates on the input and output variables x and y. The crucial step is to use fixpoints to formulate the existence of paths in the set Π used in the definition of B. These definitions are similar to the fixpoint definition of the CTL modality EF. We use $A(q, (x, y), q')$ to denote the predicate on (x, y) describing the transition from q to q' in automaton A.

Fixed Don't-Care Path. Let $\mathsf{EfixedY}(q, y, q')$ hold if there is a path of length 0 or more from q to q' in A where the value of y is fixed. This is the least fixpoint (in Z) of the following implications:

- $(q' = q) \Rightarrow Z(q, y, q')$, and
- $(\exists x, r : A(q, (x, y), r) \land Z(r, y, q')) \Rightarrow Z(q, y, q')$

The predicate $A^{\perp}(q, y, r) = (\exists x : A(q, (x, y), r))$ is pre-computed. Then, the least fixpoint is computed iteratively as follows.

$$\mathsf{EfixedY}^0(q, y, q') = (q = q')$$

$$\mathsf{EfixedY}^{i+1}(q, y, q') = \mathsf{EfixedY}^i(q, y, q') \lor (\exists r : A^{\perp}(q, y, r) \land \mathsf{EfixedY}^i(r, y, q'))$$

Let predicate $\mathsf{green}_A(r)$ be true for an accepting state r of A. The predicate $\mathsf{Efixedgreen}(q, y, q')$ holds if there is a fixed y-path from q to q' where one of the states on it is green:

$$\mathsf{Efixedgreen}(q, y, q') = (\exists r : \mathsf{EfixedY}(q, y, r) \land \mathsf{green}_A(r) \land \mathsf{EfixedY}(r, y, q'))$$

Paths and Green Paths. Let $\mathsf{Epath}(q, (x, y), q')$ hold if there is a path following the block pattern $(\perp, y)^*(x, y)(\perp, y)^*$ from q to q' in A. Then,

$$\mathsf{Epath}(q, (x, y), q') = (\exists r, r' : \mathsf{EfixedY}(q, y, r) \land A(r, (x, y), r') \land \mathsf{EfixedY}(r', y, q'))$$

Similarly, let $\mathsf{Egreenpath}(q, (x, y), q')$ hold if there is a path following the block pattern $(\perp, y)^*(x, y)(\perp, y)^*$ from q to q' in A, with an intermediate green state.

$$\mathsf{Egreenpath}(q, (x, y), q') =$$
$$(\exists r, r' : \mathsf{Efixedgreen}(q, y, r) \land A(r, (x, y), r') \land \mathsf{EfixedY}(r', y, q')) \lor$$
$$(\exists r, r' : \mathsf{EfixedY}(q, y, r) \land A(r, (x, y), r') \land \mathsf{Efixedgreen}(r', y, q'))$$

State Space of $\hat{B}$. The state space of $\hat{B}$ is formed by pairs (q, g), where q is a state of A and g is a Boolean indicating whether it is a new green state. The accepting condition $\mathsf{green}_{\hat{B}}(q, g)$ of $\hat{B}$ is given by $\mathsf{green}_A(q) \lor g$.

Initial States. The initial predicate $I_{\hat{B}}(q, g)$ is $I_A(q) \land \neg g$, where $I_A(q)$ is true for initial states of the input automata A.

Transition Relation of $\hat{B}$. The transition relation $\hat{B}((q, g), (x, y), (q', g'))$ is

$$\hat{B}((q, g), (x, y), (q', g')) = \mathsf{Epath}(q, (x, y), q') \land (g' \equiv \mathsf{Egreenpath}(q, (x, y), q'))$$

4   Implementation and Experiments

The PR algorithm has been implemented in a framework called BAS (Bounded Asynchronous Synthesis). It uses the LTL-to-automaton converter LTL3BA [3, 6], and follows the modular method, connecting to either of two solvers, BoSy [2, 12] and Acacia+ [1,8] to solve the synchronous realizability of $PR(\varphi)$. The PR construction is implemented in about 1200 lines of OCaml, using an external BDD library. (The core construction requires only about 400 lines of code.) For an LTL specification φ, the BAS workflow for asynchronous synthesis is as follows:

1. Check whether φ is synchronously realizable; if not, return UNREALIZABLE,
2. Construct Büchi automata A for $\neg\varphi$, and $\hat{A}$ for φ,
3. Concurrently
   (a) Construct $PR(\varphi)$ from A and check whether it is synchronously realizable; if so, return REALIZABLE and synthesize the implementation.
   (b) Construct $PR(\neg\varphi)$ from $\hat{A}$ and check whether it is synchronously realizable for the environment; if so, return UNREALIZABLE.
   Upon termination of any, terminate the other execution as well.

The synchronous synthesis tools successively increase a bound until a limit (computed based on automaton structure) is reached. Thus, in theory, only the check in step 3(a) is needed. However, the checks in steps 1 and 3(b) may allow the tool to terminate early (before reaching the limit bound), if a winning strategy for the environment can be discovered.

To evaluate BAS we consider the list of examples presented in Table 1. The reported experiments were performed on a VM configured to have 8 CPU cores at 2.4 GHz, 8 GB RAM, running 64-bit Linux. The running times are reported in milliseconds. For each specification (presented in the second column) we report whether it is asynchronously realizable (third column), the time for the PR construction (our contribution), and the time for checking whether the specification is realizable using BoSy and Acacia+ solvers (resp., fifth and sixth columns).

The first set of examples (Specifications 1–11) list specifications discussed in this paper and in related works. As parameterized example we consider 2 variants of arbiter specifications. The arbiter has n inputs in which clients request permissions, and n outputs in which the clients are granted permissions. In both variants of the arbiter example, no two grants are allowed to be set simultaneously. The first arbiter example (Specification 12) requires that whenever an input request r_i is set, the corresponding output grant g_i must eventually be set. The second variant (Specification 13) also requires that a grant g_i is set only if request r_i is set as well. That is, in order for a client to be granted a permission, its corresponding request must be constantly set. Since the asynchronous case cannot observe the request in between read events, this variant of the arbiter is not realizable. The results are shown for $n = 2, 4, 6$. Note that the only comparable experimental evaluation is given in [18], where they report that asynchronous synthesis of the first arbiter example (Specification 12) takes over 8 h.

Table 1. BAS asynchronous synthesis runtime evaluation (times in milliseconds). We let BoSy run upto 2 h, and Acacia+ upto 1000 iterations. "Na" denotes cases where the executions did not find a winning strategy within these boundaries.

	Specification	Asyn. Realizable?	PR constr.	Asyn. synthesis	
				BoSy	Acacia+
1	$\Box\,(x \equiv y)$	False	8	972	30
2	$\Diamond\Box x \equiv \Diamond\Box y$	False	9	Na	Na
3	$\Diamond\Box x \Rightarrow \Diamond\Box y$	True	8	899	Na
4	$\Diamond\Box y \Rightarrow \Diamond\Box x$	True	7	994	Na
5	$(\Diamond\Box x \vee \Diamond\Box \neg x) \Rightarrow \Diamond\Box x \equiv \Diamond\Box y$	True	13	1004	Na
6	$\Box\,(\neg x \Rightarrow (\neg x)\;\mathsf{U}\;(\neg y)) \Rightarrow \Diamond\Box x \equiv \Diamond\Box y$	True	10	Na	Na
7	$\Box\Diamond\,(x \wedge y) \Rightarrow (\Box\Diamond y \wedge \Box\Diamond \neg y)$	True	9	1053	30
8	$\Box\Diamond\,(x \vee y) \Rightarrow (\Box\Diamond y \wedge \Box\Diamond \neg y)$	True	9	995	40
9	$\Box\Diamond\,(x) \Rightarrow (\Box\Diamond y \wedge \Box\Diamond \neg y)$	True	8	934	30
10	$\Box\,(x \Rightarrow \Diamond y)$	True	8	960	30
11	$\Box\,(x \Rightarrow \Diamond y) \wedge \Box\,(\neg y\;\mathsf{U}\;x)$	False	10	1058	Na
Variants of parameterized arbiter (results shown are for $n = 2; 4; 6$)					
12	$\bigwedge_{i\neq j} \Box\,(\neg g_i \vee \neg g_j)\quad\wedge$ $\bigwedge_{i=1}^{n} \Box\,(r_i \Rightarrow \Diamond g_i)$	True	11; 13; 75	854; 1146; 4965	Na; Na; Na
13	$\bigwedge_{i\neq j} \Box\,(\neg g_i \vee \neg g_j)\quad\wedge$ $\bigwedge_{i=1}^{n} \Box\,(r_i \Rightarrow \Diamond g_i) \wedge \bigwedge_{i=1}^{n} \Box\,(g_i \Rightarrow r_i)$	False	17; 3124; 2024K	1129; 362K; Na	Na; Na; Na

The second specification φ is the one discussed in Sect. 2. It is surprisingly difficult to solve. Both φ and its negation are asynchronously unrealizable. Moreover, φ is synchronously realizable. Thus, the early detection tests (steps 1 and 3(b)) failed to discover a winning strategy for the environment; the bounded synthesis tools increase the considered bound monotonically without converging to an answer in a reasonable amount of time. This example highlights the need for better tests for unrealizability. The results in the following section provide simple QBF tests of unrealizability for subclasses of LTL.

5   Efficiently Solvable Subclasses of LTL

The high complexity of direct LTL (synchronous) synthesis has encouraged the search for general procedures that work well in practice, such as Safraless and bounded synthesis [24,35]. Another useful direction has been to identify fragments of LTL with efficient synthesis algorithms [5]. Among the most noteworthy is the GR(1) subclass, for which there is an efficient, symbolic synthesis procedure ([28]). We explore this direction for *asynchronous* synthesis. Surprisingly, we show that synthesis for certain fragments of LTL can be reduced to

Boolean reasoning over properties in QBF. The results cover several types of GR(1) formulae, although the question of a reduction for all of GR(1) is open.

The QBF formulae that arise have the form $\exists y \forall x.p(x,y)$, where x and y are disjoint sets of variables, and p is a propositional formula over x, y. An assignment $y = b$ for which $\forall x.p(x,b)$ holds is called a *witness* to the formula. The first such reduction is for the property $\square \lozenge P$.

Theorem 4. $\varphi = \square \lozenge P$ *is asynchronously realizable iff* $\exists y \forall x P$ *is* True.

Proof. (ping) Let b be a witness to $\exists y \forall x.P$. The function that constantly outputs $y = b$ satisfies φ for any asynchronous schedule.

(pong) Let f be a candidate implementation function and suppose that $\forall y \exists x(\neg P)$ holds. Fix any schedule. For every value $y = b$ that function f outputs at a writing point, there exists an input value $x = a$ such that $\neg P(a,b)$ holds. Thus, the environment, by issuing $x = a$ in the interval from the current writing point (with $y = b$) up to the next one, can ensure that $\neg P$ holds throughout the execution. Thus the specification $\varphi = \square \lozenge P$ does not hold on this execution. $\square$

The result in Theorem 4 applies to asynchronous synthesis, but does not apply to synchronous synthesis. For example, the property $\square \lozenge (x \equiv y)$ is asynchronously unrealizable, as $\exists y \forall x(x \equiv y)$ is False. On the other hand, it is synchronously realizable with a Mealy machine that sets y to x at each point.

Theorem 4 extends easily to conjunction and disjunction of $\square \lozenge$ properties.

Theorem 5. *Specification* $\varphi = \bigvee_{i=0}^{m} \square \lozenge P_i$ *is asynchronously realizable iff* $\exists y \forall x.(\bigvee_{i=0}^{m} P_i)$ *holds. Additionally, specification* $\varphi = \bigwedge_{i=0}^{m} \square \lozenge P_i$ *is asynchronously realizable iff for all* $i \in \{0, 1 \ldots m\}$, $\exists y \forall x.P_i$ *holds.*

Proof. The first claim follows directly from the identity $\bigvee_{i=0}^{m} \square \lozenge P_i \equiv \square \lozenge (\bigvee_{i=0}^{m} P_i)$ and Theorem 4.

For the second, for each i, let $y = b_i$ be an assignment such that $\forall x.P_i(x, b_i)$ holds. The function that generates sequence $b_0, b_1, \ldots b_m$, ad infinitum, is an asynchronous implementation of $\bigwedge_{i=0}^{m} \square \lozenge P_i$. On the other hand, suppose that for some i, $\forall y \exists x \neg P_i$ holds, then following the construction from Theorem 4, one can define an execution where P_i is always False. $\square$

Theorem 6. $\varphi = \lozenge \square P$ *is asynchronously realizable iff* $\exists y \forall x.P$ *is* True.

The proof is similar to that for Theorem 4. Theorem 6 also extends to conjunctions and disjunctions of $\lozenge \square$ properties, by arguments similar to those for Theorem 5. Namely, $\bigwedge_{i=0}^{m} \lozenge \square P_i$ is asynchronously realizable iff $\exists y \forall x(\bigwedge_{i=0}^{m} P_i)$ is True, and, $\bigvee_{i=0}^{m} \lozenge \square P_i$ is asynchronously realizable iff for some $i \in \{0, 1, \ldots m\}$, $\exists y \forall x.P_i$ is True. Theorems 4–6 apply to non-atomic reads and writes of multiple input and output variables. Proofs are in the full version of the paper.

We now consider a more general type of GR(1) formula. The *strict semantic* of GR(1) formula $\square S_e \wedge \square \lozenge P \Rightarrow \square S_s \wedge \square \lozenge Q$ is defined to be $\square(\boxminus S_e \Rightarrow S_s) \wedge (\square S_e \wedge \square \lozenge P \Rightarrow \square \lozenge Q)$ – i.e., S_s is required to hold so long as S_e has always held in the past; and if S_e holds always and P holds infinitely often, then Q holds infinitely often. This is the interpretation supported by GR(1) synchronous synthesis tools.

Theorem 7. *The strict semantics of GR(1) specification* $\Box S_e \wedge \Box \Diamond P \Rightarrow \Box S_s \wedge \Box \Diamond Q$ *is asynchronously realizable iff* $\exists y \forall x. (S_e \Rightarrow (S_s \wedge (P \Rightarrow Q)))$ *is* True.

Proof. (ping) If $y = b$ is a witness to $\exists y \forall x. (S_e \Rightarrow (S_s \wedge (P \Rightarrow Q)))$, let f be a function that always generates b. Suppose S_e holds up to point i, then as $y = b$, regardless of the x-value, S_s holds at point i. This shows that the first part of the specification holds. For the second, suppose that S_e holds always and P is true infinitely often. Then, by choice of $y = b$, $(P \Rightarrow Q)$ holds always, thus Q holds infinitely often as well.

(pong) To prove the other side of the implication, we proceed as in Theorem 4. Let f be a candidate implementation. Fix a schedule, and suppose that $\forall y \exists x. (S_e \wedge (\neg S_s \vee \neg (P \Rightarrow Q)))$ holds. Then for every step of the execution and for every value $y = b$ that function f outputs at a writing point, there exists a value $x = a$ which the environment can choose from that writing point to the next such that $S_e(a, b)$ is true, and one of $S_s(a, b)$ or $(P \Rightarrow Q)(a, b)$ is false at every point in that interval.

On this execution, S_e holds throughout. If S_s is false at some point, this violates the first part of the specification. If not, then $(P \Rightarrow Q)$ must be false everywhere; i.e., at every point P is true but Q is false. Thus, S_e holds everywhere and P holds infinitely often but Q does not hold infinitely often, violating the second part of the specification. □

Theorem 7 applies to atomic reads and writes, showing that asynchronous synthesis of GR(1) specification can be reduced to Boolean reasoning over properties in QBF. For non-atomic reads and writes, safety in asynchronous systems is more nuanced, since there is a delay between the write points of the first and last outputs in each round. This is discussed in the full version of the paper. This proof strategy does not generalize easily to the full GR(1) format, where more than one $\Box \Diamond$ property can appear on either side of the implication.

These results establish that the asynchronous synthesis problem for such specifications is easily solvable–more easily than in the synchronous setting, surprisingly avoiding entirely the need for automaton constructions and bounded synthesis. From another, equally valuable, point of view, the results show that such types of specifications may be of limited interest for automated synthesis, as solvable cases have very simple solutions.

6   Conclusions and Related Work

This work tackles the task of asynchronous synthesis from temporal specifications. The main results are a new symbolic automaton construction for general temporal properties, and the reduction of the synthesis question for several classes of specifications to QBF. These are mathematically interesting, being substantial simplifications of prior methods. Moreover, they make it feasible to implement an asynchronous synthesis tool following the modular process suggested by Pnueli and Rosner in 1989, by reducing asynchronous synthesis to a synchronous synthesis question. To the best of our knowledge, this is the first such tool. The prototype, which builds on tools for synchronous synthesis, is able to quickly synthesize asynchronous programs for several interesting properties. There are, undoubtedly, several challenges, one of which is the quick detection of unrealizable specifications.

Our work builds upon several earlier results, which we discuss here. The synthesis question for temporal properties originates from a question posed by Church in the 1950s (see [37]). The problem of synthesizing a synchronous reactive system from a linear temporal specification was formulated and studied by Pnueli and Rosner [31], who gave a solution based on non-emptiness of tree automata. There has been much progress on the synchronous synthesis question since. Key developments include the discovery of efficient symbolic (BDD-based) solutions for the GR(1) class [7,28], the invention of "Safraless" procedures [24], the application of these ideas for bounded synthesis [15,35], and their implementation in a number of tools, e.g. [8,10,11,13,20,34]. These have been applied in many settings (cf. [9,23,25–27]).

The problem of synthesizing asynchronous programs was also formulated and studied by Pnueli and Rosner [32] but has proved to be much more challenging, with only limited progress. The original Pnueli-Rosner constructions are complex and were not implemented. Work by Klein, Piterman and Pnueli, nearly 20 years later [22], shows tractability for some GR(1) specifications. However, the class of specifications that can be so handled is characterized by semantic constraints such as stuttering-closure and memoryless-ness, which are difficult to recognize.

Finkbeiner and Schewe [18,35] present an alternative method, based on bounded synthesis, that applies to all LTL properties: it encodes the existence of a deductive proof for a bounded program into SAT/SMT constraints. However, the encoding represents inputs and outputs explicitly and is, therefore, exponential in the number of input and output bits. The exponential blowup has practical consequences: an asynchronous arbiter specification requires over 8 h to synthesize [18]; the same specification can be synthesized by our method in seconds. (Note, however, that the method in [18] is not specialized to asynchronous synthesis, and this difference may not be solely due to the explicit state representation, as the specification has only 4 bits.) Recent work gives an alternative encoding of synchronous bounded synthesis into QBF constraints, retaining input and output bits in symbolic form [12]. We believe that a similar encoding applies to asynchronous bounded synthesis as well, this is a topic for future work.

Pnueli and Rosner's model of interface communication is not the only choice. Other models for asynchrony could, for instance, be based on CCS/CSP-style rendezvous communication at the interface, or permit shared read-write variables with atomic lock/unlock actions. Petri net game models have also been suggested for distributed synthesis [16]. An orthogonal direction is to weaken the adversarial power of the environment through a probabilistic model which can be used to constrain unlikely, highly adversarial input patterns to have probability 0, thus turning the synthesis problem into one where programs satisfy their specifications with high probability. (The synthesis of multiple processes is known to be undecidable in most cases [17,33].)

In the broader context of fully automatic program synthesis, there are various approaches to the synthesis of single-threaded, terminating programs from formal pre- and post-condition specifications and from examples, using type information and other techniques to prune the search space. (We will not attempt to survey this large field, some examples are [14, 19, 36].) An intriguing question is to investigate how the techniques developed in these distinct lines of work can be fruitfully combined to aid the development of asynchronous, reactive software.

Acknowledgements. Kedar Namjoshi was supported, in part, by NSF grant CCF-1563393 from the National Science Foundation. We would like to thank Michael Emmi for many helpful discussions during the early stages of this work.

References

1. Acacia+. http://lit2.ulb.ac.be/acaciaplus//
2. BoSy. https://www.react.uni-saarland.de/tools/bosy/
3. LTL3BA. https://sourceforge.net/projects/ltl3ba/
4. Alpern, B., Schneider, F.B.: Defining liveness. Inf. Process. Lett. **21**(4), 181–185 (1985)
5. Alur, R., La Torre, S.: Deterministic generators and games for LTL fragments. ACM Trans. Comput. Log. **5**(1), 1–25 (2004)
6. Babiak, T., Křetínský, M., Řehák, V., Strejček, J.: LTL to Büchi automata translation: fast and more deterministic. In: Flanagan, C., König, B. (eds.) TACAS 2012. LNCS, vol. 7214, pp. 95–109. Springer, Heidelberg (2012). https://doi.org/10.1007/978-3-642-28756-5_8
7. Bloem, R., Jobstmann, B., Piterman, N., Pnueli, A., Sa'ar, Y.: Synthesis of reactive (1) designs. J. Comput. Syst. Sci. **78**(3), 911–938 (2012)
8. Bohy, A., Bruyère, V., Filiot, E., Jin, N., Raskin, J.-F.: Acacia+, a tool for LTL synthesis. In: Madhusudan, P., Seshia, S.A. (eds.) CAV 2012. LNCS, vol. 7358, pp. 652–657. Springer, Heidelberg (2012). https://doi.org/10.1007/978-3-642-31424-7_45
9. D'Ippolito, N., Braberman, V., Piterman, N., Uchitel, S.: Synthesizing nonanomalous event-based controllers for liveness goals. Trans. Softw. Eng. Methodol. **22**(1), 9 (2013)
10. Ehlers, R.: Symbolic bounded synthesis. In: Touili, T., Cook, B., Jackson, P. (eds.) CAV 2010. LNCS, vol. 6174, pp. 365–379. Springer, Heidelberg (2010). https://doi.org/10.1007/978-3-642-14295-6_33
11. Ehlers, R.: Unbeast: symbolic bounded synthesis. In: Abdulla, P.A., Leino, K.R.M. (eds.) TACAS 2011. LNCS, vol. 6605, pp. 272–275. Springer, Heidelberg (2011). https://doi.org/10.1007/978-3-642-19835-9_25
12. Faymonville, P., Finkbeiner, B., Rabe, M.N., Tentrup, L.: Encodings of bounded synthesis. In: Legay, A., Margaria, T. (eds.) TACAS 2017. LNCS, vol. 10205, pp. 354–370. Springer, Heidelberg (2017). https://doi.org/10.1007/978-3-662-54577-5_20
13. Faymonville, P., Finkbeiner, B., Tentrup, L.: BoSy: an experimentation framework for bounded synthesis. In: Majumdar, R., Kunčak, V. (eds.) CAV 2017. LNCS, vol. 10427, pp. 325–332. Springer, Cham (2017). https://doi.org/10.1007/978-3-319-63390-9_17

14. Feng, Y., Martins, R., Wang, Y., Dillig, I., Reps, T.W.: Component-based synthesis for complex APIs. In: Castagna, G., Gordon, A.D. (eds.) Proceedings of the 44th ACM SIGPLAN Symposium on Principles of Programming Languages, POPL 2017, Paris, France, 18–20 January 2017, pp. 599–612. ACM (2017)

15. Filiot, E., Jin, N., Raskin, J.-F.: Compositional algorithms for LTL synthesis. In: Bouajjani, A., Chin, W.-N. (eds.) ATVA 2010. LNCS, vol. 6252, pp. 112–127. Springer, Heidelberg (2010). https://doi.org/10.1007/978-3-642-15643-4_10

16. Finkbeiner, B., Olderog, E.-R.: Petri games: synthesis of distributed systems with causal memory. Inf. Comput. **253**, 181–203 (2017)

17. Finkbeiner, B., Schewe, S.: Uniform distributed synthesis. In: 20th IEEE Symposium on Logic in Computer Science (LICS 2005), 26–29 June 2005, Chicago, IL, USA, Proceedings, pp. 321–330. IEEE Computer Society (2005)

18. Finkbeiner, B., Schewe, S.: Bounded synthesis. STTT **15**(5–6), 519–539 (2013)

19. Frankle, J., Osera, P.M., Walker, D., Zdancewic, S.: Example-directed synthesis: a type-theoretic interpretation. In: Bodík, R., Majumdar, R. (eds.) Proceedings of the 43rd Annual ACM SIGPLAN-SIGACT Symposium on Principles of Programming Languages, POPL 2016, St. Petersburg, FL, USA, 20–22 January 2016, pp. 802–815. ACM (2016)

20. Jobstmann, B., Bloem, R.: Optimizations for LTL synthesis. In: 6th International Conference on Formal Methods in Computer-Aided Design, FMCAD 2006, San Jose, California, USA, 12–16 November 2006, Proceedings, pp. 117–124. IEEE Computer Society (2006)

21. Klein, U.: Topics in Formal Synthesis and Modeling. Ph.D. thesis, New York University (2011)

22. Klein, U., Piterman, N., Pnueli, A.: Effective synthesis of asynchronous systems from GR(1) specifications. In: Kuncak, V., Rybalchenko, A. (eds.) VMCAI 2012. LNCS, vol. 7148, pp. 283–298. Springer, Heidelberg (2012). https://doi.org/10.1007/978-3-642-27940-9_19

23. Kress-Gazit, H., Pappas, G.J.: Automatic synthesis of robot controllers for tasks with locative prepositions. In: International Conference on Robotics and Automation (ICRA), pp. 3215–3220 (2010)

24. Kupferman, O., Vardi, M.Y.: Safraless decision procedures. In: Proceedings of FOCS, pp. 531–540. IEEE (2005)

25. Liu, J., Ozay, N., Topcu, U., Murray, R.M.: Synthesis of reactive switching protocols from temporal logic specifications. IEEE Trans. Autom. Control **58**(7), 1771–1785 (2013)

26. Maoz, S., Sa'ar, Y.: AspectLTL: an aspect language for LTL specifications. In: Borba, P., Chiba, S. (eds.) Proceedings of the 10th International Conference on Aspect-Oriented Software Development, AOSD 2011, Porto de Galinhas, Brazil, 21–25 March 2011, pp. 19–30. ACM (2011)

27. Maoz, S., Sa'ar, Y.: Assume-guarantee scenarios: semantics and synthesis. In: France, R.B., Kazmeier, J., Breu, R., Atkinson, C. (eds.) MODELS 2012. LNCS, vol. 7590, pp. 335–351. Springer, Heidelberg (2012). https://doi.org/10.1007/978-3-642-33666-9_22

28. Piterman, N., Pnueli, A., Sa'ar, Y.: Synthesis of reactive(1) designs. In: Emerson, E.A., Namjoshi, K.S. (eds.) VMCAI 2006. LNCS, vol. 3855, pp. 364–380. Springer, Heidelberg (2005). https://doi.org/10.1007/11609773_24

29. Pnueli, A.: The temporal logic of programs. In: Proceedings of FOCS, pp. 46–57. IEEE (1977)

30. Pnueli, A., Klein, U.: Synthesis of programs from temporal property specifications. In: 2009 7th IEEE/ACM International Conference on Formal Methods and Models for Co-Design, MEMOCODE 2009, pp. 1–7. IEEE (2009)
31. Pnueli, A., Rosner, R.: On the synthesis of a reactive module. In: POPL, pp. 179–190 (1989)
32. Pnueli, A., Rosner, R.: On the synthesis of an asynchronous reactive module. In: Ausiello, G., Dezani-Ciancaglini, M., Della Rocca, S.R. (eds.) ICALP 1989. LNCS, vol. 372, pp. 652–671. Springer, Heidelberg (1989). https://doi.org/10.1007/BFb0035790
33. Pneuli, A., Rosner, R.: Distributed reactive systems are hard to synthesize. In: 31st Annual Symposium on Foundations of Computer Science, St. Louis, Missouri, USA, 22–24 October 1990, vol. II, pp. 746–757. IEEE Computer Society (1990)
34. Pnueli, A., Sa'ar, Y., Zuck, L.D.: JTLV: a framework for developing verification algorithms. In: Touili, T., Cook, B., Jackson, P. (eds.) CAV 2010. LNCS, vol. 6174, pp. 171–174. Springer, Heidelberg (2010). https://doi.org/10.1007/978-3-642-14295-6_18
35. Schewe, S., Finkbeiner, B.: Bounded synthesis. In: Namjoshi, K.S., Yoneda, T., Higashino, T., Okamura, Y. (eds.) ATVA 2007. LNCS, vol. 4762, pp. 474–488. Springer, Heidelberg (2007). https://doi.org/10.1007/978-3-540-75596-8_33
36. Srivastava, S., Gulwani, S., Foster, J.S.: From program verification to program synthesis. In: Hermenegildo, M.V., Palsberg, J. (eds.) Proceedings of the 37th ACM SIGPLAN-SIGACT Symposium on Principles of Programming Languages, POPL 2010, Madrid, Spain, 17–23 January 2010, pp. 313–326. ACM (2010)
37. Thomas, W.: Facets of synthesis: revisiting Church's problem. In: de Alfaro, L. (ed.) FoSSaCS 2009. LNCS, vol. 5504, pp. 1–14. Springer, Heidelberg (2009). https://doi.org/10.1007/978-3-642-00596-1_1

8

Learning Abstractions for Program Synthesis

Xinyu Wang[1]([⊠]), Greg Anderson[1]([⊠]), Isil Dillig[1]([⊠]), and K. L. McMillan[2]([⊠])

[1] University of Texas, Austin, USA
{xwang,ganderso,isil}@cs.utexas.edu
[2] Microsoft Research, Redmond, USA
kenmcmil@microsoft.com

Abstract. Many example-guided program synthesis techniques use *abstractions* to prune the search space. While abstraction-based synthesis has proven to be very powerful, a domain expert needs to provide a suitable abstract domain, together with the abstract transformers of each DSL construct. However, coming up with useful abstractions can be non-trivial, as it requires both domain expertise and knowledge about the synthesizer. In this paper, we propose a new technique for learning abstractions that are useful for instantiating a general synthesis framework in a new domain. Given a DSL and a small set of training problems, our method uses *tree interpolation* to infer reusable predicate templates that speed up synthesis in a given domain. Our method also learns suitable abstract transformers by solving a certain kind of second-order constraint solving problem in a data-driven way. We have implemented the proposed method in a tool called ATLAS and evaluate it in the context of the BLAZE meta-synthesizer. Our evaluation shows that (a) ATLAS can learn useful abstract domains and transformers from few training problems, and (b) the abstractions learned by ATLAS allow BLAZE to achieve significantly better results compared to manually-crafted abstractions.

1 Introduction

Program synthesis is a powerful technique for automatically generating programs from high-level specifications, such as input-output examples. Due to its myriad use cases across a wide range of application domains (e.g., spreadsheet automation [1–3], data science [4–6], cryptography [7,8], improving programming productivity [9–11]), program synthesis has received widespread attention from the research community in recent years.

Because program synthesis is, in essence, a very difficult search problem, many recent solutions prune the search space by utilizing *program abstractions* [4,12–16]. For example, state-of-the-art synthesis tools, such as BLAZE [14], MORPHEUS [4] and Scythe [16], symbolically execute (partial) programs over some abstract domain and reject those programs whose abstract behavior is inconsistent with the given specification. Because many programs share the same behavior in terms of their abstract semantics, the use of abstractions allows these synthesis tools to significantly reduce the search space.

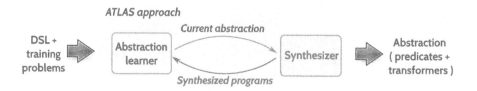

Fig. 1. Schematic overview of our approach.

While the abstraction-guided synthesis paradigm has proven to be quite powerful, a down-side of such techniques is that they require a domain expert to manually come up with a suitable abstract domain and write abstract transformers for each DSL construct. For instance, the BLAZE synthesis framework [14] expects a domain expert to manually specify a universe of predicate templates, together with sound abstract transformers for every DSL construct. Unfortunately, this process is not only time-consuming but also requires significant insight about the application domain as well as the internal workings of the synthesizer.

In this paper, we propose a novel technique for automatically learning domain-specific abstractions that are useful for instantiating an example-guided synthesis framework in a new domain. Given a DSL and a training set of synthesis problems (i.e., input-output examples), our method learns a useful abstract domain in the form of predicate templates and infers sound abstract transformers for each DSL construct. In addition to eliminating the significant manual effort required from a domain expert, the abstractions learned by our method often outperform manually-crafted ones in terms of their benefit to synthesizer performance.

The workflow of our approach, henceforth called ATLAS[1], is shown schematically in Fig. 1. Since ATLAS is meant to be used as an *off-line* training step for a general-purpose programming-by-example (PBE) system, it takes as input a DSL as well as a set of synthesis problems $\mathcal{E}$ that can be used for training purposes. Given these inputs, our method enters a refinement loop where an *Abstraction Learner* component discovers a sequence of increasingly precise abstract domains $\mathcal{A}_1, \cdots, \mathcal{A}_n$, and their corresponding abstract transformers $\mathcal{T}_1, \cdots, \mathcal{T}_n$, in order to help the *Abstraction-Guided Synthesizer* (AGS) solve all training problems. While the AGS can reject many incorrect solutions using an abstract domain $\mathcal{A}_i$, it might still return some incorrect solutions due to the insufficiency of $\mathcal{A}_i$. Thus, whenever the AGS returns an incorrect solution to any training problem, the Abstraction Learner discovers a more precise abstract domain and automatically synthesizes the corresponding abstract transformers. Upon termination of the algorithm, the final abstract domain $\mathcal{A}_n$ and transformers $\mathcal{T}_n$ are sufficient for the AGS to correctly solve *all* training problems. Furthermore, because our method learns *general* abstractions in the form of

---

[1] ATLAS stands for AuTomated Learning of AbStractions.

predicate templates, the learned abstractions are expected to be useful for solving many *other* synthesis problems beyond those in the training set.

From a technical perspective, the Abstraction Learner uses two key ideas, namely *tree interpolation* and *data-driven constraint solving*, for learning useful abstract domains and transformers respectively. Specifically, given an incorrect program $\mathcal{P}$ that cannot be refuted by the AGS using the current abstract domain $\mathcal{A}_i$, the Abstraction Learner generates a tree interpolant $\mathcal{I}_i$ that serves as a proof of $\mathcal{P}$'s incorrectness and constructs a new abstract domain $\mathcal{A}_{i+1}$ by extracting templates from the predicates used in $\mathcal{I}_i$. The Abstraction Learner also synthesizes the corresponding abstract transformers for $\mathcal{A}_{i+1}$ by setting up a *second-order constraint solving* problem where the goal is to find the unknown relationship between symbolic constants used in the predicate templates. Our method solves this problem in a data-driven way by sampling input-output examples for DSL operators and ultimately reduces the transformer learning problem to solving a system of linear equations.

We have implemented these ideas in a tool called ATLAS and evaluate it in the context of the BLAZE program synthesis framework [14]. Our evaluation shows that the proposed technique eliminates the manual effort involved in designing useful abstractions. More surprisingly, our evaluation also shows that the abstractions generated by ATLAS outperform manually-crafted ones in terms of the performance of the BLAZE synthesizer in two different application domains.

To summarize, this paper makes the following key contributions:

- We describe a method for learning abstractions (domains/transformers) that are useful for instantiating program synthesis frameworks in new domains.
- We show how tree interpolation can be used for learning abstract domains (i.e., predicate templates) from a few training problems.
- We describe a method for automatically synthesizing transformers for a given abstract domain under certain assumptions. Our method is guaranteed to find the unique best transformer if one exists.
- We implement our method in a tool called ATLAS and experimentally evaluate it in the context of the BLAZE synthesis framework. Our results demonstrate that the abstractions discovered by ATLAS outperform manually-written ones used for evaluating BLAZE in two application domains.

2   Illustrative Example

Suppose that we wish to use the BLAZE meta-synthesizer to automate the class of string transformations considered by FlashFill [1] and BlinkFill [17]. In the original version of the BLAZE framework [14], a domain expert needs to come up with a universe of suitable predicate templates as well as abstract transformers for each DSL construct. We will now illustrate how ATLAS automates this process, given a suitable DSL and its semantics (e.g., the one used in [17]).

In order to use ATLAS, one needs to provide a set of synthesis problems $\mathcal{E}$ (i.e., input-output examples) that will be used in the training process. Specifically, let us consider the three synthesis problems given below:

$$\mathcal{E} = \left\{ \begin{array}{ll} \mathcal{E}_1 : \left\{ \text{ "CAV"} \mapsto \text{"CAV2018", "SAS"} \mapsto \text{"SAS2018", "FSE"} \mapsto \text{"FSE2018" } \right\}, \\ \mathcal{E}_2 : \left\{ \text{ "510.220.5586"} \mapsto \text{"510-220-5586" } \right\}, \\ \mathcal{E}_3 : \left\{ \begin{array}{l} \text{"\textbackslash Company\textbackslash Code\textbackslash index.html"} \mapsto \text{"\textbackslash Company\textbackslash Code\textbackslash ",} \\ \text{"\textbackslash Company\textbackslash Docs\textbackslash Spec\textbackslash specs.html"} \mapsto \text{"\textbackslash Company\textbackslash Docs\textbackslash Spec\textbackslash "} \end{array} \right\} \end{array} \right\}.$$

In order to construct the abstract domain $\mathcal{A}$ and transformers $\mathcal{T}$, ATLAS starts with the trivial abstract domain $\mathcal{A}_0 = \{\top\}$ and transformers $\mathcal{T}_0$, defined as $[\![F(\top, \cdots, \top)]\!]^{\sharp} = \top$ for each DSL construct F. Using this abstraction, ATLAS invokes BLAZE to find a program $\mathcal{P}_0$ that satisfies specification $\mathcal{E}_1$ under the current abstraction $(\mathcal{A}_0, \mathcal{T}_0)$. However, since the program $\mathcal{P}_0$ returned by BLAZE is incorrect with respect to the concrete semantics, ATLAS tries to find a more precise abstraction that allows BLAZE to succeed.

Towards this goal, ATLAS enters a refinement loop that culminates in the discovery of the abstract domain $\mathcal{A}_1 = \{\top, len(\boxed{\alpha}) = \mathsf{c}, len(\boxed{\alpha}) \neq \mathsf{c}\}$, where α denotes a variable and c is an integer constant. In other words, $\mathcal{A}_1$ tracks equality and inequality constraints on the length of strings. After learning these predicate templates, ATLAS also synthesizes the corresponding abstract transformers $\mathcal{T}_1$. In particular, for each DSL construct, ATLAS learns one abstract transformer for each combination of predicate templates used in $\mathcal{A}_1$. For instance, for the Concat operator which returns the concatenation y of two strings x_1, x_2, ATLAS synthesizes the following abstract transformers, where $\star$ denotes any predicate:

$$\mathcal{T}_1 = \left\{ \begin{array}{l} [\![\text{Concat}(\top, \star)]\!]^{\sharp} = \top \\ [\![\text{Concat}(\star, \top)]\!]^{\sharp} = \top \\ [\![\text{Concat}(len(x_1) \neq \mathsf{c}_1, len(x_2) \neq \mathsf{c}_2)]\!]^{\sharp} = \top \\ [\![\text{Concat}(len(x_1) = \mathsf{c}_1, len(x_2) = \mathsf{c}_2)]\!]^{\sharp} = (len(y) = \mathsf{c}_1 + \mathsf{c}_2) \\ [\![\text{Concat}(len(x_1) = \mathsf{c}_1, len(x_2) \neq \mathsf{c}_2)]\!]^{\sharp} = (len(y) \neq \mathsf{c}_1 + \mathsf{c}_2) \\ [\![\text{Concat}(len(x_1) \neq \mathsf{c}_1, len(x_2) = \mathsf{c}_2)]\!]^{\sharp} = (len(y) \neq \mathsf{c}_1 + \mathsf{c}_2) \end{array} \right\}.$$

Since the AGS can successfully solve $\mathcal{E}_1$ using $(\mathcal{A}_1, \mathcal{T}_1)$, ATLAS now moves on to the next training problem.

For synthesis problem $\mathcal{E}_2$, the current abstraction $(\mathcal{A}_1, \mathcal{T}_1)$ is *not* sufficient for BLAZE to discover the correct program. After processing $\mathcal{E}_2$, ATLAS refines the abstract domain to the following set of predicate templates:

$$\mathcal{A}_2 = \left\{ \top, len(\boxed{\alpha}) = \mathsf{c}, len(\boxed{\alpha}) \neq \mathsf{c}, charAt(\boxed{\alpha}, \mathtt{i}) = \mathsf{c}, charAt(\boxed{\alpha}, \mathtt{i}) \neq \mathsf{c} \right\}.$$

Observe that ATLAS has discovered two additional predicate templates that track positions of characters in the string. ATLAS also learns the corresponding abstract transformers $\mathcal{T}_2$ for $\mathcal{A}_2$.

Moving on to the final training problem $\mathcal{E}_3$, BLAZE can already successfully solve it using $(\mathcal{A}_2, \mathcal{T}_2)$; thus, ATLAS terminates with this abstraction.

3 Overall Abstraction Learning Algorithm

Our top-level algorithm for learning abstractions, called LEARNABSTRACTIONS, is shown in Fig. 2. The algorithm takes two inputs, namely a domain-specific

```
1: procedure LEARNABSTRACTIONS(L, E)
   input: Domain-specific language L and a set of training problems E.
   output: Abstract domain A and transformers T.

2:     A ← { ⊤ };                                              ▷ Initialization.
3:     T ← { [[F(⊤, ··, ⊤)]]♯ = ⊤ | F ∈ Constructs(L) };
4:     for i ← 1, ··, |E| do
5:         while true do                                       ▷ Refinement loop.
6:             P ← Synthesize(L, Eᵢ, A, T);                    ▷ Invoke AGS.
7:             if P = null then break;
8:             if IsCorrect(P, Eᵢ) then break;
9:             A ← A ∪ LEARNABSTRACTDOMAIN(P, Eᵢ);
10:            T ← LEARNTRANSFORMERS(L, A);

11:    return (A, T);
```

Fig. 2. Overall learning algorithm. Constructs gives the DSL constructs in $\mathcal{L}$.

language $\mathcal{L}$ (both syntax and semantics) as well as a set of training problems $\mathcal{E}$, where each problem is specified as a *set* of input-output examples $\mathcal{E}_i$. The output of our algorithm is a pair $(\mathcal{A}, \mathcal{T})$, where $\mathcal{A}$ is an abstract domain represented by a set of predicate templates and $\mathcal{T}$ is the corresponding abstract transformers.

At a high-level, the LEARNABSTRACTIONS procedure starts with the most imprecise abstraction (just consisting of ⊤) and incrementally improves the precision of the abstract domain $\mathcal{A}$ whenever the AGS fails to synthesize the correct program using $\mathcal{A}$. Specifically, the outer loop (lines 4–10) considers each training instance $\mathcal{E}_i$ and performs a fixed-point computation (lines 5–10) that terminates when the current abstract domain $\mathcal{A}$ is good enough to solve problem $\mathcal{E}_i$. Thus, upon termination, the learned abstract domain $\mathcal{A}$ is sufficiently precise for the AGS to solve all training problems $\mathcal{E}$.

Specifically, in order to find an abstraction that is sufficient for solving $\mathcal{E}_i$, our algorithm invokes the AGS with the current abstract domain $\mathcal{A}$ and corresponding transformers $\mathcal{T}$ (line 6). We assume that Synthesize returns a program $\mathcal{P}$ that is consistent with $\mathcal{E}_i$ under abstraction $(\mathcal{A}, \mathcal{T})$. That is, symbolically executing $\mathcal{P}$ (according to $\mathcal{T}$) on inputs $\mathcal{E}_i^{in}$ yields abstract values φ that are consistent with the outputs $\mathcal{E}_i^{out}$ (i.e., $\forall j.\ \mathcal{E}_{ij}^{out} \in \gamma(\varphi_j)$). However, while $\mathcal{P}$ is guaranteed to be consistent with $\mathcal{E}_i$ under the abstract semantics, it may not satisfy $\mathcal{E}_i$ under the concrete semantics. We refer to such a program $\mathcal{P}$ as *spurious*.

Thus, whenever the call to IsCorrect fails at line 8, we invoke the LEARNAB-STRACTDOMAIN procedure (line 9) to learn additional predicate templates that are later added to $\mathcal{A}$. Since the refinement of $\mathcal{A}$ necessitates the synthesis of new transformers, we then call LEARNTRANSFORMERS (line 10) to learn a new $\mathcal{T}$. The new abstraction is guaranteed to rule out the spurious program $\mathcal{P}$ as long as there is a unique best transformer of each DSL construct for domain $\mathcal{A}$.

4 Learning Abstract Domain Using Tree Interpolation

In this section, we present the LEARNABSTRACTDOMAIN procedure: Given a spurious program $\mathcal{P}$ and a synthesis problem $\mathcal{E}$ that $\mathcal{P}$ does not solve, our goal is to find new predicate templates $\mathcal{A}'$ to add to the abstract domain $\mathcal{A}$ such that the Abstraction-Guided Synthesizer no longer returns $\mathcal{P}$ as a valid solution to the synthesis problem $\mathcal{E}$. Our key insight is that we can mine for such useful predicate templates by constructing a *tree interpolation* problem. In what follows, we first review tree interpolants (based on [18]) and then explain how we use this concept to find useful predicate templates.

Definition 1 (Tree interpolation problem). *A tree interpolation problem $T = (V, r, P, L)$ is a directed labeled tree, where V is a finite set of nodes, $r \in V$ is the root, $P : (V \backslash \{r\}) \mapsto V$ is a function that maps children nodes to their parents, and $L : V \mapsto \mathbb{F}$ is a labeling function that maps nodes to formulas from a set $\mathbb{F}$ of first-order formulas such that $\bigwedge_{v \in V} L(v)$ is unsatisfiable.*

In other words, a tree interpolation problem is defined by a tree T where each node is labeled with a formula and the conjunction of these formulas is unsatisfiable. In what follows, we write $Desc(v)$ to denote the set of all descendants of node v, including v itself, and we write $NonDesc(v)$ to denote all nodes other than those in $Desc(v)$ (i.e., $V \backslash Desc(v)$). Also, given a set of nodes V', we write $L(V')$ to denote the set of all formulas labeling nodes in V'.

Given a tree interpolation problem T, a *tree interpolant* $\mathcal{I}$ is an annotation from every node in V to a formula such that the label of the root node is *false* and the label of an internal node v is entailed by the conjunction of annotations of its children nodes. More formally, a tree interpolant is defined as follows:

Definition 2 (Tree interpolant). *Given a tree interpolation problem $T = (V, r, P, L)$, a tree interpolant for T is a function $\mathcal{I} : V \mapsto \mathbb{F}$ that satisfies the following conditions:*

1. *$\mathcal{I}(r) = \text{false}$;*
2. *For each $v \in V$: $\left(\left(\bigwedge_{P(c_i)=v} \mathcal{I}(c_i) \right) \wedge L(v) \right) \Rightarrow \mathcal{I}(v)$;*
3. *For each $v \in V$: $Vars\big(\mathcal{I}(v)\big) \subseteq Vars\big(L(Desc(v))\big) \bigcap Vars\big(L(NonDesc(v))\big)$.*

Intuitively, the first condition ensures that $\mathcal{I}$ establishes the unsatisfiability of formulas in T, and the second condition states that $\mathcal{I}$ is a valid annotation. As standard in Craig interpolation [19,20], the third condition stipulates a "shared vocabulary" condition by ensuring that the annotation at each node v refers to the common variables between the descendants and non-descendants of v.

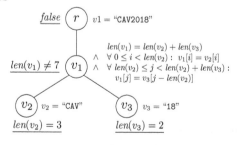

Fig. 3. A tree interpolation problem and a tree interpolant (underlined).

```
1: procedure LEARNABSTRACTDOMAIN(P, E)
     input: Program P that does not solve problem E (set of examples).
     output: Set of predicate templates A'.
2:     A' ← ∅;
3:     for each (e_in, e_out) ∈ E do
4:         if [[P]]e_in ≠ e_out then
5:             T ← CONSTRUCTTREE(P, e_in, e_out);
6:             I ← FindTreeItp(T);
7:             for each v ∈ Nodes(T)\{r} do
8:                 A' ← A' ∪ {MakeSymbolic(I(v))};
9:     return A';
```

Fig. 4. Algorithm for learning abstract domain using tree interpolation.

Example 1. Consider the tree interpolation problem $T = (V, r, P, L)$ in Fig. 3, where $L(v)$ is shown to the right of each node v. A tree interpolant I for this problem maps each node to the corresponding underlined formula. For instance, we have $I(v_1) = (len(v_1) \neq 7)$. It is easy to confirm that I is a valid interpolant according to Definition 2.

To see how tree interpolation is useful for learning predicates, suppose that the spurious program P is represented as an abstract syntax tree (AST), where each non-leaf node is labeled with the axiomatic semantics of the corresponding DSL construct. Now, since P does not satisfy the given input-output example (e_{in}, e_{out}), we are able to use this information to construct a labeled tree where the conjunction of labels is unsatisfiable. Our key idea is to mine useful predicate templates from the formulas used in the resulting tree interpolant.

With this intuition in mind, let us consider the LEARNABSTRACTDOMAIN procedure shown in Fig. 4: The algorithm uses a procedure called CONSTRUCT-TREE to generate a tree interpolation problem T for each input-output example (e_{in}, e_{out})[2] that program P does not satisfy (line 5). Specifically, letting Π denote the AST representation of P, we construct $T = (V, r, P, L)$ as follows:

- V consists of all AST nodes in Π as well as a "dummy" node d.
- The root r of T is the dummy node d.
- P is a function that maps children AST nodes to their parents and maps the root AST node to the dummy node d.
- L maps each node $v \in V$ to a formula as follows:

$$
L(v) = \begin{cases}
v' = e_{out} & v \text{ is the dummy root node with child } v'. \\
v = e_{in} & v \text{ is a leaf representing program input } e_{in}. \\
v = c & v \text{ is a leaf representing constant } c. \\
\phi_F[\boldsymbol{v'}/\boldsymbol{x}, v/y] & v \text{ represents DSL operator } F \text{ with axiomatic semantics} \\
& \phi_F(\boldsymbol{x}, y) \text{ and } \boldsymbol{v'} \text{ represents children of } v.
\end{cases}
$$

---

[2] Without loss of generality, we assume that programs take a single input x, as we can always represent multiple inputs as a list.

Essentially, the CONSTRUCTTREE procedure labels any leaf node representing the program input with the input example e_{in} and the root node with the output example e_{out}. All other internal nodes are labeled with the axiomatic semantics of the corresponding DSL operator (modulo renaming).[3] Observe that the formula $\bigwedge_{v \in V} L(v)$ is guaranteed to be unsatisfiable since $\mathcal{P}$ does not satisfy the I/O example (e_{in}, e_{out}); thus, we can obtain a tree interpolant for T.

Example 2. Consider program $\mathcal{P} :$ Concat$(x,$ "18"$)$ which concatenates constant string "18" to input x. Figure 3 shows the result of invoking CONSTRUCTTREE for $\mathcal{P}$ and input-output example ("CAV", "CAV2018"). As mentioned in Example 1, the tree interpolant $\mathcal{I}$ for this problem is indicated with the underlined formulas.

Since the tree interpolant $\mathcal{I}$ effectively establishes the incorrectness of program $\mathcal{P}$, the predicates used in $\mathcal{I}$ serve as useful abstract values that the synthesizer (AGS) should consider during the synthesis task. Towards this goal, the LEARNABSTRACTDOMAIN algorithm iterates over each predicate used in $\mathcal{I}$ (lines 7–8 in Fig. 4) and converts it to a suitable template by replacing the constants and variables used in $\mathcal{I}(v)$ with symbolic names (or "holes"). Because the original predicates used in $\mathcal{I}$ may be too specific for the current input-output example, extracting templates from the interpolant allows our method to learn reusable abstract domains.

Example 3. Given the tree interpolant $\mathcal{I}$ from Example 1, LEARNABSTRACTDO-MAIN extracts two predicate templates, namely, $len(\boxed{\alpha}) = $ c and $len(\boxed{\alpha}) \neq$ c.

5 Synthesis of Abstract Transformers

In this section, we turn our attention to the LEARNTRANSFORMERS procedure for synthesizing abstract transformers $\mathcal{T}$ for a given abstract domain $\mathcal{A}$. Following presentation in prior work [14], we consider abstract transformers that are described using equations of the following form:

$$[\![F(\chi_1(x_1, \boldsymbol{c}_1), \cdots, \chi_n(x_n, \boldsymbol{c}_n))]\!]^{\sharp} = \bigwedge_{1 \leq j \leq m} \chi'_j(y, \boldsymbol{f}_j(\boldsymbol{c})) \tag{1}$$

Here, F is a DSL construct, χ_i, χ'_j are predicate templates[4], x_i is the i'th input of F, y is F's output, $\boldsymbol{c}_1, \cdots, \boldsymbol{c}_n$ are vectors of *symbolic* constants, and $\boldsymbol{f}_j$ denotes a vector of *affine functions* over $\boldsymbol{c} = \boldsymbol{c}_1, \cdots, \boldsymbol{c}_n$. Intuitively, given concrete predicates describing the inputs to F, the transformer returns concrete predicates describing the output. Given such a transformer τ, let Outputs(τ) be the set of pairs $(\chi'_j, \boldsymbol{f}_j)$ in Eq. 1.

---

[3] Here, we assume access to the DSL's axiomatic semantics. If this is not the case (i.e., we are only given the DSL's operational semantics), we can still annotate each node as $v = c$ where c denotes the output of the partial program rooted at node v when executed on e_{in}. However, this may affect the quality of the resulting interpolant.

[4] We assume that $\chi'_1, \cdots, \chi'_m$ are distinct.

```
1: procedure LearnTransformers(L, A)
   input: DSL L and abstract domain A.
   output: A set of transformers T for constructs in L and abstract domain A.
2:    for each F ∈ Constructs(L) do
3:       for (χ₁, ··, χₙ) ∈ Aⁿ do
4:          φ ← ⊤;                                    ▷ φ is output of transformer.
5:          for χ'ⱼ ∈ A do
6:             E ← GenerateExamples(φ_F, χ'ⱼ, χ₁, ··, χₙ);
7:             fⱼ ← Solve(E);
8:             if fⱼ ≠ null ∧ Valid(Λ[fⱼ]) then φ ← (φ ∧ χ'ⱼ(y, fⱼ(c₁, ··, cₙ)))

9:          T ← T ∪ {[[F(χ₁(x₁, c₁), ··, χₙ(xₙ, cₙ))]]♯ = φ};
10:   return T;
```

Fig. 5. Algorithm for synthesizing abstract transformers. ϕ_F at line 6 denotes the axiomatic semantics of DSL construct F. Formula Λ at line 8 refers to Eq. 5.

We define the soundness of a transformer τ for DSL operator F with respect to F's axiomatic semantics ϕ_F. In particular, we say that the abstract transformer from Eq. 1 is *sound* if the following implication is valid:

$$\left(\phi_F(\boldsymbol{x}, y) \wedge \bigwedge_{1 \le i \le n} \chi_i(x_i, \boldsymbol{c}_i)\right) \Rightarrow \bigwedge_{1 \le j \le m} \chi'_j(y, \boldsymbol{f}_j(\boldsymbol{c})) \tag{2}$$

That is, the transformer for F is sound if the (symbolic) output predicate is indeed implied by the (symbolic) input predicates according to F's semantics.

Our key observation is that the problem of learning sound transformers can be reduced to solving the following *second-order constraint solving* problem:

$$\exists \boldsymbol{f}. \forall \boldsymbol{V}. \left(\left(\phi_F(\boldsymbol{x}, y) \wedge \bigwedge_{1 \le i \le n} \chi_i(x_i, \boldsymbol{c}_i)\right) \Rightarrow \bigwedge_{1 \le j \le m} \chi'_j(y, \boldsymbol{f}_j(\boldsymbol{c}))\right) \tag{3}$$

where $\boldsymbol{f} = \boldsymbol{f}_1, ··, \boldsymbol{f}_m$ and $\boldsymbol{V}$ includes all variables and functions from Eq. 2 other than $\boldsymbol{f}$. In other words, the goal of this constraint solving problem is to find interpretations of the unknown functions $\boldsymbol{f}$ that make Eq. 2 valid. Our key insight is to solve this problem in a *data-driven* way by exploiting the fact that each unknown function $f_{j,k}$ is affine.

Towards this goal, we first express each affine function $f_{j,k}(\boldsymbol{c})$ as follows:

$$f_{j,k}(\boldsymbol{c}) = p_{j,k,1} \cdot c_1 + ·· + p_{j,k,|\boldsymbol{c}|} \cdot c_{|\boldsymbol{c}|} + p_{j,k,|\boldsymbol{c}|+1}$$

where each $p_{j,k,l}$ corresponds to an unknown integer constant that we would like to learn. Now, arranging the coefficients of functions $f_{j,1}, ··, f_{j,|\boldsymbol{f}_j|}$ in $\boldsymbol{f}_j$ into a $|\boldsymbol{f}_j| \times (|\boldsymbol{c}| + 1)$ matrix P_j, we can represent $\boldsymbol{f}_j(\boldsymbol{c})$ in the following way:

$$\boldsymbol{f}_j(\boldsymbol{c})^{\mathsf{T}} = \underbrace{\begin{bmatrix} f_{j,1}(\boldsymbol{c}) \\ \cdot\cdot \\ f_{j,|\boldsymbol{f}_j|}(\boldsymbol{c}) \end{bmatrix}}_{\boldsymbol{c}_j'^{\mathsf{T}}} = \underbrace{\begin{bmatrix} p_{j,1,1} & \cdot\cdot & p_{j,1,|\boldsymbol{c}|+1} \\ \cdot\cdot & & \cdot\cdot \\ p_{j,|\boldsymbol{f}_j|,1} & \cdot\cdot & p_{j,|\boldsymbol{f}_j|,|\boldsymbol{c}|+1} \end{bmatrix}}_{P_j} \underbrace{\begin{bmatrix} c_1 \\ \cdot\cdot \\ c_{|\boldsymbol{c}|} \\ 1 \end{bmatrix}}_{\boldsymbol{c}^\dagger} \tag{4}$$

where $\boldsymbol{c}^\dagger$ is $\boldsymbol{c}^{\mathsf{T}}$ appended with the constant 1.

Given this representation, it is easy to see that the problem of synthesizing the unknown functions $\boldsymbol{f}_1, \cdots, \boldsymbol{f}_m$ from Eq. 2 boils down to finding the unknown matrices $P_1, \cdots, P_m$ such that each P_j makes the following implication valid:

$$\Lambda \equiv \left(\left((\boldsymbol{c}_j'^{\mathsf{T}} = P_j \boldsymbol{c}^\dagger) \wedge \phi_F(\boldsymbol{x}, y) \wedge \bigwedge_{1 \leq i \leq n} \chi_i(x_i, \boldsymbol{c}_i) \right) \Rightarrow \chi_j'(y, \boldsymbol{c}_j') \right) \tag{5}$$

Our key idea is to infer these unknown matrices $P_1, \cdots, P_m$ in a data-driven way by generating input-output examples of the form $[i_1, \cdots, i_{|\boldsymbol{c}|}] \mapsto [o_1, \cdots, o_{|\boldsymbol{f}_j|}]$ for each $\boldsymbol{f}_j$. In other words, $\boldsymbol{i}$ and $\boldsymbol{o}$ correspond to instantiations of $\boldsymbol{c}$ and $\boldsymbol{f}_j(\boldsymbol{c})$ respectively. Given sufficiently many such examples for every $\boldsymbol{f}_j$, we can then reduce the problem of learning each unknown matrix P_j to the problem of solving a system of linear equations.

Based on this intuition, the LEARNTRANSFORMERS procedure from Fig. 5 describes our algorithm for learning abstract transformers $\mathcal{T}$ for a given abstract domain $\mathcal{A}$. At a high-level, our algorithm synthesizes one abstract transformer for each DSL construct F and n argument predicate templates $\chi_1, \cdots, \chi_n$. In particular, given F and $\chi_1, \cdots, \chi_n$, the algorithm constructs the "return value" of the transformer as:

$$\varphi = \bigwedge_{1 \leq j \leq m} \chi_j'(y, \boldsymbol{f}_j(\boldsymbol{c}))$$

where $\boldsymbol{f}_j$ is the inferred affine function for each predicate template χ_j'.

The key part of our LEARNTRANSFORMERS procedure is the inner loop (lines 5–8) for inferring each of these $\boldsymbol{f}_j$'s. Specifically, given an output predicate template χ_j', our algorithm first generates a set of input-output examples E of the form $[p_1, \cdots, p_n] \mapsto p_0$ such that $[\![F(p_1, \cdots, p_n)]\!]^\sharp = p_0$ is a sound (albeit overly specific) transformer. Essentially, each p_i is a concrete instantiation of a predicate template, so the examples E generated at line 6 of the algorithm can be viewed as sound input-output examples for the general symbolic transformer given in Eq. 1. (We will describe the GENERATEEXAMPLES procedure in Sect. 5.1).

Once we generate these examples E, the next step of the algorithm is to learn the unknown coefficients of matrix P_j from Eq. 5 by solving a system of linear equations (line 7). Specifically, observe that we can use each input-output example $[p_1, \cdots, p_n] \mapsto p_0$ in E to construct one row of Eq. 4. In particular, we can directly extract $\boldsymbol{c} = \boldsymbol{c}_1, \cdots, \boldsymbol{c}_n$ from $p_1, \cdots, p_n$ and the corresponding value of $\boldsymbol{f}_j(\boldsymbol{c})$ from p_0. Since we have one instantiation of Eq. 4 for each of the input-output examples in E, the problem of inferring matrix P_j now reduces to solving a system of linear equations of the form $A P_j^T = B$ where A is a $|E| \times (|\boldsymbol{c}| + 1)$ (input) matrix and B is a $|E| \times |\boldsymbol{f}_j|$ (output) matrix. Thus, a solution to the

```
1: procedure GENERATEEXAMPLES(φ_F, χ_0, ··, χ_n)
     input: Semantics φ_F of operator F and templates χ_0, ··, χ_n for output and inputs.
     output: A set of valid input-output examples E for DSL construct F.
2:     E ← ∅;
3:     while ¬FullRank(E) do
4:         Draw (s_1, ··, s_n) randomly from distribution R_F over Domain(F);
5:         s_0 ← [[F(s_1, ··, s_n)]];
6:         (A_0, ··, A_n) ← Abstract(s_0, χ_0, ··, s_n, χ_n);
7:         for each (p_0, ··, p_n) ∈ A_0 × ·· ×A_n do
8:             if Valid(⋀_{1≤i≤n} p_i ∧ φ_F ⇒ p_0) then E ← E ∪ {[p_1, ··, p_n] ↦ p_0};
9:     return E;
```

Fig. 6. Example generation for learning abstract transformers.

equation $AP_j^T = B$ generated from E corresponds to a candidate solution for matrix P_j, which in turn uniquely defines $\boldsymbol{f}_j$.

Observe that the call to Solve at line 7 may return *null* if no affine function exists. Furthermore, any *non-null* $\boldsymbol{f}_j$ returned by Solve is just a *candidate* solution and may not satisfy Eq. 5. For example, this situation can arise if we do not have sufficiently many examples in E and end up discovering an affine function that is "over-fitted" to the examples. Thus, the validity check at line 8 of the algorithm ensures that the learned transformers are actually sound.

5.1 Example Generation

In our discussion so far, we assumed an oracle that is capable of generating valid input-output examples for a given transformer. We now explain our GENERATEEXAMPLES procedure from Fig. 6 that essentially implements this oracle. In a nutshell, the goal of GENERATEEXAMPLES is to synthesize input-output examples of the form $[p_1, ··, p_n] \mapsto p_0$ such that $[[F(p_1, ··, p_n)]]^\sharp = p_0$ is sound where each p_i is a concrete predicate (rather than symbolic).

Going into more detail, GENERATEEXAMPLES takes as input the semantics ϕ_F of DSL construct F for which we want to learn a transformer for as well as the input predicate templates $\chi_1, ··, \chi_n$ and output predicate template χ_0 that are supposed to be used in the transformer. For any example $[p_1, ··, p_n] \mapsto p_0$ synthesized by GENERATEEXAMPLES, each concrete predicate p_i is an instantiation of the predicate template χ_i where the symbolic constants used in χ_i are substituted with *concrete* values.

Conceptually, the GENERATEEXAMPLES algorithm proceeds as follows: First, it generates *concrete* input-output examples $[s_1, ··, s_n] \mapsto s_0$ by evaluating F on randomly-generated inputs $s_1, ··, s_n$ (lines 4–5). Now, for each concrete I/O example $[s_1, ··, s_n] \mapsto s_0$, we generate a set of *abstract* I/O examples of the form $[p_1, ··, p_n] \mapsto p_0$ (line 6). Specifically, we assume that the return value $(A_0, ··, A_n)$ of Abstract at line 6 satisfies the following properties for every $p_i \in A_i$:

- p_i is an instantiation of template χ_i.
- p_i is a sound over-approximation of s_i (i.e., $s_i \in \gamma(p_i)$).
- For any other p_i' satisfying the above two conditions, p_i' is not logically stronger than p_i.

In other words, we assume that **Abstract** returns a set of "best" sound abstractions of $(s_0, \cdots, s_n)$ under predicate templates $(\chi_0, \cdots, \chi_n)$.

Next, given abstractions $(A_0, \cdots, A_n)$ for $(s_0, \cdots, s_n)$, we consider each candidate abstract example of the form $[p_1, \cdots, p_n] \mapsto p_0$ where $p_i \in A_i$. Even though each p_i is a sound abstraction of s_i, the example $[p_1, \cdots, p_n] \mapsto p_0$ may not be valid according to the semantics of operator F. Thus, the validity check at line 8 ensures that each example added to E is in fact valid.

Example 4. Given abstract domain $\mathcal{A} = \{len(\boxed{\alpha}) = \mathsf{c}\}$, suppose we want to learn an abstract transformer τ for the **Concat** operator of the following form:

$$[\![\mathsf{Concat}\big(len(x_1) = \mathsf{c}_1, len(x_2) = \mathsf{c}_2\big)]\!]^\sharp = \big(len(y) = f([\mathsf{c}_1, \mathsf{c}_2])\big)$$

We learn the affine function f used in the transformer by first generating a set E of I/O examples for f (line 6 in LEARNTRANSFORMERS). In particular, GENERATEEXAMPLES generates concrete input values for **Concat** at random and obtains the corresponding output values by executing **Concat** on the input values. For instance, it may generate $s_1 = $ "abc" and $s_2 = $ "de" as inputs, and obtain $s_0 = $ "$abcde$" as output. Then, it abstracts these values under the given templates. In this case, we have an abstract example with $p_1 = \big(len(x_1) = 3\big)$, $p_2 = \big(len(x_2) = 2\big)$ and $p_0 = \big(len(y) = 5\big)$. Since $[p_1, p_2] \mapsto p_0$ is a valid example, it is added in E (line 8 in GENERATEEXAMPLES). At this point, E is not yet full rank, so the algorithm keeps generating more examples. Suppose it generates two more valid examples $\big(len(x_1) = 1, len(x_2) = 4\big) \mapsto \big(len(y) = 5\big)$ and $\big(len(x_1) = 6, len(x_2) = 4\big) \mapsto \big(len(y) = 10\big)$. Now E is full rank, so LEARN-TRANSFORMERS computes f by solving the following system of linear equations:

$$\begin{bmatrix} 3 & 2 & 1 \\ 1 & 4 & 1 \\ 6 & 4 & 1 \end{bmatrix} P^T = \begin{bmatrix} 5 \\ 5 \\ 10 \end{bmatrix} \xrightarrow{\text{Solve}} P = [\,1\ 1\ 0\,]$$

Here, P corresponds to the function $f([\mathsf{c}_1, \mathsf{c}_2]) = \mathsf{c}_1 + \mathsf{c}_2$, and this function defines the sound transformer: $[\![\mathsf{Concat}\big(len(x_1) = \mathsf{c}_1, len(x_2) = \mathsf{c}_2\big)]\!]^\sharp = \big(len(y) = \mathsf{c}_1 + \mathsf{c}_2\big)$ which is added to $\mathcal{T}$ at line 9 in LEARNTRANSFORMERS.

6   Soundness and Completeness

In this section we present theorems stating some of the soundness, completeness, and termination guarantees of our approach. All proofs can be found in the extended version of this paper [21].

Theorem 1 (Soundness of LEARNTRANSFORMERS). *Let $\mathcal{T}$ be the set of transformers returned by LEARNTRANSFORMERS. Then, every $\tau \in \mathcal{T}$ is sound according to Eq. 2.*

The remaining theorems are predicated on the assumptions that for each DSL construct F and input predicate templates $\chi_1, \cdots, \chi_n$ (i) there exists a unique best abstract transformer and (ii) the strongest transformer expressible in Eq. 2 is logically equivalent to the unique best transformer. Thus, before stating these theorems, we first state what we mean by a *unique best abstract transformer.*

Definition 3 (Unique best function). *Consider a family of transformers of the shape $[\![F(\chi_1(x_1, \mathbf{c}_1), \cdots, \chi_n(x_n, \mathbf{c}_n))]\!]^\sharp = \chi'(y, \star)$. We say that $\mathbf{f}$ is the unique best function for $(F, \chi_1, \cdots, \chi_n, \chi')$ if (a) replacing $\star$ with $\mathbf{f}$ yields a sound transformer, and (b) replacing $\star$ with any other $\mathbf{f}'$ yields a transformer that is either unsound or strictly worse (i.e., $\chi'(y, \mathbf{f}) \Rightarrow \chi'(y, \mathbf{f}')$ and $\chi'(y, \mathbf{f}') \not\Rightarrow \chi'(y, \mathbf{f})$).*

We now define unique best transformer in terms of unique best function:

Definition 4 (Unique best transformer). *Let F be a DSL construct and let $(\chi_1, \cdots, \chi_n) \in \mathcal{A}^n$ be the input templates for F. We say that the abstract transformer τ is a unique best transformer for $F, \chi_1, \cdots, \chi_n$ if (a) τ is sound, and (b) for any predicate template $\chi \in \mathcal{A}$, we have $(\chi, \mathbf{f}) \in \mathsf{Outputs}(\tau)$ if and only if $\mathbf{f}$ is a unique best function for $(F, \chi_1, \cdots, \chi_n, \chi)$ for some affine $\mathbf{f}$.*

Definition 5 (Complete sampling oracle). *Let F be a construct, $\mathcal{A}$ an abstract domain, and R_F a probability distribution over $\mathrm{DOMAIN}(F)$ with finite support S. Futher, for any input predicate templates $\chi_1, \cdots, \chi_n$ and output predicate template χ_0 in $\mathcal{A}$ admitting a unique best function $\mathbf{f}$, let $C(\chi_0, \cdots, \chi_n)$ be the set of tuples $(c_0, \cdots, c_n)$ such that $(\chi_0(y, c_0), \chi_1(x_1, c_1), \cdots, \chi_n(x_n, c_n)) \in A_0 \times \cdots \times A_n$ and $c_0 = \mathbf{f}(c_1, \cdots, c_n)$, where $A_0 \times \cdots \times A_n = \mathrm{ABSTRACT}(s_0, \chi_0, \cdots, s_n, \chi_n)$ and $(s_1, \cdots, s_n) \in S$ and $s_0 = [\![F(s_1, \cdots, s_n)]\!]$. The distribution R_F is a complete sampling oracle if $C(\chi_0, \cdots, \chi_n)$ has full rank for all $\chi_0, \cdots, \chi_n$.*

The following theorem states that LEARNTRANSFORMERS is guaranteed to synthesize the best transformer if a unique one exists:

Theorem 2 (Completeness of LEARNTRANSFORMERS). *Given an abstract domain $\mathcal{A}$ and a complete sampling oracle R_F for $\mathcal{A}$, LEARNTRANSFORMERS terminates. Further, let $\mathcal{T}$ be the set of transformers returned and let τ be the unique best transformer for DSL construct F and input predicate templates $\chi_1, \cdots, \chi_n \in \mathcal{A}^n$. Then we have $\tau \in \mathcal{T}$.*

Using this completeness (modulo unique best transformer) result, we can now state the termination guarantees of our LEARNABSTRACTIONS algorithm:

Theorem 3 (Termination of LEARNABSTRACTIONS). *Given a complete sampling oracle R_F for every abstract domain and the unique best transformer assumption, if there exists a solution for every problem $\mathcal{E}_i \in \mathcal{E}$, then LEARNABSTRACTIONS terminates.*

7   Implementation and Evaluation

We have implemented the proposed method as a new tool called ATLAS, which is written in Java. ATLAS takes as input a set of training problems, an Abstraction-Guided Synthesizer (AGS), and a DSL and returns an abstract domain (in the form of predicate templates) and the corresponding transformers. Internally, ATLAS uses the Z3 theorem prover [22] to compute tree interpolants and the JLinAlg linear algebra library [23] to solve linear equations.

To assess the usefulness of ATLAS, we conduct an experimental evaluation in which our goal is to answer the following two questions:

1. How does ATLAS perform during training? That is, how many training problems does it require and how long does training take?
2. How useful are the abstractions learned by ATLAS in the context of synthesis?

7.1   Abstraction Learning

To answer our first question, we use ATLAS to automatically learn abstractions for two application domains: (i) string manipulations and (ii) matrix transformations. We provide ATLAS with the DSLs used in [14] and employ BLAZE as the underlying Abstraction-Guided Synthesizer. Axiomatic semantics for each DSL construct were given in the theory of equality with uninterpreted functions.

Training Set Information. For the string domain, our training set consists of exactly the four problems used as motivating examples in the BlinkFill paper [17]. Specifically, each training problem consists of 4–6 examples that demonstrate the desired string transformation. For the matrix domain, our training set consists of four (randomly selected) synthesis problems taken from online forums. Since almost all online posts contain a single input-output example, each training problem includes one example illustrating the desired matrix transformation.

Main Results. Our main results are summarized in Fig. 7. The main takeaway message is that ATLAS can learn abstractions quite efficiently and does not require a large training set. For example, ATLAS learns 5 predicate templates and 30 abstract transformers for the string domain in a total of 10.2 s. Interestingly, ATLAS does not need all the training problems to infer these four predicates and converges to the final abstraction after just processing the first training instance. Furthermore, for the first training instance, it takes ATLAS 4 iterations in the learning loop (lines 5–10 from Fig. 2) before it converges to the final abstraction. Since this abstraction is sufficient, it takes just one iteration for each following training problem to synthesize a correct program.

Looking at the right side of Fig. 7, we also observe similar results for the matrix domain. In particular, ATLAS learns 10 predicate templates and 59 abstract transformers in a total of 22.5 s. Furthermore, ATLAS converges to the final abstract domain after processing the first three problems[5] and the number of iterations for each training instance is also quite small (ranging from 1 to 3).

---

[5] The learned abstractions can be found in the extended version of this paper [21].

String domain

	$\|\mathcal{A}\|$	$\|\mathcal{T}\|$	Iters.	Running time (sec)			
				T_{AGS}	$T_\mathcal{A}$	$T_\mathcal{T}$	T_{total}
$\mathcal{E}_1$	5	30	4	0.6	0.2	0.2	1.0
$\mathcal{E}_2$	5	30	1	4.9	0	0	4.9
$\mathcal{E}_3$	5	30	1	0.2	0	0	0.2
$\mathcal{E}_4$	5	30	1	4.1	0	0	4.1
Total	5	30	7	9.8	0.2	0.2	**10.2**

Matrix domain

	$\|\mathcal{A}\|$	$\|\mathcal{T}\|$	Iters.	Running time (sec)			
				T_{AGS}	$T_\mathcal{A}$	$T_\mathcal{T}$	T_{total}
$\mathcal{E}_1$	8	45	3	2.9	0.7	0.5	4.1
$\mathcal{E}_2$	8	45	1	2.8	0	0	2.8
$\mathcal{E}_3$	10	59	2	0.5	0.3	0.2	1.0
$\mathcal{E}_4$	10	59	1	14.6	0	0	14.6
Total	10	59	7	20.8	1.0	0.7	**22.5**

Fig. 7. Training results. $\|\mathcal{A}\|, \|\mathcal{T}\|$, Iters denote the number of predicate templates, abstract transformers, and iterations taken per training instance (lines 5–10 from Fig. 2), respectively. $T_{\text{AGS}}, T_\mathcal{A}, T_\mathcal{T}$ denote the times for invoking the synthesizer (AGS), learning the abstract domain, and learning the abstract transformers, respectively. T_{total} shows the total training time in seconds.

	Original BLAZE[†] benchmarks				Additional benchmarks				All benchmarks		
	#Solved		Running time improvement		#Solved		Running time improvement		Time (sec)	Running time improvement	
	BLAZE*	BLAZE[†]	max.	avg.	BLAZE*	BLAZE[†]	max.	avg.	avg.	max.	avg.
String	**93**	91	15.7×	2.1×	**40**	40	56×	22.3×	**2.8**	56×	**8.3×**
Matrix	**39**	39	6.1×	3.1×	**20**	19	83×	21.5×	**5.0**	83×	**9.2×**

Fig. 8. Improvement of BLAZE* over BLAZE[†] on string and matrix benchmarks.

7.2 Evaluating the Usefulness of Learned Abstractions

To answer our second question, we integrated the abstractions synthesized by ATLAS into the BLAZE meta-synthesizer. In the remainder of this section, we refer to all instantiations of BLAZE using the ATLAS-generated abstractions as BLAZE*. To assess how useful the automatically generated abstractions are, we compare BLAZE* against BLAZE[†], which refers to the manually-constructed instantiations of BLAZE described in [14].

Benchmark Information. For the string domain, our benchmark suite consists of (1) *all* 108 string transformation benchmarks that were used to evaluate BLAZE[†] and (2) 40 additional challenging problems that are collected from online forums which involve manipulating file paths, URLs, etc. The number of examples for each benchmark ranges from 1 to 400, with a median of 7 examples. For the matrix domain, our benchmark set includes (1) *all* 39 matrix transformation benchmarks in the BLAZE[†] benchmark suite and (2) 20 additional challenging problems collected from online forums. *We emphasize that the set of benchmarks used for evaluating* BLAZE* *are completely* disjoint *from the set of synthesis problems used for training* ATLAS.

Experimental Setup. We evaluate $\text{BLAZE}^{\star}$ and $\text{BLAZE}^{\dagger}$ using the same DSLs from the BLAZE paper [14]. For each benchmark, we provide the same set of input-output examples to $\text{BLAZE}^{\star}$ and $\text{BLAZE}^{\dagger}$, and use a time limit of 20 min per synthesis task.

Main Results. Our main evaluation results are summarized in Fig. 8. The key observation is that $\text{BLAZE}^{\star}$ consistently improves upon $\text{BLAZE}^{\dagger}$ for both string and matrix transformations. In particular, $\text{BLAZE}^{\star}$ not only solves more benchmarks than $\text{BLAZE}^{\dagger}$ for both domains, but also achieves about an order of magnitude speed-up on average for the common benchmarks that both tools can solve. Specifically, for the string domain, $\text{BLAZE}^{\star}$ solves 133 (out of 148) benchmarks within an average of 2.8 s and achieves an average 8.3× speed-up over $\text{BLAZE}^{\dagger}$. For the matrix domain, we also observe a very similar result where $\text{BLAZE}^{\star}$ leads to an overall speed-up of 9.2× on average.

In summary, this experiment confirms that the abstractions discovered by ATLAS are indeed useful and that they outperform manually-crafted abstractions despite eliminating human effort.

8 Related Work

To our knowledge, this paper is the first one to automatically learn abstract domains and transformers that are useful for program synthesis. We also believe it is the first to apply interpolation to program synthesis, although interpolation has been used to synthesize other artifacts such as circuits [24] and strategies for infinite games [25]. In what follows, we briefly survey existing work related to program synthesis, abstraction learning, and abstract transformer computations.

Program Synthesis. Our work is intended to complement example-guided program synthesis techniques that utilize program abstractions to prune the search space [4, 14–16]. For example, SIMPL [15] uses abstract interpretation to speed up search-based synthesis and applies this technique to the generation of imperative programs for introductory programming assignments. Similarly, SCYTHE [16] and MORPHEUS [4] perform enumeration over program sketches and use abstractions to reject sketches that do not have any valid completion. Somewhat different from these techniques, BLAZE constructs a finite tree automaton that accepts all programs whose behavior is consistent with the specification according to the DSL's abstract semantics. We believe that the method described in this paper can be useful to all such abstraction-guided synthesizers.

Abstraction Refinement. In verification, as opposed to synthesis, there have been many works that use Craig interpolants to refine abstractions [20, 26, 27]. Typically, these techniques generalize the interpolants to abstract domains by extracting a vocabulary of predicates, but they do not generalize by adding parameters to form templates. In our case, this is essential because interpolants derived from fixed input values are too specific to be directly useful. Moreover, we *reuse* the resulting abstractions for subsequent synthesis problems. In verification, this would be analogous to re-using an abstraction from one property or program to the next. It is conceivable that template-based generalization could be applied in verification to facilitate such reuse.

Abstract Transformers. Many verification techniques use logical abstract domains [28–32]. Some of these, following Yorsh, *et al.* [33] use sampling with a decision procedure to evaluate the abstract transformer [34]. Interpolation has also been used to compile efficient symbolic abstract transformers [35]. However, these techniques are restricted to finite domains or domains of finite height to allow convergence. Here, we use infinite parameterized domains to obtain better generalization; hence, the abstract transformer computation is more challenging. Nonetheless, the approach might also be applicable in verification.

9   Limitations

While this paper takes a first step towards automatically inferring useful abstractions for synthesis, our proposed method has the following limitations:

Shapes of Transformers. Following prior work [14], our algorithm assumes that abstract transformers have the shape given in Eq. 1. We additionally assume that constants c used in predicate templates are numeric values and that functions in Eq. 1 are affine. This assumption holds in several domains considered in prior work [4,14] and allows us to develop an efficient learning algorithm that reduces the problem to solving a system of linear equations.

DSL Semantics. Our method requires the DSL designer to provide the DSL's logical semantics. We believe that giving logical semantics is much easier than coming up with useful abstractions, as it does not require insights about the internal workings of the synthesizer. Furthermore, our technique could, in principle, also work without logical specifications although the learned abstract domain may not be as effective (see Footnote 3 in Sect. 4) and the synthesized transformers would not be provably sound.

UBT Assumption. Our completeness and termination theorems are predicated on the *unique best transformer (UBT)* assumption. While this assumption holds in our evaluation, it may not hold in general. However, as mentioned in Sect. 6, we can always guarantee termination by including the concrete predicates used in the interpolant $\mathcal{I}$ in addition to the symbolic templates extracted from $\mathcal{I}$.

10   Conclusion

We proposed a new technique for automatically instantiating abstraction-guided synthesis frameworks in new domains. Given a DSL and a few training problems, our method automatically discovers a useful abstract domain and the corresponding transformers for each DSL construct. From a technical perspective, our method uses tree interpolation to extract reusable templates from failed synthesis attempts and automatically synthesizes unique best transformers if they exist. We have incorporated the proposed approach into the BLAZE meta-synthesizer and show that the abstractions discovered by ATLAS are very useful.

While we have applied the proposed technique to program synthesis, we believe that some of the ideas introduced here are more broadly applicable. For instance, the idea of extracting reusable predicate templates from interpolants and synthesizing transformers in a data-driven way could also be useful in the context of program verification.

References

1. Gulwani, S.: Automating string processing in spreadsheets using input-output examples. In: Proceedings of the 38th Annual ACM SIGPLAN-SIGACT Symposium on Principles of Programming Languages, POPL, pp. 317–330. ACM (2011)
2. Singh, R., Gulwani, S.: Transforming spreadsheet data types using examples. In: Proceedings of the 43rd Annual ACM SIGPLAN-SIGACT Symposium on Principles of Programming Languages, POPL, pp. 343–356. ACM (2016)
3. Wang, X., Gulwani, S., Singh, R.: FIDEX: filtering spreadsheet data using examples. In: OOPSLA, pp. 195–213. ACM (2016)
4. Feng, Y., Martins, R., Van Geffen, J., Dillig, I., Chaudhuri, S.: Component-based synthesis of table consolidation and transformation tasks from examples. In: PLDI, pp. 422–436. ACM (2017)
5. Wang, X., Dillig, I., Singh, R.: Synthesis of data completion scripts using finite tree automata. Proc. ACM Program. Lang. 1(OOPSLA), 62:1–62:26 (2017)
6. Yaghmazadeh, N., Wang, X., Dillig, I.: Automated migration of hierarchical data to relational tables using programming-by-example. In: Proceedings of the VLDB Endowment (2018)
7. Gascón, A., Tiwari, A., Carmer, B., Mathur, U.: Look for the proof to find the program: decorated-component-based program synthesis. In: Majumdar, R., Kunčak, V. (eds.) CAV 2017. LNCS, vol. 10427, pp. 86–103. Springer, Cham (2017). https://doi.org/10.1007/978-3-319-63390-9_5
8. Tiwari, A., Gascón, A., Dutertre, B.: Program synthesis using dual interpretation. In: Felty, A.P., Middeldorp, A. (eds.) CADE 2015. LNCS (LNAI), vol. 9195, pp. 482–497. Springer, Cham (2015). https://doi.org/10.1007/978-3-319-21401-6_33
9. Feng, Y., Martins, R., Wang, Y., Dillig, I., Reps, T.W.: Component-based synthesis for complex APIs. In: POPL, vol. 52, pp. 599–612. ACM (2017)
10. Gvero, T., Kuncak, V., Kuraj, I., Piskac, R.: Complete completion using types and weights. In: Proceedings of the 34th ACM SIGPLAN Conference on Programming Language Design and Implementation, PLDI, pp. 27–38. ACM (2013)
11. Mandelin, D., Xu, L., Bodík, R., Kimelman, D.: Jungloid mining: helping to navigate the API jungle. In: Proceedings of the 26th ACM SIGPLAN Conference on Programming Language Design and Implementation, PLDI, pp. 48–61. ACM (2005)
12. Feser, J.K., Chaudhuri, S., Dillig, I.: Synthesizing data structure transformations from input-output examples. In: Proceedings of the 36th ACM SIGPLAN Conference on Programming Language Design and Implementation, PLDI, pp. 229–239. ACM (2015)

13. Polikarpova, N., Kuraj, I., Solar-Lezama, A.: Program synthesis from polymorphic refinement types. In: Proceedings of the 37th ACM SIGPLAN Conference on Programming Language Design and Implementation, PLDI, pp. 522–538. ACM (2016)
14. Wang, X., Dillig, I., Singh, R.: Program synthesis using abstraction refinement, vol. 2, pp. 63:1–63:30. ACM (2017)
15. So, S., Oh, H.: Synthesizing imperative programs from examples guided by static analysis. In: Ranzato, F. (ed.) SAS 2017. LNCS, vol. 10422, pp. 364–381. Springer, Cham (2017). https://doi.org/10.1007/978-3-319-66706-5_18
16. Wang, C., Cheung, A., Bodik, R.: Synthesizing highly expressive SQL queries from input-output examples. In: Proceedings of the 38th ACM SIGPLAN Conference on Programming Language Design and Implementation, PLDI, pp. 452–466. ACM (2017)
17. Singh, R.: BlinkFill: semi-supervised programming by example for syntactic string transformations. Proc. VLDB Endow. 9(10), 816–827 (2016)
18. Blanc, R., Gupta, A., Kovács, L., Kragl, B.: Tree interpolation in vampire. In: McMillan, K., Middeldorp, A., Voronkov, A. (eds.) LPAR 2013. LNCS, vol. 8312, pp. 173–181. Springer, Heidelberg (2013). https://doi.org/10.1007/978-3-642-45221-5_13
19. McMillan, K.L.: Applications of craig interpolants in model checking. In: Halbwachs, N., Zuck, L.D. (eds.) TACAS 2005. LNCS, vol. 3440, pp. 1–12. Springer, Heidelberg (2005). https://doi.org/10.1007/978-3-540-31980-1_1
20. McMillan, K.L.: Interpolation and SAT-based model checking. In: Hunt, W.A., Somenzi, F. (eds.) CAV 2003. LNCS, vol. 2725, pp. 1–13. Springer, Heidelberg (2003). https://doi.org/10.1007/978-3-540-45069-6_1
21. Wang, X., Dillig, I., Singh, R.: Learning Abstractions for Program Synthesis. arXiv preprint arXiv:1804.04152 (2018)
22. Z3. https://github.com/Z3Prover/z3
23. Keilhauer, A., Levy, S., Lochbihler, A., Ökmen, S., Thimm, G., Würzebesser, C.: JLinAlg: a java-library for linear algebra without rounding errors. Technical report (2003–2010). http://jlinalg.sourceforge.net/
24. Bloem, R., Egly, U., Klampfl, P., Könighofer, R., Lonsing, F.: Sat-based methods for circuit synthesis. In: Formal Methods in Computer-Aided Design, FMCAD 2014, 21–24 October 2014, Lausanne, Switzerland, pp. 31–34. IEEE (2014)
25. Farzan, A., Kincaid, Z.: Strategy synthesis for linear arithmetic games. Proc. ACM Program. Lang. 2(POPL), 61 (2017)
26. Beyer, D., Henzinger, T.A., Jhala, R., Majumdar, R.: The software model checker BLAST. Int. J. Softw. Tools Technol. Transf. 9(5–6), 505–525 (2007)
27. Albarghouthi, A., Li, Y., Gurfinkel, A., Chechik, M.: UFO: a framework for abstraction- and interpolation-based software verification. In: Madhusudan, P., Seshia, S.A. (eds.) CAV 2012. LNCS, vol. 7358, pp. 672–678. Springer, Heidelberg (2012). https://doi.org/10.1007/978-3-642-31424-7_48
28. Lev-Ami, T., Manevich, R., Sagiv, M.: TVLA: a system for generating abstract interpreters. In: Jacquart, R. (ed.) Building the Information Society. IIFIP, vol. 156, pp. 367–375. Springer, Boston, MA (2004). https://doi.org/10.1007/978-1-4020-8157-6_28
29. Lev-Ami, T., Sagiv, M.: TVLA: a system for implementing static analyses. In: Palsberg, J. (ed.) SAS 2000. LNCS, vol. 1824, pp. 280–301. Springer, Heidelberg (2000). https://doi.org/10.1007/978-3-540-45099-3_15

30. Pnueli, A., Ruah, S., Zuck, L.: Automatic deductive verification with invisible invariants. In: Margaria, T., Yi, W. (eds.) TACAS 2001. LNCS, vol. 2031, pp. 82–97. Springer, Heidelberg (2001). https://doi.org/10.1007/3-540-45319-9_7

31. Lahiri, S.K., Bryant, R.E.: Constructing quantified invariants via predicate abstraction. In: Steffen, B., Levi, G. (eds.) VMCAI 2004. LNCS, vol. 2937, pp. 267–281. Springer, Heidelberg (2004)

32. Reps, T., Thakur, A.: Automating abstract interpretation. In: Jobstmann, B., Leino, K.R.M. (eds.) VMCAI 2016. LNCS, vol. 9583, pp. 3–40. Springer, Heidelberg (2016). https://doi.org/10.1007/978-3-662-49122-5_1

33. Reps, T., Sagiv, M., Yorsh, G.: Symbolic implementation of the best transformer. In: Steffen, B., Levi, G. (eds.) VMCAI 2004. LNCS, vol. 2937, pp. 252–266. Springer, Heidelberg (2004)

34. Thakur, A., Reps, T.: A method for symbolic computation of abstract operations. In: Madhusudan, P., Seshia, S.A. (eds.) CAV 2012. LNCS, vol. 7358, pp. 174–192. Springer, Heidelberg (2012). https://doi.org/10.1007/978-3-642-31424-7_17

35. Jhala, R., McMillan, K.L.: Interpolant-based transition relation approximation. In: Etessami, K., Rajamani, S.K. (eds.) CAV 2005. LNCS, vol. 3576, pp. 39–51. Springer, Heidelberg (2005). https://doi.org/10.1007/11513988_6

9

Reachable Set Over-Approximation for Nonlinear Systems Using Piecewise Barrier Tubes

Hui Kong[1]([✉]), Ezio Bartocci[2], and Thomas A. Henzinger[1]

[1] IST Austria, Klosterneuburg, Austria
hui.kong@ist.ac.at
[2] TU Wien, Vienna, Austria

Abstract. We address the problem of analyzing the reachable set of a polynomial nonlinear continuous system by over-approximating the flow-pipe of its dynamics. The common approach to tackle this problem is to perform a numerical integration over a given time horizon based on Taylor expansion and interval arithmetic. However, this method results to be very conservative when there is a large difference in speed between trajectories as time progresses. In this paper, we propose to use combinations of barrier functions, which we call piecewise barrier tube (PBT), to over-approximate flowpipe. The basic idea of PBT is that for each segment of a flowpipe, a coarse box which is big enough to contain the segment is constructed using sampled simulation and then in the box we compute by linear programming a set of barrier functions (called barrier tube or BT for short) which work together to form a tube surrounding the flow-pipe. The benefit of using PBT is that (1) BT is independent of time and hence can avoid being stretched and deformed by time; and (2) a small number of BTs can form a tight over-approximation for the flowpipe, which means that the computation required to decide whether the BTs intersect the unsafe set can be reduced significantly. We implemented a prototype called PBTS in C++. Experiments on some benchmark systems show that our approach is effective.

1 Introduction

Hybrid systems [17] are widely used to model dynamical systems which exhibit both discrete and continuous behaviors. The reachability analysis of hybrid systems has been a challenging problem over the last few decades. The hard core of this problem lies in dealing with the continuous behavior of systems that are described by ordinary differential equations (ODEs). Although there are currently several quite efficient and scalable approaches for reachability analysis of linear systems [8–10,14,16,19,20,26,34], nonlinear ODEs are much harder to handle and the current approaches can be characterized into the following groups.

Invariant Generation [18, 21, 22, 27, 28, 36, 37, 39]. An invariant I for a system S is a set such that any trajectory of S originating from I never escapes from I. Therefore, finding an invariant I such that the initial set $I_0 \subseteq I$ and the unsafe set $U \cap I = \emptyset$ indicates the safety of the system. In this way, there is no need to compute the flowpipe. The main problem with invariant generation is that it is hard to define a set of high quality constraints which can be solved efficiently.

Abstraction and Hybridization [2, 11, 24, 31, 35]. The basic idea of the abstraction-based approach is first constructing a linear model which over-approximates the original nonlinear dynamics and then applying techniques for linear systems to the abstraction model. However, how to construct an abstraction with the fewest discrete states and sufficiently high accuracy is still a challenging issue.

Satisfiability Modulo Theory (SMT) Over Reals [6, 7, 23]. This approach encodes the reachability problem for nonlinear systems as first-order logic formulas over the real numbers. These formulas can be solved using for example $\delta-$complete decision procedures that overcome the theoretical limits in nonlinear theories over the reals, by choosing a desired precision δ. An SMT implementing such procedures can return either *unsat* if the reachability problem is unsatisfiable or δ-sat if the problem is satisfiable given the chosen precision. The δ-sat verdict does not guarantee that the dynamics of the system will reach a particular region. It may happens that by increasing the precision the problem would result *unsat*. In general the limit of this approach is that it does not provide as a result a complete and comprehensive description of the reachability set.

Bounded Time Flowpipe Computation [1, 3–5, 25, 32]. The common technique to compute a bounded flowpipe is based on interval method or Taylor model. Interval-based approach is quite efficient even for high dimensional systems [29], but it suffers the wrapping effect of intervals and can quickly accumulate over-approximation errors. In contrast, the Taylor-model-based approach is more precise in that it uses a vector of polynomials plus a vector of small intervals to symbolically represent the flowpipe. However, for the purpose of safety verification or reachability analysis, the Taylor model has to be further over-approximated by intervals, which may bring back the wrapping effect. In particular, the wrapping effect can explode easily when the flowpipe segment over a time interval is stretched drastically due to a large difference in speed between individual trajectories. This case is demonstrated by the following example.

Example 1 (Running example). Consider the 2D system [30] described by $\dot{x} = y$ and $\dot{y} = x^2$. Let the initial set X_0 be a line segment $x \in [1.0, 1.0]$ and $y \in [-1.05, -0.95]$, Fig. 1a shows the simulation result on three points in X_0 over time interval $[0, 6.6]$. The reachable set at $t = 6.6\,\mathrm{s}$ is a smooth curve connecting the end points of the three trajectories. As can be seen, the trajectory originating from the top is left far behind the one originating from the bottom, which means that the tiny initial line segment is being stretched into a huge curve very quickly,

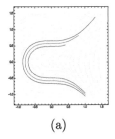
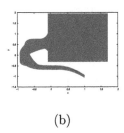

(a)   (b)

Fig. 1. (a) Simulation for Example 1 showing flowpipe segment being extremely stretched and deformed, (b) Interval over-approximation of the Taylor model computed by *Flow** [3].

while the width of the flowpipe is actually converging to 0. As a result, the interval over-approximation of this huge curve can be extremely conservative even if its Taylor model representation is precise, and reducing the time step size is not helpful. To prove this point, we computed with *Flow** [3] a Taylor model series for the time horizon of 6.6 s which consists of 13200 Taylor models. Figure 1b shows the interval approximation of the Taylor model series, which apparently starts exploding.

In this paper, we propose to use piecewise barrier tubes (PBTs) to over-approximate flowpipes of polynomial nonlinear systems, which can avoid the issue caused by the excessive stretching of a flowpipe segment. The idea of PBT is inspired from barrier certificate [22,33]. A barrier certificate $B(x)$ is a real-valued function such that (1) $B(x) \geq 0$ for all x in the initial set X_0; (2) $B(x) < 0$ for all x in the unsafe set X_U; (3) no trajectory can escape from $\{x \in \mathbb{R}^n \mid B(x) \geq 0\}$ through the boundary $\{x \in \mathbb{R}^n \mid B(x) = 0\}$. A sufficient condition for this constraint is that the Lie derivative of $B(x)$ w.r.t the dynamics $\dot{x} = f$ is positive all over the invariant region, i.e., $\mathcal{L}_f B(x) > 0$, which means that all the trajectories must move in the increasing direction of the level sets of $B(x)$.

Barrier certificates can be used to verify safety properties without computing the flowpipe explicitly. The essential idea is to use the zero level set of $B(x)$ as a barrier to separate the flowpipe from the unsafe set. Moreover, if the unsafe set is very close to the boundary of the flowpipe, the barrier has to fit the shape of the flowpipe to make sure that all components of the constraint are satisfied. However, the zero level set of a polynomial of fixed degree may not have the power to mimic the shape of the flowpipe, which means that there may exist no solution for the above constraints even if the system is safe. This problem might be addressed using piecewise barrier certificate, i.e., cutting the flowpipe into small pieces so that every piece is straight enough to have a barrier certificate of simple form. Unfortunately, this is infeasible because we know nothing about the flowpipe locally. Therefore, we have to find another way to proceed.

Instead of computing a single barrier certificate, we propose to compute barrier tubes to piecewise over-approximate the flowpipe. Concretely, in the beginning, we first construct a containing box, called **enclosure**, for the initial set using interval approach [29] and simulation, then, using linear programming, we compute a group of barrier functions which work together to form a tight tube (called barrier tube) around the flowpipe. Similarly, taking the intersection of the barrier tube and the boundary of the box as the new initial set, we repeat the previous operations to obtain successive barrier tubes step by step. The key point here is how to compute a group of tightly enclosing barriers around the flowpipe without a constraint on the unsafe set inside the box. Our basic idea is to construct a group of auxiliary state sets U around the flowpipe and then, for each $U_i \in U$, we compute a barrier certificate between U_i and the flowpipe. If a barrier certificate is found, we expand U_i towards the flowpipe iteratively until no more barrier certificate can be found; otherwise, we shrink U_i away from the flowpipe until a barrier certificate is found. Since the auxiliary sets are distributed around the flowpipe, so is the barrier tube. The benefit of such piecewise barrier tubes is that they are time independent, and hence can avoid the issue of stretched flowpipe segments caused by speed differences between trajectories. Moreover, usually a small number of BTs can form a tight over-approximation of the flowpipe, which means that less computation is needed to decide the intersection of PBT and the unsafe set.

The main contributions of this paper are as follows:

1. We transform the constraint-solving problem for barrier certificates into a linear programming problem using Handelman representation [15];
2. We introduce PBT to over-approximate the flowpipe of nonlinear systems, thus dealing with flowpipes independent of time and hence avoiding the error explosion caused by stretched flowpipe segments;
3. We implement a prototype in C++ to compute PTB automatically and we show the effectiveness of our approach by providing a comparison with the state-of-the-art tools for reachability analysis of polynomial nonlinear systems such as *CORA* [1] and *Flow** [3].

The paper is organized as follows. Section 2 is devoted to the preliminaries. Section 3 shows how to compute barrier certificates using Handelman representation, while in Sect. 4 we present a method to compute Piecewise Barrier Tubes. Section 5 provides our experimental results and we conclude in Sect. 6.

2   Preliminaries

In this section, we recall some concepts used throughout the paper. We first clarify some notation conventions. If not specified otherwise, we use boldface lower case letters to denote vectors, we use $\mathbb{R}$ for the real number field and $\mathbb{N}$ for the set of natural numbers, and we consider multivariate polynomials in $\mathbb{R}[\boldsymbol{x}]$, where the components of $\boldsymbol{x}$ act as indeterminates. In addition, for all the polynomials $B(\boldsymbol{u}, \boldsymbol{x})$, we denote by $\boldsymbol{u}$ the vector composed of all the u_i and denote by $\boldsymbol{x}$ the vector composed of all the remaining variables x_i that occur in the polynomial. We use $\mathbb{R}_{\geq 0}$ and $\mathbb{R}_{>0}$ to denote the domain of nonnegative real number and positive real number respectively.

Let $P \subseteq \mathbb{R}^n$ be a convex and compact polyhedron with non-empty interior, bounded by linear polynomials $p_1, \cdots, p_m \in \mathbb{R}[x]$. Without lose of generality, we may assume $P = \{x \in \mathbb{R}^n \mid p_i(x) \geq 0, i = 1, \cdots, m\}$.

Next, we present the notation of the Lie derivative, which is widely used in the discipline of differential geometry. Let $f : \mathbb{R}^n \to \mathbb{R}^n$ be a continuous vector field such that $\dot{x}_i = f_i(x)$ where $\dot{x}_i$ is the time derivative of $x_i(t)$.

Definition 1 (Lie derivative). *For a given polynomial $p \in \mathbb{R}[x]$ over $x = (x_1, \ldots, x_n)$ and a continuous system $\dot{x} = f$, where $f = (f_1, \ldots, f_n)$, the **Lie derivative** of $p \in \mathbb{R}[x]$ along f of order k is defined as follows.*

$$\mathcal{L}_f^k p \overset{def}{=} \begin{cases} p, & k = 0 \\ \sum_{i=1}^n \frac{\partial \mathcal{L}_f^{k-1} p}{\partial x_i} \cdot f_i, & k \geq 1 \end{cases}$$

Essentially, the k-th order Lie derivative of p is the k-th derivative of p w.r.t. time, i.e., reflects the change of p over time. We write $\mathcal{L}_f p$ for $\mathcal{L}_f^1 p$.

In this paper, we focus on semialgebraic nonlinear systems, which are defined as follows.

Definition 2 (Semialgebraic system). *A **semialgebraic system** is a triple $M \overset{def}{=} \langle X, f, X_0, I \rangle$, where*

1. *$X \subseteq \mathbb{R}^n$ is the state space of the system M,*
2. *$f \in \mathbb{R}[x]^n$ is locally Lipschitz continuous vector function,*
3. *$X_0 \subseteq X$ is the initial set, which is semialgebraic [40],*
4. *I is the invariant of the system.*

The local Lipschitz continuity guarantees the existence and uniqueness of the differential equation $\dot{x} = f$ locally. A trajectory of a semialgebraic system is defined as follows.

Definition 3 (Trajectory). *Given a semialgebraic system M, a **trajectory** originating from a point $x_0 \in X_0$ to time $T > 0$ is a continuous and differentiable function $\zeta(x_0, t) : [0, T) \to \mathbb{R}^n$ such that (1) $\zeta(x_0, 0) = x_0$, and (2) $\forall \tau \in [0, T)$: $\frac{d\zeta}{dt}\big|_{t=\tau} = f(\zeta(x_0, \tau))$. T is assumed to be within the maximal interval of existence of the solution from x_0.*

For ease of readability, we also use $\zeta(t)$ for $\zeta(x_0, t)$. In addition, we use $Flow_f(X_0)$ to denote the flowpipe of initial set X_0, i.e.,

$$Flow_f(X_0) \overset{def}{=} \{\zeta(x_0, t) \mid x_0 \in X_0, t \in \mathbb{R}_{\geq}, \dot{\zeta} = f(\zeta)\} \tag{1}$$

Definition 4 (Safety). *Given an unsafe set $X_U \subseteq X$, a semialgebraic system $M = \langle X, f, X_0, I \rangle$ is said to be **safe** if no trajectory $\zeta(x_0, t)$ of M satisfies that $\exists \tau \in \mathbb{R}_{\geq 0} : x(\tau) \in X_U$, where $x_0 \in X_0$.*

3   Computing Barrier Certificates

Given a semialgebraic system M, a barrier certificate is a real-valued function $B(\boldsymbol{x})$ such that (1) $B(\boldsymbol{x}) \geq 0$ for all $\boldsymbol{x}$ in the initial set; (2) $B(\boldsymbol{x}) < 0$ for all $\boldsymbol{x}$ in the unsafe set; (3) no trajectory can escape from the region of $B(\boldsymbol{x}) \geq 0$. Then, the hyper-surface $\{\boldsymbol{x} \in \mathbb{R}^n \mid B(\boldsymbol{x}) = 0\}$ forms a barrier separating the flowpipe from the unsafe set. To compute such a barrier certificate, the most common approach is template based constraint solving, i.e., firstly figure out a sufficient condition for the above condition and then, set up a template polynomial $B(\boldsymbol{u}, \boldsymbol{x})$ of fixed degree, and finally solve the constraint on $\boldsymbol{u}$ derived from the sufficient condition on $B(\boldsymbol{u}, \boldsymbol{x})$. There are a couple of sufficient conditions available for this purpose [13, 22, 27]. In order to have an efficient constraint solving method, we adopt the following condition [33].

Theorem 1. *Given a semialgebraic system M, let X_0 and U be the initial set and the unsafe set respectively, the system is guaranteed to be safe if there exists a real-valued function $B(\boldsymbol{x})$ such that*

$$\forall \boldsymbol{x} \in X_0 : B(\boldsymbol{x}) > 0 \tag{2}$$
$$\forall \boldsymbol{x} \in I : \mathcal{L}_f B > 0 \tag{3}$$
$$\forall \boldsymbol{x} \in X_U : B(\boldsymbol{x}) < 0 \tag{4}$$

In Theorem 1, the condition (3) means that all the trajectories of the system always point in the increasing direction of the level sets of $B(\boldsymbol{x})$ in the region I. Therefore, no trajectory starting from the initial set would cross the zero level set. The benefit of this condition is that it can be solved more efficiently than other existing conditions [13, 22] although it is relatively conservative. The most widely used approach is to transform the constraint-solving problem into a sum-of-squares (SOS) programming problem [33], which can be solved in polynomial time. However, a serious problem with SOS programming based approach is that automatic generation of polynomial templates is very hard to perform. We now show an example to demonstrate the reason. For simplicity, we assume that the initial set, the unsafe set and the invariant are defined by the polynomial inequalities $X_0(\boldsymbol{x}) \geq 0$, $X_U(\boldsymbol{x}) \geq 0$ and $I(\boldsymbol{x}) \geq 0$ respectively, then the SOS relaxation of Theorem 1 is that the following polynomials are all SOS

$$B(\boldsymbol{x}) - \mu_1(\boldsymbol{x})X_0(\boldsymbol{x}) + \epsilon_1 \tag{5}$$
$$\mathcal{L}_f B - \mu_2(\boldsymbol{x})I(\boldsymbol{x}) + \epsilon_2 \tag{6}$$
$$- B(\boldsymbol{x}) - \mu_3(\boldsymbol{x})X_U(\boldsymbol{x}) + \epsilon_3 \tag{7}$$

where $\mu_i(\boldsymbol{x}), i = 1, \cdots, 3$ are SOS polynomials as well and $\epsilon_i > 0, i = 1, \cdots, 3$. Suppose the degrees of $X_0(\boldsymbol{x})$, $I(\boldsymbol{x})$ and $X_U(\boldsymbol{x})$ are all odd numbers. Then, the degree of the template for $B(\boldsymbol{x})$ must be an odd number too. The reason is that, if $deg(B)$ is an even number, in order for the first and third polynomials to be SOS polynomials, $deg(B)$ must be greater than both $deg(\mu_3 X_U)$ and $deg(\mu_1 X_0)$, which are odd numbers. However, since the first and third condition contain $B(\boldsymbol{x})$

and $-B(\boldsymbol{x})$ respectively, their leading monomials must have the opposite sign, which means that they cannot be *SOS* polynomial simultaneously. Moreover, the degrees of the templates for the auxiliary polynomials $\mu_1(\boldsymbol{x}), \mu_3(\boldsymbol{x})$ must also be chosen properly so that $deg(\mu_1 X_0) = deg(\mu_3 X_U) = deg(B)$, because only in this way the leading monomials (which has an odd degree) of (5) and (7) have the chance to be resolved so that the resultant polynomial can be a *SOS*. Similarly, in order to make the second polynomial a *SOS* as well, one has to choose an appropriate degree for $\mu_2(\boldsymbol{x})$ according to the degree of $\mathcal{L}_f B$ and $I(\boldsymbol{x})$. As a result, the tangled constraints on the relevant template polynomials reduce the power of *SOS* programming significantly.

Due to the above reason, inspired by the work [38], we use Handelman representation to relax Theorem 1. We assume that the initial set X_0, the unsafe set X_U and the invariant I are all convex and compact polyhedra, i.e., $X_0 = \{\boldsymbol{x} \in \mathbb{R}^n \mid p_1(\boldsymbol{x}) \geq 0, \cdots, p_{m_1}(\boldsymbol{x}) \geq 0\}$, $I = \{\boldsymbol{x} \in \mathbb{R}^n \mid q_1(\boldsymbol{x}) \geq 0, \cdots, q_{m_2}(\boldsymbol{x}) \geq 0\}$ and $X_U = \{\boldsymbol{x} \in \mathbb{R}^n \mid r_1(\boldsymbol{x}) \geq 0, \cdots, r_{m_3}(\boldsymbol{x}) \geq 0\}$, where $p_i(\boldsymbol{x}), q_j(\boldsymbol{x}), r_k(\boldsymbol{x})$ are linear polynomials. Then, we have the following theorem.

Theorem 2. *Given a semialgebraic system M, let X_0, X_U and I be defined as above, the system is guaranteed to be safe if there exists a real-valued polynomial function $B(\boldsymbol{x})$ such that*

$$B(\boldsymbol{x}) \equiv \sum_{|\alpha| \leq M_1} \lambda_\alpha p_1^{\alpha_1} \cdots p_{m_1}^{\alpha_{m_1}} + \epsilon_1 \tag{8}$$

$$\mathcal{L}_f B \equiv \sum_{|\beta| \leq M_2} \lambda_\beta q_1^{\beta_1} \cdots q_{m_2}^{\beta_{m_2}} + \epsilon_2 \tag{9}$$

$$-B(\boldsymbol{x}) \equiv \sum_{|\gamma| \leq M_3} \lambda_\gamma r_1^{\gamma_1} \cdots r_{m_3}^{\gamma_{m_3}} + \epsilon_3 \tag{10}$$

where $\lambda_\alpha, \lambda_\beta, \lambda_\gamma \in \mathbb{R}_{\geq 0}$, $\epsilon_i \in \mathbb{R}_{>0}$ and $M_i \in \mathbb{N}, i = 1, \cdots, 3$.

Theorem 2 provides us with an alternative to *SOS* programming to find barrier certificate $B(\boldsymbol{x})$ by transforming it into a linear programming problem. The basic idea is that we first set up a template $B(\boldsymbol{u}, \boldsymbol{x})$ of fixed degree as well as the appropriate $M_i, i = 1, \cdots, 3$ that make the both sides of the three identities (8)–(10) have the same degree. Since (8)–(10) are identities, the coefficients of the corresponding monomials on both sides must be identical as well. Thus, we derive a system S of linear equations and inequalities over $\boldsymbol{u}, \lambda_\alpha, \lambda_\beta, \lambda_\gamma$. Now, finding a barrier certificate is just to find a feasible solution for S, which can be solved by linear programming. Compared to *SOS* programming based approach, this approach is more flexible in choosing the polynomial template as well as other parameters. We consider now a linear system to show how it works.

Example 2. Given a 2D system defined by $\dot{x} = 2x + 3y, \dot{y} = -4x + 2y$, let $X_0 = \{(x, y) \in \mathbb{R}^2 \mid p_1 = x + 100 \geq 0, p_2 = -90 - x \geq 0, p_3 = y + 45 \geq 0, p_4 = -40 - y \geq 0\}$, $I = \{(x, y) \in \mathbb{R}^2 \mid q_1 = x + 110 \geq 0, q_2 = -80 - x \geq 0, q_3 = y + 45 \geq 0, q_4 = -20 - y \geq 0\}$ and $X_U = \{(x, y) \in \mathbb{R}^2 \mid r_1 = x + 98 \geq 0, r_2 = $

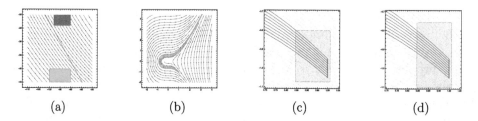

(a)   (b)   (c)   (d)

Fig. 2. (a) Linear barrier certificate (straight red line) for Example 2. Rectangle in green: initial set, rectangle in red: unsafe set. (b) PBT for the running Example 5, consisting of 45 BTs. (c) Enclosure (before bloating) for flowpipe of Example 3 (green shadow region). (d) Enclosure (after bloating) for flowpipe of Example 3. (Color figure online)

$-90-x \geq 0, r_3 = y+24 \geq 0, r_4 = -20-y \geq 0\}$. Assume $B(\boldsymbol{u}, \boldsymbol{x}) = u_1+u_2x+u_3y$, $M_i = \epsilon_i = 1$ for $i = 1, \cdots, 3$, then we obtain the following polynomial identities according to Theorem 2

$$u_1 + u_2x + u_3y - \sum_{i=1}^{4} \lambda_{1i}p_i - \epsilon_1 \equiv 0$$

$$u_2(2x + 3y) + u_3(-4x + 2y) - \sum_{j=1}^{4} \lambda_{2j}q_j - \epsilon_2 \equiv 0$$

$$- (u_1 + u_2x + u_3y) - \sum_{k=1}^{4} \lambda_{3k}r_k - \epsilon_3 \equiv 0$$

where $\lambda_{ij} \geq 0$ for $i = 1, \cdots, 3$, $j = 1, \cdots, 4$. By collecting the coefficients of x, y in the above polynomials, we obtain a system S of linear polynomial equations and inequalities over u_i, λ_{jk}. By solving S using linear programming, we obtain a feasible solution and Fig. 2a shows the computed linear barrier certificate. Note that, for the aforementioned reason, it is impossible to find a linear barrier certificate using *SOS* programming for this example.

4   Piecewise Barrier Tubes

In this section, we introduce how to construct PBTs for nonlinear polynomial systems. The basic idea of constructing PBT is that, for each segment of the flowpipe, an enclosure box is first constructed and then, a BT is constructed to form a tighter over-approximation for the flowpipe segment inside the box.

4.1   Constructing an Enclosure Box

Given an initial set, the first task is to construct an enclosure box for the initial set and the following segment of the flowpipe. As pointed out in Sect. 1, one principle to construct an enclosure box is to simplify the shape of the flowpipe segment, or in other words, to approximately bound the twisting of trajectories by some θ in the box, where the *twisting* of a trajectory is defined as follows.

Definition 5 (Twisting of a trajectory). *Let M be a continuous system and $\zeta(t)$ be a trajectory of M. Then, $\zeta(t)$ is said to have a twisting of θ on the time interval $I = [T_1, T_2]$, written as $\xi_I(\zeta)$, if it satisfies that $\xi_I(\zeta) = \theta$, where*

$$\xi_I(\zeta) \stackrel{def}{=} \sup_{t_1, t_2 \in I} \arccos\left(\frac{\langle \dot{\zeta}(t_1), \dot{\zeta}(t_2) \rangle}{\|\dot{\zeta}(t_1)\| \|\dot{\zeta}(t_2)\|} \right).$$

The basic idea to construct an enclosure box is depicted in Algorithm 1.

Algorithm 1. Algorithm to construct an enclosure box

---

   input : M: dynamics of the system; n: dimension of system; X_0: initial set
           θ_1: twisting of simulation; d: maximum distance of simulation;
   output: E: an enclosure box containing X_0; P: plane where flowpipe exits ;
    G: range of intersection of $Flow_f(X_0)$ with plane P by simulation

1 sample a set S_0 of points from X_0;
2 select a point $x_0 \in S_0$;
3 find a time step size ΔT_0 by (θ, d)-bounded simulation for x_0;
4 $\Delta T \longleftarrow \Delta T_0$;
5 **while** $\Delta T > \epsilon$ **do**
6     $[found, E] \longleftarrow$ find an enclosure box by interval arithmetic using ΔT;
7   **if** *found* **then**
8   do a simulation for all $x_i \in S_0$, select the plane P which intersects with the most of simulations; generate G;
9   bloat E s.t $Flow_f(X_0)$ gets out of E only through the facet in P;
10   break;
11   **else**
12         $\Delta T \longleftarrow 1/2 * \Delta T$;

Remark 1. In Algorithm 1, we use interval arithmetic [29] and simulation to construct an enclosure box E for a given initial set and its following flowpipe segment. Meanwhile, we obtain a coarse range of the intersection of the flowpipe and the boundary of the enclosure, which helps to accelerate the construction of barrier tube. To be simple, the enclosure is constructed in a way such that the flowpipe gets out of the box through a single facet. Given an initial set X_0, we first sample a set S_0 of points from X_0 for simulation. Then, we select a point x_0 from S_0 and do (θ, d)-simulation on x_0 to obtain a time step ΔT. A (θ, d)-simulation is a simulation that stops either when the twisting of the simulation reaches θ or when the distance between x_0 and the end point reaches d. On the one hand, by using a small θ, we aim to achieve a straight flowpipe segment. On the other hand, by specifying a maximal distance d, we make sure that the simulation can stop for a long and straight flowpipe. At each iteration of the *while* loop in line 5, we first try to construct an enclosure box by interval arithmetic over ΔT. If such an enclosure box is created, we then perform a simulation (see line 8) for all the points in S_0 to find out the plane P of facet which intersects with the most of the simulations. The idea behind line 9 is that in order to better over-approximate the intersection of the flowpipe with the boundary of the box using intervals, we push the other planes outwards to make P the only plane where the flowpipe get out of the box. Certainly, simply by simulation we cannot guarantee that the flowpipe does not intersect the other facets. Therefore, we have the following theorem for the decision.

Theorem 3. *Given a semialgebraic system M and an initial set X_0, a box E is an enclosure of X_0 and F_i is a facet of E. Then, $(Flow_f(X_0) \cap E) \cap F_i = \emptyset$ if there exists a barrier certificate $B_i(\boldsymbol{x})$ for X_0 and F_i inside E.*

Remark 2. According to the definition of barrier certificate, the proof of Theorem 3 is straightforward, which is ignored here. Therefore, to make sure that the flowpipe does not intersect the facet F_i, we only need to find a barrier certificate, which can be done using the approach presented in Sect. 3. Moreover, if no barrier certificate can be found, we further bloat the facet. Next, we still use the running Example 1 to demonstrate the process of constructing an enclosure.

Example 3 (running example). Consider the system in Example 1 and the initial set $x = 1.0, -1.05 \leq y \leq -0.95$, let the bounding twisting of simulation be $\theta = \pi/18$, then the time step size we computed for interval evaluation is $\Delta T = 0.2947$. The corresponding enclosure computed by interval arithmetic is shown in Fig. 2c. Furthermore, by simulation, we know that the flowpipe can reach both left facet and top facet. Therefore, we have two options to bloat the facet: bloat the left facet to make the flowpipe intersects the top facet only or bloat the top facet to make the flowpipe intersects left facet only. In this example, we choose the latter option and the bloated enclosure is shown in Fig. 2d. In this way, we can over-approximate the intersection of the flowpipe and the facet by intervals if we can obtain its boundary on every side. This can be achieved by finding barrier tube.

4.2   Compute a Barrier Tube Inside a Box

An important fact about the flowpipe of continuous system is that it tends to be straight if it is short enough, given that the initial set is straight as well (otherwise, we can split it). Suppose there is a small box E around a straight flowpipe, it will be easy to compute a barrier certificate for a given initial set and unsafe set inside E. A barrier tube for the flowpipe in E is a group of barrier certificates which form a tube around a flowpipe inside E. Formally,

Definition 6 (Barrier Tube). *Given a semialgebraic system M, a box E and an initial set $X_0 \subseteq E$, a barrier tube is a set of real-valued functions $BT = \{B_i(\boldsymbol{x}), i = 1, \cdots, m\}$ such that for all $B_i(\boldsymbol{x}) \in BT$: (1) $\forall \boldsymbol{x} \in X_0 : B_i(\boldsymbol{x}) > 0$ and, (2) $\forall \boldsymbol{x} \in E : \mathcal{L}_f B_i > 0$.*

According to Definition 6, a barrier tube BT is defined by a set of real-valued functions and every function inequality $B_i(\boldsymbol{x}) > 0$ is an invariant of M in E and so do their conjunction. The property of a barrier tube BT is formally described in the following theorem.

Theorem 4. *Given a semialgebraic system M, a box E and an initial set $X_0 \subseteq E$, let $BT = \{B_i(\boldsymbol{x}) : i = 1, \cdots, m\}$ be a barrier tube of M and $\Omega = \{\boldsymbol{x} \in \mathbb{R}^n \mid \bigwedge B_i(\boldsymbol{x}) > 0, B_i \in BT\}$, then $Flow_f(X_0) \cap E \subseteq \Omega \cap E$.*

Remark 3. Theorem 4 states that an arbitrary barrier tube is able to form an over-approximation for the reach pipe in the box E. Compared to a single barrier certificate, multiple barrier certificates could over-approximate the flowpipe more precisely. However, since there is no constraint on unsafe sets in Definition 6, a barrier tube satisfying the definition could be very conservative. In order to obtain an accurate approximation for the flowpipe, we choose to create additional auxiliary constraints.

Auxiliary Unsafe Set (AUS). To obtain an accurate barrier tube, there are two main questions to be answered: (1) How many barrier certificates are needed? and (2) How do we control their positions to make the tube well-shaped to better over-approximate the flowpipe? The answer for the first question is quite simple: the more, the better. This will be explained later on. For the second question, the answer is to construct a group of properly distributed auxiliary state sets (AUSs). Each set of the AUSs is used as an unsafe set U_i for the system and then we compute a barrier certificate B_i for U_i according to Theorem 2. Since the zero level set of B_i serves as a barrier between the flowpipe and U_i, the space where a barrier could appear is fully determined by the position of U_i. Roughly speaking, when U_i is far away from the flowpipe, the space for a barrier to exist is wide as well. Correspondingly, the barrier certificate found would usually locate far away from the flowpipe as well. Certainly, as U_i gets closer to the flowpipe, the space for barrier certificates also contracts towards the flowpipe accordingly. Therefore, by expanding U_i towards the flowpipe, we can get more precise over-approximations for the flowpipe.

Why Multiple AUS? Although the accuracy of the barrier certificate over-approximation can be improved by expanding the AUS towards the flowpipe, the capability of a single barrier certificate is very limited because it can erect a barrier which only matches a single profile of the flow pipe. However, if we have a set U of AUSs which are distributed evenly around the flowpipe and there is a barrier certificate B_i for each $U_i \in U$, these barrier certificates would be able to over-approximate the flowpipe from a number of profiles. Therefore, increasing the number of AUSs can increase the quality of the over-approximation as well. Furthermore, if all these auxiliary sets are connected, all the barriers would form a tube surrounding the flowpipe. Therefore, if we can create a series of boxes piecewise covering the flowpipe and then construct a barrier tube for every piece of the flowpipe, we obtain an over-approximation for the flowpipe by PBT.

Based on the above idea, we provide Algorithm 2 to compute barrier tube.

Algorithm 2. Algorithm to compute barrier tube

---

    input : M: dynamics of the system; X_0: Initial set;
               E: interval enclosure of initial set;
               G: interval approx. of $(\partial E \cap Flow_f(X_0))$ by simulation;
               P: plane where flowpipe exits from box;
               D: candidate degree list for template polynomial;
               ϵ: difference in size between AUS (auxiliary unsafe set)
    output: BT: barrier tube; X_0': interval over-approximation of $(BT \cap E)$

---

1 **foreach** G_{ij}: an facet of G **do**
2 | *found* $\longleftarrow$ *false* ;
3 | **foreach** $d \in D$ **do**
4 | | AUS $\longleftarrow$ CreateAUS(G, P, G_{ij});
5 | | **while** *true* **do**
6 | | | $[found, B_{ij}] \longleftarrow$ ComputeBarrierCert(X_0, E, AUS, d) ;
7 | | | **if** *found* **then** AUS' $\longleftarrow$ Expand (AUS);
8 | | | **else** AUS' $\longleftarrow$ Contract (AUS) ;
9 | | | **if** Diff(AUS', AUS) $\leq \epsilon$ **then** break;
10 | | | **else** AUS' $\longleftarrow$ AUS;
11 | **if** *found* **then** BT $\longleftarrow$ Push(BT, B_{ij}); break;
12 | **else** return FAIL;
13 **return** SUCCEED;

Remark 4. In Algorithm 2, for an n-dimensional flowpipe segment, we aim to build a barrier tube composed of $2(n-1)$ barrier certificates, which means we need to construct $2(n-1)$ AUSs. According to Algorithm 1, we know that the plane P is the only exit of the flowpipe from the enclosure E and G is roughly the region where they intersect. Let F^G be the facet of E that contains G, then for every facet F_{ij}^G of F^G, we can take an $(n-1)$-dimensional rectangle between F_{ij}^G and G_{ij} as an AUS, where G_{ij} is the facet of G adjacent to F_G^{ij}. Therefore, enumerating all the facets of G in line 1 would produce $2(n-1)$ positions for AUS. The loop in line 3 is attempting to find a polynomial barrier certificate of different degrees in D. In the while loop 5, we iteratively compute the best barrier certificate by adjusting the width of AUS through binary search until the difference in width between two successive AUSs is less than the specified threshold ϵ.

Example 4 (Running example). Consider the initial set and the enclosure computed in Example 3, we use Algorithm 2 to compute a barrier tube. The initial set is $X_0 = [1.0, 1.0] \times [-1.05, -0.95]$ and the enclosure of X_0 is $E = [0.84, 1.01] \times [-1.1, -0.75]$, $G = [0.84, 0.84] \times [-0.91, -0.80]$, the plane P is $x = 0.84$, $D = \{2\}$ and $\epsilon = 0.001$. The barrier tube consists of two barrier certificates. As shown in Fig. 3, each of the barrier certificates is derived from an AUS (red line segment) which is located respectively on the bottom-left and top-left boundary of E.

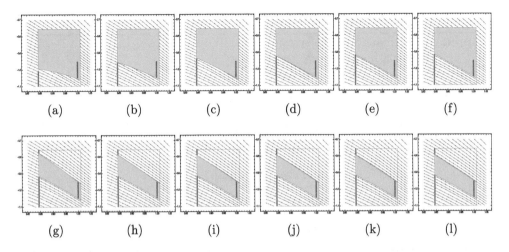

Fig. 3. Computing process of BT for Example 4. Blue line segment: initial set, red line segment: AUS. Figure a–l show how intermediate barrier certificates changed with the width of the AUSs and Fig. l shows the final BT (shadow region in green). (Color figure online)

4.3   Compute Piecewise Barrier Tube

During the computation of a barrier tube by Algorithm 2, we create a series of AUSs around the flowpipe, which build up a rectangular enclosure for the intersection of the flowpipe and the facet of the enclosure box. As a result, such a rectangular enclosure can be taken as an initial set for the following flowpipe segment and then Algorithm 2 can be applied repeatedly to compute a PBT. The basic procedure to compute PBT is presented in Algorithm 3.

Remark 5. In Algorithm 3, initially a box that contains the initial set X_0 is constructed using Algorithm 1. The loop in line 2 consists of 3 major parts: (1) In lines 3–6, a barrier tube BT is firstly computed using Algorithm 2. The **while** loop keeps shrinking the box until a barrier tube is found; (2) In line 8, the initial set X_0 is updated for the next box; (3) In line 9, a new box is constructed to contain X_0 and the process is repeated.

Example 5 (Running example). Let us consider again the running example. We set the length of PBT to 45 and the PBT we obtained is shown in Fig. 2b. Compared to the interval over-approximation of the Taylor model obtained using *Flow**, the computed PBT consists of a significantly reduced number of segments and is more precise for the absence of stretching.

Safety Verification Based on PBT. The idea of safety verification based on PBT is straightforward. Given an unsafe set X_U, for each intermediate initial set X_0 and the corresponding enclosure box E, we first check whether $X_U \cap E = \emptyset$. If not empty, we would further find a barrier certificate between X_U and the flowpipe of X_0 inside E. If empty or barrier found, we continue to compute

---

Algorithm 3. Algorithm to compute PBT

---

   input : M: dynamics of the system; X_0: Initial set;
             N: length of piecewise barrier tube
   output: PBT: piecewise barrier tube

1   E ← construct an initial box containing X_0;
2   **for** $i \leftarrow 1$ **to** N **do**
3      $[Found, \mathsf{BT}] \leftarrow \texttt{findBarrierTube}\ (\mathsf{E}, X_0)$;
4   **while** *not Found* **do**
5   E ← $\texttt{Shrink}\ (\mathsf{E})$;
6         $[Found, \mathsf{BT}] \leftarrow \texttt{findBarrierTube}\ (\mathsf{E}, X_0)$;
7   **if** *Found* **then**
8         $X_0 \leftarrow \texttt{OverApprox}(\mathsf{BT} \cap \texttt{Facet}(\mathsf{E}))$;
9   E ← construct the next box containing X_0;

Table 1. Model definitions

Model	Dynamics	Initial set X_0	Time horizon (TH)
Controller 2D	$\dot{x} = xy + y^3 + 2$	$x \in [29.9, 30.1]$	0.0125
	$\dot{y} = x^2 + 2x - 3y$	$y \in [-38, -36]$	
Van der Pol	$\dot{x} = y$	$x \in [1, 1.5]$	6.74
Oscillator	$\dot{y} = y - x - x^2 y$	$y \in [2.0, 2.45]$	
Lotka-Volterra	$\dot{x} = x(1.5 - y)$	$x \in [4.5, 5.2]$	3.2
	$\dot{y} = -y(3 - x)$	$y \in [1.8, 2.2]$	
	$\dot{x} = 10(y - x)$	$x \in [1.79, 1.81]$	0.51
Controller 3D	$\dot{y} = x^3$	$y \in [1.0, 1.1]$	
	$\dot{z} = xy - 2.667z$	$y \in [0.5, 0.6]$	

longer PBT. The refinement of PBT computation can be achieved by using smaller E and higher d for template polynomial.

5   Implementation and Experiments

We have implemented the proposed approach as a C++ prototype called Piecewise Barrier Tube Solver (*PBTS*), choosing *Gurobi* [12] as our internal linear programming solver. We have also performed some experiments on a benchmark of four nonlinear polynomial dynamical systems (described in Table 1) to compare the efficiency and the effectiveness of our approach w.r.t. other tools. Our experiments were performed on a desktop computer with a 3.6 GHz *Intel Core i7-7700* 8 Core CPU and 32 GB memory. The results are presented in Table 2.

Remark 6. There are a number of outstanding tools for flowpipe computation [1,3–5]. Since our approach is to perform flowpipe computation for polynomial

Table 2. Tool Comparison on Nonlinear Systems. #var: number of variables; T: computing time; NFS: number of flowpipe segments; DEG: candidate degrees for template polynomial (only for *PBTS*); TH: time horizon for flowpipe (only for *Flow** and *CORA*). FAIL: failed to terminate under 30 min.

Model	#var	PBTS			TH	Flow*		CORA	
		T	NFS	DEG		T	NFS	T	NFS
Controller 2D	2	5.62	46	2	0.0125	22.17	6250	FAIL	-
Van der Pol	2	13.38	110	2,3	6.74	15.28	337	212.51	12523
Lotka-Volterra	2	6.65	30	3,4	3.2	10.59	3200	35.84	2903
Controller 3D	3	83.65	15	4	0.51	11.61	5100	65.18	6767

nonlinear systems, we pick two of the most relevant state-of-the-art tools for comparison: *CORA* [1] and *Flow** [3]. Note that a big difference between our approach and the other two approaches is that *PBTS* is time-independent, which means that we cannot compare PBTS with *CORA* or *Flow** over the exactly same time horizon. To be fair enough, for *Flow** and *CORA*, we have used the same time horizon for the flowpipe computation, while we have computed a slightly longer flowpipe using *PBTS*. To guide the reader, we have also used different plotting colors to visualize the difference between the flowpipes obtained from the three different tools.

Evaluation. As pointed out in Sect. 1, a common problem with the bounded-time integration based approaches is that the flowpipe segment of a dynamics system can be extremely stretched with time so that the interval over-approximation of the flowpipe segment is very conservative and usually the solver has to stop prematurely due to the error explosion. This fact can be found easily from the figures Fig. 4, 5, 6 and 7. In particular, for *Controller 2D*, *Flow** can give quite nice result in the beginning but started producing an exploding flowpipe very quickly (Note that *Flow** offers options to produce better plotting which however is expensive and was not used for safety verification. *CORA* even failed to give a result after over 30 min of running). This phenomenon reappeared with both *Flow** and *CORA* for *Controller 3D*. Notice that most of the time horizons used in the experiment are basically the time limits that *Flow** and *CORA* can reach, i.e., a slightly larger value for the time horizon would cause the solvers to fail. In comparison, our tool has no such problem and can survive a much longer flowpipe before exploding or even without exploding as shown in Fig. 4a.

Another important factor of the approaches is the efficiency. As is shown in Table 2, our approach is more efficient on the first three examples but slower on the last example than the other two tools. The reason for this phenomenon is that the degree d of the template polynomial used in the last example is higher than the others and increasing d led to an increase in the number of decision variables in the linear constraint. This suggests that using smaller d on shorter flowpipe segment would be better. In addition, we can also see in Table 2 that the number of the flowpipe segments produced by *PBTS* is much fewer than that

(a) PBTS   (b) Flow*

Fig. 4. Flowpipe for Controller 2D.

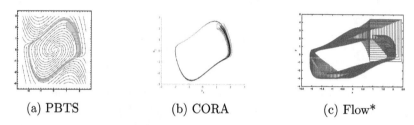

(a) PBTS   (b) CORA   (c) Flow*

Fig. 5. Flowpipe for Van der Pol Oscillator.

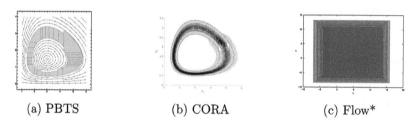

(a) PBTS   (b) CORA   (c) Flow*

Fig. 6. Flowpipe for Lotka-Volterra.

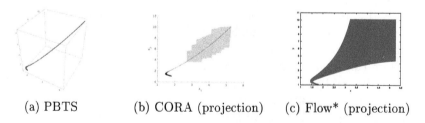

(a) PBTS   (b) CORA (projection)   (c) Flow* (projection)

Fig. 7. Flowpipe (projection) for Controller 3D.

produced by *Flow** and *CORA*. In this respect, *PBTS* would be more efficient on safety verification.

6   Conclusion

We have presented PBTS, a novel approach to over-approximate flowpipes of nonlinear systems with polynomial dynamics. The benefit of using BTs is that they are time-independent and hence cannot be stretched or deformed by time.

Moreover, this approach only results in a small number of BTs which are sufficient to form a tight over-approximation for the flowpipe, hence the safety verification with PBT can be very efficient.

References

1. Althoff, M., Grebenyuk, D.: Implementation of interval arithmetic in CORA 2016. In: Proceedings of ARCH@CPSWeek 2016: The 3rd International Workshop on Applied Verification for Continuous and Hybrid Systems, EPiC Series in Computing, vol. 43, pp. 91–105. EasyChair (2017)
2. Asarin, E., Dang, T., Girard, A.: Hybridization methods for the analysis of nonlinear systems. Acta Inform. **43**(7), 451–476 (2007)
3. Chen, X., Ábrahám, E., Sankaranarayanan, S.: Flow*: an analyzer for non-linear hybrid systems. In: Sharygina, N., Veith, H. (eds.) CAV 2013. LNCS, vol. 8044, pp. 258–263. Springer, Heidelberg (2013). https://doi.org/10.1007/978-3-642-39799-8_18
4. Dang, T., Le Guernic, C., Maler, O.: Computing reachable states for nonlinear biological models. In: Degano, P., Gorrieri, R. (eds.) CMSB 2009. LNCS, vol. 5688, pp. 126–141. Springer, Heidelberg (2009). https://doi.org/10.1007/978-3-642-03845-7_9
5. Duggirala, P.S., Mitra, S., Viswanathan, M., Potok, M.: C2E2: a verification tool for stateflow models. In: Baier, C., Tinelli, C. (eds.) TACAS 2015. LNCS, vol. 9035, pp. 68–82. Springer, Heidelberg (2015). https://doi.org/10.1007/978-3-662-46681-0_5
6. Fränzle, M., Herde, C.: HySAT: an efficient proof engine for bounded model checking of hybrid systems. Form. Methods Syst. Des. **30**(3), 179–198 (2007)
7. Fränzle, M., Herde, C., Teige, T., Ratschan, S., Schubert, T.: Efficient solving of large non-linear arithmetic constraint systems with complex boolean structure. JSAT **1**(3–4), 209–236 (2007)
8. Frehse, G., et al.: SpaceEx: scalable verification of hybrid systems. In: Gopalakrishnan, G., Qadeer, S. (eds.) CAV 2011. LNCS, vol. 6806, pp. 379–395. Springer, Heidelberg (2011). https://doi.org/10.1007/978-3-642-22110-1_30
9. Girard, A.: Reachability of uncertain linear systems using zonotopes. In: Morari, M., Thiele, L. (eds.) HSCC 2005. LNCS, vol. 3414, pp. 291–305. Springer, Heidelberg (2005). https://doi.org/10.1007/978-3-540-31954-2_19
10. Girard, A., Le Guernic, C.: Efficient reachability analysis for linear systems using support functions. In: Proceedings of IFAC World Congress, vol. 41, no. 2, pp. 8966–8971 (2008)
11. Grosu, R., et al.: From cardiac cells to genetic regulatory networks. In: Gopalakrishnan, G., Qadeer, S. (eds.) CAV 2011. LNCS, vol. 6806, pp. 396–411. Springer, Heidelberg (2011). https://doi.org/10.1007/978-3-642-22110-1_31
12. Gu, Z., Rothberg, E., Bixby, R.: Gurobi optimizer reference manual (2017). http://www.gurobi.com/documentation/7.5/refman/refman.html
13. Gulwani, S., Tiwari, A.: Constraint-based approach for analysis of hybrid systems. In: Gupta, A., Malik, S. (eds.) CAV 2008. LNCS, vol. 5123, pp. 190–203. Springer, Heidelberg (2008). https://doi.org/10.1007/978-3-540-70545-1_18
14. Gurung, A., Ray, R., Bartocci, E., Bogomolov, S., Grosu, R.: Parallel reachability analysis of hybrid systems in xspeed. Int. J. Softw. Tools Technol. Transf. (2018)
15. Handelman, D.: Representing polynomials by positive linear functions on compact convex polyhedra. Pac. J. Math. **132**(1), 35–62 (1988)

16. Hartmanns, A., Hermanns, H.: The modest toolset: an integrated environment for quantitative modelling and verification. In: Ábrahám, E., Havelund, K. (eds.) TACAS 2014. LNCS, vol. 8413, pp. 593–598. Springer, Heidelberg (2014). https://doi.org/10.1007/978-3-642-54862-8_51

17. Henzinger, T.A.: The theory of hybrid automata. In: Proceedings of IEEE Symposium on Logic in Computer Science, pp. 278–292 (1996)

18. Huang, Z., Fan, C., Mereacre, A., Mitra, S., Kwiatkowska, M.: Invariant verification of nonlinear hybrid automata networks of cardiac cells. In: Biere, A., Bloem, R. (eds.) CAV 2014. LNCS, vol. 8559, pp. 373–390. Springer, Cham (2014). https://doi.org/10.1007/978-3-319-08867-9_25

19. Jiang, Y., Yang, Y., Liu, H., Kong, H., Gu, M., Sun, J., Sha, L.: From state-flow simulation to verified implementation: a verification approach and a real-time train controller design. In: 2016 IEEE Real-Time and Embedded Technology and Applications Symposium (RTAS), pp. 1–11. IEEE (2016)

20. Jiang, Y., Zhang, H., Li, Z., Deng, Y., Song, X., Ming, G., Sun, J.: Design and optimization of multiclocked embedded systems using formal techniques. IEEE Trans. Ind. Electron. **62**(2), 1270–1278 (2015)

21. Kong, H., Bogomolov, S., Schilling, C., Jiang, Y., Henzinger, T.A.: Safety verification of nonlinear hybrid systems based on invariant clusters. In: Proceedings of HSCC 2017: The 20th International Conference on Hybrid Systems: Computation and Control, pp. 163–172. ACM (2017)

22. Kong, H., He, F., Song, X., Hung, W.N.N., Gu, M.: Exponential-condition-based barrier certificate generation for safety verification of hybrid systems. In: Sharygina, N., Veith, H. (eds.) CAV 2013. LNCS, vol. 8044, pp. 242–257. Springer, Heidelberg (2013). https://doi.org/10.1007/978-3-642-39799-8_17

23. Kong, S., Gao, S., Chen, W., Clarke, E.: dReach: δ-reachability analysis for hybrid systems. In: Baier, C., Tinelli, C. (eds.) TACAS 2015. LNCS, vol. 9035, pp. 200–205. Springer, Heidelberg (2015). https://doi.org/10.1007/978-3-662-46681-0_15

24. Krilavicius, T.: Hybrid techniques for hybrid systems. Ph.D. thesis, University of Twente, Enschede, Netherlands (2006)

25. Lal, R., Prabhakar, P.: Bounded error flowpipe computation of parameterized linear systems. In: Proceedings of EMSOFT 2015: The International Conference on Embedded Software, pp. 237–246. IEEE (2015)

26. Le Guernic, C., Girard, A.: Reachability analysis of hybrid systems using support functions. In: Bouajjani, A., Maler, O. (eds.) CAV 2009. LNCS, vol. 5643, pp. 540–554. Springer, Heidelberg (2009). https://doi.org/10.1007/978-3-642-02658-4_40

27. Liu, J., Zhan, N., Zhao, H.: Computing semi-algebraic invariants for polynomial dynamical systems. In: Proceedings of EMSOFT 2011: The 11th International Conference on Embedded Software, pp. 97–106. ACM (2011)

28. Matringe, N., Moura, A.V., Rebiha, R.: Generating invariants for non-linear hybrid systems by linear algebraic methods. In: Cousot, R., Martel, M. (eds.) SAS 2010. LNCS, vol. 6337, pp. 373–389. Springer, Heidelberg (2010). https://doi.org/10.1007/978-3-642-15769-1_23

29. Nedialkov, N.S.: Interval tools for ODEs and DAEs. In: Proceedings of SCAN 2006: The 12th GAMM - IMACS International Symposium on Scientific Computing, Computer Arithmetic and Validated Numerics, p. 4. IEEE (2006)

30. Neher, M., Jackson, K.R., Nedialkov, N.S.: On Taylor model based integration of ODEs. SIAM J. Numer. Anal. **45**(1), 236–262 (2007)

31. Prabhakar, P., Soto, M.G.: Hybridization for stability analysis of switched linear systems. In: Proceedings of HSCC 2016: The 19th International Conference on Hybrid Systems: Computation and Control, pp. 71–80. ACM (2016)

32. Prabhakar, P., Viswanathan, M.: A dynamic algorithm for approximate flow computations. In: Proceedings of HSSC 2011: The 14th International Conference on Hybrid Systems: Computation and Control, pp. 133–142. ACM (2011)
33. Prajna, S., Jadbabaie, A.: Safety verification of hybrid systems using barrier certificates. In: Alur, R., Pappas, G.J. (eds.) HSCC 2004. LNCS, vol. 2993, pp. 477–492. Springer, Heidelberg (2004). https://doi.org/10.1007/978-3-540-24743-2_32
34. Ray, R., et al.: XSpeed: accelerating reachability analysis on multi-core processors. In: Piterman, N. (ed.) HVC 2015. LNCS, vol. 9434, pp. 3–18. Springer, Cham (2015). https://doi.org/10.1007/978-3-319-26287-1_1
35. Roohi, N., Prabhakar, P., Viswanathan, M.: Hybridization based CEGAR for hybrid automata with affine dynamics. In: Chechik, M., Raskin, J.-F. (eds.) TACAS 2016. LNCS, vol. 9636, pp. 752–769. Springer, Heidelberg (2016). https://doi.org/10.1007/978-3-662-49674-9_48
36. Sankaranarayanan, S.: Automatic invariant generation for hybrid systems using ideal fixed points. In: Proceedings of HSCC 2010: The 13th ACM International Conference on Hybrid Systems: Computation and Control, pp. 221–230. ACM (2010)
37. Sankaranarayanan, S., Sipma, H.B., Manna, Z.: Constructing invariants for hybrid systems. In: Alur, R., Pappas, G.J. (eds.) HSCC 2004. LNCS, vol. 2993, pp. 539–554. Springer, Heidelberg (2004). https://doi.org/10.1007/978-3-540-24743-2_36
38. Sankaranarayanan, S., Chen, X., et al.: Lyapunov function synthesis using handelman representations. In: IFAC Proceedings Volumes, vol. 46, no. 23, pp. 576–581 (2013)
39. Sogokon, A., Ghorbal, K., Jackson, P.B., Platzer, A.: A method for invariant generation for polynomial continuous systems. In: Jobstmann, B., Leino, K.R.M. (eds.) VMCAI 2016. LNCS, vol. 9583, pp. 268–288. Springer, Heidelberg (2016). https://doi.org/10.1007/978-3-662-49122-5_13
40. Stengle, G.: A nullstellensatz and a positivstellensatz in semialgebraic geometry. Math. Ann. 207(2), 87–97 (1974)

10

Start Pruning When Time Gets Urgent: Partial Order Reduction for Timed Systems

Frederik M. Bønneland, Peter Gjøl Jensen,
Kim Guldstrand Larsen, Marco Muñiz,
and Jiří Srba[✉]

Department of Computer Science,
Aalborg University, Aalborg, Denmark
{frederikb,pgj,kgl,muniz,srba}@cs.aau.dk

Abstract. Partial order reduction for timed systems is a challenging topic due to the dependencies among events induced by time acting as a global synchronization mechanism. So far, there has only been a limited success in finding practically applicable solutions yielding significant state space reductions. We suggest a working and efficient method to facilitate stubborn set reduction for timed systems with urgent behaviour. We first describe the framework in the general setting of timed labelled transition systems and then instantiate it to the case of timed-arc Petri nets. The basic idea is that we can employ classical untimed partial order reduction techniques as long as urgent behaviour is enforced. Our solution is implemented in the model checker TAPAAL and the feature is now broadly available to the users of the tool. By a series of larger case studies, we document the benefits of our method and its applicability to real-world scenarios.

1 Introduction

Partial order reduction techniques for untimed systems, introduced by Godefroid, Peled, and Valmari in the nineties (see e.g. [6]), have since long proved successful in combating the notorious state space explosion problem. For *timed* systems, the success of partial order reduction has been significantly challenged by the strong dependencies between events caused by time as a global synchronizer. Only recently—and moreover in combination with *approximate* abstraction techniques—stubborn set techniques have demonstrated a true reduction potential for systems modelled by timed automata [23].

We pursue an orthogonal solution to the current partial order approaches for timed systems and, based on a stubborn set reduction [28,39], we target a general class of timed systems with *urgent behaviour*. In a modular modelling approach for timed systems, urgency is needed to realistically model behaviour in a component that should be unobservable to other components [36]. Examples of such instantaneously evolving behaviours include, among others, cases like behaviour detection in a part of a sensor (whose duration is assumed to be negligible) or handling of release and completion of periodic tasks in a real-time operating system. We observe that focusing on the urgent part of the behaviour of a timed system allows us to exploit the full range of partial order reduction techniques already validated for untimed systems. This leads to an exact and broadly applicable reduction technique, which we shall demonstrate on a series of industrial case studies showing significant space and time reduction. In order to highlight the generality of the approach, we first describe our reduction technique in the setting of timed labelled transition systems. We shall then instantiate it to timed-arc Petri nets and implement and experimentally validate it in the model checker TAPAAL [19].

Let us now briefly introduce the model of timed-arc Peri nets and explain our reduction ideas. In timed-arc Petri nets, each token is associated with a nonnegative integer representing its age and input arcs to transitions contain intervals, restricting the ages of tokens available for transition firing (if an interval is missing, we assume the default interval $[0, \infty]$ that accepts all token ages). In Fig. 1a we present a simple monitoring system modelled as a timed-arc Petri net. The system consists of two identical sensors where sensor i, $i \in \{1, 2\}$, is represented by the places b_i and m_i, and the transitions s_i and r_i. Once a token of age 0 is placed into the place b_i, the sensor gets started by executing the transition s_i and moving the token from place b_i to m_i where the monitoring process starts. As the place b_i has an associated age invariant ≤ 0, meaning that all tokens in b_i must be of age at most 0, no time delay is allowed and the firing of s_i becomes urgent. In the monitoring place m_i we have to delay one time unit before the transition r_i reporting the reading of the sensor becomes enabled. Due to the age invariant ≤ 1 in the place m_i, we cannot wait longer than one time unit, after which r_i becomes also urgent.

The places c_1, c_2 and c_3 together with the transitions i_1, i_2 and t are used to control the initialization of the sensors. At the execution start, only the transition i_1 is enabled and because it is an urgent transition (denoted by the white circle), no delay is initially possible and i_1 must be fired immediately while removing the token of age 0 from c_1 and placing a new token of age 0 into c_2. At the same time, the first sensor gets started as i_1 also places a fresh token of age 0 into b_1. Now the control part of the net can decide to fire without any delay the transition i_2 and start the second sensor, or it can delay one unit of time after which i_2 becomes urgent due to the age invariant ≤ 1 as the token in c_2 is now of age 1. If i_2 is fired now, it will place a fresh token of age 0 into b_2. However, the token that is moved from c_2 to c_3 by the pair of transport arcs with the diamond-shaped arrow tips preserves its age 1, so now we have to wait precisely one more time unit before t becomes enabled. Moreover, before t can be fired, the places m_1 and m_2 must be empty as otherwise the firing of t is disabled due to inhibitor arcs with circle-shaped arrow tips.

In Fig. 1b we represent the reachable state space of the simple monitoring system where markings are represented using the notation like $c_3 : 1 + b_2 : 2$ that stands for one token of age 1 in place c_3 and one token of age 2 in place b_2. The dashed boxes represent the markings that can be avoided during the state space exploration when we apply our partial order reduction method for checking if

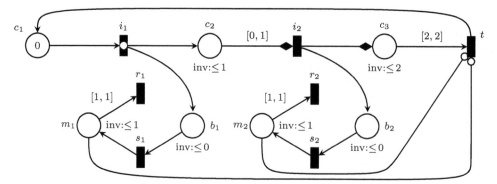

(a) TAPN model of a simple monitoring system

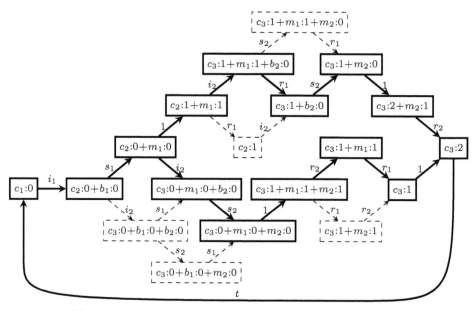

(b) Reachable state space generated by the net in Figure 1a

Fig. 1. Simple monitoring system

the termination transition t can become enabled from the initial marking. We can see that the partial order reduction is applied such that it preserves at least one path to all configurations where our goal is reached (transition t is enabled) and where time is not urgent anymore (i.e. to the configurations that allow the delay of 1 time unit). The basic idea of our approach is to apply the stubborn set reduction on the commutative diamonds where time is not allowed to elapse.

Related Work. Our stubborn set reduction is based on the work of Valmari et al. [28,39]. We formulate their stubborn set method in the abstract framework of labelled transition systems with time and add further axioms for time elapsing in order to guarantee preservation of the reachability properties.

For Petri nets, Yoneda and Schlingloff [41] apply a partial order reduction to one-safe time Petri nets, however, as claimed in [38], the method is mainly suitable for small to medium models due to a computational overhead, confirmed also in [29]. The experimental evaluation in [41] shows only one selected example. Sloan and Buy [38] try to improve on the efficiency of the method, at the expense of considering only a rather limited model of *simple time Petri nets* where each transition has a statically assigned duration. Lilius [29] suggests to instead use alternative semantics of timed Petri nets to remove the issues related to the global nature of time, allowing him to apply directly the untimed partial order approaches. However, the semantics is nonstandard and no experiments are reported. Another approach is by Virbitskaite and Pokozy [40], who apply a partial order method on the *region graph* of bounded time Petri nets. Region graphs are in general not an efficient method for state space representation and the method is demonstrated only on a small buffer example with no further experimental validation. Recently, partial order techniques were suggested by André et al. for parametric time Petri nets [5], however, the approach is working only for safe and acyclic nets. Boucheneb and Barkaoui [12–14] discuss a partial order reduction technique for timed Petri nets based on *contracted state class graphs* and present a few examples on a prototype implementation (the authors do not refer to any publicly available tool). Their method is different from ours as it aims at adding timing constrains to the independence relation, but it does not exploit urgent behaviour. Moreover, the models of time Petri nets and timed-arc Petri nets are, even on the simplest nets, incomparable due to the different way to modelling time.

The fact that we are still lacking a practically applicable method for the time Petri net model is documented by a missing implementation of the technique in leading tools for time Petri net model checking like TINA [9] and Romeo [22]. We are not aware of any work on partial order reduction technique for the class of timed-arc Petri nets that we consider in this paper. This is likely because this class of nets provides even more complex timing behaviour, as we consider unbounded nets where each token carries its timing information (and needs a separate clock to remember the timing), while in time Petri nets timing is associated only to a priory fixed number of transitions in the net.

In the setting of timed automata [3], early work on partial order reduction includes Bengtsson et al. [8] and Minea [32] where they introduce the notion of local as well as global clocks but provide no experimental evaluation. Dams et al. [18] introduce the notion of *covering* in order to generalize dependencies but also here no empirical evaluation is provided. Lugiez, Niebert et al. [30,34] study the notion of *event zones* (capturing time-durations between events) and use it to implement Mazurkiewicz-trace reductions. Salah et al. [37] introduce and implement an exact method based on merging zones resulting from different interleavings. The method achieves performance comparable with the approximate convex-hull abstraction which is by now superseded by the exact LU-abstraction [7]. Most recently, Hansen et al. [23] introduce a variant of stubborn sets for reducing an *abstracted zone graph*, thus in general offering overapproximate analysis. Our technique is orthogonal to the other approaches mentioned above; not only is the model different but also the application of our reduction gives exact results and is based on new reduction ideas. Finally, the idea of applying partial order reduction for independent events that happen at the same time appeared also in [15] where the authors, however, use a static method that declares actions as independent only if they do not communicate, do not emit signals and do not access any shared variables. Our realization of the method to the case of timed-arc Petri nets applies a dynamic (on-the-fly) reduction, while executing a detailed timing analysis that allows us to declare more transitions as independent—sometimes even in the case when they share resources.

2   Partial Order Reduction for Timed Systems

We shall now describe the general idea of our partial order reduction technique (based on stubborn sets [28, 39]) in terms of timed transition systems. We consider real-time delays in the rest of this section, as these results are not specific only to discrete time semantics. Let A be a given set of actions such that $A \cap \mathbb{R}_{\geq 0} = \emptyset$ where $\mathbb{R}_{\geq 0}$ stands for the set of nonnegative real numbers.

Definition 1 (Timed Transition System). *A timed transition system is a tuple $(S, s_0, \rightarrow)$ where S is a set of states, $s_0 \in S$ is the initial state, and $\rightarrow \subseteq S \times (A \cup \mathbb{R}_{\geq 0}) \times S$ is the transition relation.*

If $(s, \alpha, s') \in \rightarrow$ we write $s \xrightarrow{\alpha} s'$. We implicitly assume that if $s \xrightarrow{0} s'$ then $s = s'$, i.e. zero time delays do not change the current state. The set of *enabled actions* at a state $s \in S$ is defined as $\mathsf{En}(s) \overset{\text{def}}{=} \{a \in A \mid \exists s' \in S.\ s \xrightarrow{a} s'\}$. Given a sequence of actions $w = \alpha_1 \alpha_2 \alpha_3 \dots \alpha_n \in (A \cup \mathbb{R}_{\geq 0})^*$ we write $s \xrightarrow{w} s'$ iff $s \xrightarrow{\alpha_1} \dots \xrightarrow{\alpha_n} s'$. If there is a sequence w of length n such that $s \xrightarrow{w} s'$, we also write $s \rightarrow^n s'$. Finally, let $\rightarrow^*$ be the reflexive and transitive closure of the relation $\rightarrow$ such that $s \rightarrow s'$ iff there is $\alpha \in \mathbb{R}_{\geq 0} \cup A$ and $s \xrightarrow{\alpha} s'$.

For the rest of this section, we assume a fixed transition system $(S, s_0, \rightarrow)$ and a set of goal states $G \subseteq S$. The *reachability problem*, given a timed transition system $(S, s_0, \rightarrow)$ and a set of goal states G, is to decide whether there is $s' \in G$ such that $s_0 \rightarrow^* s'$.

We now develop the theoretical foundations of stubborn sets for timed transition systems. A state $s \in S$ is *zero time* if time can not elapse at s. We denote the zero time property of a state s by the predicate $\mathsf{zt}(s)$ and define it as $\mathsf{zt}(s)$ iff for all $s' \in S$ and all $d \in \mathbb{R}_{\geq 0}$ if $s \xrightarrow{d} s'$ then $d = 0$. A *reduction* of a timed transition system is a function $\mathsf{St} : S \rightarrow 2^A$. A reduction defines a reduced transition relation $\underset{\mathsf{St}}{\rightarrow} \subseteq \rightarrow$ such that $s \underset{\mathsf{St}}{\xrightarrow{\alpha}} s'$ iff $s \xrightarrow{\alpha} s'$ and $\alpha \in \mathsf{St}(s) \cup \mathbb{R}_{\geq 0}$. For a given state $s \in S$ we define $\overline{\mathsf{St}(s)} \overset{\text{def}}{=} A \setminus \mathsf{St}(s)$ as the set of all actions that are not in $\mathsf{St}(s)$.

Definition 2 (Reachability Conditions). *A reduction St on a timed transition system $(S, s_0, \rightarrow)$ is* reachability preserving *if it satisfies the following four conditions.*

$(\mathcal{Z})$ $\forall s \in S.\ \neg zt(s) \implies En(s) \subseteq St(s)$

$(\mathcal{D})$ $\forall s, s' \in S.\ \forall w \in \overline{St(s)}^{*}.\ zt(s) \wedge s \xrightarrow{w} s' \implies zt(s')$

$(\mathcal{R})$ $\forall s, s' \in S.\ \forall w \in \overline{St(s)}^{*}.\ zt(s) \wedge s \xrightarrow{w} s' \wedge s \notin G \implies s' \notin G$

$(\mathcal{W})$ $\forall s, s' \in S.\ \forall w \in \overline{St(s)}^{*}.\ \forall a \in St(s).\ zt(s) \wedge s \xrightarrow{wa} s' \implies s \xrightarrow{aw} s'$

Condition $\mathcal{Z}$ declares that in a state where a delay is possible, all enabled actions become stubborn actions. Condition $\mathcal{D}$ guarantees that in order to enable a time delay from a state where delaying is not allowed, a stubborn action must be executed. Similarly, Condition $\mathcal{R}$ requires that a stubborn action must be executed before a goal state can be reached from a non-goal state. Finally, Condition $\mathcal{W}$ allows us to commute stubborn actions with non-stubborn actions. The following theorem shows that reachability preserving reductions generate pruned transition systems where the reachability of goal states is preserved.

Theorem 1 (Shortest-Distance Reachability Preservation). *Let* St *be a reachability preserving reduction satisfying* $\mathcal{Z}$, $\mathcal{D}$, $\mathcal{R}$ *and* $\mathcal{W}$. *Let* $s \in S$. *If* $s \to^{n} s'$ *for some* $s' \in G$ *then also* $s \xrightarrow[St]{}^{m} s''$ *for some* $s'' \in G$ *where* $m \leq n$.

Proof. We proceed by induction on n. *Base step.* If $n = 0$, then $s = s'$ and $m = n = 0$. *Inductive step.* Let $s_0 \xrightarrow{\alpha_0} s_1 \xrightarrow{\alpha_1} \ldots \xrightarrow{\alpha_n} s_{n+1}$ where $s_0 \notin G$ and $s_{n+1} \in G$. Without loss of generality we assume that for all i, $0 \leq i \leq n$, we have $\alpha_i \neq 0$ (otherwise we can simply skip these 0-delay actions and get a shorter sequence). We have two cases. Case $\neg zt(s_0)$: by condition $\mathcal{Z}$ we have $En(s_0) \subseteq St(s_0)$ and by the definition of $\xrightarrow[St]{}$ we have $s_0 \xrightarrow[St]{\alpha_0} s_1$ since $\alpha_0 \in En(s_0) \cup \mathbb{R}_{\geq 0}$. By the induction hypothesis we have $s_1 \xrightarrow[St]{}^{m} s''$ with $s'' \in G$ and $m \leq n$ and $m + 1 \leq n + 1$. Case $zt(s_0)$: let $w = \alpha_0 \alpha_1 \ldots \alpha_n$ and α_i be such that $\alpha_i \in St(s_0)$ and for all $k < i$ holds that $\alpha_k \notin St(s_0)$, i.e. α_i is the first stubborn action in w. Such an α_i has to exist otherwise $s_{n+1} \notin G$ due to condition $\mathcal{R}$. Because of condition $\mathcal{D}$ we get $zt(s_k)$ for all k, $0 \leq k < i$, otherwise α_i cannot be the first stubborn action in w. We can split w as $w = u\alpha_i v$ with $u \in \overline{St(s_0)}^{*}$. Since all states in the path to s_i are zero time, by $\mathcal{W}$ we can swap α_i as $s_0 \xrightarrow{\alpha_i} s'_1 \xrightarrow{u} s_i \xrightarrow{v} s'$ with $|uv| = n$. Since $\alpha_i \in St(s_0)$ we get $s_0 \xrightarrow[St]{\alpha_i} s'_1$ and by the induction hypothesis we have $s'_1 \xrightarrow[St]{}^{m} s''$ where $s'' \in G$, $m \leq n$, and $m + 1 \leq n + 1$. $\square$

3 Timed-Arc Petri Nets

We shall now define the model of timed-arc Petri nets (as informally described in the introduction) together with a reachability logic and a few technical lemmas needed later on. Let $\mathbb{N}_0 = \mathbb{N} \cup \{0\}$ and $\mathbb{N}_0^{\infty} = \mathbb{N}_0 \cup \{\infty\}$. We define the set of *well-formed closed time intervals* as $\mathcal{I} \overset{\text{def}}{=} \{[a, b] \mid a \in \mathbb{N}_0, b \in \mathbb{N}_0^{\infty}, a \leq b\}$ and its subset $\mathcal{I}^{\text{inv}} \overset{\text{def}}{=} \{[0, b] \mid b \in \mathbb{N}_0^{\infty}\}$ used in age invariants.

Definition 3 (Timed-Arc Petri Net). *A* timed-arc Petri net *(TAPN) is a 9-tuple* $N = (P, T, T_{urg}, IA, OA, g, w, Type, I)$ *where*

- P is a finite set of places,
- T is a finite set of transitions such that $P \cap T = \emptyset$,
- $T_{urg} \subseteq T$ is the set of urgent transitions,
- $IA \subseteq P \times T$ is a finite set of input arcs,
- $OA \subseteq T \times P$ is a finite set of output arcs,
- $g : IA \to \mathcal{I}$ is a time constraint function assigning guards (time intervals) to input arcs s.t.
  - if $(p,t) \in IA$ and $t \in T_{urg}$ then $g((p,t)) = [0,\infty]$,
- $w : IA \cup OA \to \mathbb{N}$ is a function assigning weights to input and output arcs,
- $Type : IA \cup OA \to \textbf{Types}$ is a type function assigning a type to all arcs where $\textbf{Types} = \{Normal, Inhib\} \cup \{Transport_j \mid j \in \mathbb{N}\}$ such that
  - if $Type(z) = Inhib$ then $z \in IA$ and $g(z) = [0,\infty]$,
  - if $Type((p,t)) = Transport_j$ for some $(p,t) \in IA$ then there is exactly one $(t,p') \in OA$ such that $Type((t,p')) = Transport_j$,
  - if $Type((t,p')) = Transport_j$ for some $(t,p') \in OA$ then there is exactly one $(p,t) \in IA$ such that $Type((p,t)) = Transport_j$,
  - if $Type((p,t)) = Transport_j = Type((t,p'))$ then $w((p,t)) = w((t,p'))$,
- $I : P \to \mathcal{I}^{inv}$ is a function assigning age invariants to places.

Note that for transport arcs we assume that they come in pairs (for each type $Transport_j$) and that their weights match. Also for inhibitor arcs and for input arcs to urgent transitions, we require that the guards are $[0,\infty]$.

Before we give the formal semantics of the model, let us fix some notation. Let $N = (P,T,T_{urg}, IA, OA, g, w, Type, I)$ be a TAPN. We denote by ${}^\bullet x \stackrel{\text{def}}{=} \{y \in P \cup T \mid (y,x) \in IA \cup OA, \ Type((y,x)) \neq Inhib\}$ the preset of a transition or a place x. Similarly, the postset is defined as $x^\bullet \stackrel{\text{def}}{=} \{y \in P \cup T \mid (x,y) \in (IA \cup OA)\}$. We denote by ${}^\circ t \stackrel{\text{def}}{=} \{p \in P \mid (p,t) \in IA \wedge Type((p,t)) = Inhib\}$ the inhibitor preset of a transition t. The inhibitor postset of a place p is defined as $p^\circ \stackrel{\text{def}}{=} \{t \in T \mid (p,t) \in IA \wedge Type((p,t)) = Inhib\}$. Let $\mathcal{B}(\mathbb{R}^{\geq 0})$ be the set of all finite multisets over $\mathbb{R}^{\geq 0}$. A marking M on N is a function $M : P \longrightarrow \mathcal{B}(\mathbb{R}^{\geq 0})$ where for every place $p \in P$ and every token $x \in M(p)$ we have $x \in I(p)$, in other words all tokens have to satisfy the age invariants. The set of all markings in a net N is denoted by $\mathcal{M}(N)$.

We write (p,x) to denote a token at a place p with the age $x \in \mathbb{R}^{\geq 0}$. Then $M = \{(p_1,x_1),(p_2,x_2),\ldots,(p_n,x_n)\}$ is a multiset representing a marking M with n tokens of ages x_i in places p_i. We define the size of a marking as $|M| = \sum_{p \in P} |M(p)|$ where $|M(p)|$ is the number of tokens located in the place p. A marked TAPN (N, M_0) is a TAPN N together with an initial marking M_0 with all tokens of age 0.

Definition 4 (Enabledness). Let $N = (P,T,T_{urg}, IA, OA, g, w, Type, I)$ be a TAPN. We say that a transition $t \in T$ is enabled in a marking M by the multisets of tokens $In = \{(p,x_p^1),(p,x_p^2),\ldots,(p,x_p^{w((p,t))}) \mid p \in {}^\bullet t\} \subseteq M$ and $Out = \{(p',x_{p'}^1),(p',x_{p'}^2),\ldots,(p',x_{p'}^{w((t,p'))}) \mid p' \in t^\bullet\}$ if

– *for all input arcs except the inhibitor arcs, the tokens from In satisfy the age guards of the arcs, i.e.*

$$\forall p \in {}^{\bullet}t.\ x_p^i \in g((p,t))\ for\ 1 \le i \le w((p,t))$$

– *for any inhibitor arc pointing from a place p to the transition t, the number of tokens in p is smaller than the weight of the arc, i.e.*

$$\forall (p,t) \in IA.\ Type((p,t)) = Inhib \Rightarrow |M(p)| < w((p,t))$$

– *for all input arcs and output arcs which constitute a transport arc, the age of the input token must be equal to the age of the output token and satisfy the invariant of the output place, i.e.*

$$\forall (p,t) \in IA.\forall (t,p') \in OA.\ Type((p,t)) = Type((t,p')) = Transport_j$$
$$\Rightarrow \left(x_p^i = x_{p'}^i \land x_{p'}^i \in I(p') \right)\ for\ 1 \le i \le w((p,t))$$

– *for all normal output arcs, the age of the output token is 0, i.e.*

$$\forall (t,p') \in OA.\ Type((t,p')) = Normal \Rightarrow x_{p'}^i = 0\ for\ 1 \le i \le w((t,p')).$$

A given marked TAPN (N, M_0) defines a timed transition system $T(N) \overset{\text{def}}{=} (\mathcal{M}(N), M_0, \rightarrow)$ where the states are markings and the transitions are as follows.

– If $t \in T$ is enabled in a marking M by the multisets of tokens In and Out then t can *fire* and produce the marking $M' = (M \setminus In) \uplus Out$ where $\uplus$ is the multiset sum operator and $\setminus$ is the multiset difference operator; we write $M \overset{t}{\rightarrow} M'$ for this action transition.
– A time *delay* $d \in \mathbb{N}_0$ is allowed in M if
   • $(x + d) \in I(p)$ for all $p \in P$ and all $x \in M(p)$, i.e. by delaying d time units no token violates any of the age invariants, and
   • if $M \overset{t}{\rightarrow} M'$ for some $t \in T_{urg}$ then $d = 0$, i.e. enabled urgent transitions disallow time passing.
By delaying d time units in M we reach the marking M' defined as $M'(p) = \{x + d \mid x \in M(p)\}$ for all $p \in P$; we write $M \overset{d}{\rightarrow} M'$ for this delay transition.

Note that the semantics above defines the discrete-time semantics as the delays are restricted to nonnegative integers. It is well known that for timed-arc Petri nets with nonstrict intervals, the marking reachability problem on discrete and continuous time nets coincide [31]. This is, however, not the case for more complex properties like liveness that can be expressed in the CTL logic (for counter examples that can be expressed in CTL see e.g. [25]).

3.1 Reachability Logic and Interesting Sets of Transitions

We now describe a logic for expressing the properties of markings based on the number of tokens in places and transition enabledness, inspired by the logic

Table 1. Interesting transitions of φ (assuming $M \not\models \varphi$, otherwise $A_M(\varphi) = \emptyset$)

Formula φ	$A_M(\varphi)$	$A_M(\neg\varphi)$
deadlock	$({}^\bullet t)^\bullet \cup {}^\bullet({}^\circ t)$ for some $t \in \mathsf{En}(M)$	$\emptyset$
t	${}^\bullet p$ for some $p \in {}^\bullet t$ where $M(p) < w((p,t))$ or $p^\bullet$ for some $p \in {}^\circ t$ where $M(p) \geq w((p,t))$	$({}^\bullet t)^\bullet \cup {}^\bullet({}^\circ t)$
$e_1 < e_2$	$decr_M(e_1) \cup incr_M(e_2)$	$A_M(e_1 \geq e_2)$
$e_1 \leq e_2$	$decr_M(e_1) \cup incr_M(e_2)$	$A_M(e_1 > e_2)$
$e_1 > e_2$	$incr_M(e_1) \cup decr_M(e_2)$	$A_M(e_1 \leq e_2)$
$e_1 \geq e_2$	$incr_M(e_1) \cup decr_M(e_2)$	$A_M(e_1 < e_2)$
$e_1 = e_2$	$decr_M(e_1) \cup incr_M(e_2)$ if $eval_M(e_1) > eval_M(e_2)$ $incr_M(e_1) \cup decr_M(e_2)$ if $eval_M(e_1) < eval_M(e_2)$	$A_M(e_1 \neq e_2)$
$e_1 \neq e_2$	$incr_M(e_1) \cup decr_M(e_1) \cup incr_M(e_2) \cup decr_M(e_2)$	$A_M(e_1 = e_2)$
$\varphi_1 \wedge \varphi_2$	$A_M(\varphi_i)$ for some $i \in \{1,2\}$ where $M \not\models \varphi_i$	$A_M(\neg\varphi_1 \vee \neg\varphi_2)$
$\varphi_1 \vee \varphi_2$	$A_M(\varphi_1) \cup A_M(\varphi_2)$	$A_M(\neg\varphi_1 \wedge \neg\varphi_2)$

Table 2. Increasing and decreasing transitions of expression e

Expression e	$incr_M(e)$	$decr_M(e)$
c	$\emptyset$	$\emptyset$
p	${}^\bullet p$	$p^\bullet$
$e_1 + e_2$	$incr_M(e_1) \cup incr_M(e_2)$	$decr_M(e_1) \cup decr_M(e_2)$
$e_1 - e_2$	$incr_M(e_1) \cup decr_M(e_2)$	$decr_M(e_1) \cup incr_M(e_2)$
$e_1 * e_2$	$incr_M(e_1) \cup decr_M(e_1) \cup incr_M(e_2) \cup decr_M(e_2)$	$incr_M(e_1) \cup decr_M(e_1) \cup incr_M(e_2) \cup decr_M(e_2)$

used in the Model Checking Contest (MCC) Property Language [27]. Let $N = (P, T, T_{urg}, IA, OA, g, w, Type, I)$ be a TAPN. The formulae of the logic are given by the abstract syntax:

$$\varphi ::= deadlock \mid t \mid e_1 \bowtie e_2 \mid \varphi_1 \wedge \varphi_2 \mid \varphi_1 \vee \varphi_2 \mid \neg\varphi$$
$$e ::= c \mid p \mid e_1 \oplus e_2$$

where $t \in T$, $\bowtie \in \{<, \leq, =, \neq, >, \geq\}$, $c \in \mathbb{Z}$, $p \in P$, and $\oplus \in \{+, -, *\}$. Let Φ be the set of all such formulae and let E_N be the set of arithmetic expressions over the net N. The semantics of φ in a marking $M \in \mathcal{M}(N)$ is given by

$$
\begin{aligned}
M &\models deadlock & &\text{if } \mathsf{En}(M) = \emptyset \\
M &\models t & &\text{if } t \in \mathsf{En}(M) \\
M &\models e_1 \bowtie e_2 & &\text{if } eval_M(e_1) \bowtie eval_M(e_2)
\end{aligned}
$$

assuming a standard semantics for Boolean operators and where the semantics of arithmetic expressions in a marking M is as follows: $eval_M(c) = c$, $eval_M(p) = |M(p)|$, and $eval_M(e_1 \oplus e_2) = eval_M(e_1) \oplus eval_M(e_2)$.

Let φ be a formula. We are interested in the question, whether we can reach from the initial marking some of the goal markings from $G_\varphi = \{M \in \mathcal{M}(N) \mid M \models \varphi\}$. In order to guide the reduction such that transitions that lead to the goal markings are included in the generated stubborn set, we define the notion of *interesting* transitions for a marking M relative to φ, and we let $A_M(\varphi) \subseteq T$ denote the set of interesting transitions. Formally, we shall require that whenever $M \xrightarrow{w} M'$ via a sequence of transitions $w = t_1 t_2 \ldots t_n \in T^*$ where $M \notin G_\varphi$ and $M' \in G_\varphi$, then there must exist i, $1 \leq i \leq n$, such that $t_i \in A_M(\varphi)$.

Table 1 gives a possible definition of $A_M(\varphi)$. Let us remark that the definition is at several places nondeterministic, allowing for a variety of sets of interesting transitions. Table 1 uses the functions $incr_M : E_N \to 2^T$ and $decr_M : E_N \to 2^T$ defined in Table 2. These functions take as input an expression e, and return all transitions that can possibly, when fired, increase resp. decrease the evaluation of e. The following lemma formally states the required property of the functions $incr_M$ and $decr_M$.

Lemma 1. *Let* $N = (P, T, T_{urg}, IA, OA, g, w, Type, I)$ *be a TAPN and* $M \in \mathcal{M}(N)$ *a marking. Let* $e \in E_N$ *and let* $M \xrightarrow{w} M'$ *where* $w = t_1 t_2 \ldots t_n \in T^*$.

- *If* $eval_M(e) < eval_{M'}(e)$ *then there is* i, $1 \leq i \leq n$, *such that* $t_i \in incr_M(e)$.
- *If* $eval_M(e) > eval_{M'}(e)$ *then there is* i, $1 \leq i \leq n$, *such that* $t_i \in decr_M(e)$.

We finish this section with the main technical lemma, showing that at least one interesting transition must be fired before we can reach a marking satisfying a given reachability formula.

Lemma 2. *Let* $N = (P, T, T_{urg}, IA, OA, g, w, Type, I)$ *be a TAPN, let* $M \in \mathcal{M}(N)$ *be its marking and let* $\varphi \in \Phi$ *be a given formula. If* $M \not\models \varphi$ *and* $M \xrightarrow{w} M'$ *where* $w \in \overline{A_M(\varphi)}^*$ *then* $M' \not\models \varphi$.

4 Partial Order Reductions for TAPN

We are now ready to state the main theorem that provides sufficient syntax-driven conditions for a reduction in order to guarantee preservation of reachability. Let $N = (P, T, T_{urg}, IA, OA, g, w, Type, I)$ be a TAPN, let $M \in \mathcal{M}(N)$ be a marking of N, and let $\varphi \in \Phi$ be a formula. We recall that $A_M(\varphi)$ is the set of interesting transitions as defined earlier.

Theorem 2 (Reachability Preserving Closure). *Let* St *be a reduction such that for all* $M \in \mathcal{M}(N)$ *it satisfies the following conditions.*

1. *If* $\neg zt(M)$ *then* $En(M) \subseteq St(M)$.
2. *If* $zt(M)$ *then* $A_M(\varphi) \subseteq St(M)$.
3. *If* $zt(M)$ *then either*
    (a) *there is* $t \in T_{urg} \cap En(M) \cap St(M)$ *where* $^\bullet(^\circ t) \subseteq St(M)$, *or*
    (b) *there is* $p \in P$ *where* $I(p) = [a, b]$ *and* $b \in M(p)$ *such that* $t \in St(M)$ *for every* $t \in p^\bullet$ *where* $b \in g((p, t))$.

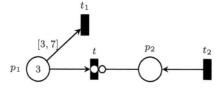 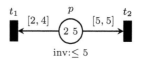

(a) Transitions t_1 and t_2 can disable resp. inhibit the urgent transition t

(b) Transition t_2 can remove the token of age 5 from p

Fig. 2. Cases for Condition 3

4 *For all $t \in \mathsf{St}(M) \setminus \mathsf{En}(M)$ either*
  (a) there is $p \in {}^\bullet t$ such that $|\{x \in M(p) \mid x \in g((p,t))\}| < w((p,t))$ and
         – $t' \in \mathsf{St}(M)$ for all $t' \in {}^\bullet p$ where there is $p' \in {}^\bullet t$ with $\mathit{Type}((t',p)) = \mathit{Type}((p',t')) = \mathit{Transport}_j$ and where $g((p',t')) \cap g((p,t)) \neq \emptyset$, and
         – if $0 \in g((p,t))$ then also ${}^\bullet p \subseteq \mathsf{St}(M)$, or
  (b) there is $p \in {}^\circ t$ where $|M(p)| \geq w((p,t))$ such that
         – $t' \in \mathsf{St}(M)$ for all $t' \in p^\bullet$ where $M(p) \cap g((p,t')) \neq \emptyset$.
5 *For all $t \in \mathsf{St}(M) \cap \mathsf{En}(M)$ we have*
  (a) $t' \in \mathsf{St}(M)$ for every $t' \in p^\bullet$ where $p \in {}^\bullet t$ and $g((p,t)) \cap g((p,t')) \neq \emptyset$, and
  (b) $(t^\bullet)^\circ \subseteq \mathsf{St}(M)$.

Then St satisfies $\mathcal{Z}$, $\mathcal{D}$, $\mathcal{R}$, and $\mathcal{W}$.

Let us now briefly discuss the conditions of Theorem 2. Clearly, Condition 1 ensures that if time can elapse, we include all enabled transitions into the stubborn set and Condition 2 guarantees that all interesting transitions (those that can potentially make the reachability proposition true) are included as well.

Condition 3 makes sure that if time elapsing is disabled then any transition that can possibly enable time elapsing will be added to the stubborn set. There are two situations how time progress can be disabled. Either, there is an urgent enabled transition, like the transition t in Fig. 2a. Since t_2 can add a token to p_2 and by that inhibit t, Condition 3a makes sure that t_2 is added into the stubborn set in order to satisfy $\mathcal{D}$. As t_1 can remove the token of age 3 from p_1 and hence disable t, we must add t_1 to the stubborn set too (guaranteed by Condition 5a). The other situation when time gets stopped is when a place with an age invariant contains a token that disallows time passing, like in Fig. 2b where time is disabled because the place p has a token of age 5, which is the maximum possible age of tokens in p due to the age invariant. Since t_2 can remove the token of age 5 from p, we include it to the stubborn set due to Condition 3b. On the other hand t_1 does not have to be included in the stubborn set as its firing cannot remove the token of age 5 from p.

Condition 4 makes sure that an disabled stubborn transition can never be enabled by a non-stubborn transition. There are two reasons why a transition is disabled. Either, as in Fig. 3a where t is disabled, there is an insufficient number of tokens of appropriate age to fire the transition. In this case, Condition 4a

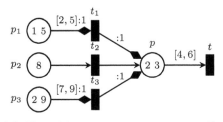 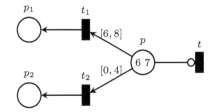

(a) Transition t_1 can transport well-aged tokens into p and enable t

(b) Transition t_1 can enable t by removing tokens from p

Fig. 3. Cases for Condition 4

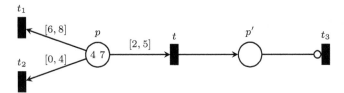

(a) Stubborn transition t can disable both t_2 and t_3

Fig. 4. Cases for Condition 5

makes sure that transitions that can add tokens of a suitable age via transport arcs are included in the stubborn set. This is the case for the transition t_1 in our example, as $[2, 5]$ has a nonempty intersection with $[4, 6]$. On the other hand, t_3 does not have to be added. As the transition t_2 only adds fresh tokens of age 0 to p via normal arcs, there is no need to add t_2 into the stubborn set either. The other reason for a transition to be disabled is due to inhibitor arcs, as shown on the transition t in Fig. 3b. Condition 4b makes sure that t_1 is added to the stubborn set, as it can enable t (the interval $[6, 8]$ has a nonempty intersection with the tokens of age 6 and 7 in the place p). As this is not the case for t_2, this transition can be left out from the stubborn set.

Finally, Condition 5 guarantees that enabled stubborn transitions can never disable any non-stubborn transitions. For an illustration, take a look at Fig. 4a and assume that t is an enabled stubborn transition. Firing of t can remove the token of age 4 from p and disable t_2, hence t_2 must become stubborn by Condition 5a in order to satisfy $\mathcal{W}$. On the other hand, the intervals $[6, 8]$ and $[2, 5]$ have empty intersection, so there is no need to declare t_1 as a stubborn transition. Moreover, firing of t can also disable the transition t_3 due to the inhibitor arc, so we must add t_3 to the stubborn set by Condition 5b.

The conditions of Theorem 2 can be turned into an iterative saturation algorithm for the construction of stubborn sets as shown in Algorithm 1. When running this algorithm for the net in our running example, we can reduce the state space exploration for fireability of the transition t as depicted in Fig. 1b. Our last theorem states that the algorithm returns stubborn subsets of enabled

---

Algorithm 1. Construction of a reachability preserving stubborn set

---

input   : $N = (P, T, T_{urg}, IA, OA, g, w, Type, I)$, $M \in \mathcal{M}(N)$, $\varphi \in \Phi$
output   : $\mathsf{St}(M) \cap \mathsf{En}(M)$

1 **if** $\neg \mathsf{zt}(M)$ **then**
2 $\quad$ **return** $\mathsf{En}(M)$;

3 $X := \emptyset$; $Y := A_M(\varphi)$;
4 **if** $T_{urg} \cap \mathsf{En}(M) \neq \emptyset$ **then**
5 $\quad$ pick any $t \in T_{urg} \cap \mathsf{En}(M)$;
6 $\quad$ **if** $t \notin Y$ **then**
7 $\quad\quad$ $Y := Y \cup \{t\}$;
8 $\quad$ $Y := Y \cup {}^\bullet({}^\circ t)$;

9 **else**
10 $\quad$ pick any $p \in P$ where $I(p) = [a, b]$ and $b \in M(p)$
11 $\quad$ **forall** $t \in p^\bullet$ **do**
12 $\quad\quad$ **if** $b \in g((p, t))$ **then**
13 $\quad\quad\quad$ $Y := Y \cup \{t\}$;

14 **while** $Y \neq \emptyset$ **do**
15 $\quad$ pick any $t \in Y$;
16 $\quad$ **if** $t \notin \mathsf{En}(M)$ **then**
17 $\quad\quad$ **if** $\exists p \in {}^\bullet t.\ |\{x \in M(p) \mid x \in g((p, t))\}| < w((p, t))$ **then**
18 $\quad\quad\quad$ pick any such p;
19 $\quad\quad\quad$ **forall** $t' \in {}^\bullet p \setminus X$ **do**
20 $\quad\quad\quad\quad$ **forall** $p' \in {}^\bullet t'$ **do**
21 $\quad\quad\quad\quad\quad$ **if** $Type((t', p)) = Type((p', t')) = Transport_j \wedge g((p', t')) \cap g((p, t)) \neq \emptyset$ **then**
22 $\quad\quad\quad\quad\quad\quad$ $Y := Y \cup \{t'\}$;

23 $\quad\quad\quad$ **if** $0 \in g((p, t))$ **then**
24 $\quad\quad\quad\quad$ $Y := Y \cup ({}^\bullet p \setminus X)$;

25 $\quad\quad$ **else**
26 $\quad\quad\quad$ pick any $p \in {}^\circ t$ s.t. $|M(p)| \geq w((p, t))$;
27 $\quad\quad\quad$ **forall** $t' \in p^\bullet \setminus X$ **do**
28 $\quad\quad\quad\quad$ **if** $M(p) \cap g((p, t')) \neq \emptyset$ **then**
29 $\quad\quad\quad\quad\quad$ $Y := Y \cup \{t'\}$;

30 $\quad$ **else**
31 $\quad\quad$ **forall** $p \in {}^\bullet t$ **do**
32 $\quad\quad\quad$ $Y := Y \cup (\{t' \in p^\bullet | g((p, t)) \cap g((p, t')) \neq \emptyset\} \setminus X)$;
33 $\quad\quad$ $Y := Y \cup ((t^\bullet)^\circ \setminus X)$;

34 $\quad$ $Y := Y \setminus \{t\}$;
35 $\quad$ $X := X \cup \{t\}$;

36 **return** $X \cap \mathsf{En}(M)$;

---

transitions that satisfy the four conditions of Theorem 1 and hence we preserve the reachability property as well as the minimum path to some reachable goal.

Theorem 3. *Algorithm 1 terminates and returns* $\mathsf{St}(M) \cap \mathsf{En}(M)$ *for some reduction* St *that satisfies* $\mathcal{Z}$, $\mathcal{D}$, $\mathcal{R}$, *and* $\mathcal{W}$.

5   Implementation and Experiments

We implemented our partial order method in C++ and integrated it within the model checker TAPAAL [19] and its discrete time engine `verifydtapn` [4,11]. We evaluate our partial order reduction on a wide range of case studies.

PatientMonitoring. The patient monitoring system [17] models a medical system that through sensors periodically scans patient's vital functions, making sure that abnormal situations are detected and reported within given deadlines. The timed-arc Petri net model was described in [17] for two sensors monitoring patient's pulse rate and oxygen saturation level. We scale the case study by adding additional sensors. *BloodTransfusion.* This case study models a larger blood transfusion workflow [16], the benchmarking case study of the little-JIL language. The timed-arc Petri net model was described in [10] and we verify that the workflow is free of deadlocks (unless all sub-workflows correctly terminate). The problem is scaled by the number of patients receiving a blood transfusion. *FireAlarm.* This case study uses a modified (due to trade secrets) fire alarm system owned by a German company [20,21]. It models a four-channel round-robin frequency-hopping transmission scheduling in order to ensure a reliable communication between a number of wireless sensors (by which the case study is scaled) and a central control unit. The protocol is based on time-division multiple access (TDMA) channel access and we verify that for a given frequency-jammer, it takes never more than three cycles before a fire alarm is communicated to the central unit. *BAwPC.* Business Activity with Participant Completion (BAwPC) is a web-service coordination protocol from WS-BA specification [33] that ensures a consistent agreement on the outcome of long-running distributed applications. In [26] it was shown that the protocol is flawed and a correct, enhanced variant was suggested. We model check this enhanced protocol and scale it by the capacity of the communication buffer. *Fischer.* Here we consider a classical Fischer's protocol for ensuring mutual exclusion for a number of timed processes. The timed-arc Petri net model is taken from [2] and it is scaled by the number of processes. *LynchShavit.* This is another timed-based mutual exclusion algorithm by Lynch and Shavit, with the timed-arc Petri net model taken from [1] and scaled by the number of processes. *MPEG2.* This case study describes the workflow of the MPEG-2 video encoding algorithm run on a multicore processor (the timed-arc Petri net model was published in [35]) and we verify the maximum duration of the workflow. The model is scaled by the number of B frames in the IB^nP frame sequence. *AlternatingBit.* This is a classical case study of alternating bit protocol, based on the timed-arc Petri net model given in [24]. The purpose of the protocol is to ensure a safe communication between a sender and a receiver over an unreliable medium. Messages are time-stamped in order to compensate

Table 3. Experiments with and without partial order reduction (POR)

Model	Time (seconds)		Markings ×1000		Reduction	
	NORMAL	POR	NORMAL	POR	%Time	%Markings
PatientMonitoring 3	5.88	0.35	333	28	94	92
PatientMonitoring 4	22.06	0.48	1001	36	98	96
PatientMonitoring 5	80.76	0.65	3031	44	99	99
PatientMonitoring 6	305.72	0.85	9248	54	100	99
PatientMonitoring 7	5516.93	5.75	130172	318	100	100
BloodTransfusion 2	0.32	0.41	48	43	−28	11
BloodTransfusion 3	7.88	6.45	792	546	18	31
BloodTransfusion 4	225.18	109.30	14904	7564	51	49
BloodTransfusion 5	5256.01	1611.14	248312	94395	69	62
FireAlarm 10	28.95	14.17	796	498	51	37
FireAlarm 12	116.97	17.51	1726	526	85	70
FireAlarm 14	598.89	21.65	5367	554	96	90
FireAlarm 16	5029.25	29.48	19845	582	99	97
FireAlarm 18	27981.90	34.55	77675	610	100	99
FireAlarm 20	154495.29	41.47	308914	638	100	100
FireAlarm 80	>2 days	602.71	−	1522	−	−
FireAlarm 125	>2 days	1957.00	−	2260	−	−
BAwPC 2	0.21	0.41	19	16	−95	15
BAwPC 4	3.45	4.04	193	125	−17	35
BAwPC 6	23.01	17.08	900	452	26	50
BAwPC 8	73.73	39.29	2294	952	47	58
BAwPC 10	135.62	60.66	3819	1412	55	63
BAwPC 12	173.09	73.53	4736	1665	58	65
Fischer-9	3.24	2.37	281	233	27	17
Fischer-11	12.68	8.73	923	738	31	20
Fischer-13	42.52	28.53	2628	2041	33	22
Fischer-15	121.31	77.50	6700	5066	36	24
Fischer-17	313.69	198.36	15622	11536	37	26
Fischer-19	748.52	456.30	33843	24469	39	28
Fischer-21	1622.69	985.07	68934	48904	39	29
LynchShavit 9	3.98	3.31	282	234	17	17
LynchShavit 11	15.73	12.19	925	740	23	20
LynchShavit 13	51.08	37.97	2631	2043	26	22
LynchShavit 15	146.63	103.63	6703	5069	29	24
LynchShavit 17	384.52	258.09	15626	11540	33	26
LynchShavit 19	907.60	597.68	33848	24474	34	28
LynchShavit 21	2011.58	1307.72	68940	48910	35	29
MPEG2 3	13.17	15.43	2188	2187	−17	0
MPEG2 4	109.62	125.45	15190	15180	−14	0
MPEG2 5	755.54	840.84	87568	87478	−11	0
MPEG2 6	4463.19	5092.58	435023	434354	−14	0
AlternatingBit 20	9.17	9.51	617	617	−4	0
AlternatingBit 30	48.20	49.13	2804	2804	−2	0
AlternatingBit 40	161.18	162.94	8382	8382	−1	0
AlternatingBit 50	408.34	408.86	19781	19781	0	0

(via retransmission) for the possibility of losing messages. The case study is scaled by the maximum number of messages in transfer.

All experiments were run on AMD Opteron 6376 Processors with 500 GB memory. In Table 3 we compare the time to verify a model without (NORMAL) and with (POR) partial order reduction, the number of explored markings (in thousands) and the percentage of time and memory reduction. We can observe clear benefits of our technique on PatientMonitoring, BloodTransfusion and Fire-Alarm where we are both exponentially faster and explore only a fraction of all reachable markings. For example in FireAlarm, we are able to verify its correctness for all 125 sensors, as it is required by the German company [21]. This would be clearly unfeasible without the use of partial order reduction.

In BAwPC, we can notice that for the smallest instances, there is some computation overhead from computing the stubborn sets, however, it clearly pays off for the larger instances where the percentages of reduced state space are closely followed by the percentages of the verification times and in fact improve with the larger instances. Fischer and LynchShavit case studies demonstrate that even moderate reductions of the state space imply considerable reduction in the running time and computing the stubborn sets is well worth the extra effort.

MPEG2 is an example of a model that allows only negligible reduction of the state space size, and where we observe an actual slowdown in the running time due to the computation of the stubborn sets. Nevertheless, the overhead stays constant in the range of about 15%, even for increasing instance sizes. Finally, AlternatingBit protocol does not allow for any reduction of the state space (even though it contains age invariants) but the overhead in the running time is negligible.

We observed similar performance of our technique also for the cases where the reachability property does not hold and a counter example can be generated.

6 Conclusion

We suggested a simple, yet powerful and application-ready partial order reduction for timed systems. The reduction comes into effect as soon as the timed system enters an urgent configuration where time cannot elapse until a nonempty sequence of transitions gets executed. The method is implemented and fully integrated, including GUI support, into the open-source tool TAPAAL. We demonstrated its practical applicability on several case studies and conclude that computing the stubborn sets causes only a minimal overhead while providing large benefits for reducing the state space in numerous models. The method is not specific to stubborn reduction technique only and it preserves the shortest execution sequences. Moreover, once the time gets urgent, other classical (untimed) partial order approaches should be applicable too. Our method was instantiated to (unbounded) timed-arc Petri nets with discrete time semantics, however, we claim that the technique allows for general application to other modelling formalisms like timed automata and timed Petri nets, as well as an extension to continuous time. We are currently working on adapting the theory and providing an efficient implementation for UPPAAL-style timed automata with continuous time semantics.

Acknowledgements. We thank Mads Johannsen for his help with the GUI support for partial order reduction. The work was funded by the center IDEA4CPS, Innovation Fund Denmark center DiCyPS and ERC Advanced Grant LASSO. The last author is partially affiliated with FI MU in Brno.

References

1. Abdulla, P., Deneux, J., Mahata, P., Nylén, A.: Using forward reachability analysis for verification of timed Petri nets. Nord. J. Comput. **14**, 1–42 (2007)
2. Abdulla, P.A., Nylén, A.: Timed Petri nets and BQOs. In: Colom, J.-M., Koutny, M. (eds.) ICATPN 2001. LNCS, vol. 2075, pp. 53–70. Springer, Heidelberg (2001). https://doi.org/10.1007/3-540-45740-2_5
3. Alur, R., Dill, D.L.: A theory of timed automata. Theor. Comput. Sci. **126**(2), 183–235 (1994)
4. Andersen, M., Gatten Larsen, H., Srba, J., Grund Sørensen, M., Haahr Taankvist, J.: Verification of liveness properties on closed timed-arc Petri nets. In: Kučera, A., Henzinger, T.A., Nešetřil, J., Vojnar, T., Antoš, D. (eds.) MEMICS 2012. LNCS, vol. 7721, pp. 69–81. Springer, Heidelberg (2013). https://doi.org/10.1007/978-3-642-36046-6_8
5. André, E., Chatain, T., Rodríguez, C.: Preserving partial-order runs in parametric time Petri nets. ACM Trans. Embed. Comput. Syst. **16**(2), 43:1–43:26 (2017)
6. Baier, C., Katoen, J.-P.: Principles of Model Checking. The MIT Press, Cambridge (2008)
7. Behrmann, G., Bouyer, P., Larsen, K.G., Pelánek, R.: Lower and upper bounds in zone-based abstractions of timed automata. STTT **8**(3), 204–215 (2006)
8. Bengtsson, J., Jonsson, B., Lilius, J., Yi, W.: Partial order reductions for timed systems. In: Sangiorgi, D., de Simone, R. (eds.) CONCUR 1998. LNCS, vol. 1466, pp. 485–500. Springer, Heidelberg (1998). https://doi.org/10.1007/BFb0055643
9. Berthomieu, B., Vernadat, F.: Time Petri nets analysis with TINA. In: Third International Conference on Quantitative Evaluation of Systems, pp. 123–124. IEEE Computer Society (2006)
10. Bertolini, C., Liu, Z., Srba, J.: Verification of timed healthcare workflows using component timed-arc Petri nets. In: Weber, J., Perseil, I. (eds.) FHIES 2012. LNCS, vol. 7789, pp. 19–36. Springer, Heidelberg (2013). https://doi.org/10.1007/978-3-642-39088-3_2
11. Viesmose Birch, S., Stig Jacobsen, T., Jon Jensen, J., Moesgaard, C., Nørgaard Samuelsen, N., Srba, J.: Interval abstraction refinement for model checking of timed-arc Petri nets. In: Legay, A., Bozga, M. (eds.) FORMATS 2014. LNCS, vol. 8711, pp. 237–251. Springer, Cham (2014). https://doi.org/10.1007/978-3-319-10512-3_17
12. Boucheneb, H., Barkaoui, K.: Reducing interleaving semantics redundancy in reachability analysis of time Petri nets. ACM Trans. Embed. Comput. Syst. **12**(1), 7:1–7:24 (2013)
13. Boucheneb, H., Barkaoui, K.: Stubborn sets for time Petri nets. ACM Trans. Embed. Comput. Syst. **14**(1), 11:1–11:25 (2015)

14. Boucheneb, H., Barkaoui, K.: Delay-dependent partial order reduction technique for real time systems. Real-Time Syst. **54**, 278–306 (2017)
15. Bozga, M., Graf, S., Ober, I., Ober, I., Sifakis, J.: The IF toolset. In: Bernardo, M., Corradini, F. (eds.) SFM-RT 2004. LNCS, vol. 3185, pp. 237–267. Springer, Heidelberg (2004). https://doi.org/10.1007/978-3-540-30080-9_8
16. Christov, S., Avrunin, G., Clarke, A., Osterweil, L., Henneman, E.: A benchmark for evaluating software engineering techniques for improving medical processes. In: SEHC 2010, pp. 50–56. ACM (2010)
17. Cicirelli, F., Furfaro, A., Nigro, L.: Model checking time-dependent system specifications using time stream Petri nets and UPPAAL. Appl. Math. Comput. **218**(16), 8160–8186 (2012)
18. Dams, D., Gerth, R., Knaack, B., Kuiper, R.: Partial-order reduction techniques for real-time model checking. Form. Asp. Comput. **10**(5–6), 469–482 (1998)
19. David, A., Jacobsen, L., Jacobsen, M., Jørgensen, K.Y., Møller, M.H., Srba, J.: TAPAAL 2.0: integrated development environment for timed-arc Petri nets. In: Flanagan, C., König, B. (eds.) TACAS 2012. LNCS, vol. 7214, pp. 492–497. Springer, Heidelberg (2012). https://doi.org/10.1007/978-3-642-28756-5_36
20. Feo-Arenis, S., Westphal, B., Dietsch, D., Muñiz, M., Andisha, A.S.: The wireless fire alarm system: ensuring conformance to industrial standards through formal verification. In: Jones, C., Pihlajasaari, P., Sun, J. (eds.) FM 2014. LNCS, vol. 8442, pp. 658–672. Springer, Cham (2014). https://doi.org/10.1007/978-3-319-06410-9_44
21. Feo-Arenis, S., Westphal, B., Dietsch, D., Muñiz, M., Andisha, S., Podelski, A.: Ready for testing: ensuring conformance to industrial standards through formal verification. Form. Asp. Comput. **28**(3), 499–527 (2016)
22. Gardey, G., Lime, D., Magnin, M., Roux, O.H.: Romeo: a tool for analyzing time Petri nets. In: Etessami, K., Rajamani, S.K. (eds.) CAV 2005. LNCS, vol. 3576, pp. 418–423. Springer, Heidelberg (2005). https://doi.org/10.1007/11513988_41
23. Hansen, H., Lin, S.-W., Liu, Y., Nguyen, T.K., Sun, J.: Diamonds are a girl's best friend: partial order reduction for timed automata with abstractions. In: Biere, A., Bloem, R. (eds.) CAV 2014. LNCS, vol. 8559, pp. 391–406. Springer, Cham (2014). https://doi.org/10.1007/978-3-319-08867-9_26
24. Jacobsen, L., Jacobsen, M., Møller, M.H., Srba, J.: Verification of timed-arc Petri Nets. In: Černá, I., Gyimóthy, T., Hromkovič, J., Jefferey, K., Královič, R., Vukolić, M., Wolf, S. (eds.) SOFSEM 2011. LNCS, vol. 6543, pp. 46–72. Springer, Heidelberg (2011). https://doi.org/10.1007/978-3-642-18381-2_4
25. Jensen, P., Larsen, K., Srba, J.: Discrete and continuous strategies for timed-arc Petri net games. Int. J. Softw. Tools Technol. Transf. (STTT), 1–18 (2017, to appear). Online since September 2017
26. Marques Jr., A., Ravn, A., Srba, J., Vighio, S.: Model-checking web services business activity protocols. Int. J. Softw. Tools Technol. Transf. (STTT) **15**(2), 125–147 (2012)
27. Kordon, F., Garavel, H., Hillah, L.M., Hulin-Hubard, F., Chiardo, G., Hamez, A., Jezequel, L., Miner, A., Meijer, J., Paviot-Adet, E., Racordon, D., Rodriguez, C., Rohr, C., Srba, J., Thierry-Mieg, Y., Trịnh, G., Wolf, K.: Complete Results for the 2016 Edition of the Model Checking Contest, June 2016. http://mcc.lip6.fr/2016/results.php
28. Kristensen, L.M., Schmidt, K., Valmari, A.: Question-guided stubborn set methods for state properties. Form. Methods Syst. Des. **29**(3), 215–251 (2006)
29. Lilius, J.: Efficient state space search for time Petri nets. Electron. Notes Theo. Comput. Sci. **18**, 113–133 (1998). MFCS 1998 Workshop on Concurrency

30. Lugiez, D., Niebert, P., Zennou, S.: A partial order semantics approach to the clock explosion problem of timed automata. Theor. Comput. Sci. **345**(1), 27–59 (2005)
31. Mateo, J., Srba, J., Sørensen, M.: Soundness of timed-arc workflow nets in discrete and continuous-time semantics. Fundam. Inform. **140**(1), 89–121 (2015)
32. Minea, M.: Partial order reduction for model checking of timed automata. In: Baeten, J.C.M., Mauw, S. (eds.) CONCUR 1999. LNCS, vol. 1664, pp. 431–446. Springer, Heidelberg (1999). https://doi.org/10.1007/3-540-48320-9_30
33. Newcomer, E., Robinson, I.: Web services business activity (WS-businessactivity) version 1.2 (2009). http://docs.oasis-open.org/ws-tx/wstx-wsba-1.2-spec-os/wstx-wsba-1.2-spec-os.html
34. Niebert, P., Qu, H.: Adding invariants to event zone automata. In: Asarin, E., Bouyer, P. (eds.) FORMATS 2006. LNCS, vol. 4202, pp. 290–305. Springer, Heidelberg (2006). https://doi.org/10.1007/11867340_21
35. Pelayo, F., Cuartero, F., Valero, V., Macia, H., Pelayo, M.: Applying timed-arc Petri nets to improve the performance of the MPEG-2 encoding algorithm. In: 10th International Multimedia Modelling Conference, pp. 49–56. IEEE Computer Society (2004)
36. Perin, M., Faure, J.: Coupling timed plant and controller models with urgent transitions without introducing deadlocks. In: 17th International Conference on Emerging Technologies and Factory Automation (ETFA 2012), pp. 1–9. IEEE (2012)
37. Salah, R.B., Bozga, M., Maler, O.: On interleaving in timed automata. In: Baier, C., Hermanns, H. (eds.) CONCUR 2006. LNCS, vol. 4137, pp. 465–476. Springer, Heidelberg (2006). https://doi.org/10.1007/11817949_31
38. Sloan, R.H., Buy, U.: Stubborn sets for real-time Petri nets. Form. Methods Syst. Des. **11**(1), 23–40 (1997)
39. Valmari, A., Hansen, H.: Stubborn set intuition explained. In: Koutny, M., Kleijn, J., Penczek, W. (eds.) Transactions on Petri Nets and Other Models of Concurrency XII. LNCS, vol. 10470, pp. 140–165. Springer, Heidelberg (2017). https://doi.org/10.1007/978-3-662-55862-1_7
40. Virbitskaite, I., Pokozy, E.: A partial order method for the verification of time Petri nets. In: Ciobanu, G., Păun, G. (eds.) FCT 1999. LNCS, vol. 1684, pp. 547–558. Springer, Heidelberg (1999). https://doi.org/10.1007/3-540-48321-7_46
41. Yoneda, T., Schlingloff, B.-H.: Efficient verification of parallel real-time systems. Form. Methods Syst. Des. **11**(2), 187–215 (1997)

Strix: Explicit Reactive Synthesis Strikes Back!

Philipp J. Meyer🆔, Salomon Sickert$^{(\boxtimes)}$🆔,
and Michael Luttenberger

Technical University of Munich, Munich, Germany
{meyerphi,sickert,luttenbe}@in.tum.de

Abstract. STRIX is a new tool for reactive LTL synthesis combining
a direct translation of LTL formulas into deterministic parity automata
(DPA) and an efficient, multi-threaded explicit state solver for parity
games. In brief, STRIX (1) decomposes the given formula into simpler
formulas, (2) translates these on-the-fly into DPAs based on the queries
of the parity game solver, (3) composes the DPAs into a parity game, and
at the same time already solves the intermediate games using strategy
iteration, and (4) finally translates the winning strategy, if it exists, into
a Mealy machine or an AIGER circuit with optional minimization using
external tools. We experimentally demonstrate the applicability of our
approach by a comparison with PARTY, BoSY, and LTLSYNT using the
SYNTCOMP2017 benchmarks. In these experiments, our prototype can
compete with BoSY and LTLSYNT with only PARTY performing slightly
better. In particular, our prototype successfully synthesizes the full and
unmodified LTL specification of the AMBA protocol for $n = 2$ masters.

1 Introduction

Reactive synthesis refers to the problem of finding for a formal specification of
an input-output relation, in our case a *linear temporal logic (LTL)*, a matching implementation [22], e.g. a *Mealy machine* or an *and-inverter-graph (AIG)*.
Since the automata-theoretic approach to synthesis involves the construction of
a potentially double exponentially sized automaton (in the length of the specification) [13], most existing tools focus on symbolic and bounded methods in
order to combat the state-space explosion [5,9,11,18]. A beneficial side effect of
these approaches is that they tend to yield succinct implementations.

In contrast to these approaches, we present a prototype implementation of
an LTL synthesis tool which follows the automata theoretic approach using parity games as an intermediate step. STRIX[1] uses the LTL-to-DPA translation

presented in [10,23] and the multi-threaded explicit-state parity game solver
presented in [14,20]: First, the given formula is decomposed into much simpler
requirements, often resulting in a large number of safety and co-safety conditions and only a few requiring Büchi or parity acceptance conditions, which is
comparable to the approach of [5,21]. These requirements are then translated
on-the-fly into automata, keeping the invariant that the parity game solver can
easily compose the actual parity game. Further, by querying only for states that
are actually required for deciding the winner, the implementation avoids unnecessary work.

The parity game solver is based on the *strategy iteration* of [19] which iteratively improves non-deterministic strategies, i.e. strategies that can allow several
actions for a given state as long as they all are guaranteed to lead to the specified
system behaviour. When translating the winning strategy into a Mealy automaton or an AIG this non-determinism can be used similarly to "don't cares" when
minimizing boolean circuits. Strategy iteration offers us two additional advan-
tages, first, we can directly take advantage of multi-core systems; second, we
can reuse the winning strategies which have been computed for the intermediate
arenas.

Related Work and Experimental Evaluation. From the tools submitted to SYNT-
COMP2017, LTLSYNT [15] is closest to our approach: it also combines an LTL-
to-DPA-translation with an explicit-state parity game solver, but it does not
intertwine the two steps, instead it uses a different approach for the translation
leading to one monolithic DPA which is then turned in a parity game. In contrast, the two best performing tools from SYNTCOMP2017, BoSy and PARTY,
use bounded synthesis, by reduction either to SAT, SMT, or safety games.

In order to give a realistic estimation of how our tool would have faired at
SYNTCOMP2017 (TLSF/LTL track), we tried to re-create the benchmark environment of SYNTCOMP2017 as close as possible on our hardware: in its current
state, our tool would have been ranked below PARTY, but before LTLSYNT and
BoSy. Due to time and resource constraints, we could only do an in-depth comparison with the current version of LTLSYNT; in particular we used the TLSF
specification of the complete[2] AMBA protocol for $n = 2$ as a benchmark. We
refer to Sect. 3 for details on the benchmarking procedure.

2 Design and Implementation

STRIX is implemented in Java and C++. It supports LTL and TLSF [16] (only
the reduced *basic* variant) as input languages, while the latter one is preferred,
since it contains more information about the specification. We describe the main
steps of the tool in the following paragraphs with examples given in Fig. 1.

---

[2] i.e. no decomposition in masters and clients or structural properties were used.

Splitting and Translation. As a preprocessing step the specification is split into syntactic (co)safety and (co)Büchi formulas, and one remaining general LTL formula. These are then translated into the simplest deterministic automaton class using the constructions of [10, 23]. To speed up the process these automata are constructed on-the-fly, i.e., states are created only if requested by later stages. Furthermore, since DPAs can be easily complemented, the implementation translates the formula and its negation and chooses the faster obtained one.

$$\varphi = \underbrace{\mathbf{G}(\neg g_0 \vee \neg g_1)}_{\psi_1} \wedge \underbrace{\mathbf{G}(r_0 \to \mathbf{F}g_0)}_{\psi_2} \wedge \underbrace{\mathbf{G}(r_1 \to \mathbf{F}g_1)}_{\psi_3} \quad I = \{r_0, r_1\} \quad O = \{g_0, g_1\}$$

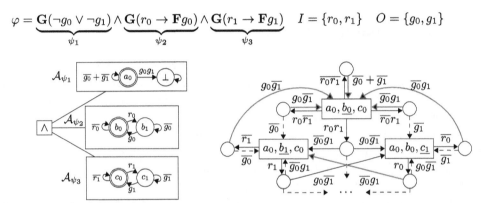

Splitted specification with one safety and two Büchi automata.

Partial min-even parity arena. Red thick edges have parity 0 and thin black edges parity 1.

Fig. 1. Synthesis of a simple arbiter with two clients. Here, a winning strategy is already obtained on the partial arena: always take any of the non-dashed edges.

Arena Construction. Here we construct one product automaton and combine the various acceptance conditions into a single parity acceptance condition: for this, we use the idea underlying the last-appearance-record construction, known from the translation of Muller to parity games, to directly obtain a parity game again.

Parity Game Solving. The parity game solver runs in parallel to the arena construction on the partially constructed game in order to guide the translation process, with the possibility for early termination when a winning strategy for the system player is found. It uses strategy iteration that supports non-deterministic strategies [19] from which we can benefit in several ways: First, in the translation process, the current strategy stays valid when adding nodes to the arena and thus can be used as initial strategy when solving the extended arena. Second, the non-deterministic strategies allow us to later heuristically select actions of the strategy that minimize the generated controller and to identify irrelevant output signals (similar to "don't care"-cells in Karnaugh maps). Finally, the strategy iteration can easily take advantage of multi-core architectures [14, 20].

Controller Generation and Minimization. From the non-deterministic strategy we obtain an incompletely specified Mealy machine and optionally pass it to the external SAT-based minimizer MeMin [1] for Mealy machines and extract a more compact description.

AIGER Circuit Generation and Minimization. We translate the minimized Mealy machine with the tool Speculoos[3] into an AIGER circuit. In parallel, we also construct an AIGER circuit out of the non-minimized Mealy machine, since this can sometimes result in smaller circuits. The two AIGER circuits are then further compressed using ABC [6], and the smaller one is returned.

3 Experimental Evaluation

We evaluate STRIX on the TLFS/LTL-track benchmark of the SYNTCOMP2017 competition, which consists of 177 realizable and 67 unrealizable temporal logic synthesis specifications [15]. The experiment was run on a server with an Intel E5-2630 v4 clocked at 2.2 GHz (boost disabled). To mimic SYNTCOMP2017 we imposed a limit of 8 threads for parallelization, a memory limit of 32 GB and a timeout of one hour for each specification. Every specification for that a tool correctly decides realizability within these limits is counted as solved for the category **Realizability**, and every specification for that it can additionally produce an AIGER circuit that is successfully verified is counted as solved for the category **Synthesis**. For this we verified the circuits with an additional time limit of one hour using the NUXMV model checker [7] with the `check_ltlspec` and `check_ltlspec_klive` routines in parallel.

We compared STRIX with LTLSYNT in the latest available release (version 2.5) at time of writing. This version differs from the one used during SYNTCOMP2017 as it contains several improvements, but also performs worse in a few cases and exhibits erroneous behaviour: for **Realizability**, it produced one wrong answer, and for **Synthesis**, it failed in 72 cases to produce AIGER circuits due to a program error.

Additionally, we compare our results with the best configuration of the top tools competing in SYNTCOMP2017: PARTY (portfolio), LTLSYNT and BoSY (spot). Due to the difficulty of recreating the SYNTCOMP2017 hardware setup[4], we compiled the results for these tools in Table 1 from the SYNTCOMP2017 webpage[5] combining them with our results.

---

[3] https://github.com/romainbrenguier/Speculoos

[4] SYNTCOMP2017 was run on an Intel E3-1271 v3 (4 cores/8 threads) at 3.6 GHz with 32 GB of RAM available for the tools. As stated above, we imposed the same constraints regarding timeout, maximal number of threads, and memory limit; but the Intel E3-1271 v3 runs at 3.6 GHz (with boost 4.0 GHz), while the Intel E5-2630 v4 used by us runs at only 2.2 GHz (boost disabled) resulting in a lower per-thread-performance (potentially 30% slower); on the other hand our system has a larger cache and a theoretically much higher memory bandwidth from up to 68.3 GB/s compared to 25.6 GB/s (for random reads, as in the case of dynamically generated parity games, these numbers are much closer). It seems therefore likely that for some benchmark-tool combinations our system is faster while for others it is slower.

[5] http://syntcomp.cs.uni-saarland.de/syntcomp2017/experiments/

The **Quality** rating compares the size of the solutions according to the SYNT-COMP2017 formula, where a tool gets $2 - \log_{10} \frac{n+1}{r+1}$ quality points for each verified solution of size n for a specification with reference size r. We now move on to a detailed discussion of the results and their interpretation.

Table 1. Results for STRIX compared with LTLSYNT and selected results from SYNT-COMP2017 on the TLSF/LTL-track benchmark and on noteable instances. We mark timeouts by TIME, memouts by MEM, and errors by ERR.

| | | Our system | | SYNTCOMP2017 | | |
		STRIX	LTLSYNT (2.5)	PARTY	LTLSYNT	BOSY
Solved	Realizability	214	204	224	195	181
	Synthesis	197	123	203	182	181
	Quality	330	136	308	180	298
	Avg. Quality	1.68	1.10	1.52	0.99	1.64
Time (s) Realizability	full_arbiter_7	11.34	MEM	8.77	MEM	TIME
	prioritized_arbiter_7	58.53	TIME	372.95	TIME	TIME
	round_robin_arbiter_6	8.45	158.33	TIME	733.92	TIME
	ltl2dba_E_10	6.79	324.84	TIME	TIME	TIME
	ltl2dba_Q_8	2.13	346.12	TIME	TIME	TIME
Size (AIG)	amba_...._encode_12	89	ERR	1040	3251	369
	full_arbiter_5	531	ERR	2257	7393	TIME
	full_arbiter_6	626	ERR	7603	26678	TIME
	ltl2dba_E_4	7	406	243	406	TIME
	ltl2dba_E_6	11	3952	1955	3952	TIME

Realizability. We were able to correctly decide realizability for 163 and unrealizability for 51 specifications, resulting in 214 solved instances. We solve five instances that were previously unsolved in SYNTCOMP2017.

Synthesis. We produced AIGER circuits for 148 of the realizable specifications. In 15 cases, we only constructed a Mealy machine, but the subsequent steps (MEMIN for minimization or SPECULOOS for circuit generation) reached the time or memory limit. We were able to verify correctness for 146 of the circuits, reaching the model checking time limit in two case. Together with the 51 specifications for which we determined unrealizability, this results in 197 solved instances.

Quality. We produced 36 solutions that are smaller than any solution during SYNTCOMP2017. The most significant reductions are for the AMBA encoder and the full arbiter, with reductions of over 75%, and for ltl2dba_E_4 and ltl2dba_E_6, where we produce indeed the smallest implementation there is.

3.1 Effects of Minimization

We could reduce the size of the Mealy machine in 80 cases, and on average by 45%. However the data showed that this did not always reduce the size of the generated AIGER circuit: in 13 cases (most notably for several arbiter specifications) the size of the circuit generated from the Mealy machine actually increased when applying minimization (on average by 190%), while it decreased in 62 cases (on average by 55%).

We conjecture that the structure of the product-arena is sometimes amenable to compact representation in an AIGER circuit, while after the (SAT-based) minimization this is lost. In these cases the SAT/SMT-based bounded synthesis tools such as BoSy and Party also have difficulties producing a small solution, if any at all.

3.2 Synthesis of Complete AMBA AHB Arbiter

To test maturity and scalability of our tool, we synthesized the AMBA AHB arbiter [2], a common case study for reactive synthesis. We used the parameterized specification from [17] for $n = 2$ masters, which was also part of SYNT-COMP2016, but was left unsolved by any tool. With a memory limit of 128 GB, we could decide realizability within 26 min and produce a Mealy machine with 83 states after minimization. While specialised GR(1) solvers [2, 4, 12] or decompositional approaches [3] are able to synthesize the specification in a matter of minutes, to the best of our knowledge we are the first full LTL synthesis tool that can handle the complete non-decomposed specification in a reasonable amount of time. For comparison, LTLSYNT (2.5) needs more than 2.5 days on our system and produces a Mealy machine with 340 states.

3.3 Discussion

The LTLSYNT tool is part of Spot [8], which uses a Safra-style determinization procedure for NBAs. Conceptually, it also uses DPAs and a parity game solver as a decision procedure. However, as shown in [10] the produced automata tend to be larger compared to our translation, which probably results in the lower quality score. Our approach has similar performance and scales better on certain cases. The instances where LTLSYNT performs better than STRIX are specifications that we cannot split efficiently and the DPA construction becomes the bottleneck.

Bounded synthesis approaches (BoSy, Party) tend to produce smaller Mealy machines and to be able to handle larger alphabets. However, they fail when the minimal machine implementing the desired property is large, even if there is a compact implementation as a circuit. In our approach, we can often solve these cases and still regain compactness of the implementation through minimization afterwards. The strength of the Party portfolio is the combination of traditional bounded synthesis and a novel approach by reduction to safety games, which results in a large number of solved instances, but reduces the avg. quality score.

Future Work. STRIX combines Java (LTL simplification and automata translations) and C++ (parity game construction and solving). We believe that a pure C++ implementation will further improve the overall runtime and reduce the memory footprint. Next, there are several algorithmic questions we want to investigate going forward, especially expanding parallelization of the tool. Furthermore, we want to reduce the dependency on external tools for circuit generation in order to be able to fine-tune this step better. Especially replacing SPECULOOS is important, since it turned out that it was unable to handle complex transition systems.

References

1. Abel, A., Reineke, J.: MeMin: SAT-based exact minimization of incompletely specified mealy machines. In: Proceedings of the IEEE/ACM International Conference on Computer-Aided Design, ICCAD 2015, Austin, TX, USA, 2–6 November 2015, pp. 94–101 (2015). https://doi.org/10.1109/ICCAD.2015.7372555
2. Bloem, R., Galler, S.J., Jobstmann, B., Piterman, N., Pnueli, A., Weiglhofer, M.: Specify, compile, run: hardware from PSL. Electr. Notes Theor. Comput. Sci. **190**(4), 3–16 (2007). https://doi.org/10.1016/j.entcs.2007.09.004
3. Bloem, R., Jacobs, S., Khalimov, A.: Parameterized synthesis case study: AMBA AHB. In: Proceedings of the 3rd Workshop on Synthesis, SYNT 2014, Vienna, Austria, 23–24 July 2014, pp. 68–83 (2014). https://doi.org/10.4204/EPTCS.157.9
4. Bloem, R., Jobstmann, B., Piterman, N., Pnueli, A., Sa'ar, Y.: Synthesis of reactive(1) designs. J. Comput. Syst. Sci. **78**(3), 911–938 (2012). https://doi.org/10.1016/j.jcss.2011.08.007
5. Bohy, A., Bruyère, V., Filiot, E., Jin, N., Raskin, J.-F.: Acacia+, a tool for LTL synthesis. In: Madhusudan, P., Seshia, S.A. (eds.) CAV 2012. LNCS, vol. 7358, pp. 652–657. Springer, Heidelberg (2012). https://doi.org/10.1007/978-3-642-31424-7_45
6. Brayton, R., Mishchenko, A.: ABC: an academic industrial-strength verification tool. In: Touili, T., Cook, B., Jackson, P. (eds.) CAV 2010. LNCS, vol. 6174, pp. 24–40. Springer, Heidelberg (2010). https://doi.org/10.1007/978-3-642-14295-6_5
7. Cavada, R., et al.: The NUXMV symbolic model checker. In: Biere, A., Bloem, R. (eds.) CAV 2014. LNCS, vol. 8559, pp. 334–342. Springer, Cham (2014). https://doi.org/10.1007/978-3-319-08867-9_22
8. Duret-Lutz, A., Lewkowicz, A., Fauchille, A., Michaud, T., Renault, É., Xu, L.: Spot 2.0 — a framework for LTL and ω-automata manipulation. In: Artho, C., Legay, A., Peled, D. (eds.) ATVA 2016. LNCS, vol. 9938, pp. 122–129. Springer, Cham (2016). https://doi.org/10.1007/978-3-319-46520-3_8
9. Ehlers, R.: Unbeast: symbolic bounded synthesis. In: Abdulla, P.A., Leino, K.R.M. (eds.) TACAS 2011. LNCS, vol. 6605, pp. 272–275. Springer, Heidelberg (2011). https://doi.org/10.1007/978-3-642-19835-9_25
10. Esparza, J., Křetínský, J., Raskin, J.-F., Sickert, S.: From LTL and limit-deterministic Büchi automata to deterministic parity automata. In: Legay, A., Margaria, T. (eds.) TACAS 2017. LNCS, vol. 10205, pp. 426–442. Springer, Heidelberg (2017). https://doi.org/10.1007/978-3-662-54577-5_25

11. Faymonville, P., Finkbeiner, B., Tentrup, L.: BoSy: an experimentation framework for bounded synthesis. In: Majumdar, R., Kunčak, V. (eds.) CAV 2017. LNCS, vol. 10427, pp. 325–332. Springer, Cham (2017). https://doi.org/10.1007/978-3-319-63390-9_17

12. Godhal, Y., Chatterjee, K., Henzinger, T.A.: Synthesis of AMBA AHB from formal specification: a case study. STTT **15**(5–6), 585–601 (2013). https://doi.org/10.1007/s10009-011-0207-9

13. Grädel, E., Thomas, W., Wilke, T. (eds.): Automata Logics, and Infinite Games: A Guide to Current Research. LNCS, vol. 2500. Springer, Heidelberg (2002). https://doi.org/10.1007/3-540-36387-4

14. Hoffmann, P., Luttenberger, M.: Solving parity games on the GPU. In: Van Hung, D., Ogawa, M. (eds.) ATVA 2013. LNCS, vol. 8172, pp. 455–459. Springer, Cham (2013). https://doi.org/10.1007/978-3-319-02444-8_34

15. Jacobs, S., Basset, N., Bloem, R., Brenguier, R., Colange, M., Faymonville, P., Finkbeiner, B., Khalimov, A., Klein, F., Michaud, T., Pérez, G.A., Raskin, J., Sankur, O., Tentrup, L.: The 4th reactive synthesis competition (SYNTCOMP 2017): benchmarks, participants and results. arXiv:1711.11439 [cs.LO] (2017)

16. Jacobs, S., Klein, F., Schirmer, S.: A high-level LTL synthesis format: TLSF v1.1. In: Proceedings of the Fifth Workshop on Synthesis, SYNT@CAV 2016, Toronto, Canada, 17–18 July 2016, pp. 112–132 (2016). https://doi.org/10.4204/EPTCS.229.10

17. Jobstmann, B.: Applications and optimizations for LTL synthesis. Ph.D. thesis, Graz University of Technology (2007)

18. Khalimov, A., Jacobs, S., Bloem, R.: PARTY parameterized synthesis of token rings. In: Sharygina, N., Veith, H. (eds.) CAV 2013. LNCS, vol. 8044, pp. 928–933. Springer, Heidelberg (2013). https://doi.org/10.1007/978-3-642-39799-8_66

19. Luttenberger, M.: Strategy iteration using non-deterministic strategies for solving parity games. arXiv:0806.2923 [cs.GT] (2008)

20. Meyer, P.J., Luttenberger, M.: Solving mean-payoff games on the GPU. In: Artho, C., Legay, A., Peled, D. (eds.) ATVA 2016. LNCS, vol. 9938, pp. 262–267. Springer, Cham (2016). https://doi.org/10.1007/978-3-319-46520-3_17

21. Morgenstern, A., Schneider, K.: Exploiting the temporal logic hierarchy and the non-confluence property for efficient LTL synthesis. In: Proceedings of the First Symposium on Games, Automata, Logic, and Formal Verification, GANDALF 2010, Minori (Amalfi Coast), Italy, 17–18 June 2010, pp. 89–102 (2010). https://doi.org/10.4204/EPTCS.25.11

22. Pnueli, A., Rosner, R.: On the synthesis of a reactive module. In: Proceedings of the 16th ACM SIGPLAN-SIGACT Symposium on Principles of Programming Languages, POPL 1989, pp. 179–190. ACM, New York (1989). https://doi.org/10.1145/75277.75293

23. Sickert, S., Esparza, J., Jaax, S., Křetínský, J.: Limit-deterministic Büchi automata for linear temporal logic. In: Chaudhuri, S., Farzan, A. (eds.) CAV 2016. LNCS, vol. 9780, pp. 312–332. Springer, Cham (2016). https://doi.org/10.1007/978-3-319-41540-6_17

12

Nagini: A Static Verifier for Python

Marco Eilers$^{(\boxtimes)}$ and Peter Müller

Department of Computer Science, ETH Zurich,
Zurich, Switzerland
{marco.eilers,peter.mueller}@inf.ethz.ch

Abstract. We present Nagini, an automated, modular verifier for statically-typed, concurrent Python 3 programs, built on the Viper verification infrastructure. Combining established concepts with new ideas, Nagini can verify memory safety, functional properties, termination, deadlock freedom, and input/output behavior. Our experiments show that Nagini is able to verify non-trivial properties of real-world Python code.

1 Introduction

Dynamic languages have become widely used because of their expressiveness and ease of use. The Python language in particular is popular in domains like teaching, prototyping, and more recently data science. Python's lack of safety guarantees can be problematic when, as is increasingly the case, it is used for critical applications with high correctness demands. The Python community has reacted to this trend by integrating type annotations and optional static type checking into the language [20]. However, there is currently virtually no tool support for reasoning about Python programs beyond type safety.

We present Nagini, a sound verifier for statically-typed, concurrent Python programs. Nagini can prove memory safety, data race freedom, and user-supplied assertions. Nagini performs *modular* verification, which is important for verification to scale and to be able to verify libraries, and *automates* the verification process for programs annotated with specifications.

Nagini builds on many techniques established in existing tools: (1) Like VeriFast [10] and other tools [4,19,22], it uses separation logic style permissions [16] in order to locally reason about concurrent programs. (2) Like .NET Code Contracts [7], it uses a contract library to enable users to write code-level specifications. (3) Like many verification tools [2,6,11,13], it verifies programs by encoding the program and its specification into an intermediate verification language [1,8], namely Viper [14], for which automatic verifiers already exist.

Nagini combines these techniques with new ideas in order to verify advanced properties and handle the dynamic aspects of Python. In particular, Nagini implements a comprehensive system for verifying finite blocking [5] and input/output behavior [18], and builds on Mypy [12] to verify safety while also supporting important dynamic language features. Nagini is intended for verifying substantial, real-world code, and is currently used to verify the Python

implementation of the SCION internet architecture [3]. To our knowledge, it
is the first tool to enable automatic verification of Python code. Existing tools
for JavaScript [21,24] also target a dynamic language, but focus on faithfully
modeling JavaScript's complex semantics rather than practical verification of
high-level properties.

Due to its wide range of verifiable properties, Nagini has applications in
many domains: In addition to memory safety, programmers can choose to prove
that a server implementation will stay responsive, that data science code has
desired functional properties, or that algorithms terminate and preserve certain
invariants, for example in a teaching context. Nagini is open-source and available
online[1], and can be used from the popular PyCharm IDE via a prototype plugin.

In this paper, we describe Nagini's supported Python subset and specification
language, give an overview of its implementation and the encoding from Python
to Viper, and provide an experimental evaluation of Nagini on real-world code.

2   Language and Specifications

Python Subset: Nagini requires input programs to comply to the static, nominal type system defined in PEP 484 [20] as implemented in the Mypy type
checker [12], which requires type annotations for function parameters and return
types, but can normally infer types of local variables. Nagini fully supports the
non-gradual part of Mypy's type system, including generics and union types.

The Python subset accepted by Mypy and Nagini can accommodate most
real Python programs, potentially via some workarounds like using union types
instead of structural typing. While our subset is statically typed, it includes many
features and potential pitfalls not found in static languages, such as dynamic
addition and removal fields from objects. Some other features like reflection and
dynamic code generation are not supported.

Where compromises are necessary, Nagini aims for modularity, performance,
and completeness for features typically found in user code over general support for all language features. As an example, Nagini works with a simplified
model of Python's object attribute lookup behavior: A simple attribute access
in Python leads to the invocation of several "magic" methods, which, if modelled correctly, would result in an overhead that would likely make automatic
verification intractable. Nagini exploits the fact that these methods are mostly
used to implement decorators, metaclasses, and system libraries, but rarely in
user code. It assumes the default behavior of those methods, and implements
direct support for frequently-used decorators and metaclasses that change their
behavior. Importantly, Nagini flags an error if verified programs override these
methods or are otherwise outside the supported subset, and is therefore sound.

Specification Language: Nagini includes a library of specification functions similar to .NET Code Contracts [7] to express pre- and postconditions, loop invariants, and other assertions. Calls to these functions are interpreted as specifications by Nagini, but can be automatically removed before execution. Users can

---

[1] https://github.com/marcoeilers/nagini.

```
1    from nagini_contracts.contracts import *
2    from typing import List
3    import db
4
5    class Ticket:
6        def __init__(self, show: int, row: int, seat: int) -> None:
7            self.show_id = show
8            self.row, self.seat = row, seat
9            Fold(self.state())
10           Ensures(self.state() and MayCreate(self, 'discount_code'))
11
12       @Predicate
13       def state(self) -> bool:
14           return Acc(self.show_id) and Acc(self.row) and Acc(self.seat)
15
16   def order_tickets(num: int, show_id: int, code: str=None) -> List[Ticket]:
17       Requires(num > 0)
18       Exsures(SoldoutException, True)
19       seats = db.get_seats(show_id, num)
20       res = []  # type: List[Ticket]
21       for row, seat in seats:
22           Invariant(list_pred(res))
23           Invariant(Forall(res, lambda t: t.state() and
24                                 Implies(code is not None, Acc(t.discount_code))))
25           Invariant(MustTerminate(len(seats) - len(res)))
26           ticket = Ticket(show_id, row, seat)
27           if code:
28               ticket.discount_code = code
29           res.append(ticket)
30       return res
```

Fig. 1. Example program demonstrating Nagini's specification language. Contract functions are highlighted in italics. Note that functional specifications and postconditions are largely omitted to highlight the different specification constructs.

annotate Mypy-style type stub files for external libraries with specifications; the program will then be verified assuming they are correct. A detailed explanation of the specification language can be found in Nagini's Wiki[2].

An example of an annotated program is shown in Fig. 1. The first two lines import the contract library and Python's library for type annotations. Pre- and postconditions are declared via calls to the contract functions **Requires** and **Ensures** in lines 17 and 10, respectively. The arguments of these functions are interpreted as assertions, which can be side-effect free boolean Python expressions or calls to other contract functions. Similarly, loops must be annotated with invariants (line 22), and special *exceptional* postconditions specify which exceptions a method may raise, and what postconditions must hold in this case. The **Exsures** annotation in line 18 states that a **SoldoutException** may be raised and makes no guarantees in this case. The invariant **MustTerminate** in line 25 specifies that the loop terminates; the argument represents a ranking function [5].

Like the underlying Viper language, Nagini uses Implicit Dynamic Frames (IDF) [23], a variation of separation logic [16], to achieve framing and allow local reasoning in the presence of concurrency. IDF establishes a system of *permissions* for heap locations that roughly corresponds to separation logic's points-to predicates. Methods may only read or write heap locations they currently hold a permission for, and can specify which permissions they require from and give

---

[2] https://github.com/marcoeilers/nagini/wiki.

back to their caller in their pre- and postconditions. Since there is only ever a single permission per heap location, holding a permission guarantees that neither other threads nor called methods can modify the respective location.

In Nagini, a permission is created when a field is assigned to for the first time; e.g., when executing line 9, the __init__ method will have permission to three fields. Permission assertions are expressed using the Acc function (line 14). Assertions can be abstracted over using predicates [17], declared in Nagini by using annotated functions (line 12). In the example, the constructor of Ticket bundles all available permissions in the predicate state using the ghost statement Fold in line 9 and subsequently returns this predicate to its caller via its postcondition.

In addition, Nagini offers a second kind of permission that allows *creating* a field that does not currently exist, but cannot be used for reading (since that would cause a runtime error). Constructors implicitly get this kind of permission for every field mentioned in a class; in the example, such a permissions is returned to the caller (line 10) and used in line 28. The loop invariant contains the permission to modify the res list using one of several built-in predicates for Python's standard data types (line 22) as well as permissions to the fields of all objects in the list (line 23). This kind of *quantified permission* [15], corresponding to separation logic's iterated separating conjunction, is one of two supported ways to express permissions over unbounded numbers of heap locations.

Other contract functions allow specifying, e.g., I/O behavior, and some have variations for advanced users, e.g., the Forall function can take trigger expressions to specify when the underlying SMT solver should instantiate the quantifier.

Verified properties: Nagini verifies some safety properties by default: Verified programs will not raise runtime errors or undeclared exceptions. The permission system guarantees that verified code is memory safe and free of data races. Nagini also verifies some properties that Mypy only checks optimistically, e.g., that referenced names are defined before they are used. As an example, if the Ticket class were defined after the order_tickets function, Nagini would not allow calls to the function *before* the class definition, because of the call in line 26.

Beyond this, Nagini can verify (1) functional properties, (2) input/output properties, i.e., which I/O operations may or must occur, using a generalization of the method by Penninckx et al. [18], and (3) finite blocking [5], i.e., that no thread blocks indefinitely when trying to acquire a lock or join another thread, which includes deadlock freedom and termination. Verification is modular in the sense that adding code to a program only requires verifying the added parts; any code that verified before is guaranteed to still verify. Top level statements are an exception and have to be reverified when any part of the program changes, since Python's import mechanism is inherently non-modular.

3   Implementation

Nagini's verification workflow is depicted in Fig. 2. After parsing, Nagini invokes the Mypy type checker on the input and rejects the program if errors are found.

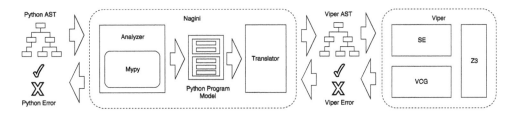

Fig. 2. Nagini verification workflow.

It then analyzes the input program and extracts structural information into an internal model, which is then encoded into a Viper program. The program is verified using one of the two Viper backends, based on either symbolic execution (SE) or verification condition generation (VCG), respectively. Any resulting Viper-level error messages are mapped back to a Python-level error.

Encoding: Nagini encodes Python programs into Viper programs that verify only if the original program was correct. At the top level, Viper programs consist of *methods*, whose bodies contain imperative code, side-effect free *functions*, and the aforementioned *predicates*, as well as *domains*, which can be used to declare and axiomatize custom data types. The structure of a created Viper program roughly follows the structure of the Python program: Each function in the Python program corresponds to either a method, a function, or a predicate in the Viper program, depending on its annotation. Additional Viper methods are generated to check proof obligations like behavioral subtyping and to model the execution of all top level statements.

Nagini maintains various kinds of ghost state, e.g., for verifying finite blocking and to represent which names are currently defined. It models Python's type system using a Viper domain axiomatized to reflect subtype relations. Nagini desugars complex Python language constructs into simple ones that exist in Viper, but subtle language differences often require additional effort in the encoding. As an example, Viper distinguishes references from primitive values whereas Python does not, requiring boxing and unboxing operations in the encoding.

Tool interaction: Nagini is invoked on an annotated Python file, and verifies this file and all (transitive) imports without user interaction. It then outputs either a success message or Python-level error messages that indicate type or verification errors, use of unsupported features, or invalid specifications, along with the source location. As an example, removing the **Fold** statement in line 9 of Fig. 1 yields the error message "Postcondition of __init__ might not hold. There might be insufficient permission to access self.state(). (example.py@10.16)".

4   Evaluation

In addition to having a comprehensive test suite of over 12,500 lines of code, we have evaluated Nagini on a set of examples containing (parts of) implemen-

	Example	LOC / Spec.	Viper LOC	SF	FC	FB	IO	T_{Seq}	T_{Par}
1	rosetta/quicksort	31 / 10	635	✓	-	✓	-	8.48	8.31
2	interactivepython/bst	145 / 65	947	✓	✓	-	-	57.44	41.80
3	keon/knapsack	33 / 10	864	✓	-	-	-	19.39	14.49
4	wikipedia/duck_typing	19 / 0	486	✓	-	-	-	1.82	1.92
5	scion/path_store	207 / 94	2133	✗	-	-	-	51.37	35.26
6	example	40 / 19	736	✓	-	✓	-	6.11	5.91
7	verifast/brackets_checker	143 / 82	1081	✓	✓	✓	✓	7.66	6.63
8	verifast/putchar_with_buffer	139 / 88	865	✓	-	✓	✓	4.74	4.29
9	chalice2viper/watchdog	66 / 22	769	✓	-	✓	-	3.66	3.41
10	parkinson/recell	46 / 25	561	✓	✓	-	-	2.09	2.07

Fig. 3. Experiments. For each example, we list the lines of code (excluding whitespace and comments), the number of those lines that are used for specifications, the length of the resulting Viper program, properties (SF = safety, FC = functional correctness, FB = finite blocking, IO = input/output behavior) that could be verified (✓), could not be verified (✗) or were not attempted (-), and the verification times with Viper's SE backend, sequential and parallelized, in seconds.

tations of standard algorithms from the internet[3], the example from Fig. 1, a class from the SCION implementation, as well as examples from other verifiers translated to Python. Figure 3 shows the examples and which properties were verified; the functional property we proved for the binary search tree implementation is that it maintains a sorted tree. The examples cover language features like inheritance (example 10), comprehensions (3), dynamic field addition (6), operator overloading (3), union types (4), threads and locks (9), as well as specification constructs like quantified permissions (6) and predicate families (10). Nagini correctly finds an error in the SCION example and successfully verifies all other examples.

The runtimes shown in Fig. 3 were measured by averaging over ten runs on a Lenovo Thinkpad T450s running Ubuntu 16.04, Python 3.5 and OpenJDK 8 on a warmed-up JVM. They show that Nagini can effectively verify non-trivial properties of real-life Python programs in reasonable time. Due to modular verification, parts of a program can be verified independently and in parallel (which Nagini does by default), so that larger programs will not inherently lead to performance problems. This is demonstrated by the speedup achieved via parallelization on the two larger examples; for the smaller ones, verification time is dominated by a single complex method. Additionally, the annotation overhead is well within the range of other verification tools [9].

Acknowledgements. Thanks to Vytautas Astrauskas, Samuel Hitz, and Fábio Pakk Selmi-Dei for their contributions to Nagini. We gratefully acknowledge support from the Zurich Information Security and Privacy Center (ZISC).

---

[3] We chose examples that do not make use of dynamic features or external libraries from rosettacode.org, interactivepython.org and github.com/keon/algorithms.

References

1. Barnett, M., Chang, B.-Y.E., DeLine, R., Jacobs, B., Leino, K.R.M.: Boogie: a modular reusable verifier for object-oriented programs. In: de Boer, F.S., Bonsangue, M.M., Graf, S., de Roever, W.-P. (eds.) FMCO 2005. LNCS, vol. 4111, pp. 364–387. Springer, Heidelberg (2006). https://doi.org/10.1007/11804192_17
2. Barnett, M., Fähndrich, M., Leino, K.R.M., Müller, P., Schulte, W., Venter, H.: Specification and verification: the Spec# experience. Commun. ACM **54**(6), 81–91 (2011)
3. Barrera, D., Chuat, L., Perrig, A., Reischuk, R.M., Szalachowski, P.: The scion internet architecture. Commun. ACM **60**(6), 56–65 (2017)
4. Berdine, J., Calcagno, C., O'Hearn, P.W.: Smallfoot: modular automatic assertion checking with separation logic. In: de Boer, F.S., Bonsangue, M.M., Graf, S., de Roever, W.-P. (eds.) FMCO 2005. LNCS, vol. 4111, pp. 115–137. Springer, Heidelberg (2006). https://doi.org/10.1007/11804192_6
5. Boström, P., Müller, P.: Modular verification of finite blocking in non-terminating programs. In: Boyland, J.T. (ed.) European Conference on Object-Oriented Programming (ECOOP). LIPIcs, vol. 37, pp. 639–663. Schloss Dagstuhl (2015)
6. Dahlweid, M., Moskal, M., Santen, T., Tobies, S., Schulte, W.: VCC: contract-based modular verification of concurrent C. In: 2009 31st International Conference on Software Engineering - Companion Volume, pp. 429–430, May 2009
7. Fähndrich, M., Barnett, M., Logozzo, F.: Code contracts (2008). http://research.microsoft.com/contracts
8. Filliâtre, J.-C., Paskevich, A.: Why3—where programs meet provers. In: Felleisen, M., Gardner, P. (eds.) ESOP 2013. LNCS, vol. 7792, pp. 125–128. Springer, Heidelberg (2013). https://doi.org/10.1007/978-3-642-37036-6_8
9. Hawblitzel, C., Howell, J., Lorch, J.R., Narayan, A., Parno, B., Zhang, D., Zill, B.: Ironclad apps: end-to-end security via automated full-system verification. In: 11th USENIX Symposium on Operating Systems Design and Implementation, OSDI 2014, Broomfield, CO, USA, 6–8 October 2014, pp. 165–181 (2014)
10. Jacobs, B., Smans, J., Philippaerts, P., Vogels, F., Penninckx, W., Piessens, F.: VeriFast: a powerful, sound, predictable, fast verifier for C and Java. In: Bobaru, M., Havelund, K., Holzmann, G.J., Joshi, R. (eds.) NFM 2011. LNCS, vol. 6617, pp. 41–55. Springer, Heidelberg (2011). https://doi.org/10.1007/978-3-642-20398-5_4
11. Kirchner, F., Kosmatov, N., Prevosto, V., Signoles, J., Yakobowski, B.: Frama-C: a software analysis perspective. Formal Aspects Comput. **27**(3), 573–609 (2015)
12. Lehtosalo, J., et al.: Mypy - optional static typing for python (2017). http://mypy-lang.org
13. Leino, K.R.M.: Dafny: an automatic program verifier for functional correctness. In: Clarke, E.M., Voronkov, A. (eds.) LPAR 2010. LNCS (LNAI), vol. 6355, pp. 348–370. Springer, Heidelberg (2010). https://doi.org/10.1007/978-3-642-17511-4_20
14. Müller, P., Schwerhoff, M., Summers, A.J.: Viper: a verification infrastructure for permission-based reasoning. In: Jobstmann, B., Leino, K.R.M. (eds.) VMCAI 2016. LNCS, vol. 9583, pp. 41–62. Springer, Heidelberg (2016). https://doi.org/10.1007/978-3-662-49122-5_2
15. Müller, P., Schwerhoff, M., Summers, A.J.: Automatic verification of iterated separating conjunctions using symbolic execution. In: Chaudhuri, S., Farzan, A. (eds.) CAV 2016. LNCS, vol. 9779, pp. 405–425. Springer, Cham (2016). https://doi.org/10.1007/978-3-319-41528-4_22

16. O'Hearn, P., Reynolds, J., Yang, H.: Local reasoning about programs that alter data structures. In: Fribourg, L. (ed.) CSL 2001. LNCS, vol. 2142, pp. 1–19. Springer, Heidelberg (2001). https://doi.org/10.1007/3-540-44802-0_1
17. Parkinson, M., Bierman, G.: Separation logic and abstraction. In: Proceedings of the 32nd ACM SIGPLAN-SIGACT Symposium on Principles of Programming Languages, POPL 2005, pp. 247–258. ACM, New York (2005)
18. Penninckx, W., Jacobs, B., Piessens, F.: Sound, modular and compositional verification of the input/output behavior of programs. In: Vitek, J. (ed.) ESOP 2015. LNCS, vol. 9032, pp. 158–182. Springer, Heidelberg (2015). https://doi.org/10.1007/978-3-662-46669-8_7
19. Piskac, R., Wies, T., Zufferey, D.: GRASShopper: complete heap verification with mixed specifications. In: Ábrahám, E., Havelund, K. (eds.) TACAS 2014. LNCS, vol. 8413, pp. 124–139. Springer, Heidelberg (2014). https://doi.org/10.1007/978-3-642-54862-8_9
20. van Rossum, G., Lehtosalo, J., Langa, Ł.: Type Hints (2014). https://www.python.org/dev/peps/pep-0484/
21. Santos, J.F., Maksimovic, P., Naudziuniene, D., Wood, T., Gardner, P.: JaVert: JavaScript verification toolchain. PACMPL **2**(POPL), 50:1–50:33 (2018)
22. Smans, J., Jacobs, B., Piessens, F.: VeriCool: an automatic verifier for a concurrent object-oriented language. In: Barthe, G., de Boer, F.S. (eds.) FMOODS 2008. LNCS, vol. 5051, pp. 220–239. Springer, Heidelberg (2008). https://doi.org/10.1007/978-3-540-68863-1_14
23. Smans, J., Jacobs, B., Piessens, F.: Implicit dynamic frames. ACM Trans. Program. Lang. Syst. **34**(1), 2:1–2:58 (May 2012)
24. Stefanescu, A., Park, D., Yuwen, S., Li, Y., Rosu, G.: Semantics-based program verifiers for all languages. In: Proceedings of the 2016 ACM SIGPLAN International Conference on Object-Oriented Programming, Systems, Languages, and Applications, OOPSLA 2016, Part of SPLASH 2016, Amsterdam, The Netherlands, 30 October–4 November 2016, pp. 74–91 (2016)

13

Sound Value Iteration

Tim Quatmann$^{(\boxtimes)}$ⓘ and Joost-Pieter Katoenⓘ

RWTH Aachen University, Aachen, Germany
`tim.quatmann@cs.rwth-aachen.de`

Abstract. Computing reachability probabilities is at the heart of probabilistic model checking. All model checkers compute these probabilities in an iterative fashion using value iteration. This technique approximates a fixed point from below by determining reachability probabilities for an increasing number of steps. To avoid results that are significantly off, variants have recently been proposed that converge from both below and above. These procedures require starting values for both sides. We present an alternative that does not require the a priori computation of starting vectors and that converges faster on many benchmarks. The crux of our technique is to give tight and safe bounds—whose computation is cheap—on the reachability probabilities. Lifting this technique to expected rewards is trivial for both Markov chains and MDPs. Experimental results on a large set of benchmarks show its scalability and efficiency.

1 Introduction

Markov decision processes (MDPs) [1,2] have their roots in operations research and stochastic control theory. They are frequently used for stochastic and dynamic optimization problems and are widely applicable in, e.g., stochastic scheduling and robotics. MDPs are also a natural model in randomized distributed computing where coin flips by the individual processes are mixed with non-determinism arising from interleaving the processes' behaviors. The central problem for MDPs is to find a policy that determines what action to take in the light of what is known about the system at the time of choice. The typical aim is to optimize a given objective, such as minimizing the expected cost until a given number of repairs, maximizing the probability of being operational for 1,000 steps, or minimizing the probability to reach a "bad" state.

Probabilistic model checking [3,4] provides a scalable alternative to tackle these MDP problems, see the recent surveys [5,6]. The central computational issue in MDP model checking is to solve a system of linear inequalities. In absence of non-determinism—the MDP being a Markov Chain (MC)—a linear equation system is obtained. After appropriate pre-computations, such as determining the states for which no policy exists that eventually reaches the goal state, the (in)equation system has a unique solution that coincides with the extremal value that is sought for. Possible solution techniques to compute such solutions include policy iteration, linear programming, and value iteration. Modern probabilistic model checkers such as PRISM [7] and Storm [8] use value iteration by default. This approximates a fixed point from below by determining the probabilities to reach a target state within k steps in the k-th iteration. The iteration is typically stopped if the difference between the value vectors of two successive (or vectors that are further apart) is below the desired accuracy ε.

This procedure however can provide results that are significantly off, as the iteration is stopped prematurely, e.g., since the probability mass in the MDP only changes slightly in a series of computational steps due to a "slow" movement. This problem is not new; similar problems, e.g., occur in iterative approaches to compute long-run averages [9] and transient measures [10] and pop up in statistical model checking to decide when to stop simulating for unbounded reachability properties [11]. As recently was shown, this phenomenon does not only occur for hypothetical cases but affects practical benchmarks of MDP model checking too [12]. To remedy this, Haddad and Monmege [13] proposed to iteratively approximate the (unique) fixed point from both below and above; a natural termination criterion is to halt the computation once the two approximations differ less than $2 \cdot \varepsilon$. This scheme requires two starting vectors, one for each approximation. For reachability probabilities, the conservative values zero and one can be used. For expected rewards, it is non-trivial to find an appropriate upper bound—how to "guess" an adequate upper bound to the expected reward to reach a goal state? Baier *et al.* [12] recently provided an algorithm to solve this issue.

This paper takes an alternative perspective to obtaining a sound variant of value iteration. *Our approach does not require the a priori computation of starting vectors and converges faster on many benchmarks.* The crux of our technique is to give tight and safe bounds—whose computation is cheap and that are obtained during the course of value iteration—on the reachability probabilities. The approach is simple and can be lifted straightforwardly to expected rewards. The central idea is to split the desired probability for reaching a target state into the sum of

(i) the probability for reaching a target state *within* k steps and
(ii) the probability for reaching a target state *only after* k steps.

We obtain (i) via k iterations of (standard) value iteration. A second instance of value iteration computes the probability that a target state is still reachable after k steps. We show that from this information safe lower and upper bounds for (ii) can be derived. We illustrate that the same idea can be applied to expected rewards, topological value iteration [14], and Gauss-Seidel value iteration. We also discuss in detail its extension to MDPs and provide extensive experimental evaluation using our implementation in the model checker Storm [8]. Our experiments show that on many practical benchmarks we need significantly fewer iterations, yielding a speed-up of about 20% on average. More importantly though, is the conceptual simplicity of our approach.

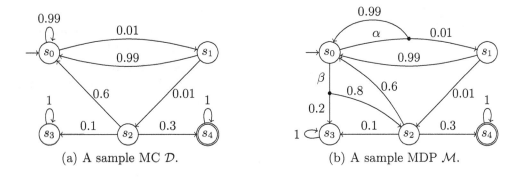

(a) A sample MC $\mathcal{D}$.   (b) A sample MDP $\mathcal{M}$.

Fig. 1. Example models.

2 Preliminaries

For a finite set S and vector $x \in \mathbb{R}^{|S|}$, let $x[s] \in \mathbb{R}$ denote the entry of x that corresponds to $s \in S$. Let $S' \subseteq S$ and $a \in \mathbb{R}$. We write $x[S'] = a$ to denote that $x[s] = a$ for all $s \in S'$. Given $x, y \in \mathbb{R}^{|S|}$, $x \le y$ holds iff $x[s] \le y[s]$ holds for all $s \in S$. For a function $f \colon \mathbb{R}^{|S|} \to \mathbb{R}^{|S|}$ and $k \ge 0$ we write f^k for the function obtained by applying f k times, i.e., $f^0(x) = x$ and $f^k(x) = f(f^{k-1}(x))$ if $k > 0$.

2.1 Probabilistic Models and Measures

We briefly present probabilistic models and their properties. More details can be found in, e.g., [15].

Definition 1 (Probabilistic Models). *A* Markov Decision Process (MDP) *is a tuple* $\mathcal{M} = (S, Act, \mathbf{P}, s_I, \rho)$, *where*

– *S is a finite set of states, Act is a finite set of actions, s_I is the initial state,*
– $\mathbf{P} \colon S \times Act \times S \to [0,1]$ *is a transition probability function satisfying* $\sum_{s' \in S} \mathbf{P}(s, \alpha, s') \in \{0,1\}$ *for all* $s \in S, \alpha \in Act$, *and*
– $\rho \colon S \times Act \to \mathbb{R}$ *is a reward function.*

$\mathcal{M}$ *is a* Markov Chain (MC) *if* $|Act| = 1$.

Example 1. Figure 1 shows an example MC and an example MDP.

We often simplify notations for MCs by omitting the (unique) action. For an MDP $\mathcal{M} = (S, Act, \mathbf{P}, s_I, \rho)$, the set of *enabled actions* of state $s \in S$ is given by $Act(s) = \{\alpha \in Act \mid \sum_{s' \in S} \mathbf{P}(s, \alpha, s') = 1\}$. We assume that $Act(s) \ne \emptyset$ for each $s \in S$. Intuitively, upon performing action α at state s reward $\rho(s, \alpha)$ is collected and with probability $\mathbf{P}(s, \alpha, s')$ we move to $s' \in S$. Notice that rewards can be positive or negative.

A state $s \in S$ is called *absorbing* if $\mathbf{P}(s, \alpha, s) = 1$ for every $\alpha \in Act(s)$. A *path* of $\mathcal{M}$ is an infinite alternating sequence $\pi = s_0 \alpha_0 s_1 \alpha_1 \ldots$ where $s_i \in S$, $\alpha_i \in$

$Act(s_i)$, and $\mathbf{P}(s_i, \alpha_i, s_{i+1}) > 0$ for all $i \geq 0$. The set of paths of $\mathcal{M}$ is denoted by $Paths^{\mathcal{M}}$. The set of paths that start at $s \in S$ is given by $Paths^{\mathcal{M},s}$. A *finite path* $\hat{\pi} = s_0 \alpha_0 \ldots \alpha_{n-1} s_n$ is a finite prefix of a path ending with $last(\hat{\pi}) = s_n \in S$. $|\hat{\pi}| = n$ is the length of $\hat{\pi}$, $Paths^{\mathcal{M}}_{fin}$ is the set of finite paths of $\mathcal{M}$, and $Paths^{\mathcal{M},s}_{fin}$ is the set of finite paths that start at state $s \in S$. We consider LTL-like notations for sets of paths. For $k \in \mathbb{N} \cup \{\infty\}$ and $G, H \subseteq S$ let

$$H \mathcal{U}^{\leq k} G = \{s_0 \alpha_0 s_1 \cdots \in Paths^{\mathcal{M},s_I} \mid s_0, \ldots, s_{j-1} \in H, \; s_j \in G \text{ for some } j \leq k\}$$

denote the set of paths that, starting from the initial state s_I, only visit states in H until after at most k steps a state in G is reached. Sets $H \mathcal{U}^{>k} G$ and $H \mathcal{U}^{=k} G$ are defined similarly. We use the shorthands $\Diamond^{\leq k} G := S \mathcal{U}^{\leq k} G$, $\Diamond G := \Diamond^{\leq \infty} G$, and $\Box^{\leq k} G := Paths^{\mathcal{M},s_I} \setminus \Diamond^{\leq k}(S \setminus G)$.

A *(deterministic) scheduler* for $\mathcal{M}$ is a function $\sigma \colon Paths^{\mathcal{M}}_{fin} \to Act$ such that $\sigma(\hat{\pi}) \in Act(last(\hat{\pi}))$ for all $\hat{\pi} \in Paths^{\mathcal{M}}_{fin}$. The set of (deterministic) schedulers for $\mathcal{M}$ is $\mathfrak{S}^{\mathcal{M}}$. $\sigma \in \mathfrak{S}^{\mathcal{M}}$ is called *positional* if $\sigma(\hat{\pi})$ only depends on the last state of $\hat{\pi}$, i.e., for all $\hat{\pi}, \hat{\pi}' \in Paths^{\mathcal{M}}_{fin}$ we have $last(\hat{\pi}) = last(\hat{\pi}')$ implies $\sigma(\hat{\pi}) = \sigma(\hat{\pi}')$. For MDP $\mathcal{M}$ and scheduler $\sigma \in \mathfrak{S}^{\mathcal{M}}$ the *probability measure* over finite paths is given by $\mathrm{Pr}^{\mathcal{M},\sigma}_{fin} \colon Paths^{\mathcal{M},s_I}_{fin} \to [0,1]$ with $\mathrm{Pr}^{\mathcal{M},\sigma}_{fin}(s_0 \ldots s_n) = \prod_{i=0}^{n-1} \mathbf{P}(s_i, \sigma(s_0 \ldots s_i), s_{i+1})$. The probability measure $\mathrm{Pr}^{\mathcal{M},\sigma}$ over measurable sets of infinite paths is obtained via a standard cylinder set construction [15].

Definition 2 (Reachability Probability). *The* reachability probability *of MDP $\mathcal{M} = (S, Act, \mathbf{P}, s_I, \rho)$, $G \subseteq S$, and $\sigma \in \mathfrak{S}^{\mathcal{M}}$ is given by $\mathrm{Pr}^{\mathcal{M},\sigma}(\Diamond G)$.*

For $k \in \mathbb{N} \cup \{\infty\}$, the function $\blacklozenge^{\leq k} G \colon \Diamond G \to \mathbb{R}$ yields the k-bounded reachability reward of a path $\pi = s_0 \alpha_0 s_1 \cdots \in \Diamond G$. We set $\blacklozenge^{\leq k} G(\pi) = \sum_{i=0}^{j-1} \rho(s_i, \alpha_i)$, where $j = \min(\{i \geq 0 \mid s_i \in G\} \cup \{k\})$. We write $\blacklozenge G$ instead of $\blacklozenge^{\leq \infty} G$.

Definition 3 (Expected Reward). *The* expected (reachability) reward *of MDP $\mathcal{M} = (S, Act, \mathbf{P}, s_I, \rho)$, $G \subseteq S$, and $\sigma \in \mathfrak{S}^{\mathcal{M}}$ with $\mathrm{Pr}^{\mathcal{M},\sigma}(\Diamond G) = 1$ is given by the expectation $\mathbb{E}^{\mathcal{M},\sigma}(\blacklozenge G) = \int_{\pi \in \Diamond G} \blacklozenge G(\pi) \, d\mathrm{Pr}^{\mathcal{M},\sigma}(\pi)$.*

We write $\mathrm{Pr}^{\mathcal{M},\sigma}_s$ and $\mathbb{E}^{\mathcal{M},\sigma}_s$ for the probability measure and expectation obtained by changing the initial state of $\mathcal{M}$ to $s \in S$. If $\mathcal{M}$ is a Markov chain, there is only a single scheduler. In this case we may omit the superscript σ from $\mathrm{Pr}^{\mathcal{M},\sigma}$ and $\mathbb{E}^{\mathcal{M},\sigma}$. We also omit the superscript $\mathcal{M}$ if it is clear from the context. The maximal reachability probability of $\mathcal{M}$ and G is given by $\mathrm{Pr}^{\max}(\Diamond G) = \max_{\sigma \in \mathfrak{S}^{\mathcal{M}}} \mathrm{Pr}^{\sigma}(\Diamond G)$. There is a a positional scheduler that attains this maximum [16]. The same holds for minimal reachability probabilities and maximal or minimal expected rewards.

Example 2. Consider the MDP $\mathcal{M}$ from Fig. 1(b). We are interested in the maximal probability to reach state s_4 given by $\mathrm{Pr}^{\max}(\Diamond\{s_4\})$. Since s_4 is not reachable from s_3 we have $\mathrm{Pr}^{\max}_{s_3}(\Diamond\{s_4\}) = 0$. Intuitively, choosing action β at state s_0 makes reaching s_3 more likely, which should be avoided in order to maximize the probability to reach s_4. We therefore assume a scheduler σ that always chooses action α at state s_0. Starting from the initial state s_0, we then eventually take the transition from s_2 to s_3 or the transition from s_2 to s_4 with probability one. The resulting probability to reach s_4 is given by $\mathrm{Pr}^{\max}(\lozenge\{s_4\}) = \mathrm{Pr}^\sigma(\lozenge\{s_4\}) = 0.3/(0.1 + 0.3) = 0.75$.

2.2   Probabilistic Model Checking via Interval Iteration

In the following we present approaches to compute reachability probabilities and expected rewards. We consider approximative computations. Exact computations are handled in e.g. [17,18] For the sake of clarity, we focus on reachability probabilities and sketch how the techniques can be lifted to expected rewards.

Reachability Probabilities. We fix an MDP $\mathcal{M} = (S, Act, \mathbf{P}, s_I, \rho)$, a set of goal states $G \subseteq S$, and a precision parameter $\varepsilon > 0$.

Problem 1. Compute an ε-approximation of the maximal reachability probability $\mathrm{Pr}^{\max}(\lozenge G)$, i.e., compute a value $r \in [0, 1]$ with $|r - \mathrm{Pr}^{\max}(\lozenge G)| < \varepsilon$.

We briefly sketch how to compute such a value r via *interval iteration* [12,13,19]. The computation for minimal reachability probabilities is analogous.

W.l.o.g. it is assumed that the states in G are absorbing. Using graph algorithms, we compute $S_0 = \{s \in S \mid \mathrm{Pr}_s^{\max}(\lozenge G) = 0\}$ and partition the state space of $\mathcal{M}$ into $S = S_0 \uplus G \uplus S_?$ with $S_? = S \setminus (G \cup S_0)$. If $s_I \in S_0$ or $s_I \in G$, the probability $\mathrm{Pr}^{\max}(\lozenge G)$ is 0 or 1, respectively. From now on we assume $s_I \in S_?$.

We say that $\mathcal{M}$ is *contracting* with respect to $S' \subseteq S$ if $\mathrm{Pr}_s^\sigma(\lozenge S') = 1$ for all $s \in S$ and for all $\sigma \in \mathfrak{S}^\mathcal{M}$. We assume that $\mathcal{M}$ is contracting with respect to $G \cup S_0$. Otherwise, we apply a transformation on the so-called *end components*[1] of $\mathcal{M}$, yielding a contracting MDP $\mathcal{M}'$ with the same maximal reachability probability as $\mathcal{M}$. Roughly, this transformation replaces each end component of $\mathcal{M}$ with a single state whose enabled actions coincide with the actions that previously lead outside of the end component. This step is detailed in [13,19].

We have $x^*[s] = \mathrm{Pr}_s^{\max}(\lozenge G)$ for $s \in S$ and the unique fixpoint x^* of the function $f \colon \mathbb{R}^{|S|} \to \mathbb{R}^{|S|}$ with $f(x)[S_0] = 0$, $f(x)[G] = 1$, and

$$f(x)[s] = \max_{\alpha \in Act(s)} \sum_{s' \in S} \mathbf{P}(s, \alpha, s') \cdot x[s']$$

for $s \in S_?$. Hence, computing $\mathrm{Pr}^{\max}(\lozenge G)$ reduces to finding the fixpoint of f.

A popular technique for this purpose is the *value iteration* algorithm [1]. Given a starting vector $x \in \mathbb{R}^{|S|}$ with $x[S_0] = 0$ and $x[G] = 1$, standard value iteration computes $f^k(x)$ for increasing k until $\max_{s \in S} |f^k(x)[s] - f^{k-1}(x)[s]| < \varepsilon$ holds for a predefined precision $\varepsilon > 0$. As pointed out in, e.g., [13], there is no

---

[1] Intuitively, an end component is a set of states $S' \subseteq S$ such that there is a scheduler inducing that from any $s \in S'$ exactly the states in S' are visited infinitely often.

guarantee on the preciseness of the result $r = f^k(x)[s_I]$, i.e., standard value iteration does not give any evidence on the error $|r - \mathrm{Pr}^{\max}(\Diamond G)|$. The intuitive reason is that value iteration only approximates the fixpoint x^* from one side, yielding no indication on the distance between the current result and x^*.

Example 3. Consider the MDP $\mathcal{M}$ from Fig. 1(b). We invoked standard value iteration in PRISM [7] and Storm [8] to compute the reachability probability $\mathrm{Pr}^{\max}(\Diamond\{s_4\})$. Recall from Example 2 that the correct solution is 0.75. With (absolute) precision $\varepsilon = 10^{-6}$ both model checkers returned 0.7248. Notice that the user can improve the precision by considering, e.g., $\varepsilon = 10^{-8}$ which yields 0.7497. However, there is no guarantee on the preciseness of a given result.

The *interval iteration* algorithm [12,13,19] addresses the impreciseness of value iteration. The idea is to approach the fixpoint x^* from below and from above. The first step is to find starting vectors $x_\ell, x_u \in \mathbb{R}^{|S|}$ satisfying $x_\ell[S_0] = x_u[S_0] = 0$, $x_\ell[G] = x_u[G] = 1$, and $x_\ell \leq x^* \leq x_u$. As the entries of x^* are probabilities, it is always valid to set $x_\ell[S_?] = 0$ and $x_u[S_?] = 1$. We have $f^k(x_\ell) \leq x^* \leq f^k(x_u)$ for any $k \geq 0$. Interval iteration computes $f^k(x_\ell)$ and $f^k(x_u)$ for increasing k until $\max_{s \in S}|f^k(x_\ell)[s] - f^k(x_u)[s]| < 2\varepsilon$. For the result $r = 1/2 \cdot (f^k(x_\ell)[s_I] + f^k(x_u)[s_I])$ we obtain that $|r - \mathrm{Pr}^{\max}(\Diamond G)| < \varepsilon$, i.e., we get a sound approximation of the maximal reachability probability.

Example 4. We invoked interval iteration in PRISM and Storm to compute the reachability probability $\mathrm{Pr}^{\max}(\Diamond\{s_4\})$ for the MDP $\mathcal{M}$ from Fig. 1(b). Both implementations correctly yield an ε-approximation of $\mathrm{Pr}^{\max}(\Diamond\{s_4\})$, where we considered $\varepsilon = 10^{-6}$. However, both PRISM and Storm required roughly 300,000 iterations for convergence.

Expected Rewards. Whereas [13,19] only consider reachability probabilities, [12] extends interval iteration to compute expected rewards. Let $\mathcal{M}$ be an MDP and G be a set of absorbing states such that $\mathcal{M}$ is contracting with respect to G.

Problem 2. Compute an ε-approximation of the maximal expected reachability reward $\mathbb{E}^{\max}(\blacklozenge G)$, i.e., compute a value $r \in \mathbb{R}$ with $|r - \mathbb{E}^{\max}(\blacklozenge G)| < \varepsilon$.

We have $x^*[s] = \mathbb{E}_s^{\max}(\blacklozenge G)$ for the unique fixpoint x^* of $g\colon \mathbb{R}^{|S|} \to \mathbb{R}^{|S|}$ with

$$g(x)[G] = 0 \quad \text{and} \quad g(x)[s] = \max_{\alpha \in Act(s)} \rho(s, \alpha) + \sum_{s' \in S} \mathbf{P}(s, \alpha, s') \cdot x[s']$$

for $s \notin G$. As for reachability probabilities, interval iteration can be applied to approximate this fixpoint. The crux lies in finding appropriate starting vectors $x_\ell, x_u \in \mathbb{R}^{|S|}$ guaranteeing $x_\ell \leq x^* \leq x_u$. To this end, [12] describe graph based algorithms that give an upper bound on the expected number of times each individual state $s \in S \setminus G$ is visited. This then yields an approximation of the expected amount of reward collected at the various states.

3 Sound Value Iteration for MCs

We present an algorithm for computing reachability probabilities and expected rewards as in Problems 1 and 2. The algorithm is an alternative to the interval iteration approach [12,20] but (i) does not require an a priori computation of starting vectors $x_\ell, x_u \in \mathbb{R}^{|S|}$ and (ii) converges faster on many practical benchmarks as shown in Sect. 5. For the sake of simplicity, we first restrict to computing reachability probabilities on MCs.

In the following, let $\mathcal{D} = (S, \mathbf{P}, s_I, \rho)$ be an MC, $G \subseteq S$ be a set of absorbing goal states and $\varepsilon > 0$ be a precision parameter. We consider the partition $S = S_0 \cup G \cup S_?$ as in Sect. 2.2. The following theorem captures the key insight of our algorithm.

Theorem 1. *For MC $\mathcal{D}$ let G and $S_?$ be as above and $k \geq 0$ with $\mathrm{Pr}_s(\square^{\leq k} S_?) < 1$ for all $s \in S_?$. We have*

$$\mathrm{Pr}(\lozenge^{\leq k} G) + \mathrm{Pr}(\square^{\leq k} S_?) \cdot \min_{s \in S_?} \frac{\mathrm{Pr}_s(\lozenge^{\leq k} G)}{1 - \mathrm{Pr}_s(\square^{\leq k} S_?)}$$

$$\leq \mathrm{Pr}(\lozenge G) \leq \mathrm{Pr}(\lozenge^{\leq k} G) + \mathrm{Pr}(\square^{\leq k} S_?) \cdot \max_{s \in S_?} \frac{\mathrm{Pr}_s(\lozenge^{\leq k} G)}{1 - \mathrm{Pr}_s(\square^{\leq k} S_?)}.$$

Theorem 1 allows us to approximate $\mathrm{Pr}(\lozenge G)$ by computing for increasing $k \in \mathbb{N}$

- $\mathrm{Pr}(\lozenge^{\leq k} G)$, the probability to reach a state in G within k steps, and
- $\mathrm{Pr}(\square^{\leq k} S_?)$, the probability to stay in $S_?$ during the first k steps.

This can be realized via a value-iteration based procedure. The obtained bounds on $\mathrm{Pr}(\lozenge G)$ can be tightened arbitrarily since $\mathrm{Pr}(\square^{\leq k} S_?)$ approaches 0 for increasing k. In the following, we address the correctness of Theorem 1, describe the details of our algorithm, and indicate how the results can be lifted to expected rewards.

3.1 Approximating Reachability Probabilities

To approximate the reachability probability $\mathrm{Pr}(\lozenge G)$, we consider the step bounded reachability probability $\mathrm{Pr}(\lozenge^{\leq k} G)$ for $k \geq 0$ and provide a lower and an upper bound for the 'missing' probability $\mathrm{Pr}(\lozenge G) - \mathrm{Pr}(\lozenge^{\leq k} G)$. Note that $\lozenge G$ is the disjoint union of the paths that reach G *within* k steps (given by $\lozenge^{\leq k} G$) and the paths that reach G only *after* k steps (given by $S_? \mathcal{U}^{>k} G$).

Lemma 1. *For any $k \geq 0$ we have $\mathrm{Pr}(\lozenge G) = \mathrm{Pr}(\lozenge^{\leq k} G) + \mathrm{Pr}(S_? \mathcal{U}^{>k} G)$.*

A path $\pi \in S_? \mathcal{U}^{>k} G$ reaches some state $s \in S_?$ after *exactly* k steps. This yields the partition $S_? \mathcal{U}^{>k} G = \biguplus_{s \in S_?} (S_? \mathcal{U}^{=k} \{s\} \cap \lozenge G)$. It follows that

$$\mathrm{Pr}(S_? \mathcal{U}^{>k} G) = \sum_{s \in S_?} \mathrm{Pr}(S_? \mathcal{U}^{=k} \{s\}) \cdot \mathrm{Pr}_s(\lozenge G).$$

Consider $\ell, u \in [0,1]$ with $\ell \leq \Pr_s(\lozenge G) \leq u$ for all $s \in S_?$, i.e., ℓ and u are lower and upper bounds for the reachability probabilities within $S_?$. We have

$$\sum_{s \in S_?} \Pr(S_? \, \mathcal{U}^{=k}\{s\}) \cdot \Pr_s(\lozenge G) \leq \sum_{s \in S_?} \Pr(S_? \, \mathcal{U}^{=k}\{s\}) \cdot u = \Pr(\square^{\leq k} S_?) \cdot u.$$

We can argue similar for the lower bound ℓ. With *Lemma* 1 we get the following.

Proposition 1. *For MC* $\mathcal{D}$ *with* G, $S_?$, ℓ, u *as above and any* $k \geq 0$ *we have*

$$\Pr(\lozenge^{\leq k} G) + \Pr(\square^{\leq k} S_?) \cdot \ell \leq \Pr(\lozenge G) \leq \Pr(\lozenge^{\leq k} G) + \Pr(\square^{\leq k} S_?) \cdot u.$$

Remark 1. The bounds for $\Pr(\lozenge G)$ given by Proposition 1 are similar to the bounds obtained after performing k iterations of interval iteration with starting vectors $x_\ell, x_u \in \mathbb{R}^{|S|}$, where $x_\ell[S_?] = \ell$ and $x_u[S_?] = u$.

We now discuss how the bounds ℓ and u can be obtained from the step bounded probabilities $\Pr_s(\lozenge^{\leq k} G)$ and $\Pr_s(\square^{\leq k} S_?)$ for $s \in S_?$. We focus on the upper bound u. The reasoning for the lower bound ℓ is similar.

Let $s_{\max} \in S_?$ be a state with maximal reachability probability, that is $s_{\max} \in \arg\max_{s \in S_?} \Pr_s(\lozenge G)$. From Proposition 1 we get

$$\Pr_{s_{\max}}(\lozenge G) \leq \Pr_{s_{\max}}(\lozenge^{\leq k} G) + \Pr_{s_{\max}}(\square^{\leq k} S_?) \cdot \Pr_{s_{\max}}(\lozenge G).$$

We solve the inequality for $\Pr_{s_{\max}}(\lozenge G)$ (assuming $\Pr_s(\square^{\leq k} S_?) < 1$ for all $s \in S_?$):

$$\Pr_{s_{\max}}(\lozenge G) \leq \frac{\Pr_{s_{\max}}(\lozenge^{\leq k} G)}{1 - \Pr_{s_{\max}}(\square^{\leq k} S_?)} \leq \max_{s \in S_?} \frac{\Pr_s(\lozenge^{\leq k} G)}{1 - \Pr_s(\square^{\leq k} S_?)}.$$

Proposition 2. *For MC* $\mathcal{D}$ *let* G *and* $S_?$ *be as above and* $k \geq 0$ *such that* $\Pr_s(\square^{\leq k} S_?) < 1$ *for all* $s \in S_?$. *For every* $\hat{s} \in S_?$ *we have*

$$\min_{s \in S_?} \frac{\Pr_s(\lozenge^{\leq k} G)}{1 - \Pr_s(\square^{\leq k} S_?)} \leq \Pr_{\hat{s}}(\lozenge G) \leq \max_{s \in S_?} \frac{\Pr_s(\lozenge^{\leq k} G)}{1 - \Pr_s(\square^{\leq k} S_?)}.$$

Theorem 1 is a direct consequence of Propositions 1 and 2.

3.2   Extending the Value Iteration Approach

Recall the standard value iteration algorithm for approximating $\Pr(\lozenge G)$ as discussed in Sect. 2.2. The function $f \colon \mathbb{R}^{|S|} \to \mathbb{R}^{|S|}$ for MCs simplifies to $f(x)[S_0] = 0$, $f(x)[G] = 1$, and $f(x)[s] = \sum_{s' \in S} \mathbf{P}(s, s') \cdot x[s']$ for $s \in S_?$. We can compute the k-step bounded reachability probability at every state $s \in S$

Input : MC $\mathcal{D} = (S, \mathbf{P}, s_I, \rho)$, absorbing states $G \subseteq S$, precision $\varepsilon > 0$
Output : $r \in \mathbb{R}$ with $|r - \text{Pr}(\lozenge G)| < \varepsilon$
1   $S_? \leftarrow S \setminus (\{s \in S \mid \text{Pr}_s(\lozenge G) = 0\} \cup G)$
2   initialize $x_0, y_0 \in \mathbb{R}^{|S|}$ with $x_0[G] = 1$, $x_0[S \setminus G] = 0$, $y_0[S_?] = 1$, $y_0[S \setminus S_?] = 0$
3   $\ell_0 \leftarrow -\infty$; $u_0 \leftarrow +\infty$
4   $k \leftarrow 0$
5   **repeat**
6      $k \leftarrow k + 1$
7      $x_k \leftarrow f(x_{k-1})$; $y_k \leftarrow h(y_{k-1})$
8   **if** $y_k[s] < 1$ for all $s \in S_?$ **then**
9        $\ell_k \leftarrow \max(\ell_{k-1}, \min_{s \in S_?} \frac{x_k[s]}{1 - y_k[s]})$; $u_k \leftarrow \min(u_{k-1}, \max_{s \in S_?} \frac{x_k[s]}{1 - y_k[s]})$
10 **until** $y_k[s_I] \cdot (u_k - \ell_k) < 2 \cdot \varepsilon$
11 **return** $x_k[s_I] + y_k[s_I] \cdot \frac{\ell_k + u_k}{2}$

Algorithm 1: Sound value iteration for MCs.

by performing k iterations of value iteration [15, Remark 10.104]. More precisely, when applying f k times on starting vector $x \in \mathbb{R}^{|S|}$ with $x[G] = 1$ and $x[S \setminus G] = 0$ we get $\text{Pr}_s(\lozenge^{\leq k} G) = f^k(x)[s]$. The probabilities $\text{Pr}_s(\square^{\leq k} S_?)$ for $s \in S$ can be computed similarly. Let $h: \mathbb{R}^{|S|} \to \mathbb{R}^{|S|}$ with $h(y)[S \setminus S_?] = 0$ and $h(y)[s] = \sum_{s' \in S} \mathbf{P}(s, s') \cdot y[s']$ for $s \in S_?$. For starting vector $y \in \mathbb{R}^{|S|}$ with $y[S_?] = 1$ and $y[S \setminus S_?] = 0$ we get $\text{Pr}_s(\square^{\leq k} S_?) = h^k(y)[s]$.

Algorithm 1 depicts our approach. It maintains vectors $x_k, y_k \in \mathbb{R}^{|S|}$ which, after k iterations of the loop, store the k-step bounded probabilities $\text{Pr}_s(\lozenge^{\leq k} G)$ and $\text{Pr}_s(\square^{\leq k} S_?)$, respectively. Additionally, the algorithm considers lower bounds ℓ_k and upper bounds u_k such that the following invariant holds.

Lemma 2. *After executing the loop of Algorithm 1 k times we have for all $s \in S_?$ that $x_k[s] = \text{Pr}_s(\lozenge^{\leq k} G)$, $y_k[s] = \text{Pr}_s(\square^{\leq k} S_?)$, and $\ell_k \leq \text{Pr}_s(\lozenge G) \leq u_k$.*

The correctness of the algorithm follows from Theorem 1. Termination is guaranteed since $\text{Pr}(\lozenge(S_0 \cup G)) = 1$ and therefore $\lim_{k \to \infty} \text{Pr}(\square^{\leq k} S_?) = \text{Pr}(\square S_?) = 0$.

Theorem 2. *Algorithm 1 terminates for any MC $\mathcal{D}$, goal states G, and precision $\varepsilon > 0$. The returned value r satisfies $|r - \text{Pr}(\lozenge G)| < \varepsilon$.*

Example 5. We apply Algorithm 1 for the MC in Fig. 1(a) and the set of goal states $G = \{s_4\}$. We have $S_? = \{s_0, s_1, s_2\}$. After $k = 3$ iterations it holds that

$$x_3[s_0] = 0.00003 \quad x_3[s_1] = 0.003 \quad x_3[s_2] = 0.3$$
$$y_3[s_0] = 0.99996 \quad y_3[s_1] = 0.996 \quad y_3[s_2] = 0.6$$

Hence, $\frac{x_3[s]}{1 - y_3[s]} = \frac{3}{4} = 0.75$ for all $s \in S_?$. We get $\ell_3 = u_3 = 0.75$. The algorithm converges for any $\varepsilon > 0$ and returns the correct solution $x_3[s_0] + y_3[s_0] \cdot 0.75 = 0.75$.

3.3   Sound Value Iteration for Expected Rewards

We lift our approach to expected rewards in a straightforward manner. Let $G \subseteq S$ be a set of absorbing goal states of MC $\mathcal{D}$ such that $\Pr(\lozenge G) = 1$. Further let $S_? = S \setminus G$. For $k \geq 0$ we observe that the expected reward $\mathbb{E}(\blacklozenge G)$ can be split into the expected reward collected within k steps and the expected reward collected only after k steps, i.e., $\mathbb{E}(\blacklozenge G) = \mathbb{E}(\blacklozenge^{\leq k} G) + \sum_{s \in S_?} \Pr(S_? \, \mathcal{U}^{=k} \{s\}) \cdot \mathbb{E}_s(\blacklozenge G)$. Following a similar reasoning as in Sect. 3.1 we can show the following.

Theorem 3. *For MC $\mathcal{D}$ let G and $S_?$ be as before and $k \geq 0$ such that $\Pr_s(\square^{\leq k} S_?) < 1$ for all $s \in S_?$. We have*

$$\mathbb{E}(\blacklozenge^{\leq k} G) + \Pr(\square^{\leq k} S_?) \cdot \min_{s \in S_?} \frac{\mathbb{E}_s(\blacklozenge^{\leq k} G)}{1 - \Pr_s(\square^{\leq k} S_?)}$$

$$\leq \mathbb{E}(\blacklozenge G) \leq \mathbb{E}(\blacklozenge^{\leq k} G) + \Pr(\square^{\leq k} S_?) \cdot \max_{s \in S_?} \frac{\mathbb{E}_s(\blacklozenge^{\leq k} G)}{1 - \Pr_s(\square^{\leq k} S_?)}.$$

Recall the function $g \colon \mathbb{R}^{|S|} \to \mathbb{R}^{|S|}$ from Sect. 2.2, given by $g(x)[G] = 0$ and $g(x)[s] = \rho(s) + \sum_{s' \in S} \mathbf{P}(s, s') \cdot x[s']$ for $s \in S_?$. For $s \in S$ and $x \in \mathbb{R}^{|S|}$ with $x[S] = 0$ we have $\mathbb{E}_s(\blacklozenge^{\leq k} G) = g^k(x)[s]$. We modify Algorithm 1 such that it considers function g instead of function f. Then, the returned value r satisfies $|r - \mathbb{E}(\blacklozenge G)| < \varepsilon$.

3.4   Optimizations

Algorithm 1 can make use of *initial bounds* $\ell_0, u_0 \in \mathbb{R}$ with $\ell_0 \leq \Pr_s(\lozenge G) \leq u_0$ for all $s \in S_?$. Such bounds could be derived, e.g., from domain knowledge or during preprocessing [12]. The algorithm always chooses the largest available lower bound for ℓ_k and the lowest available upper bound for u_k, respectively. If Algorithm 1 and interval iteration are initialized with the same bounds, Algorithm 1 always requires as most as many iterations compared to interval iteration (cf. Remark 1).

Gauss-Seidel value iteration [1,12] is an optimization for standard value iteration and interval iteration that potentially leads to faster convergence. When computing $f(x)[s]$ for $s \in S_?$, the idea is to consider already computed results $f(x)[s']$ from the current iteration. Formally, let $\prec \subseteq S \times S$ be some strict total ordering of the states. Gauss-Seidel value iteration considers instead of function f the function $f_\prec \colon \mathbb{R}^{|S|} \to \mathbb{R}^{|S|}$ with $f_\prec[S_0] = 0$, $f_\prec[G] = 1$, and

$$f_\prec(x)[s] = \sum_{s' \prec s} \mathbf{P}(s, s') \cdot f_\prec(x)[s'] + \sum_{s' \nprec s} \mathbf{P}(s, s') \cdot x[s'].$$

Values $f_\prec(x)[s]$ for $s \in S$ are computed in the order defined by $\prec$. This idea can also be applied to our approach. To this end, we replace f by $f_\prec$ and h by $h_\prec$, where $h_\prec$ is defined similarly. More details are given in [21].

Topological value iteration [14] employs the graphical structure of the MC $\mathcal{D}$. The idea is to decompose the states S of $\mathcal{D}$ into strongly connected components[2]

---

[2] $S' \subseteq S$ is a connected component if s can be reached from s' for all $s, s' \in S'$. S' is a strongly connected component if no superset of S' is a connected component.

(SCCs) that are analyzed individually. The procedure can improve the runtime of classical value iteration since for a single iteration only the values for the current SCC have to be updated. A topological variant of interval iteration is introduced in [12]. Given these results, sound value iteration can be extended similarly.

4 Sound Value Iteration for MDPs

We extend sound value iteration to compute reachability probabilities in MDPs. Assume an MDP $\mathcal{M} = (S, Act, \mathbf{P}, s_I, \rho)$ and a set of absorbing goal states G. For simplicity, we focus on maximal reachability probabilities, i.e., we compute $\mathrm{Pr}^{\max}(\Diamond G)$. Minimal reachability probabilities and expected rewards are analogous. As in Sect. 2.2 we consider the partition $S = S_0 \uplus G \uplus S_?$ such that $\mathcal{M}$ is contracting with respect to $G \cup S_0$.

4.1 Approximating Maximal Reachability Probabilities

We argue that our results for MCs also hold for MDPs under a given scheduler $\sigma \in \mathfrak{S}^{\mathcal{M}}$. Let $k \geq 0$ such that $\mathrm{Pr}_s^\sigma(\Box^{\leq k} S_?) < 1$ for all $s \in S_?$. Following the reasoning as in Sect. 3.1 we get

$$\mathrm{Pr}^\sigma(\Diamond^{\leq k}G) + \mathrm{Pr}^\sigma(\Box^{\leq k}S_?) \cdot \min_{s \in S_?} \frac{\mathrm{Pr}_s^\sigma(\Diamond^{\leq k}G)}{1 - \mathrm{Pr}_s^\sigma(\Box^{\leq k}S_?)} \leq \mathrm{Pr}^\sigma(\Diamond G) \leq \mathrm{Pr}^{\max}(\Diamond G).$$

Next, assume an upper bound $u \in \mathbb{R}$ with $\mathrm{Pr}_s^{\max}(\Diamond G) \leq u$ for all $s \in S_?$. For a scheduler $\sigma_{\max} \in \mathfrak{S}^{\mathcal{M}}$ that attains the maximal reachability probability, i.e., $\sigma_{\max} \in \arg\max_{\sigma \in \mathfrak{S}^{\mathcal{M}}} \mathrm{Pr}^\sigma(\Diamond G)$ it holds that

$$\mathrm{Pr}^{\max}(\Diamond G) = \mathrm{Pr}^{\sigma_{\max}}(\Diamond G) \leq \mathrm{Pr}^{\sigma_{\max}}(\Diamond^{\leq k}G) + \mathrm{Pr}^{\sigma_{\max}}(\Box^{\leq k}S_?) \cdot u$$
$$\leq \max_{\sigma \in \mathfrak{S}^{\mathcal{M}}} \left(\mathrm{Pr}^\sigma(\Diamond^{\leq k}G) + \mathrm{Pr}^\sigma(\Box^{\leq k}S_?) \cdot u \right).$$

We obtain the following theorem which is the basis of our algorithm.

Theorem 4. *For MDP $\mathcal{M}$ let G, $S_?$, and u be as above. Assume $\sigma \in \mathfrak{S}^{\mathcal{M}}$ and $k \geq 0$ such that $\sigma \in \arg\max_{\sigma' \in \mathfrak{S}^{\mathcal{M}}} \mathrm{Pr}^{\sigma'}(\Diamond^{\leq k}G) + \mathrm{Pr}^{\sigma'}(\Box^{\leq k}S_?) \cdot u$ and $\mathrm{Pr}_s^\sigma(\Box^{\leq k}S_?) < 1$ for all $s \in S_?$. We have*

$$\mathrm{Pr}^\sigma(\Diamond^{\leq k}G) + \mathrm{Pr}^\sigma(\Box^{\leq k}S_?) \cdot \min_{s \in S_?} \frac{\mathrm{Pr}_s^\sigma(\Diamond^{\leq k}G)}{1 - \mathrm{Pr}_s^\sigma(\Box^{\leq k}S_?)}$$
$$\leq \mathrm{Pr}^{\max}(\Diamond G) \leq \mathrm{Pr}^\sigma(\Diamond^{\leq k}G) + \mathrm{Pr}^\sigma(\Box^{\leq k}S_?) \cdot u.$$

Similar to the results for MCs it also holds that $\mathrm{Pr}^{\max}(\Diamond G) \leq \max_{\sigma \in \mathfrak{S}^{\mathcal{M}}} \hat{u}_k^\sigma$ with

$$\hat{u}_k^\sigma := \mathrm{Pr}^\sigma(\Diamond^{\leq k}G) + \mathrm{Pr}^\sigma(\Box^{\leq k}S_?) \cdot \max_{s \in S_?} \frac{\mathrm{Pr}_s^\sigma(\Diamond^{\leq k}G)}{1 - \mathrm{Pr}_s^\sigma(\Box^{\leq k}S_?)}.$$

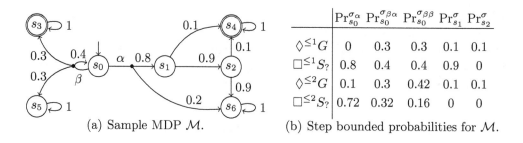

(a) Sample MDP $\mathcal{M}$.   (b) Step bounded probabilities for $\mathcal{M}$.

Fig. 2. Example MDP with corresponding step bounded probabilities.

However, this upper bound can not trivially be embedded in a value iteration based procedure. Intuitively, in order to compute the upper bound for iteration k, one can not necessarily build on the results for iteration $k - 1$.

Example 6. Consider the MDP $\mathcal{M}$ given in Fig. 2(a). Let $G = \{s_3, s_4\}$ be the set of goal states. We therefore have $S_? = \{s_0, s_1, s_2\}$. In Fig. 2(b) we list step bounded probabilities with respect to the possible schedulers, where σ_α, $\sigma_{\beta\alpha}$, and $\sigma_{\beta\beta}$ refer to schedulers with $\sigma_\alpha(s_0) = \alpha$ and for $\gamma \in \{\alpha, \beta\}$, $\sigma_{\beta\gamma}(s_0) = \beta$ and $\sigma_{\beta\gamma}(s_0\beta s_0) = \gamma$. Notice that the probability measures $\mathrm{Pr}^\sigma_{s_1}$ and $\mathrm{Pr}^\sigma_{s_2}$ are independent of the considered scheduler σ. For step bounds $k \in \{1, 2\}$ we get

- $\max_{\sigma \in \mathfrak{S}_\mathcal{M}} \hat{u}_1^\sigma = \hat{u}_1^{\sigma_\alpha} = 0 + 0.8 \cdot \max(0, 1, 0) = 0.8$ and
- $\max_{\sigma \in \mathfrak{S}_\mathcal{M}} \hat{u}_2^\sigma = \hat{u}_2^{\sigma_{\beta\beta}} = 0.42 + 0.16 \cdot \max(0.5, 0.19, 1) = 0.5$.

4.2 Extending the Value Iteration Approach

The idea of our algorithm is to compute the bounds for $\mathrm{Pr}^{\max}(\Diamond G)$ as in Theorem 4 for increasing $k \geq 0$. Algorithm 2 outlines the procedure. Similar to Algorithm 1 for MCs, vectors $x_k, y_k \in \mathbb{R}^{|S|}$ store the step bounded probabilities $\mathrm{Pr}^{\sigma_k}_s(\Diamond^{\leq k} G)$ and $\mathrm{Pr}^{\sigma_k}_s(\Box^{\leq k} S_?)$ for any $s \in S$. In addition, schedulers σ_k and upper bounds $u_k \geq \max_{s \in S_?} \mathrm{Pr}^{\max}_s(\Diamond G)$ are computed in a way that Theorem 4 is applicable.

Lemma 3. *After executing k iterations of Algorithm 2 we have for all $s \in S_?$ that $x_k[s] = \mathrm{Pr}^{\sigma_k}_s(\Diamond^{\leq k} G)$, $y_k[s] = \mathrm{Pr}^{\sigma_k}_s(\Box^{\leq k} S_?)$, and $\ell_k \leq \mathrm{Pr}^{\max}_s(\Diamond G) \leq u_k$, where $\sigma_k \in \arg\max_{\sigma \in \mathfrak{S}_\mathcal{M}} \mathrm{Pr}^\sigma_s(\Diamond^{\leq k} G) + \mathrm{Pr}^\sigma_s(\Box^{\leq k} S_?) \cdot u_k$.*

The lemma holds for $k = 0$ as x_0, y_0, and u_0 are initialized accordingly. For $k > 0$ we assume that the claim holds after $k - 1$ iterations, i.e., for x_{k-1}, y_{k-1}, u_{k-1} and scheduler σ_{k-1}. The results of the kth iteration are obtained as follows.

The function *findAction* illustrated in Algorithm 3 determines the choices of a scheduler $\sigma_k \in \arg\max_{\sigma \in \mathfrak{S}_\mathcal{M}} \mathrm{Pr}^\sigma_s(\Diamond^{\leq k} G) + \mathrm{Pr}^\sigma_s(\Box^{\leq k} S_?) \cdot u_{k-1}$ for $s \in S_?$. The idea is to consider at state s an action $\sigma_k(s) = \alpha \in Act(s)$ that maximizes

$$\mathrm{Pr}^{\sigma_k}_s(\Diamond^{\leq k} G) + \mathrm{Pr}^{\sigma_k}_s(\Box^{\leq k} S_?) \cdot u_{k-1} = \sum_{s' \in S} \mathbf{P}(s, \alpha, s') \cdot (x_{k-1}[s'] + y_{k-1}[s'] \cdot u_{k-1}).$$

Input : MDP $\mathcal{M} = (S, Act, \mathbf{P}, s_I, \rho)$, absorbing states $G \subseteq S$, precision $\varepsilon > 0$
Output : $r \in \mathbb{R}$ with $|r - \text{Pr}^{\max}(\lozenge G)| < \varepsilon$

1 $S_0 \leftarrow \{s \in S \mid \text{Pr}_s^{\max}(\lozenge G) = 0\}$
2 assert that $\mathcal{M}$ is contracting with respect to $G \cup S_0$
3 $S_? \leftarrow S \setminus (S_0 \cup G)$
4 initialize $x_0, y_0 \in \mathbb{R}^{|S|}$ with $x_0[G] = 1, x_0[S \setminus G] = 0, y_0[S_?] = 1, y_0[S \setminus S_?] = 0$
5 $\ell_0 \leftarrow -\infty; u_0 \leftarrow +\infty; d_0 \leftarrow -\infty$
6 $k \leftarrow 0$
7 **repeat**
8 $\quad k \leftarrow k + 1$
9 $\quad$ initialize $x_k, y_k \in \mathbb{R}^{|S|}$ with $x_k[G] = 1, x_k[S_0] = 0, y_k[S \setminus S_?] = 0$
10 $\quad d_k \leftarrow d_{k-1}$
11 $\quad$ **foreach** $s \in S_?$ **do**
12 $\quad\quad \alpha \leftarrow findAction(x_{k-1}, y_{k-1}, s, u_{k-1})$
13 $\quad\quad d_k \leftarrow \max(d_k, decisionValue(x_{k-1}, y_{k-1}, s, \alpha))$
14 $\quad\quad x_k[s] \leftarrow \sum_{s' \in S} \mathbf{P}(s, \alpha, s') \cdot x_{k-1}[s']$
15 $\quad\quad y_k[s] \leftarrow \sum_{s' \in S} \mathbf{P}(s, \alpha, s') \cdot y_{k-1}[s']$
16 $\quad$ **if** $y_k[s] < 1$ for all $s \in S_?$ **then**
17 $\quad\quad \ell_k \leftarrow \max(\ell_{k-1}, \min_{s \in S_?} \frac{x_k[s]}{1 - y_k[s]})$
18 $\quad\quad u_k \leftarrow \min(u_{k-1}, \max(d_k, \max_{\in S_?} \frac{x_k[s]}{1 - y_k[s]}))$
19 **until** $y_k[s_I] \cdot (u_k - \ell_k) < 2 \cdot \varepsilon$
20 **return** $x_k[s_I] + y_k[s_I] \cdot \frac{\ell_k + u_k}{2}$

Algorithm 2: Sound value iteration for MDPs

For the case where no real upper bound is known (i.e., $u_{k-1} = \infty$) we implicitly assume a sufficiently large value for u_{k-1} such that $\text{Pr}_s^\sigma(\lozenge^{\leq k} G)$ becomes negligible. Upon leaving state s, σ_k mimics σ_{k-1}, i.e., we set $\sigma_k(s\alpha s_1 \alpha_1 \ldots s_n) = \sigma_{k-1}(s_1 \alpha_1 \ldots s_n)$. After executing Line 15 of Algorithm 2 we have $x_k[s] = \text{Pr}_s^{\sigma_k}(\lozenge^{\leq k} G)$ and $y_k[s] = \text{Pr}_s^{\sigma_k}(\square^{\leq k} S_?)$.

It remains to derive an upper bound u_k. To ensure that Lemma 3 holds we require (i) $u_k \geq \max_{s \in S_?} \text{Pr}_s^{\max}(\lozenge G)$ and (ii) $u_k \in U_k$, where

$$U_k = \{u \in \mathbb{R} \mid \sigma_k \in \arg\max_{\sigma \in \mathfrak{S}^{\mathcal{M}}} \text{Pr}_s^\sigma(\lozenge^{\leq k} G) + \text{Pr}_s^\sigma(\square^{\leq k} S_?) \cdot u \text{ for all } s \in S_?\}.$$

Intuitively, the set $U_k \subseteq \mathbb{R}$ consists of all possible upper bounds u for which σ_k is still optimal. $U_k \subseteq$ is convex as it can be represented as a conjunction of inequalities with $U_0 = \mathbb{R}$ and $u \in U_k$ if and only if $u \in U_{k-1}$ and for all $s \in S_?$ with $\sigma_k(s) = \alpha$ and for all $\beta \in Act(s) \setminus \{\alpha\}$

$$\sum_{s' \in S} \mathbf{P}(s, \alpha, s') \cdot (x_{k-1}[s'] + y_{k-1}[s'] \cdot u) \geq \sum_{s' \in S} \mathbf{P}(s, \beta, s') \cdot (x_{k-1}[s'] + y_{k-1}[s'] \cdot u).$$

The algorithm maintains the so-called *decision value* d_k which corresponds to the minimum of U_k (or $-\infty$ if the minimum does not exist). Algorithm 4 outlines the

```
1  function findAction(x, y, s, u)
2      if u ≠ ∞ then
3          return α ∈ arg max_{α∈Act(s)} Σ_{s'∈S} P(s, α, s') · (x[s'] + y[s'] · u)
4      else
5          return α ∈ arg max_{α∈Act(s)} Σ_{s'∈S} P(s, α, s') · (y[s'])
```

Algorithm 3: Computation of optimal action.

```
1  function decisionValue(x, y, s, α)
2      d ← -∞
3      foreach β ∈ Act(s) \ {α} do
4          y_Δ ← Σ_{s'∈S}(P(s, α, s') - P(s, β, s')) · y[s']
5          if y_Δ > 0 then
6              x_Δ ← Σ_{s'∈S}(P(s, β, s') - P(s, α, s')) · x[s']
7              d ← max(d, x_Δ/y_Δ)
8      return d
```

Algorithm 4: Computation of decision value.

procedure to obtain the decision value at a given state. Our algorithm ensures that u_k is only set to a value in $[d_k, u_{k-1}] \subseteq U_k$.

Lemma 4. *After executing Line 18 of Algorithm 2:* $u_k \geq \max_{s \in S_?} \Pr_s^{\max}(\Diamond G)$.

To show that u_k is a valid upper bound, let $s_{\max} \in \arg\max_{s \in S_?} \Pr_s^{\max}(\Diamond G)$ and $u^* = \Pr_{s_{\max}}^{\max}(\Diamond G)$. From Theorem 4, $u_{k-1} \geq u^*$, and $u_{k-1} \in U_k$ we get

$$u^* \leq \max_{\sigma \in \mathfrak{S}^\mathcal{M}} \Pr_{s_{\max}}^\sigma (\Diamond^{\leq k} G) + \Pr_{s_{\max}}^\sigma (\Box^{\leq k} S_?) \cdot u_{k-1}$$

$$= \Pr_{s_{\max}}^{\sigma_k} (\Diamond^{\leq k} G) + \Pr_{s_{\max}}^{\sigma_k} (\Box^{\leq k} S_?) \cdot u_{k-1} = x_k[s_{\max}] + y_k[s_{\max}] \cdot u_{k-1}$$

which yields a new upper bound $x_k[s_{\max}] + y_k[s_{\max}] \cdot u_{k-1} \geq u^*$. We repeat this scheme as follows. Let $v_0 := u_{k-1}$ and for $i > 0$ let $v_i := x_k[s_{\max}] + y_k[s_{\max}] \cdot v_{i-1}$. We can show that $v_{i-1} \in U_k$ implies $v_i \geq u^*$. Assuming $y_k[s_{\max}] < 1$, the sequence $v_0, v_1, v_2, \dots$ converges to $v_\infty := \lim_{i \to \infty} v_i = \frac{x_k[s_{\max}]}{1 - y_k[s_{\max}]}$. We distinguish three cases to show that $u_k = \min(u_{k-1}, \max(d_k, \max_{s \in S_?} \frac{x_k[s]}{1 - y_k[s]})) \geq u^*$.

- If $v_\infty > u_{k-1}$, then also $\max_{s \in S_?} \frac{x_k[s]}{1 - y_k[s]} > u_{k-1}$. Hence $u_k = u_{k-1} \geq u^*$.
- If $d_k \leq v_\infty \leq u_{k-1}$, we can show that $v_i \leq v_{i-1}$. It follows that for all $i > 0$, $v_{i-1} \in U_k$, implying $v_i \geq u^*$. Thus we get $u_k = \max_{s \in S_?} \frac{x_k[s]}{1 - y_k[s]} \geq v_\infty \geq u^*$.
- If $v_\infty < d_k$ then there is an $i \geq 0$ with $v_i \geq d_k$ and $u^* \leq v_{i+1} < d_k$. It follows that $u_k = d_k \geq u^*$.

Example 7. Reconsider the MDP $\mathcal{M}$ from Fig. 2(a) and goal states $G = \{s_3, s_4\}$. The maximal reachability probability is attained for a scheduler that always chooses β at state s_0, which results in $\mathrm{Pr}^{\max}(\lozenge G) = 0.5$. We now illustrate how Algorithm 2 approximates this value by sketching the first two iterations. For the first iteration *findAction* yields action α at s_0. We obtain:

$$x_1[s_0] = 0, \ x_1[s_1] = 0.1, \ x_1[s_2] = 0.1, \ y_1[s_0] = 0.8, \ y_1[s_1] = 0.9, \ y_1[s_2] = 0,$$
$$d_1 = 0.3/(0.8 - 0.4) = 0.75, \ \ell_1 = \min(0, 1, 0) = 0, \ u_1 = \max(0.75, 0, 1, 0) = 1.$$

In the second iteration *findAction* yields again α for s_0 and we get:

$$x_2[s_0] = 0.08, \ x_2[s_1] = 0.19, \ x_2[s_2] = 0.1, \ y_2[s_0] = 0.72, \ y_2[s_1] = 0, \ y_2[s_2] = 0,$$
$$d_2 = 0.75, \ \ell_2 = \min(0.29, 0.19, 0.1) = 0.1, \ u_2 = \max(0.75, 0.29, 0.19, 0.1) = 0.75.$$

Due to the decision value we do not set the upper bound u_2 to $0.29 < \mathrm{Pr}^{\max}(\lozenge G)$.

Theorem 5. *Algorithm 2 terminates for any MDP $\mathcal{M}$, goal states G and precision $\varepsilon > 0$. The returned value r satisfies $|r - \mathrm{Pr}^{\max}(\lozenge G)| \leq \varepsilon$.*

The correctness of the algorithm follows from Theorem 4 and Lemma 3. Termination follows since $\mathcal{M}$ is contracting with respect to $S_0 \cup G$, implying $\lim_{k \to \infty} \mathrm{Pr}^\sigma(\square^{\leq k} S_?) = 0$. The optimizations for Algorithm 1 mentioned in Sect. 3.4 can be applied to Algorithm 2 as well.

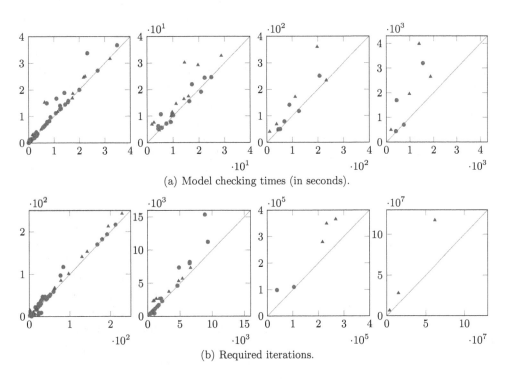

(a) Model checking times (in seconds).

(b) Required iterations.

Fig. 3. Comparison of sound value iteration (x-axis) and interval iteration (y-axis).

5   Experimental Evaluation

Implementation. We implemented sound value iteration for MCs and MDPs into the model checker `Storm` [8]. The implementation computes reachability probabilities and expected rewards using explicit data structures such as sparse matrices and vectors. Moreover, Multi-objective model checking is supported, where we straightforwardly extend the value iteration-based approach of [22] to sound value iteration. We also implemented the optimizations given in Sect. 3.4.

Experimental Results. We considered a wide range of case studies including

- all MCs, MDPs, and CTMCs from the `PRISM` benchmark suite [23],
- several case studies from the `PRISM` website www.prismmodelchecker.org,
- Markov automata accompanying `IMCA` [24], and
- multi-objective MDPs considered in [22].

In total, 130 model and property instances were considered. For CTMCs and Markov automata we computed (untimed) reachability probabilities or expected rewards on the underlying MC and the underlying MDP, respectively. In all experiments the precision parameter was given by $\varepsilon = 10^{-6}$.

We compare sound value iteration (SVI) with interval iteration (II) as presented in [12,13]. We consider the Gauss-Seidel variant of the approaches and compute initial bounds ℓ_0 and u_0 as in [12]. For a better comparison we consider the implementation of II in `Storm`. [21] gives a comparison with the implementation of II in `PRISM`. The experiments were run on a single core (2GHz) of an HP BL685C G7 with 192GB of available memory. However, almost all experiments required less than 4GB. We measured model checking times and required iterations. All logfiles and considered benchmarks are available at [25].

Figure 3(a) depicts the model checking times for SVI (x-axis) and II (y-axis). For better readability, the benchmarks are divided into four plots with different scales. Triangles (▲) and circles (●) indicate MC and MDP benchmarks, respectively. Similarly, Fig. 3(b) shows the required iterations of the approaches. We observe that SVI converged faster and required fewer iterations for almost all MCs and MDPs. SVI performed particularly well on the challenging instances where many iterations are required. Similar observations were made when comparing the topological variants of SVI and II. Both approaches were still competitive if no a priori bounds are given to SVI. More details are given in [21].

Figure 4 indicates the model checking times of SVI and II as well as their topological variants. For reference, we also consider standard (unsound) value iteration (VI). The x-axis depicts the number of instances that have been solved by the corresponding approach within the time limit indicated on the y-axis. Hence, a point (x, y) means that for x instances the model checking time was less or equal than y. We observe that the topological variant of SVI yielded the best run times among all sound approaches and even competes with (unsound) VI.

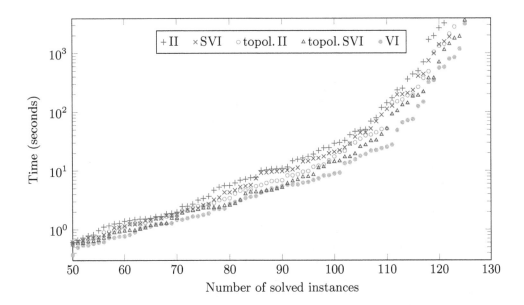

Fig. 4. Runtime comparison between different approaches.

6   Conclusion

In this paper we presented a sound variant of the value iteration algorithm which safely approximates reachability probabilities and expected rewards in MCs and MDPs. Experiments on a large set of benchmarks indicate that our approach is a reasonable alternative to the recently proposed interval iteration algorithm.

References

1. Puterman, M.L.: Markov Decision Processes: Discrete Stochastic Dynamic Programming. Wiley, Hoboken (1994)
2. Feinberg, E.A., Shwartz, A.: Handbook of Markov Decision Processes: Methods and Applications. Kluwer, Dordrecht (2002)
3. Katoen, J.P.: The probabilistic model checking landscape. In: LICS, pp. 31–45. ACM (2016)
4. Baier, C.: Probabilistic model checking. In: Dependable Software Systems Engineering. NATO Science for Peace and Security Series - D: Information and Communication Security, vol. 45, pp. 1–23. IOS Press (2016)
5. Etessami, K.: Analysis of probabilistic processes and automata theory. In: Handbook of Automata Theory. European Mathematical Society (2016, to appear)
6. Baier, C., de Alfaro, L., Forejt, V., Kwiatkowska, M.: Probabilistic model checking. In: Clarke, E., Henzinger, T., Veith, H., Bloem, R. (eds.) Handbook of Model Checking, pp. 963–999. Springer, Cham (2018)
7. Kwiatkowska, M., Norman, G., Parker, D.: PRISM 4.0: verification of probabilistic real-time systems. In: Gopalakrishnan, G., Qadeer, S. (eds.) CAV 2011. LNCS, vol. 6806, pp. 585–591. Springer, Heidelberg (2011). https://doi.org/10.1007/978-3-642-22110-1_47

8. Dehnert, C., Junges, S., Katoen, J.-P., Volk, M.: A STORM is coming: a modern probabilistic model checker. In: Majumdar, R., Kunčak, V. (eds.) CAV 2017. LNCS, vol. 10427, pp. 592–600. Springer, Cham (2017). https://doi.org/10.1007/978-3-319-63390-9_31

9. Katoen, J., Zapreev, I.S.: Safe on-the-fly steady-state detection for time-bounded reachability. In: QEST, pp. 301–310. IEEE Computer Society (2006)

10. Malhotra, M.: A computationally efficient technique for transient analysis of repairable markovian systems. Perform. Eval. **24**(4), 311–331 (1996)

11. Daca, P., Henzinger, T.A., Kretínský, J., Petrov, T.: Faster statistical model checking for unbounded temporal properties. ACM Trans. Comput. Log. **18**(2), 12:1–12:25 (2017)

12. Baier, C., Klein, J., Leuschner, L., Parker, D., Wunderlich, S.: Ensuring the reliability of your model checker: interval iteration for markov decision processes. In: Majumdar, R., Kunčak, V. (eds.) CAV 2017. LNCS, vol. 10426, pp. 160–180. Springer, Cham (2017). https://doi.org/10.1007/978-3-319-63387-9_8

13. Haddad, S., Monmege, B.: Interval iteration algorithm for MDPs and IMDPs. Theor. Comput. Sci. **735**, 111–131 (2017)

14. Dai, P., Weld, D.S., Goldsmith, J.: Topological value iteration algorithms. J. Artif. Intell. Res. **42**, 181–209 (2011)

15. Baier, C., Katoen, J.P.: Principles of Model Checking. The MIT Press, Cambridge (2008)

16. Bertsekas, D.P., Tsitsiklis, J.N.: An analysis of stochastic shortest path problems. Math. Oper. Res. **16**(3), 580–595 (1991)

17. Giro, S.: Efficient computation of exact solutions for quantitative model checking. In: QAPL. EPTCS, vol. 85, pp. 17–32 (2012)

18. Bauer, M.S., Mathur, U., Chadha, R., Sistla, A.P., Viswanathan, M.: Exact quantitative probabilistic model checking through rational search. In: FMCAD, pp. 92–99. IEEE (2017)

19. Brázdil, T., et al.: Verification of Markov decision processes using learning algorithms. In: Cassez, F., Raskin, J.-F. (eds.) ATVA 2014. LNCS, vol. 8837, pp. 98–114. Springer, Cham (2014). https://doi.org/10.1007/978-3-319-11936-6_8

20. Haddad, S., Monmege, B.: Reachability in MDPs: refining convergence of value iteration. In: Ouaknine, J., Potapov, I., Worrell, J. (eds.) RP 2014. LNCS, vol. 8762, pp. 125–137. Springer, Cham (2014). https://doi.org/10.1007/978-3-319-11439-2_10

21. Quatmann, T., Katoen, J.P.: Sound value iteration. Technical report, CoRR abs/1804.05001 (2018)

22. Forejt, V., Kwiatkowska, M., Parker, D.: Pareto curves for probabilistic model checking. In: Chakraborty, S., Mukund, M. (eds.) ATVA 2012. LNCS, pp. 317–332. Springer, Heidelberg (2012). https://doi.org/10.1007/978-3-642-33386-6_25

23. Kwiatkowska, M., Norman, G., Parker, D.: The PRISM benchmark suite. In: Proceedings of QEST, pp. 203–204. IEEE CS (2012)

24. Guck, D., Timmer, M., Hatefi, H., Ruijters, E., Stoelinga, M.: Modelling and analysis of markov reward automata. In: Cassez, F., Raskin, J.-F. (eds.) ATVA 2014. LNCS, vol. 8837, pp. 168–184. Springer, Cham (2014). https://doi.org/10.1007/978-3-319-11936-6_13

25. Quatmann, T., Katoen, J.P.: Experimental Results for Sound Value Iteration. figshare (2018). https://doi.org/10.6084/m9.figshare.6139052

14

Semantic Adversarial Deep Learning

Tommaso Dreossi[1], Somesh Jha[2(✉)], and Sanjit A. Seshia[1]

[1] University of California at Berkeley, Berkeley, USA
{dreossi,sseshia}@berkeley.edu
[2] University of Wisconsin, Madison, Madison, USA
jha@cs.wisc.edu

Abstract. Fueled by massive amounts of data, models produced by machine-learning (ML) algorithms, especially deep neural networks, are being used in diverse domains where trustworthiness is a concern, including automotive systems, finance, health care, natural language processing, and malware detection. Of particular concern is the use of ML algorithms in cyber-physical systems (CPS), such as self-driving cars and aviation, where an adversary can cause serious consequences.

However, existing approaches to generating adversarial examples and devising robust ML algorithms mostly ignore the *semantics* and *context* of the overall system containing the ML component. For example, in an autonomous vehicle using deep learning for perception, not every adversarial example for the neural network might lead to a harmful consequence. Moreover, one may want to prioritize the search for adversarial examples towards those that significantly modify the desired semantics of the overall system. Along the same lines, existing algorithms for constructing robust ML algorithms ignore the specification of the overall system. In this paper, we argue that the semantics and specification of the overall system has a crucial role to play in this line of research. We present preliminary research results that support this claim.

1 Introduction

Machine learning (ML) algorithms, fueled by massive amounts of data, are increasingly being utilized in several domains, including healthcare, finance, and transportation. Models produced by ML algorithms, especially *deep neural networks* (DNNs), are being deployed in domains where trustworthiness is a big concern, such as automotive systems [35], finance [25], health care [2], computer vision [28], speech recognition [17], natural language processing [38], and cyber-security [8,42]. Of particular concern is the use of ML (including deep learning) in *cyber-physical systems* (CPS) [29], where the presence of an adversary can cause serious consequences. For example, much of the technology behind autonomous and driver-less vehicle development is "powered" by machine learning [4,14]. DNNs have also been used in airborne collision avoidance systems for unmanned aircraft (ACAS Xu) [22]. However, *in designing and deploying these algorithms in critical cyber-physical systems, the presence of an active adversary is often ignored.*

Adversarial machine learning (AML) is a field concerned with the analysis of ML algorithms to adversarial attacks, and the use of such analysis in making ML algorithms robust to attacks. It is part of the broader agenda for safe and verified ML-based systems [39, 41]. In this paper, we first give a brief survey of the field of AML, with a particular focus on deep learning. We focus mainly on attacks on outputs or models that are produced by ML algorithms that occur *after training* or "external attacks", which are especially relevant to cyber-physical systems (e.g., for a driverless car the ML algorithm used for navigation has been already trained by the manufacturer once the "car is on the road"). These attacks are more realistic and are distinct from other type of attacks on ML models, such as attacks that poison the training data (see the paper [18] for a survey of such attacks). We survey attacks caused by *adversarial examples*, which are inputs crafted by adding small, often imperceptible, perturbations to force a trained ML model to misclassify.

We contend that the work on adversarial ML, while important and useful, is not enough. In particular, we advocate for the increased use of *semantics* in adversarial analysis and design of ML algorithms. *Semantic adversarial learning* explores a space of semantic modifications to the data, uses system-level semantic specifications in the analysis, utilizes semantic adversarial examples in training, and produces not just output labels but also additional semantic information. Focusing on deep learning, we explore these ideas and provide initial experimental data to support them.

Roadmap. Section 2 provides the relevant background. A brief survey of adversarial analysis is given in Sect. 3. Our proposal for semantic adversarial learning is given in Sect. 4.

2 Background

Background on Machine Learning. Next we describe some general concepts in machine learning (ML). We will consider the supervised learning setting. Consider a sample space Z of the form $X \times Y$, and an ordered training set $S = ((x_i, y_i))_{i=1}^m$ (x_i is the data and y_i is the corresponding label). Let H be a hypothesis space (e.g., weights corresponding to a logistic-regression model). There is a loss function $\ell : H \times Z \mapsto \mathbb{R}$ so that given a hypothesis $w \in H$ and a sample $(x, y) \in Z$, we obtain a loss $\ell(w, (x, y))$. We consider the case where we want to minimize the loss over the training set S,

$$L_S(w) = \frac{1}{m} \sum_{i=1}^m \ell(w, (x_i, y_i)) + \lambda \mathcal{R}(w).$$

In the equation given above, $\lambda > 0$ and the term $\mathcal{R}(w)$ is called the *regularizer* and enforces "simplicity" in w. Since S is fixed, we sometimes denote $\ell_i(w) = \ell(w, (x_i, y_i))$ as a function only of w. We wish to find a w that minimizes $L_S(w)$ or we wish to solve the following optimization problem:

$$\min_{w \in H} L_S(w)$$

Example: We will consider the example of logistic regression. In this case $X = \mathbb{R}^n$, $Y = \{+1, -1\}$, $H = \mathbb{R}^n$, and the loss function $\ell(w, (x, y))$ is as follows ($\cdot$ represents the dot product of two vectors):

$$\log\left(1 + e^{-y(w^T \cdot x)}\right)$$

If we use the L_2 regularizer (i.e. $\mathcal{R}(w) = \|w\|_2$), then $L_S(w)$ becomes:

$$\frac{1}{m}\sum_{i=1}^{m}\log\left(1 + e^{-y_i(w^T \cdot x_i)}\right) + \lambda \|w\|_2$$

Stochastic Gradient Descent. *Stochastic Gradient Descent (SGD)* is a popular method for solving optimization tasks (such as the optimization problem $\min_{w \in H} L_S(w)$ we considered before). In a nutshell, SGD performs a series of updates where each update is a gradient descent update with respect to a small set of points sampled from the training set. Specifically, suppose that we perform SGD T times. There are two typical forms of SGD: in the first form, which we call **Sample-SGD**, we uniformly and randomly sample $i_t \sim [m]$ at time t, and perform a gradient descent based on the i_t-th sample (x_{i_t}, y_{i_t}):

$$w_{t+1} = G_{\ell_t, \eta_t}(w_t) = w_t - \eta_t \ell'_{i_t}(w_t) \tag{1}$$

where w_t is the hypothesis at time t, η_t is a parameter called the *learning rate*, and $\ell'_{i_t}(w_t)$ denotes the derivative of $\ell_{i_t}(w)$ evaluated at w_t. We will denote G_{ℓ_t, η_t} as G_t. In the second form, which we call **Perm-SGD**, we first perform a random permutation of S, and then apply Eq. 1 T times by cycling through S according to the order of the permutation. The process of SGD can be summarized as a diagram:

$$w_0 \xrightarrow{G_1} w_1 \xrightarrow{G_2} \cdots \xrightarrow{G_t} w_t \xrightarrow{G_{t+1}} \cdots \xrightarrow{G_T} w_T$$

Classifiers. The output of the learning algorithm gives us a *classifier*, which is a function from $\mathfrak{R}^n$ to $\mathcal{C}$, where $\mathfrak{R}$ denotes the set of reals and $\mathcal{C}$ is the set of class labels. To emphasize that a classifier depends on a hypothesis $w \in H$, which is the output of the learning algorithm described earlier, we will write it as F_w (if w is clear from the context, we will sometimes simply write F). For example, after training in the case of logistic regression we obtain a function from $\mathfrak{R}^n$ to $\{-1, +1\}$. Vectors will be denoted in boldface, and the r-th component of a vector $\mathbf{x}$ is denoted by $\mathbf{x}[r]$.

Throughout the paper, we refer to the function $s(F_w)$ as the *softmax layer* corresponding to the classifier F_w. In the case of logistic regression, $s(F_w)(\mathbf{x})$ is the following tuple (the first element is the probability of -1 and the second one is the probability of $+1$):

$$\langle \frac{1}{1 + e^{w^T \cdot \mathbf{x}}}, \frac{1}{1 + e^{-w^T \cdot \mathbf{x}}} \rangle$$

Formally, let $c = |\mathcal{C}|$ and F_w be a classifier, we let $s(F_w)$ be the function that maps $\mathbb{R}^n$ to $\mathbb{R}_+^c$ such that $\|s(F_w)(\mathbf{x})\|_1 = 1$ for any $\mathbf{x}$ (i.e., $s(F_w)$ computes a probability vector). We denote $s(F_w)(\mathbf{x})[l]$ to be the probability of $s(F_w)(\mathbf{x})$ at label l. Recall that the softmax function from $\mathbb{R}^k$ to a probability distribution over $\{1, \cdots, k\} = [k]$ such that the probability of $j \in [k]$ for a vector $\mathbf{x} \in \mathbb{R}^k$ is

$$\frac{e^{\mathbf{x}[j]}}{\sum_{r=1}^k e^{\mathbf{x}[r]}}$$

Some classifiers $F_w(\mathbf{x})$ are of the form $\arg\max_l s(F_w)(\mathbf{x})[l]$ (i.e., the classifier F_w outputs the label with the maximum probability according to the "softmax layer"). For example, in several deep-neural network (DNN) architectures the last layer is the *softmax* layer. We are assuming that the reader is a familiar with basics of deep-neural networks (DNNs). For readers not familiar with DNNs we can refer to the excellent book by Goodfellow et al. [15].

Background on Logic. Temporal logics are commonly used for specifying desired and undesired properties of systems. For cyber-physical systems, it is common to use temporal logics that can specify properties of real-valued signals over real time, such as *signal temporal logic* (STL) [30] or *metric temporal logic* (MTL) [27].

A *signal* is a function $s : D \to S$, with $D \subseteq \mathbb{R}_{\geq 0}$ an interval and either $S \subseteq \mathbb{B}$ or $S \subseteq \mathbb{R}$, where $\mathbb{B} = \{\top, \bot\}$ and $\mathbb{R}$ is the set of reals. Signals defined on $\mathbb{B}$ are called *booleans*, while those on $\mathbb{R}$ are said *real-valued*. A *trace* $w = \{s_1, \ldots, s_n\}$ is a finite set of real-valued signals defined over the same interval D. We use variables x_i to denote the value of a real-valued signal at a particular time instant.

Let $\Sigma = \{\sigma_1, \ldots, \sigma_k\}$ be a finite set of predicates $\sigma_i : \mathbb{R}^n \to \mathbb{B}$, with $\sigma_i \equiv p_i(x_1, \ldots, x_n) \lhd 0$, $\lhd \in \{<, \leq\}$, and $p_i : \mathbb{R}^n \to \mathbb{R}$ a function in the variables $x_1, \ldots, x_n$. An STL formula is defined by the following grammar:

$$\varphi := \sigma \mid \neg\varphi \mid \varphi \wedge \varphi \mid \varphi \, \mathsf{U}_I \, \varphi \tag{2}$$

where $\sigma \in \Sigma$ is a predicate and $I \subset \mathbb{R}_{\geq 0}$ is a closed non-singular interval. Other common temporal operators can be defined as syntactic abbreviations in the usual way, like for instance $\varphi_1 \vee \varphi_2 := \neg(\neg\varphi_1 \wedge \neg\varphi_2)$, $\mathsf{F}_I \, \varphi := \top \, \mathsf{U}_I \, \varphi$, or $\mathsf{G}_I \, \varphi := \neg\mathsf{F}_I \, \neg\varphi$. Given a $t \in \mathbb{R}_{\geq 0}$, a shifted interval I is defined as $t + I = \{t + t' \mid t' \in I\}$. The qualitative (or Boolean) semantics of STL is given in the usual way:

Definition 1 (Qualitative semantics). *Let w be a trace, $t \in \mathbb{R}_{\geq 0}$, and φ be an STL formula. The qualitative semantics of φ is inductively defined as follows:*

$$
\begin{aligned}
w, t &\models \sigma \;\; \text{iff } \sigma(w(t)) \text{ is true} \\
w, t &\models \neg\varphi \;\; \text{iff } w, t \not\models \varphi \\
w, t &\models \varphi_1 \wedge \varphi_2 \;\; \text{iff } w, t \models \varphi_1 \text{ and } w, t \models \varphi_2 \\
w, t &\models \varphi_1 \mathsf{U}_I \varphi_2 \;\; \text{iff } \exists t' \in t + I \text{ s.t. } w, t' \models \varphi_2 \text{ and } \forall t'' \in [t, t'], w, t'' \models \varphi_1
\end{aligned}
\tag{3}
$$

A trace w satisfies a formula φ if and only if $w, 0 \models \varphi$, in short $w \models \varphi$. STL also admits a quantitative or robust semantics, which we omit for brevity. This provides quantitative information on the formula, telling how strongly the specification is satisfied or violated for a given trace.

3   Attacks

There are several types of attacks on ML algorithms. For excellent material on various attacks on ML algorithms we refer the reader to [3, 18]. For example, in *training time* attacks an adversary wishes to poison a data set so that a "bad" hypothesis is learned by an ML-algorithm. This attack can be modeled as a game between the algorithm ML and an adversary A as follows:

- ML picks an ordered training set $S = ((x_i, y_i))_{i=1}^{m}$.
- A picks an ordered training set $\widehat{S} = ((\hat{x}_i, \hat{y}_i))_{i=1}^{r}$, where r is $\lfloor \epsilon m \rfloor$.
- ML learns on $S \cup \widehat{S}$ by essentially minimizing

$$\min_{w \in H} L_{S \cup \widehat{S}}(w).$$

The attacker wants to maximize the above quantity and thus chooses $\widehat{S}$ such that $\min_{w \in H} L_{S \cup \widehat{S}}(w)$ is maximized. For a recent paper on certified defenses for such attacks we refer the reader to [44]. In *model extraction* attacks an adversary with black-box access to a classifier, but no prior knowledge of the parameters of a ML algorithm or training data, aims to duplicate the functionality of (i.e., steal) the classifier by querying it on well chosen data points. For an example, model-extraction attacks see [45].

In this paper, we consider *test-time attacks*. We assume that the classifier F_w has been trained without any interference from the attacker (i.e. no training time attacks). Roughly speaking, an attacker has an image $\mathbf{x}$ (e.g. an image of stop sign) and wants to craft a perturbation δ so that the label of $\mathbf{x} + \delta$ is what the attacker desires (e.g. yield sign). The next sub-section describes test-time attacks in detail. We will sometimes refer to F_w as simply F, but the hypothesis w is lurking in the background (i.e., whenever we refer to w, it corresponds to the classifier F).

3.1   Test-Time Attacks

The adversarial goal is to take any input vector $\mathbf{x} \in \Re^n$ and produce a minimally altered version of $\mathbf{x}$, *adversarial sample* denoted by $\mathbf{x}^{\star}$, that has the property of being misclassified by a classifier $F : \Re^n \to \mathcal{C}$. Formally speaking, an adversary wishes to solve the following optimization problem:

$$\begin{aligned} &\min_{\delta \in \Re^n} & \mu(\delta) \\ &\text{such that } F(\mathbf{x} + \delta) \in T \\ & & \delta \cdot \mathbf{M} = 0 \end{aligned}$$

The various terms in the formulation are μ is a metric on $\Re^n$, $T \subseteq \mathcal{C}$ is a subset of the labels (the reader should think of T as the target labels for the attacker), and $\mathbf{M}$ (called the *mask*) is a n-dimensional 0–1 vector of size n. The objective function minimizes the metric μ on the perturbation δ. Next we describe various constraints in the formulation.

- $F(\mathbf{x} + \delta) \in T$
  The set T constrains the perturbed vector $\mathbf{x} + \delta$[1] to have the label (according to F) in the set T. For *mis-classification* problems the label of $\mathbf{x}$ and $\mathbf{x} + \delta$ are different, so we have $T = \mathcal{C} - \{F(\mathbf{x})\}$. For *targeted mis-classification* we have $T = \{t\}$ (for $t \in \mathcal{C}$), where t is the target that an attacker wants (e.g., the attacker wants t to correspond to a yield sign).
- $\delta \cdot \mathbf{M} = 0$
  The vector M can be considered as a mask (i.e., an attacker can only perturb a dimension i if $M[i] = 0$), i.e., if $M[i] = 1$ then $\delta[i]$ is forced to be 0. Essentially the attacker can only perturb dimension i if the i-th component of M is 0, which means that δ lies in k-dimensional space where k is the number of non-zero entries in Δ. This constraint is important if an attacker wants to target a certain area of the image (e.g., glasses of in a picture of person) to perturb.
- *Convexity*
  Notice that even if the metric μ is convex (e.g., μ is the L_2 norm), because of the constraint involving F, the optimization problem is *not convex* (the constraint $\delta \cdot \mathbf{M} = 0$ is convex). In general, solving convex optimization problems is more tractable non-convex optimization [34].

Note that the constraint $\delta \cdot \mathbf{M} = 0$ essentially constrains the vector to be in a lower-dimensional space and does add additional complexity to the optimization problem. Therefore, for the rest of the section we will ignore that constraint and work with the following formulation:

$$\min_{\delta \in \Re^n} \quad \mu(\delta)$$
$$\text{such that } F(\mathbf{x} + \delta) \in T$$

FGSM Mis-classification Attack - This algorithm is also known as the *fast gradient sign method (FGSM)* [16]. The adversary crafts an adversarial sample $\mathbf{x}^\star = \mathbf{x} + \delta$ for a given legitimate sample $\mathbf{x}$ by computing the following perturbation:

$$\delta = \varepsilon \, \text{sign}(\nabla_{\mathbf{x}} L_F(\mathbf{x})) \tag{4}$$

The function $L_F(\mathbf{x})$ is a shorthand for $\ell(w, \mathbf{x}, l(\mathbf{x}))$, where w is the hypothesis corresponding to the classifier F, $\mathbf{x}$ is the data point and $l(\mathbf{x})$ is the label of $\mathbf{x}$ (essentially we evaluate the loss function at the hypothesis corresponding to the classifier). The gradient of the function L_F is computed with respect to

---

[1] The vectors are added component wise.

$\mathbf{x}$ using sample $\mathbf{x}$ and label $y = l(\mathbf{x})$ as inputs. Note that $\nabla_{\mathbf{x}} L_F(\mathbf{x})$ is an n-dimensional vector and $\mathrm{sign}(\nabla_{\mathbf{x}} L_F(\mathbf{x}))$ is a n-dimensional vector whose i-th element is the sign of the $\nabla_{\mathbf{x}} L_F(\mathbf{x})[i]$. The value of the *input variation parameter* ε factoring the sign matrix controls the perturbation's amplitude. Increasing its value increases the likelihood of $\mathbf{x}^\star$ being misclassified by the classifier F but on the contrary makes adversarial samples easier to detect by humans. The key idea is that FGSM takes a step *in the direction of the gradient of the loss function* and thus tries to maximize it. Recall that SGD takes a step in the direction that is opposite to the gradient of the loss function because it is trying to minimize the loss function.

JSMA Targeted Mis-classification Attack - This algorithm is suitable for targeted misclassification [37]. We refer to this attack as JSMA throughout the rest of the paper. To craft the perturbation δ, components are sorted by decreasing *adversarial saliency value*. The adversarial saliency value $S(\mathbf{x}, t)[i]$ of component i for an adversarial target class t is defined as:

$$S(\mathbf{x}, t)[i] = \begin{cases} 0 \text{ if } \frac{\partial s(F)[t](\mathbf{x})}{\partial \mathbf{x}[i]} < 0 \text{ or } \sum_{j \neq t} \frac{\partial s(F)[j](\mathbf{x})}{\partial \mathbf{x}[i]} > 0 \\ \frac{\partial s(F)[t](\mathbf{x})}{\partial \mathbf{x}[i]} \left| \sum_{j \neq t} \frac{\partial s(F)[j](\mathbf{x})}{\partial \mathbf{x}[i]} \right| \text{ otherwise} \end{cases} \tag{5}$$

where matrix $J_F = \left[\frac{\partial s(F)[j](\mathbf{x})}{\partial \mathbf{x}[i]} \right]_{ij}$ is the Jacobian matrix for the output of the softmax layer $s(F)(\mathbf{x})$. Since $\sum_{k \in \mathcal{C}} s(F)[k](\mathbf{x}) = 1$, we have the following equation:

$$\frac{\partial s(F)[t](\mathbf{x})}{\partial \mathbf{x}[i]} = - \sum_{j \neq t} \frac{\partial s(F)[j](\mathbf{x})}{\partial \mathbf{x}[i]}$$

The first case corresponds to the scenario if changing the i-th component of $\mathbf{x}$ takes us further away from the target label t. Intuitively, $S(\mathbf{x}, t)[i]$ indicates how likely is changing the i-th component of $\mathbf{x}$ going to "move towards" the target label t. Input components i are added to perturbation δ in order of decreasing adversarial saliency value $S(\mathbf{x}, t)[i]$ until the resulting adversarial sample $\mathbf{x}^\star = \mathbf{x} + \delta$ achieves the target label t. The perturbation introduced for each selected input component can vary. Greater individual variations tend to reduce the number of components perturbed to achieve misclassification.

CW Targeted Mis-classification Attack. The CW-attack [5] is widely believed to be one of the most "powerful" attacks. The reason is that CW cast their problem as an unconstrained optimization problem, and then use state-of-the art solver (i.e. Adam [24]). In other words, they leverage the advances in optimization for the purposes of generating adversarial examples.

In their paper Carlini-Wagner consider a wide variety of formulations, but we present the one that performs best according to their evaluation. The optimization problem corresponding to CW is as follows:

$$\min_{\delta \in \Re^n} \quad \mu(\delta)$$
$$\text{such that } F(\mathbf{x} + \delta) = t$$

CW use an existing solver (Adam [24]) and thus need to make sure that each component of $\mathbf{x} + \delta$ is between 0 and 1 (i.e. valid pixel values). Note that the other methods did not face this issue because they control the "internals" of the algorithm (i.e., CW used a solver in a "black box" manner). We introduce a new vector $\mathbf{w}$ whose i-th component is defined according to the following equation:

$$\delta[i] = \frac{1}{2}(\tanh(\mathbf{w}[i]) + 1) - \mathbf{x}[i]$$

Since $-1 \leq \tanh(\mathbf{w}[i]) \leq 1$, it follows that $0 \leq \mathbf{x}[i] + \delta[i] \leq 1$. In terms of this new variable the optimization problem becomes:

$$\min_{\mathbf{w} \in \Re^n} \ \mu(\tfrac{1}{2}(\tanh(\mathbf{w}) + 1) - \mathbf{x})$$
$$\text{such that } F(\tfrac{1}{2}(\tanh(\mathbf{w}) + 1)) = t$$

Next they approximate the constraint $(F(\mathbf{x}) = \mathbf{t})$ with the following function:

$$g(\mathbf{x}) = \max\left(\max_{i \neq t} Z(F)(\mathbf{x})[i] - Z(F)(\mathbf{x})[t], -\kappa\right)$$

In the equation given above $Z(F)$ is the input of the DNN to the softmax layer (i.e. $s(F)(\mathbf{x}) = \text{softmax}(Z(F)(\mathbf{x}))$) and κ is a confidence parameter (higher κ encourages the solver to find adversarial examples with higher confidence). The new optimization formulation is as follows:

$$\min_{\mathbf{w} \in \Re^n} \ \mu(\tfrac{1}{2}(\tanh(\mathbf{w}) + 1) - \mathbf{x})$$
$$\text{such that } g(\tfrac{1}{2}(\tanh(\mathbf{w}) + 1)) \leq 0$$

Next we incorporate the constraint into the objective function as follows:

$$\min_{\mathbf{w} \in \Re^n} \mu(\tfrac{1}{2}(\tanh(\mathbf{w}) + 1) - \mathbf{x}) + c\, g(\tfrac{1}{2}(\tanh(\mathbf{w}) + 1))$$

In the objective given above, the "Lagrangian variable" $c > 0$ is a suitably chosen constant (from the optimization literature we know that there exists $c > 0$ such that the optimal solutions of the last two formulations are the same).

3.2 Adversarial Training

Once an attacker finds an adversarial example, then the algorithm can be retrained using this example. Researchers have found that retraining the model with adversarial examples produces a more robust model. For this section, we will work with attack algorithms that have a target label t (i.e. we are in the targeted mis-classification case, such as JSMA or CW). Let $\mathcal{A}(w, \mathbf{x}, t)$ be the attack algorithm, where its inputs are as follows: $w \in H$ is the current hypothesis, $\mathbf{x}$ is the data point, and $t \in \mathcal{C}$ is the target label. The output of $\mathcal{A}(w, \mathbf{x}, t)$ is a perturbation δ such that $F(\mathbf{x} + \delta) = t$. If the attack algorithm is simply a mis-classification algorithm (e.g. FGSM or Deepfool) we will drop the last parameter t.

An *adversarial training* algorithm $\mathcal{R}_{\mathcal{A}}(w, \mathbf{x}, t)$ is parameterized by an attack algorithm $\mathcal{A}$ and outputs a new hypothesis $w' \in H$. Adversarial training works by taking a datapoint $\mathbf{x}$ and an attack algorithm $\mathcal{A}(w, \mathbf{x}, t)$ as its input and then retraining the model using a specially designed loss function (essentially one performs a single step of the SGD using the new loss function). The question arises: what loss function to use during the training? Different methods use different loss functions.

Next, we discuss some adversarial training algorithms proposed in the literature. At a high level, an important point is that the more sophisticated an adversarial perturbation algorithm is, harder it is to turn it into adversarial training. The reason is that it is hard to "encode" the adversarial perturbation algorithm as an objective function and optimize it. We will see this below, especially for the virtual adversarial training (VAT) proposed by Miyato et al. [32].

Retraining for FGSM. We discussed the FGSM attack method earlier. In this case $\mathcal{A} = \text{FGSM}$. The loss function used by the retraining algorithm $\mathcal{R}_{\text{FGSM}}(w, \mathbf{x}, t)$ is as follows:

$$\ell_{\text{FGSM}}(w, \mathbf{x}_i, y_i) = \ell(w, \mathbf{x}_i, y_i) + \lambda \ell\left(w, \mathbf{x}_i + \text{FGSM}(w, \mathbf{x}_i), y_i\right)$$

Recall that $\text{FGSM}(w, \mathbf{x})$ was defined earlier, and λ is a regularization parameter. The simplicity of $\text{FGSM}(w, \mathbf{x}_i)$ allows taking its gradient, but this objective function requires label y_i because we are reusing the same loss function ℓ used to train the original model. Further, $\text{FGSM}(w, \mathbf{x}_i)$ may not be very good because it may not produce good adversarial perturbation direction (i.e. taking a bigger step in this direction might produce a distorted image). The retraining algorithm is simply as follows: *take one step in the SGD using the loss function ℓ_{FGSM} at the data point $\mathbf{x}_i$.*

A caveat is needed for taking gradient during the SGD step. At iteration t suppose we have model parameters w_t, and we need to compute the gradient of the objective. Note that $\text{FGSM}(w, \mathbf{x})$ depends on w so by chain rule we need to compute $\partial \text{FGSM}(w, \mathbf{x})/\partial w|_{w=w_t}$. However, this gradient is volatile[2], and so instead Goodfellow et al. only compute:

$$\left.\frac{\partial \ell\left(w, \mathbf{x}_i + \text{FGSM}(w_t, \mathbf{x}_i), y_i\right)}{\partial w}\right|_{w=w_t}$$

Essentially they treat $\text{FGSM}(w_t, \mathbf{x}_i)$ as a constant while taking the derivative.

Virtual Adversarial Training (VAT). Miyato et al. [32] observed the drawback of requiring label y_i for the adversarial example. Their intuition is that one wants the classifier to behave "similarly" on $\mathbf{x}$ and $\mathbf{x}+\delta$, where δ is the adversarial perturbation. Specifically, the distance of the distribution corresponding to the output of the softmax layer F_w on $\mathbf{x}$ and $\mathbf{x}+\delta$ is small. VAT uses *KullbackLeibler*

---

[2] In general, second-order derivatives of a classifier corresponding to a DNN vanish at several points because several layers are piece-wise linear.

(KL) *divergence* as the measure of the distance between two distributions. Recall that KL divergence of two distributions P and Q over the same finite domain D is given by the following equation:

$$\text{KL}(P, Q) = \sum_{i \in D} P(i) \log \left(\frac{P(i)}{Q(i)} \right)$$

Therefore, they propose that, instead of reusing ℓ, they propose to use the following for the regularizer,

$$\Delta(r, \mathbf{x}, w) = \text{KL}\left(s(F_w)(\mathbf{x})[y], s(F_w)(\mathbf{x} + r)[y] \right)$$

for some r such that $\|r\| \leq \delta$. As a result, the label y_i is *no longer* required. The question is: what r to use? Miyato et al. [32] propose that in theory we should use the "best" one as

$$\max_{r : \|r\| \leq \delta} \text{KL}\left(s(F_w)(\mathbf{x})[y], s(F_w)(\mathbf{x} + r)[y] \right)$$

This thus gives rise to the following loss function to use during retraining:

$$\ell_{\text{VAT}}(w, \mathbf{x}_i, y_i) = \ell(w, \mathbf{x}_i, y_i) + \lambda \max_{r : \|r\| \leq \delta} \Delta(r, \mathbf{x}_i, w)$$

However, one cannot easily compute the gradient for the regularizer. Hence the authors perform an approximation as follows:

1. Compute the Taylor expansion of $\Delta(r, \mathbf{x}_i, w)$ at $r = 0$, so $\Delta(r, \mathbf{x}_i, w) = r^T H(\mathbf{x}_i, w) \, r$ where $H(\mathbf{x}_i, w)$ is the Hessian matrix of $\Delta(r, \mathbf{x}_i, w)$ with respect to r at $r = 0$.
2. Thus $\max_{\|r\| \leq \delta} \Delta(r, \mathbf{x}_i, w) = \max_{\|r\| \leq \delta} \left(r^T H(\mathbf{x}_i, w) \, r \right)$. By variational characterization of the symmetric matrix ($H(\mathbf{x}_i, w)$ is symmetric), $r^* = \delta \bar{v}$ where $\bar{v} = \overline{v(\mathbf{x}_i, w)}$ is the unit eigenvector of $H(\mathbf{x}_i, w)$ corresponding to its largest eigenvalue. Note that r^* depends on $\mathbf{x}_i$ and w. Therefore the loss function becomes:

$$\ell_{\text{VAT}}(\theta, \mathbf{x}_i, y_i) = \ell(\theta, \mathbf{x}_i, y_i) + \lambda \Delta(r^*, \mathbf{x}_i, w)$$

3. Now suppose in the process of SGD we are at iteration t with model parameters w_t, and we need to compute $\partial \ell_{\text{VAT}} / \partial w |_{w=w_t}$. By chain rule we need to compute $\partial r^* / \partial w |_{w=w_t}$. However the authors find that such gradients are volatile, so they instead fix r^* as a constant at the point θ_t, and compute

$$\frac{\partial \text{KL}\left(s(F_w)(\mathbf{x})[y], s(F_w)(\mathbf{x} + r)[y] \right)}{\partial w} \Bigg|_{w=w_t}$$

3.3   Black Box Attacks

Recall that earlier attacks (e.g. FGSM and JSMA) needed white-box access to the classifier F (essentially because these attacks require first order information about the classifier). In this section, we present black-box attacks. In this case, an attacker can *only* ask for the labels $F(\mathbf{x})$ for certain data points. Our presentation is based on [36], but is more general.

Let $\mathcal{A}(w, \mathbf{x}, t)$ be the attack algorithm, where its inputs are: $w \in H$ is the current hypothesis, $\mathbf{x}$ is the data point, and $t \in \mathcal{C}$ is the target label. The output of $\mathcal{A}(w, \mathbf{x}, t)$ is a perturbation δ such that $F(\mathbf{x} + \delta) = t$. If the attack algorithm is simply a mis-classification algorithm (e.g. FGSM or Deepfool) we will drop the last parameter t (recall that in this case the attack algorithm returns a δ such that $F(\mathbf{x} + \delta) \neq F(\mathbf{x})$). An *adversarial training* algorithm $\mathcal{R}_\mathcal{A}(w, \mathbf{x}, t)$ is parameterized by an attack algorithm $\mathcal{A}$ and outputs a new hypothesis $w' \in H$ (this was discussed in the previous subsection).

Initialization: We pick a substitute classifier G and an initial seed data set S_0 and train G. For simplicity, we will assume that the sample space $Z = X \times Y$ and the hypothesis space H for G is same as that of F (the classifier under attack). However, this is not crucial to the algorithm. We will call G the *substitute classifier* and F the *target classifier*. Let $S = S_0$ be the initial data set, which will be updated as we iterate.

Iteration: Run the attack algorithm $\mathcal{A}(w, \mathbf{x}, t)$ on G and obtain a δ. If $F(\mathbf{x} + \delta) = t$, then **stop** we are done. If $F(\mathbf{x} + \delta) = t'$ but not equal to t, we augment the data set S as follows:

$$S = S \cup (\mathbf{x} + \delta, t')$$

We now retrain G on this new data set, which essentially means running the SGD on the new data point $(\mathbf{x} + \delta, t')$. Notice that we can also use adversarial training $\mathcal{R}_\mathcal{A}(w, \mathbf{x}, t)$ to update G (to our knowledge this has been not tried out in the literature).

3.4 Defenses

Defenses with formal guarantees against test-time attacks have proven elusive. For example, Carlini and Wagner [6] have a recent paper that breaks *ten recent defense proposals*. However, defenses that are based on robust-optimization objectives have demonstrated promise [26, 33, 43]. Several techniques for verifying properties of a DNN (in isolation) have appeared recently (e.g., [12, 13, 19, 23]). Due to space limitations we will not give a detailed account of all these defenses.

4 Semantic Adversarial Analysis and Training

A central tenet of this paper is that the analysis of deep neural networks (and machine learning components, in general) must be more *semantic*. In particular, we advocate for the increased use of semantics in several aspects of adversarial analysis and training, including the following:

- *Semantic Modification Space:* Recall that the goal of adversarial attacks is to modify an input vector **x** with an adversarial modification δ so as to achieve a target misclassification. Such modifications typically do not incorporate the application-level semantics or the context within which the neural network is deployed. We argue that it is essential to incorporate more application-level, contextual semantics into the modification space. Such *semantic modifications* correspond to modifications that may arise more naturally within the context of the target application. We view this not as ignoring arbitrary modifications (which are indeed worth considering with a security mind set), but as prioritizing the design and analysis of DNNs towards semantic adversarial modifications. Sect. 4.1 discusses this point in more detail.
- *System-Level Specifications:* The goal of much of the work in adversarial attacks has been to generate misclassifications. However, not all misclassifications are made equal. We contend that it is important to find misclassifications that lead to violations of desired properties of the system within which the DNN is used. Therefore, one must identify such *system-level specifications* and devise analysis methods to verify whether an erroneous behavior of the DNN component can lead to the violation of a system-level specification. System-level counterexamples can be valuable aids to repair and re-design machine learning models. See Sect. 4.1 for a more detailed discussion of this point.
- *Semantic (Re-)Training:* Most machine learning models are trained with the main goal of reducing misclassifications as measured by a suitably crafted loss function. We contend that it is also important to train the model to avoid undesirable behaviors at the system level. For this, we advocate using methods for *semantic training*, where system-level specifications, counterexamples, and other artifacts are used to improve the semantic quality of the ML model. Sect. 4.2 explores a few ideas.
- *Confidence-Based Analysis and Decision Making:* Deep neural networks (and other ML models) often produce not just an output label, but also an associated confidence level. We argue that *confidence levels* must be used within the design of ML-based systems. They provide a way of exposing more information from the DNN to the surrounding system that uses its decisions. Such confidence levels can also be useful to prioritize analysis towards cases that are more egregious failures of the DNN. More generally, any *explanations* and *auxiliary information* generated by the DNN that accompany its main output decisions can be valuable aids in their design and analysis.

4.1   Compositional Falsification

We discuss the problem of performing system-level analysis of a deep learning component, using recent work by the authors [9, 10] to illustrate the main points. The material in this section is mainly based on [40].

We begin with some basic notation. Let S denote the model of the full system S under verification, E denote a model of its environment, and Φ denote the specification to be verified. C is an ML model (e.g. DNN) that is part of S. As in Sect. 3, let $\mathbf{x}$ be an input to C. We assume that Φ is a trace property – a set of behaviors of the closed system obtained by composing S with E, denoted $S\|E$. The goal of falsification is to find one or more counterexamples showing how the composite system $S\|E$ violates Φ. In this context, *semantic analysis of C is about finding a modification δ from a space of semantic modifications Δ such that C, on $\mathbf{x} + \delta$, produces a misclassification that causes $S\|E$ to violate Φ.*

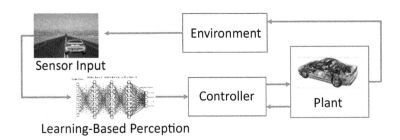

Fig. 1. Automatic Emergency Braking System (AEBS) in closed loop. An image classifier based on deep neural networks is used to perceive objects in the ego vehicle's frame of view.

Example Problem. As an illustrative example, consider a simple model of an Automatic Emergency Braking System (AEBS), that attempts to detect objects in front of a vehicle and actuate the brakes when needed to avert a collision. Figure 1 shows the AEBS as a system composed of a controller (automatic braking), a plant (vehicle sub-system under control, including transmission), and an advanced sensor (camera along with an obstacle detector based on deep learning). The AEBS, when combined with the vehicle's environment, forms a closed loop control system. The controller regulates the acceleration and braking of the plant using the velocity of the subject (ego) vehicle and the distance between it and an obstacle. The sensor used to detect the obstacle includes a camera along with an image classifier based on DNNs. In general, this sensor can provide noisy measurements due to incorrect image classifications which in turn can affect the correctness of the overall system.

Suppose we want to verify whether the distance between the ego vehicle and a preceding obstacle is always larger than 2 m. In STL, this requirement Φ can be written as $\mathbf{G}_{0,T}(\|\mathbf{x}_{\text{ego}} - \mathbf{x}_{\text{obs}}\|_2 \geq 2)$. Such verification requires the exploration of a very large input space comprising of the control inputs (e.g., acceleration and braking pedal angles) and the machine learning (ML) component's feature space (e.g., all the possible pictures observable by the camera). The latter space is particularly large—for example, note that the feature space of RGB images of dimension 1000×600 px (for an image classifier) contains $256^{1000 \times 600 \times 3}$ elements.

In the above example, $S\|E$ is the closed loop system in Fig. 1 where S comprises the DNN and the controller, and E comprises everything else. C is the DNN used for object detection and classification.

This case study has been implemented in Matlab/Simulink[3] in two versions that use two different Convolutional Neural Networks (CNNs): the Caffe [20] version of AlexNet [28] and the Inception-v3 model created with Tensorflow [31], both trained on the ImageNet database [1]. Further details about this example can be obtained from [9].

Approach. A key idea in our approach is to have a *system-level verifier* that abstracts away the component C while verifying Φ on the resulting abstraction. This system-level verifier communicates with a component-level analyzer that searches for semantic modifications δ to the input $\mathbf{x}$ of C that could lead to violations of the system-level specification Φ. Figure 2 illustrates this approach.

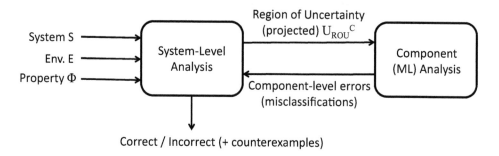

Fig. 2. Compositional verification approach. A system-level verifier cooperates with a component-level analysis procedure (e.g., adversarial analysis of a machine learning component to find misclassifications).

We formalize this approach while trying to emphasize the intuition. Let T denote the set of all possible traces of the composition of the system with its environment, $S\|E$. Given a specification Φ, let T_Φ denote the set of traces in T satisfying Φ. Let U_Φ denote the projection of these traces onto the state and interface variables of the environment E. U_Φ is termed as the *validity domain* of Φ, i.e., the set of environment behaviors for which Φ is satisfied. Similarly, the complement set $U_{\neg\Phi}$ is the set of environment behaviors for which Φ is violated.

Our approach works as follows:

1. The System-level Verifier initially performs two analyses with two extreme abstractions of the ML component. First, it performs an *optimistic* analysis, wherein the ML component is assumed to be a "perfect classifier", i.e., all feature vectors are correctly classified. In situations where ML is used for perception/sensing, this abstraction assumes perfect perception/sensing. Using this abstraction, we compute the validity domain for this abstract model of the system, denoted U_Φ^+. Next, it performs a *pessimistic* analysis where the ML component is abstracted by a "completely-wrong classifier", i.e., all feature vectors are misclassified. Denote the resulting validity domain as U_Φ^-. It is expected that $U_\Phi^+ \supseteq U_\Phi^-$.

Abstraction permits the System-level Verifier to operate on a lower-dimensional search space and identify a region in this space that may be affected by the malfunctioning of component C—a so-called "region of uncertainty" (ROU). This region, U_{ROU}^C is computed as $U_\Phi^+ \setminus U_\Phi^-$. In other words, it comprises all environment behaviors that could lead to a system-level failure when component C malfunctions. This region U_{ROU}^C, projected onto the inputs of C, is communicated to the ML Analyzer. (Concretely, in the context of our example of Sect. 4.1, this corresponds to finding a subspace of images that corresponds to U_{ROU}^C.)

2. The Component-level Analyzer, also termed as a Machine Learning (ML) Analyzer, performs a detailed analysis of the projected ROU U_{ROU}^C. A key aspect of the ML analyzer is to explore the *semantic modification space* efficiently. Several options are available for such an analysis, including the various adversarial analysis techniques surveyed earlier (applied to the semantic space), as well as systematic sampling methods [9]. Even though a component-level formal specification may not be available, each of these adversarial analyses has an implicit notion of "misclassification." We will refer to these as *component-level errors*. The working of the ML analyzer from [9] is shown in Fig. 3.

3. When the Component-level (ML) Analyzer finds component-level errors (e.g., those that trigger misclassifications of inputs whose labels are easily inferred), it communicates that information back to the System-level Verifier, which checks whether the ML misclassification can lead to a violation of the system-level property Φ. If yes, we have found a system-level counterexample. If no component-level errors are found, and the system-level verification can prove the absence of counterexamples, then it can conclude that Φ is satisfied. Otherwise, if the ML misclassification cannot be extended to a system-level counterexample, the ROU is updated and the revised ROU passed back to the Component-level Analyzer.

The communication between the System-level Verifier and the Component-level (ML) Analyzer continues thus, until we either prove/disprove Φ, or we run out of resources.

Sample Results. We have applied the above approach to the problem of *compositional falsification* of cyber-physical systems (CPS) with machine learning components [9]. For this class of CPS, including those with highly non-linear dynamics and even black-box components, simulation-based falsification of temporal logic properties is an approach that has proven effective in industrial practice (e.g., [21,46]). We present here a sample of results on the AEBS example from [9], referring the reader to more detailed descriptions in the other papers on the topic [9,10].

In Fig. 4 we show one result of our analysis for the Inception-v3 deep neural network. This figure shows both correctly classified and misclassified images on a range of synthesized images where (i) the environment vehicle is moved away from or towards the ego vehicle (along z-axis), (ii) it is moved sideways along

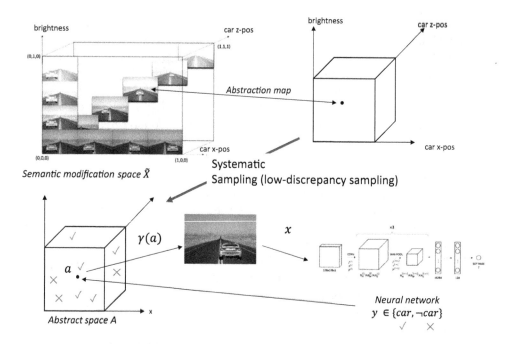

Fig. 3. Machine Learning Analyzer: Searching the Semantic Modification Space. A concrete semantic modification space (top left) is mapped into a discrete abstract space. Systematic sampling, using low-discrepancy methods, yields points in the abstract space. These points are concretized and the NN is evaluated on them to ascertain if they are correctly or wrongly classified. The misclassifications are fed back for system-level analysis.

the road (along x-axis), or (iii) the brightness of the image is modified. These modifications constitute the 3 axes of the figure. Our approach finds misclassifications that do not lead to system-level property violations and also misclassifications that do lead to such violations. For example, Fig. 4 shows two misclassified images, one with an environment vehicle that is too far away to be a safety hazard, as well as another image showing an environment vehicle driving slightly on the wrong side of the road, which is close enough to potentially cause a violation of the system-level safety property (of maintaining a safe distance from the ego vehicle).

For further details about this and other results with our approach, we refer the reader to [9, 10].

4.2 Semantic Training

In this section we discuss two ideas for *semantic training and retraining* of deep neural networks. We first discuss the use of *hinge loss* as a way of incorporating confidence levels into the training process. Next, we discuss how system-level counterexamples and associated misclassifications can be used in the retraining process to both improve the accuracy of ML models and also to gain more assurance in the overall system containing the ML component. A more detailed study

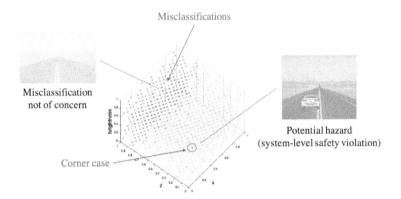

Fig. 4. Misclassified images for Inception-v3 neural network (trained on ImageNet with TensorFlow). Red crosses are misclassified images and green circles are correctly classified. Our system-level analysis finds a corner-case image that could lead to a system-level safety violation. (Color figure online)

of using misclassifications (ML component-level counterexamples) to improve the accuracy of the neural network is presented in [11]; this approach is termed *counterexample-guided data augmentation*, inspired by counterexample-guided abstraction refinement (CEGAR) [7] and similar paradigms.

Experimental Setup. As in the preceding section, we consider an Automatic Emergency Braking System (AEBS) using a DNN-based object detector. However, in these experiments we use an AEBS deployed within Udacity's self-driving car simulator, as reported in our previous work [10].[4] We modified the Udacity simulator to focus exclusively on braking. In our case studies, the car follows some predefined way-points, while accelerating and braking are controlled by the AEBS connected to a convolutional neural network (CNN). In particular, whenever the CNN detects an obstacle in the images provided by the onboard camera, the AEBS triggers a braking action that slows the vehicle down and avoids the collision against the obstacle.

We designed and implemented a CNN to predict the presence of a cow on the road. Given an image taken by the onboard camera, the CNN classifies the picture in either "cow" or "not cow" category. The CNN architecture is shown in Fig. 5. It consists of eight layers: the first six are alternations of convolutions and max-pools with ReLU activations, the last two are a fully connected layer and a softmax that outputs the network prediction (confidence level for each label).

We generated a data set of 1000 road images with and without cows. We split the data set into 80% training and 20% validation data. Our model was implemented and trained using the Tensorflow library with cross-entropy cost function and the Adam algorithm optimizer (learning rate 10^{-4}). The model

---

[4] Udacity's self-driving car simulator.

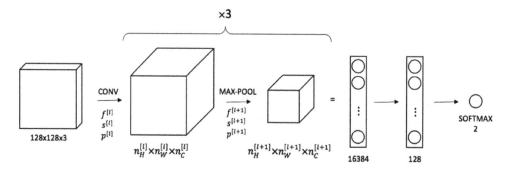

Fig. 5. CNN architecture.

Fig. 6. Udacity simulator with a CNN-based AEBS in action.

reached 95% accuracy on the test set. Finally, the resulting CNN is connected to the Unity simulator via Socket.IO protocol.[5] Figure 6 depicts a screenshot of the simulator with the AEBS in action in proximity of a cow.

Hinge Loss. In this section, we investigate the relationship between multiclass hinge loss functions and adversarial examples. *Hinge loss* is defined as follows:

$$l(\hat{y}) = \max(0, k + \max_{i \neq l}(\hat{y}_i) - \hat{y}_l) \tag{6}$$

where (x, y) is a training sample, $\hat{y} = F(x)$ is a prediction, and l is the *ground truth* label of x. For this section, the output $\hat{y}$ is a numerical value indicating the *confidence level* of the network for each class. For example, $\hat{y}$ can be the output of a softmax layer as described in Sect. 2.

---

[5] Socket.IO protocol.

Consider what happens as we vary k. Suppose there is an $i \neq l$ s.t. $\hat{y}_i > \hat{y}_l$. Pick the largest such i, call it i^*. For $k = 0$, we will incur a loss of $\hat{y}_{i^*} - \hat{y}_l$ for the example (x, y). However, as we make k more negative, we increase the tolerance for "misclassifications" produced by the DNN F. Specifically, we incur no penalty for a misclassification as long as the associated confidence level deviates from that of the ground truth label by no more than $|k|$. Larger the absolute value of k, the greater the tolerance. Intuitively, this biases the training process towards avoiding "high confidence misclassifications".

In this experiment, we investigate the role of k and explore different parameter values. At training time, we want to minimize the mean hinge loss across all training samples. We trained the CNN described above with different values of k and evaluated its precision on both the original test set and a set of counterexamples generated for the original model, i.e., the network trained with cross-entropy loss.

Table 1 reports accuracy and log loss for different values of k on both original and counterexamples test sets ($T_{original}$ and $T_{countex}$, respectively).

Table 1. Hinge loss with different k values.

k	$T_{original}$		$T_{countex}$	
	Acc	Log-loss	Acc	Log-loss
0	0.69	0.68	0.11	0.70
-0.01	0.77	0.69	0.00	0.70
-0.05	0.52	0.70	0.67	0.69
-0.1	0.50	0.70	0.89	0.68
-0.25	0.51	0.70	0.77	0.68

Table 1 shows interesting results. We note that a negative k increases the accuracy of the model on counterexamples. In other words, biasing the training process by penalizing high-confidence misclassifications improves accuracy on counterexamples! However, the price to pay is a reduction of accuracy on the original test set. This is still a very preliminary result and further experimentation and analysis is necessary.

System-Level Counterexamples. By using the composition falsification framework presented in Sect. 4.1, we identify orientations, displacements on the x-axis, and color of an obstacle that leads to a collision of the vehicle with the obstacle. Figure 7 depicts configurations of the obstacle that lead to specification violations, and hence, to collisions.

In an experiment, we augment the original training set with the elements of $T_{countex}$, i.e., images of the original test set $T_{original}$ that are misclassified by the original model (see Sect. 4.2).

We trained the model with both cross-entropy and hinge loss for 20 epochs. Both models achieve a high accuracy on the validation set ($\approx 92\%$). However,

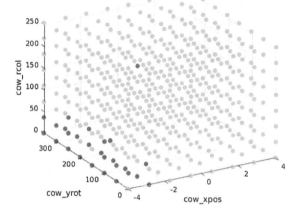

Fig. 7. Semantic counterexamples: obstacle configurations leading to property violations (in red). (Color figure online)

when plugged into the AEBS, neither of these models prevents the vehicle from colliding against the obstacle with an adversarial configuration. This seems to indicate that simply retraining with some semantic (system-level) counterexamples generated by analyzing the system containing the ML model may not be sufficient to eliminate all semantic counterexamples.

Interestingly, though, it appears that in both cases the impact of the vehicle with the obstacle happens at a slower speed than the one with the original model. In other words, the AEBS system starts detecting the obstacle earlier than with the original model, and therefore starts braking earlier as well. This means that despite the specification violations, the counterexample retraining procedure seems to help with limiting the damage in case of a collision. Coupled with a run-time assurance framework (see [41]), semantic retraining could help mitigate the impact of misclassifications on the system-level behavior.

5   Conclusion

In this paper, we surveyed the field of adversarial machine learning with a special focus on deep learning and on test-time attacks. We then introduced the idea of *semantic adversarial machine (deep) learning*, where adversarial analysis and training of ML models is performed using the semantics and context of the overall system within which the ML models are utilized. We identified several ideas for integrating semantics into adversarial learning, including using a semantic modification space, system-level formal specifications, training using semantic counterexamples, and utilizing more detailed information about the outputs produced by the ML model, including confidence levels, in the modules that use these outputs to make decisions. Preliminary experiments show the promise of these ideas, but also indicate that much remains to be done. We believe the field of semantic adversarial learning will be a rich domain for research at the intersection of machine learning, formal methods, and related areas.

Acknowledgments. The first and third author were supported in part by NSF grant 1646208, the DARPA BRASS program under agreement number FA8750-16-C0043, the DARPA Assured Autonomy program, and Berkeley Deep Drive.

References

1. Imagenet. http://image-net.org/
2. Alipanahi, B., Delong, A., Weirauch, M.T., Frey, B.J.: Predicting the sequence specificities of DNA-and RNA-binding proteins by deep learning. Nat. Biotechnol. **33**, 831–838 (2015)
3. Barreno, M., Nelson, B., Joseph, A.D., Tygar, J.D.: The security of machine learning. Mach. Learn. **81**(2), 121–148 (2010)
4. Bojarski, M., Del Testa, D., Dworakowski, D., Firner, B., Flepp, B., Goyal, P., Jackel, L., Monfort, M., Muller, U., Zhang, J., Zhang, X., Zhao, J., Zieba, K.: End to end learning for self-driving cars. Technical report (2016). CoRR, abs/1604.07316. http://arxiv.org/abs/1604.07316
5. Carlini, N., Wagner, D.: Towards evaluating the robustness of neural networks. In: IEEE Symposium on Security and Privacy (2017)
6. Carlini, N., Wagner, D.: Adversarial examples are not easily detected: bypassing ten detection methods. In: ACM Workshop on Artificial Intelligence and Security (2017)
7. Clarke, E., Grumberg, O., Jha, S., Lu, Y., Veith, H.: Counterexample-guided abstraction refinement. In: Emerson, E.A., Sistla, A.P. (eds.) CAV 2000. LNCS, vol. 1855, pp. 154–169. Springer, Heidelberg (2000). https://doi.org/10.1007/10722167_15
8. Dahl, G.E., Stokes, J.W., Deng, L., Yu, D.: Large-scale malware classification using random projections and neural networks. In: Proceedings of the IEEE International Conference on Acoustics, Speech and Signal Processing (ICASSP), pp. 3422–3426. IEEE (2013)
9. Dreossi, T., Donzé, A., Seshia, S.A.: Compositional falsification of cyber-physical systems with machine learning components. In: Barrett, C., Davies, M., Kahsai, T. (eds.) NFM 2017. LNCS, vol. 10227, pp. 357–372. Springer, Cham (2017). https://doi.org/10.1007/978-3-319-57288-8_26
10. Dreossi, T., Donzé, A., Seshia, S.A.: Compositional falsification of cyber-physical systems with machine learning components. CoRR, abs/1703.00978 (2017)
11. Dreossi, T., Ghosh, S., Yue, X., Keutzer, K., Sangiovanni-Vincentelli, A., Seshia, S.A.: Counterexample-guided data augmentation. In: International Joint Conference on Artificial Intelligence (IJCAI), July 2018
12. Dutta, S., Jha, S., Sankaranarayanan, S., Tiwari, A.: Output range analysis for deep neural networks (2018, to appear)
13. Dvijotham, K., Stanforth, R., Gowal, S., Mann, T., Kohli, P.: A Dual Approach to Scalable Verification of Deep Networks. ArXiv e-prints, March 2018
14. Eddy, N.: AI, machine learning drive autonomous vehicle development (2016). http://www.informationweek.com/big-data/big-data-analytics/ai-machine-learning-drive-autonomous-vehicle-development/d/d-id/1325906
15. Goodfellow, I., Bengio, Y., Courville, A.: Deep Learning. MIT Press (2016). http://www.deeplearningbook.org

16. Goodfellow, I.J., Shlens, J., Szegedy, C.: Explaining and harnessing adversarial examples. In: Proceedings of the 2015 International Conference on Learning Representations. Computational and Biological Learning Society (2015)
17. Hinton, G., Deng, L., Dong, Y., Dahl, G.E., Mohamed, A., Jaitly, N., Senior, A., Vanhoucke, V., Nguyen, P., Sainath, T.N., et al.: Deep neural networks for acoustic modeling in speech recognition: the shared views of four research groups. IEEE Signal Process. Mag. **29**(6), 82–97 (2012)
18. Huang, L., Joseph, A.D., Nelson, B., Rubinstein, B.I.P., Tygar, J.D.: Adversarial machine learning. In: Proceedings of the 4th ACM Workshop on Security and Artificial Intelligence, pp. 43–58. ACM (2011)
19. Huang, X., Kwiatkowska, M., Wang, S., Wu, M.: Safety verification of deep neural networks. In: Majumdar, R., Kunčak, V. (eds.) CAV 2017. LNCS, vol. 10426, pp. 3–29. Springer, Cham (2017). https://doi.org/10.1007/978-3-319-63387-9_1
20. Jia, Y., Shelhamer, E., Donahue, J., Karayev, S., Long, J., Girshick, R., Guadarrama, S., Darrell, T.: Caffe: convolutional architecture for fast feature embedding. In: ACM Multimedia Conference, ACMMM, pp. 675–678 (2014)
21. Jin, X., Donzé, A., Deshmukh, J., Seshia, S.A.: Mining requirements from closed-loop control models. IEEE Trans. Comput.-Aided Des. Circuits Syst. **34**(11), 1704–1717 (2015)
22. Julian, K., Lopez, J., Brush, J., Owen, M., Kochenderfer, M.: Policy compression for aircraft collision avoidance systems. In: Proceedings of the 35th Digital Avionics Systems Conference (DASC) (2016)
23. Katz, G., Barrett, C., Dill, D.L., Julian, K., Kochenderfer, M.J.: Reluplex: an Efficient SMT solver for verifying deep neural networks. In: Majumdar, R., Kunčak, V. (eds.) CAV 2017. LNCS, vol. 10426, pp. 97–117. Springer, Cham (2017). https://doi.org/10.1007/978-3-319-63387-9_5
24. Kingma, D.P., Ba, J.: Adam: a method for stochastic optimization (2017). https://arxiv.org/abs/1412.6980
25. Knorr, E.: How PayPal beats the bad guys with machine learning (2015). http://www.infoworld.com/article/2907877/machine-learning/how-paypal-reduces-fraud-with-machine-learning.html
26. Kolter, J.Z., Wong, E.: Provable defenses against adversarial examples via the convex outer adversarial polytope. CoRR, abs/1711.00851 (2017)
27. Koymans, R.: Specifying real-time properties with metric temporal logic. Real-Time Syst. **2**(4), 255–299 (1990)
28. Krizhevsky, A., Sutskever, I., Hinton, G.E.: Imagenet classification with deep convolutional neural networks. In: Advances in Neural Information Processing Systems, pp. 1097–1105 (2012)
29. Lee, E.A., Seshia, S.A.: Introduction to Embedded Systems: A Cyber-Physical Systems Approach, 2nd edn. MIT Press, Cambridge (2016)
30. Maler, O., Nickovic, D.: Monitoring temporal properties of continuous signals. In: Lakhnech, Y., Yovine, S. (eds.) FORMATS/FTRTFT - 2004. LNCS, vol. 3253, pp. 152–166. Springer, Heidelberg (2004). https://doi.org/10.1007/978-3-540-30206-3_12
31. Martín Abadi et al. TensorFlow: large-scale machine learning on heterogeneous systems (2015). Software: tensorflow.org
32. Miyato, T., Maeda, S., Koyama, M., Nakae, K., Ishii, S.: Distributional smoothing by virtual adversarial examples. CoRR, abs/1507.00677 (2015)
33. Mdry, A., Makelov, A., Schmidt, L., Tsipras, D., Vladu, A.: Towards deep learning models resistant to adversarial attacks. In: ICLR (2018)

34. Nocedal, J., Wright, S.: Numerical Optimization. Springer, New York (2006). https://doi.org/10.1007/978-0-387-40065-5
35. NVIDIA: Nvidia Tegra Drive PX: Self-driving Car Computer (2015)
36. Papernot, N., McDaniel, P., Goodfellow, I., Jha, S., Celik, Z.B., Swami, A.: Practical black-box attacks against machine learning. In: Proceedings of the 2017 ACM Asia Conference on Computer and Communications Security (AsiaCCS), April 2017
37. Papernot, N., McDaniel, P., Jha, S., Fredrikson, M., Celik, Z.B., Swami, A.: The limitations of deep learning in adversarial settings. In: Proceedings of the 1st IEEE European Symposium on Security and Privacy. arXiv preprint arXiv:1511.07528 (2016)
38. Pennington, J., Socher, R., Manning, C.D.: Glove: global vectors for word representation. In: Proceedings of the Empirical Methods in Natural Language Processing (EMNLP 2014), vol. 12, pp. 1532–1543 (2014)
39. Russell, S., Dietterich, T., Horvitz, E., Selman, B., Rossi, F., Hassabis, D., Legg, S., Suleyman, M., George, D., Phoenix, S.: Letter to the editor: research priorities for robust and beneficial artificial intelligence: an open letter. AI Mag. **36**(4), 3–4 (2015)
40. Seshia, S.A.: Compositional verification without compositional specification for learning-based systems. Technical report UCB/EECS-2017-164, EECS Department, University of California, Berkeley, November 2017
41. Seshia, S.A., Sadigh, D., Sastry, S.S.: Towards Verified Artificial Intelligence. ArXiv e-prints, July 2016
42. Shin, E.C.R., Song, D., Moazzezi, R.: Recognizing functions in binaries with neural networks. In: 24th USENIX Security Symposium (USENIX Security 2015), pp. 611–626 (2015)
43. Sinha, A., Namkoong, H., Duchi, J.: Certifiable distributional robustness with principled adversarial training. In: ICLR (2018)
44. Steinhardt, J., Koh, P.W., Liang, P.: Certified defenses for data poisoning attacks. In: Advances in Neural Information Processing Systems (NIPS) (2017)
45. Tramer, F., Zhang, F., Juels, A., Reiter, M., Ristenpart, T.: Stealing machine learning models via prediction APIs. In: USENIX Security (2016)
46. Yamaguchi, T., Kaga, T., Donzé, A., Seshia, S.A.: Combining requirement mining, software model checking, and simulation-based verification for industrial automotive systems. In: Proceedings of the IEEE International Conference on Formal Methods in Computer-Aided Design (FMCAD), October 2016

Permissions

The contributors of this book come from diverse backgrounds, making this book a truly international effort. This book will bring forth new frontiers with its revolutionizing research information and detailed analysis of the nascent developments around the world.

We would like to thank all the contributing authors for lending their expertise to make the book truly unique. They have played a crucial role in the development of this book. Without their invaluable contributions this book wouldn't have been possible. They have made vital efforts to compile up to date information on the varied aspects of this subject to make this book a valuable addition to the collection of many professionals and students.

This book was conceptualized with the vision of imparting up-to-date information and advanced data in this field. To ensure the same, a matchless editorial board was set up. Every individual on the board went through rigorous rounds of assessment to prove their worth. After which they invested a large part of their time researching and compiling the most relevant data for our readers.

The editorial board has been involved in producing this book since its inception. They have spent rigorous hours researching and exploring the diverse topics which have resulted in the successful publishing of this book. They have passed on their knowledge of decades through this book. To expedite this challenging task, the publisher supported the team at every step. A small team of assistant editors was also appointed to further simplify the editing procedure and attain best results for the readers.

Apart from the editorial board, the designing team has also invested a significant amount of their time in understanding the subject and creating the most relevant covers. They scrutinized every image to scout for the most suitable representation of the subject and create an appropriate cover for the book.

The publishing team has been an ardent support to the editorial, designing and production team. Their endless efforts to recruit the best for this project, has resulted in the accomplishment of this book. They are a veteran in the field of academics and their pool of knowledge is as vast as their experience in printing. Their expertise and guidance has proved useful at every step. Their uncompromising quality standards have made this book an exceptional effort. Their encouragement from time to time has been an inspiration for everyone.

The publisher and the editorial board hope that this book will prove to be a valuable piece of knowledge for researchers, students, practitioners and scholars across the globe.

List of Contributors

Byron Cook
Amazon Web Services, Seattle, USA
University College London, London, UK

Yuki Satake and Hiroshi Unno
University of Tsukuba, Tsukuba, Japan

Lauren Pick, Grigory Fedyukovich and Aarti Gupta
Princeton University, Princeton, USA

Kenneth L. McMillan
Microsoft Research, Redmond, USA

Alessandro Abate and Elizabeth Polgreen
University of Oxford, Oxford, UK

Cristina David
University of Cambridge, Cambridge, UK
Diffblue Ltd., Oxford, UK

Pascal Kesseli
Diffblue Ltd., Oxford, UK

Daniel Kroening
University of Oxford, Oxford, UK
Diffblue Ltd., Oxford, UK

Aws Albarghouthi
University of Wisconsin–Madison, Madison, WI, USA

Justin Hsu
University College London, London, UK
Cornell University, Ithaca, NY, USA

Suguman Bansal
Rice University, Houston, TX, USA

Kedar S. Namjoshi
Bell Labs, Nokia, Murray Hill, NJ, USA

Yaniv Sa'ar
Bell Labs, Nokia, Kfar Saba, Israel

Xinyu Wang, Greg Anderson and Isil Dillig
University of Texas, Austin, USA

Hui Kong and Thomas A. Henzinger
IST Austria, Klosterneuburg, Austria

Ezio Bartocci
TU Wien, Vienna, Austria

Frederik M. Bønneland, Peter Gjøl Jensen, Kim Guldstrand Larsen, Marco Muñiz and Jiří Srba
Department of Computer Science, Aalborg University, Aalborg, Denmark

Philipp J. Meyer, Salomon Sickert and Michael Luttenberger
Technical University of Munich, Munich, Germany

Marco Eilers and Peter Müller
Department of Computer Science, ETH Zurich, Zurich, Switzerland

Tim Quatmann and Joost-Pieter Katoen
RWTH Aachen University, Aachen, Germany

Tommaso Dreossi and Sanjit A. Seshia
University of California at Berkeley, Berkeley, USA

Somesh Jha
University of Wisconsin, Madison, Madison, USA

Index

Printed in the USA
CPSIA information can be obtained
at www.ICGtesting.com
JSHW051508111223
53612JS00005B/58